TREASURES

Books by Belva Plain

TREASURES
HARVEST
BLESSINGS
TAPESTRY
THE GOLDEN CUP
CRESCENT CITY
EDEN BURNING
RANDOM WINDS
EVERGREEN

BELVA PLAIN
TREASURES

**Delacorte
Press**

Published by
Delacorte Press
Bantam Doubleday Dell Publishing Group, Inc.
666 Fifth Avenue
New York, New York 10103

Library of Congress Cataloging in Publication Data

Plain, Belva.
    Treasures / Belva Plain.
        p.   cm.
        ISBN 0-385-29927-3 (hc) : $21.00. —ISBN 0-385-30610-5
    (large print) : $25.00
        I. Title.
    [PS3566.L254T7   1992]
813′.54—dc20   91-32590
                                                                CIP

Book design by Diane Stevenson·SNAP-HAUS GRAPHICS

Manufactured in the United States of America

Published simultaneously in Canada

March 1992

10   9   8   7   6   5   4   3   2   1

BVG

TREASURES

The two United States marshals, who had come to make an arrest, parked their inconspicuous black car, got out, and looked up at the ornamental neomodern roof of the sixty-five-storied tower. Somber rain clouds drooped over the city, releasing their first drops just as the pair in their plain dark suits reached the bronze doors that fronted the avenue. The younger man, who seemed almost imperceptibly to hesitate, followed the other across the marble floor to the long rank of elevators. This was no ordinary assignment today, nor was this a part of New York into which he usually was sent, and he was feeling a certain tension. It bothered him that he did. It was unprofessional.

"It seems funny in a way to handcuff the guy," he said. "Guy'll be wearing a Brooks Brothers suit probably. You know what I mean? He's not an armed thug."

"But you can't ever tell what a person will do. He could go off his nut and start punching. Or he could even head for the window. Press the forty-first floor, will you?"

The elevator slid upward silently as if on silken cords, while a red light efficiently marked each number as it passed.

"Smells of money, doesn't it, Jim?" remarked the younger.

"Sure does. And lots of it."

"Wonder what the guy really did. Really, I mean."

"God knows. You've got to be a high-priced lawyer to figure it out. I wouldn't bother to try."

"Seems kind of sad, doesn't it? Being hauled off from a place like this."

"It's always sad no matter where it is. You never feel good about it," Jim said seriously. "But it's a job, Harry. You get used to it."

The door opened and they stepped out in front of a long glass wall with many glass doors.

"Which way, Jim? Which is his?"

"He owns the whole floor. Two floors, actually. I'll get you there, don't worry." Jim grinned.

Receptionists are always pretty, reflected Harry, allowing his senior to do the talking to her while he himself examined the surroundings. He didn't know anything about rich living, he knew he didn't, and yet, when the brief opening and shutting of a door gave him a view of quiet gray carpeting and a corridor lined with paintings, he knew that he was seeing the real thing. Gold was gaudy and quietness was expensive. Maybe he had read that somewhere.

He thought: In one of these rooms, perhaps a room at the end of that very corridor, a man is going to have a terrible shock. In another minute or two. A terrible shock.

The receptionist must have telephoned because now a woman came rushing in. A fussy-looking matron with fuzzy gray hair, she was terrified.

"What? What? United States marshals?" she cried, confronting Jim.

He showed his badge, and Harry did the same.

The woman's eyes, enlarged by her glasses, sprang tears.

"It's got to be a mistake! I can't let you see him before he talks to a lawyer. This isn't right! No, you're not going in."

"Ma'am," said Jim, "here's the warrant. Read it. We can force our way in. You don't want us to do that, do you?"

TREASURES

They were moving through the door toward the gray carpet, following the frantic woman. They entered a room, spacious, with many windows, more paintings, and a great desk at which a man was seated. Upon seeing them, he stood.

The woman was almost babbling. "I couldn't stop them. I don't know what all this is, I—"

The man was young. He's about my age, thought Harry, and all this place is his. And somehow the pity he had been feeling for this stranger now turned to anger. To be my age and own all this! I hope he gets what's coming to him, whatever he did.

The man was standing on dignity, but he was scared to death, his face had gone blue-white. He stammered.

"There's a mistake here. A terrible mistake. My lawyer's working on the matter right now."

"That's all right," Jim said. "You'll be able to call your lawyer. But you'll have to come along." He took out the cuffs. "I'm sorry, but you'll need to wear these."

"You don't understand," the man said. "I'm not the sort of person—"

"Please. Make it easy for yourself," Jim told him patiently.

The woman was openly weeping. "He's a good man. Be gentle with him."

And Harry's pity flowed back. "Don't worry," he heard himself say.

In less than five minutes they were out of the building with their prisoner, whose handcuffs were hidden by the raincoat that the woman had dropped over them. Silently, stunned and proud, the prisoner climbed into the car and was driven away through the dreary rain.

On the forty-first floor in the room from which he had been taken, there had been a fire under a carved mantel, and a spray of yellow flowers on the desk.

The event made the front pages of all the papers as well as the television news. Telephones rang in the offices of the city's prestigious corporations.

"Have you heard how it happened? Well, I heard—"

At dinner parties all up and down Fifth Avenue, Park Avenue, out to the North Shore, and in Connecticut, it was the topic of the moment.

"Everybody loved him," people said, commiserating and astonished. "So bright, so charming, so kind. And no one in the world was ever more generous, we all know that. I can't believe it! What can have happened? How can you explain it?"

PART ONE
1973-1981

CHAPTER ONE

❧

T he downstairs neighbors had provided hot soup, cold meats, salad, and a home-baked pie, food enough for a dozen hungry eaters, Eddy Osborne remarked to himself. But there were only his sisters Connie and Lara and Lara's husband, Davey, at the kitchen table, none of them able to swallow more than a few mouthfuls of the good things. If anyone had told me I'd swallow even that much on the day of my mother's funeral I wouldn't have believed it, he thought.

He stood up, poured a cup of coffee from the pot on the stove, and went to stare out of the rain-beaded window at the bleak March afternoon. A shudder chilled his shoulders. Here was the ultimate desolation, the gray gloom and the grief.

Poor Peg, poor Mom! Sometimes the wig had tilted to the side, mocking her gaunt face with a rakish, jaunty look; she had been so vain, too, about the thick, tawny hair that all three of her children had inherited. . . . And Eddy's heart broke. Making a little sound like a sob, he covered it with a cough and turned his face.

Lara said softly, "One thing, anyway, should be a comfort. She was never alone. One of us was always with her. And she did appreciate that private room, Eddy. Remember how she kept asking whether you really could afford it?"

3

"She'd have had that if it had taken my last penny or if I'd had to steal, so help me!"

"Oh," Lara cried, "she must have known there was no hope for her, yet she never said a word. How brave she was!"

"No," Connie said. "The real reason is that she was afraid to admit how lousy life can be."

The grim, harsh comment shocked. But there was no sense in challenging it. Connie would defend herself by saying that she was merely looking truth in the face. She had few illusions, young Connie. The elder sister felt that was a pity, but answered only, "Let's go inside. No, leave the dishes, Connie. I'll clear them later. I'll be needing something to do tonight after you go home."

The living room had once been an upstairs sitting room when the house had been built for a banker's family a century ago, before everybody who could afford to move had left town for the new wooded suburbs in the hills. The small space was dominated by the television, whose great blank eye was staring as they all sat down. It would have been unseemly to activate it on this night, and no one did.

Connie pulled down the shades, complaining, "Damn rotten weather!" as if, on this day at least, the rain need not have been so furious or the wind so wild in the trees.

"Your mother would say," Davey responded in his mild way, "that rain like this nourishes the earth."

No one answered. Yes, Eddy knew, that would be typical of her. When, in high school, he had broken his arm she had told him to be thankful he hadn't broken it before the soccer season. But I'm not like her, he thought, nor is Connie.

Too restless to be still, he went back to a window again and raised the shade that Connie had lowered. The houses across the street were mirror images of this one where Lara lived, a tall, shingled Victorian with a second door cut into its front to accommodate an upstairs flat. Before each house lay a narrow,

4

woebegone yard bordered with neglected, weedy shrubs and dotted with piles of soiled, melting snow. Above the rooftops, in a brown sky, thin clouds raced toward evening.

"God, what a miserable way to live," he thought. "So many years gone by already in this confining town!"

He turned around into the room. Davey was reading the newspapers. The two women had laid their heads back and closed their eyes. The silence ticked in Eddy's head.

Then the street door slammed, vibrating through the walls. In the flat below, where five children were crammed, a fight exploded. Somebody was trying to start a balky engine in the driveway next door; it wheezed, it whirred, it coughed.

An impetuous fury rose in Eddy. No rest, no privacy, no beauty, no money!

His sisters had not moved. They were exhausted. And he felt compassion for them, for their tenderness in a tough, hard world. He believed that he understood them; he knew how desperately Lara longed for a child and would probably never have one; he knew how Connie, like himself, longed for betterment, for color, for life, he knew that her feet, like his, wanted to run. . . .

Now as they rested, unaware of his scrutiny, he observed his sisters. Connie had a nineteen-twenties look, one which was becoming fashionable again; her lips were a bold cupid's bow, her nose short and straight, her eyebrows two narrow, graceful curves above alert gray eyes. She was unusually vivacious and knew how to make the best of herself. People looked at her. Yet it was always said that Lara was the beauty, having what were called "good bones"; her face was a pure oval, and she had contemplative sea-blue eyes, the same color as Eddy's own.

His, however, were not contemplative, any more than Connie's were. Their eyes were quick; everything about us two, for better or for worse, is quick, he thought suddenly. And thinking so, it seemed to him that now was as good a time as any to say what had to be said, not that any time was really a good one for the dropping of a bombshell.

He said evenly, "I've something to tell you. I hope you won't be shocked too much, but I'm going to be leaving you. Leaving town. I'm moving to New York."

"You're what?" cried Connie, sitting up straight.

"There's a guy I've known since college. He's an accountant like me, only the difference is that he happens to have an uncle who's lent him enough to get started in brokerage. He wants a partner. He wants me, and he's willing to stake me, to take me in with him."

A gleam of interest shot through Connie's eyes. "Wall Street?" she asked.

"Yes, ma'am, you bet. Wall Street."

"Leaving us!" Lara cried. "Oh, Eddy!"

"Minutes away by plane, honey. I'm not leaving you. Not ever." And he repeated, "A matter of minutes. All right, a couple of hours. Not Afghanistan or the end of the world." His smile coaxed.

Lara was dismayed. "But you've been building up so nicely! I can't understand why you'd want to leave it all behind like that."

"Building? Yes. But it's too gradual, too slow, compared with this opportunity. It's small potatoes."

She thought, We're splitting apart already. Peg's six hours in her grave. Then it's true what they say: When the mother dies, the family breaks up. Couldn't he think of that, Eddy, Peg's golden boy with the bright hair, the sea-blue eyes, and the nonchalant stance? She felt suddenly hopeless.

Davey asked quietly, "How long have you known this?"

"About three months. I probably should have told you sooner, but I thought, well, we were all going through enough without having any more on our minds, so I waited." Eddy reached into his pocket. "Look. I had cards printed."

" 'Vernon Edward Osborne, Jr.,' " Lara read, and in a voice

6

that rang with sad reproach observed, "You've always hated the name Vernon."

"I know. But just for the card, it's distinguished. A little different."

Davey had another question. "Don't you have to put up any money at all, Eddy?"

"Sure, but not much. I've saved twelve thousand dollars out of my earnings, and I was incredibly lucky at cards one night a while back. Made another fifteen, believe it or not. So I've got enough to put down for my share of the partnership, and I'll pay off the balance out of what I make in the market."

Davey said slowly, "*If* you make it in the market, you mean."

"I'll make it. I have a feel for the market. I've kept a phantom investment account in my head. If I'd had the money to do it, actually I'd have made a killing." When Davey made no comment, Eddy said, "The market's on the rise, a long rise. Anybody can see that. Besides, you don't get anyplace in life without taking a few chances. You have to be willing to risk. That's what this country was built on. All the great inventors, all the industrialists, took risks."

Davey glanced at Lara, and she saw that he was reading her mind, feeling her sadness, as he always could and did.

Then he said quietly, "To each his own. I guess New York will agree with you, Eddy. It's no place for us. Lara and I have our places here. The shop's doing a whole lot better than it did when my dad had it, and I've got some inventions, some ideas I'm working on—" He stopped, took Lara's hand, and pressed it.

She could read her brother's mind. How good is "a lot better"? Eddy must be thinking as he glanced around the room. It was a pretty room, furnished with secondhand pieces that she had slipcovered herself in a scheme of pink, red, and cream, copied out of a glossy magazine. But the carpet, which had come with the flat, was threadbare. . . .

Eddy used to come home starry-eyed over some house he had

7

seen or some car he had ridden in. Like Pop before him he *aspired*; like Pop, too, he'd been quick to imitate the ways of the upper class, its dress, its speech, everything about it. But unlike Pop he was smart. He might do very well. Yes, it was possible. Oh, this was a blow all the same! To lose Eddy, for no matter what reason! To lose his native, almost invaluable good humor, the very sparkle that he brought into the room when he walked in! All this family, this family that was far too small in the first place, would miss him so. The empty space that he would leave would gape at them.

Now Connie, in her practical way, asked how soon he planned to go.

"I thought in about two weeks. First I want to help you get out of that apartment, find something nicer for you. In the first place it's too large for you alone, without Mom, and too glum besides. Do you feel up to going out with me tomorrow to look?"

"Well," she answered. "Well." Her eyes moved about the room, as if searching, then to Davey and Lara, and finally, looking down at the tear in the carpet, she said, "It looks as if we've both picked the same time to surprise each other. But maybe it's better to get it over with all at once."

Alarmed again, Lara cried, "What are you talking about?"

"Well, you see—you see—oh, you know, Lara, how I've been wanting to just—just *go* somewhere! I've never really *been* anywhere."

"Will you get to the point, Connie, please?"

Now Davey took over. "You don't need to apologize, Connie. Just tell us what's on your mind."

"Texas. I've been hearing so much about it. It's booming. You can always get a job." Emboldened, she continued, "There's something exciting just in the sound of it. Texas. Houston. I want to see it."

Lara's mouth went dry, and the palms of her hands were wet.

"You don't know a soul there, Connie. To go alone, leaving the only family you've got—it doesn't make any sense. None at all."

"But I think it does. And that's what matters, isn't it?"

"You're only twenty, Connie!"

"Yes. Twenty. Not sixteen, not twelve, or eight."

Lara tried another tack. "What kind of a job do you think you'll get without a single contact? How will you even know where to begin to find a place to live?"

"Darling, don't be a mother hen. I'll buy a newspaper and read the ads, what do you think?"

Lara's thoughts were sad and bitter. Yes, I was a mother hen. I had to be, hadn't I? All the years while Mom was too sick from chemotherapy to take real charge of things, and I with a teenage sister eight years younger than I and a lively brother five years younger than I.

"It's not so easy to find a job, Connie. You have no training. At least you do have a job here that you can depend on."

"What, selling slacks and skirts in a tenth-rate department store, when there's so much in the world to do and see?"

"You might take some courses and learn to do something better."

"I haven't the will just now, or the patience." Connie stood up and laid her hand on Lara's shoulder. "Don't look so hurt," she said. "I'm not staying away forever. Can't you make believe we're very rich, and I'm taking a year off to travel around the world?"

"She's right," Eddy said. "A young woman wants a change, a touch of adventure in her life. It's natural. Okay, you didn't want it, Lara. But if you hadn't fallen in love with Davey, probably you would have felt the same way."

Lara, knowing she was expected to smile, did so, faintly. "We'll talk some more," she replied.

Davey agreed. "Good idea. Today was a hard one, but tomorrow's another day, so let's try to lighten up a little. As Eddy says, nobody's going to the ends of the world."

Lara got the message. "Stay here for the night, Connie. It's no good going back alone to the apartment." It was a bleak place at best, sunless all day and noisy half the night because of the bar and grill beneath it. Now Mom's clothes were still hanging in the closet. "I'll go get some blankets from the spare room."

The spare room, she thought as she straightened the bed, was meant to be the nursery. It was to have had lemon-yellow walls, a frieze of Mother Goose figures, or maybe Winnie-the-Pooh, going all around. The furniture would be white, and for a girl the crib would have a canopy of dotted Swiss, or perhaps organdy. . . .

She hated the room. She kept the door closed, dusted it every week or two, then shut the door again. Seven years married, and nothing. Doctors, thermometers, hormones, sperm analyses, watching for the fertile period in the month—and nothing.

"Why don't you fix this room? You could have a nice little den," Connie remarked as she came in.

Connie doesn't know how that hurts, Lara thought, not answering.

On the dresser stood the room's sole ornament, a photograph of their parents, taken on their wedding day. The two sisters stood looking at it now. Their parents had been handsome people, Vernon dark with a sporty boutonniere and flashing teeth, Peg's sweet face tiny in its frame of lavish hair.

Connie sighed. "How happy they were that day! And how it all turned out! A good thing Mom couldn't have seen ahead."

"She loved Pop no matter what. Remember how he used to call her 'Peg o' My Heart'?"

"I don't see how she could have kept on loving him. I guess it was noble of her, but I'm not made that way. Life's too short."

"He was a good man except for the booze, and that wasn't his fault. It ran in his family. Thank God none of us has inherited it."

Pop had been a salesman, traveling back and forth through the

Midwest, selling—depending upon the company for which he happened to be working at the time—anything from shoes to toaster ovens to used tires. As often as he lost his jobs, so often did the family move from one flat to another, always in the oldest part of a town, above a hardware store, or a Laundromat, and under a crumbling pediment bearing some inscription like FERRY BUILDING, 1894, or BUMSTEAD BUILDING, 1911. The longest period that they had ever stayed in one place was when his liver and then his heart had finally failed; then Peg had opened her little beauty parlor and eked out a living for her children.

And yet . . . "He was a good man," she repeated.

Connie's look was a mingling of pity and disbelief. "I guess you've forgotten the nights when he came staggering home."

"No, but I remember the nights when he read poetry aloud to us."

Then Peg, who knew nothing about books, had nevertheless smiled in pleasure because her children were being taught to love them. Lara sighed. The ache lay heavy within her. Through all this dreadful day the memories had been aching. . . .

Once, before Lara was born, so Peg had told them, she had glanced at one of Pop's library books and seen the name Lara. "It was a Russian story he was reading, *Doctor Zhivago*, I think he said. Anyway, the name looked pretty, and so when you came along, I gave it to you."

And Connie? Well, Connie was Consuelo after the Vanderbilt heiress who married the Duke of Marlborough.

"She was forced to marry him. Isn't that awful?" Peg had been horrified. "I read it in a magazine. Went to her wedding with eyes red from crying. Isn't that awful?"

Those, then, were the parents, Vernon and Peg, a pair of tangled lives, knotted and twisted like a length of twine rolled carelessly.

Connie had begun to strip off her clothes. In bra and panty hose she stood before the mirror and stretched.

"I'm so tired, I hardly have enough strength to take a shower."

"Wait till the morning, then. You're clean enough and you need your rest."

Connie smiled. "You always used to say that. Oh, Lara darling, don't look so miserable! Don't worry about me. I'll do fine, I promise."

"I can't help worrying, can I? Besides, I'll miss you. I've never been without you."

"Don't you think I'll miss you too?"

"Are you really sure you're doing the right thing? It seems so drastic, so unnecessary."

"Lara, I need a chance to meet people." Connie spoke with unusual gravity. "In this town—you know what's here, Lara. I don't want a life like—"

Like mine, Lara said to herself. I know that. Walking home beneath the trees on a summer night, Davey asked me, "Are you willing to share almost nothing with me? I'll do my best for you, Lara. Only, my best isn't all that good." Was I willing? To go to the ends of the earth with you, Davey, to live in a tent or under the open sky. It was true then, and it is true still.

"You have such a lovely expression right now," Connie said. "What are you thinking?"

Lara shook her head. "I don't know. Just—everything."

"I love you, Lara."

"Of course you do. We all love each other. Go to sleep, dear. I'll go out and say good-night to Eddy."

He was already in his overcoat. "I waited to see whether you were feeling any better. Davey's gone down to his workbench."

"I feel all right. I guess I have to. But why, tell me why you had to encourage her?"

"She has a right to live her own life, Lara. Besides, she'll do what she wants with or without encouragement."

"She's rebellious. Yes, she's strong and clever, but she thinks she can make anything turn out exactly as she wants it to. She hasn't yet learned that that's not possible."

"Lara, you're a rock. Do you think we—Connie and I both— don't remember how you watched over us? I can still see you walking Connie to school and calling for her, I remember how you used to drive me to the barbershop and the dentist's. But, honey, a time comes when one can't cling to the rock anymore, and Connie's time has come."

"Whom have we got?" Lara blurted. "Two second cousins too old and poor even to make the trip for the funeral, and that's all. We have no roots and I'm trying to establish some, that's all."

"Money will help," Eddy said darkly. "And I'm trying to make some."

"We're not speaking the same language tonight, Eddy."

"Maybe not. We're both too tired to think." He kissed her. "I'll be going. Get some rest."

Through the window that overlooked the yard, she saw a light burning in Davey's shed behind the garage. The rain had slackened to a drizzle, and throwing an old coat over her shoulders, she ran out back.

Davey's workroom was a cramped jumble of shelves before which stood a battered table covered with a variety of implements, both delicate and solid, that had no meaning at all for Lara: tubes, filaments, calipers, chisels, fuses, and rolled copper wire, along with notebooks, pencil stubs, and oil-stained rags. Bent over all these now was Davey's dark, round head; he was apparently intent on writing in a notebook. At some time or other, when his current idea clarified itself, he would tell her what it was.

She was so proud of him! Even if nothing were ever to come of any of his inventions, she would always be proud of him. He was the first friend she had made on her first day in a strange high school in a new town. Walking home after school, she had been followed by a group of frightening toughs, but when Davey had appeared and walked next to her, they had dispersed. Later she found out why. The tall boy with the odd name, Davey Davis— Davey was his mother's maiden name—just happened to be the basketball star of the school.

She went inside and put her arms around him. He stroked her hair.

"I know. It's been a cruel day. Cruel months," he murmured.

"I've been thinking over and over how true it is that as soon as the mother's gone, the family scatters."

"No, no. We're too close for that. Anyway, plans change all the time. Nothing's written in stone."

"They'll never come back again."

"Lara! This doesn't sound like you. You're always the family optimist."

"I know. But sometimes I get to thinking that one can be a fool of an optimist too." She sighed. "You know what I mean, Davey. You know."

"The baby," he said gently.

"The baby we wait for every month and who never comes." Her voice broke. "And never will."

"Never is a long time, darling."

"Words, Davey. Just words."

He put his cheek on hers, holding her close. After a moment he said, "We could adopt."

"So you've stopped hoping too?"

"I didn't mean— Oh, Lara, it's so hard to know what to say to you. How to cope with these monthly disappointments, the doctors, the tests? I just don't know anymore. But we could adopt," he repeated.

"That's not easy either. One doesn't just walk in and select a baby. One waits for years, and even then—"

"Perhaps not a baby, but an older child who needs a home? Sad to say, there are plenty of those."

"I want a *baby*! I want to be the mother from the very start."

TREASURES

"Darling," Davey said, holding her tighter. "Then we should wait a little more. Won't you try some of your optimism again?"

She felt that she was weighing him down with her obsession while he was striving to lift her up. It wasn't fair of her.

"Okay, okay, no more. Let's go upstairs," she said.

In the familiar bed, under the quilts, they lay warmly and quietly.

"You're still the most beautiful woman I've ever seen," Davey murmured. "In a gingham apron or, better, in nothing at all."

And so, after a little time desire moved them. It fled across Lara's mind as they turned into each other's arms that this was the deepest joy and comfort of all, this total, trustful merging. This was the reality of life. All else faded away.

In the aftermath Davey fell immediately into sweet sleep. But for a long while she could only drowse, to dream and to be startled awake. In the confusion of one dream she had been sitting at the table that she always liked to picture in her head. It was a lavish table set with flowers, candles, and pink linen. Peg was well, with all her lovely hair. Pop in his best mood was reading aloud; she herself was a child, the privileged eldest, with the little brother and the baby sister next to her. But at the same time she was a young mother in a long rose skirt, sitting there with Davey and their children between them. "We couldn't have any, so we adopted them," Davey was explaining, when she opened her eyes.

But Davey hadn't stirred. She curved herself now into his back, feeling unity, feeling the safety of his presence in the silent room. A piece of sky, visible over the bulk of his shoulder, covered half the window. It seemed to be in motion, racing like the ocean she had never seen, a dark green ocean shot through with gleams of light.

CHAPTER
TWO

❧

H ouston was *hot*. Like a metal dome the bronze sky burned above the city. Dusty leaves hung through the long afternoon. Coming into the hotel from the street was like walking into a freezer room; the sweating body received a shuddering shock.

Connie's hotel was a huge commercial establishment in the downtown business district, neither expensive nor cheap, but suited to the funds that Eddy had advanced, adequate for a month or considerably longer if she were careful.

She had moved a chair over to the window. The outlook here, some fifty feet to a bank of similar windows on the opposite side of the meager courtyard, was depressing, but even such dim daylight was less depressing than was the sullen yellow lamplight next to the dingy brown bed. On the floor at her feet a pile of newspapers lay open at the want-ad section.

Column after column of Help Wanted confirmed her judgment: Texas was truly booming. With a feeling of challenge and elation she ran her eyes to the top of a page and down, when suddenly they paused, and she read,

TREASURES

Young vendeuse for exclusive shop, experienced European fashions for demanding clientele, well spoken, attractive appearance. Salary and commissions.

Vendeuse. From her slight experience with high-school French, Connie summoned up a verb: *vendre,* to sell. So what this verbiage boiled down to was being a saleswoman in a fancy dress shop. *Experienced.* Three years' worth, although not doing exactly what they were looking for. *Young. Well spoken. Attractive.* She stood up and went to the full-length mirror on the bathroom door.

The mirror showed her nothing that was not entirely familiar. Nevertheless, the sight was reassuring. Her heavy hair hung at a becoming length almost to her shoulders. The beige linen suit with coral shirt, Lara's going-away gift, was smartly slender; the gold earrings, Eddy's extravagant birthday present, were eighteen carat; her long, slender feet were shod in Italian shoes, which were her own extravagance, for she was vain about her feet and her long, slender hands. One by one, for perhaps the thousandth time since she had reached adulthood, Connie examined each feature of her face: lips just a trifle too thin, nose a trifle too short, cheekbones a trifle too wide; the whole no match for Lara's classic near-perfection. She knew that well and was not at all bothered by it, for she had the greater power to attract, and knew that well too.

The important thing was to know how to use this power to a practical end. So, before going to be interviewed, Miss Osborne, go buy a stack of magazines and make yourself familiar with European fashion. Then do your hair tomorrow morning, hail an air-conditioned taxi, and arrive coolly unruffled and speak up. There can't be much difference between selling polyester pant-suits and Chanel, can there? Selling is selling, and people are people, after all.

* * *

The shop, situated in a grand mall, was spacious and serene, carpeted in silver-gray and ornamented with sprays of gladioli. Here and there a circular rack held a dozen garments on display, but obviously, most of the stock was out of sight behind a mirrored wall.

Slowly and keenly, for half an hour, Connie was examined.

"You say you've had experience with merchandise like this?"

"Yes. In Cleveland."

"Have you a recommendation from them?"

"Unfortunately, no. The owner died of a heart attack, and everything fell apart the next day. As you can imagine," Connie added with a small sigh. She touched a lavender suit that hung where she was standing. "What they've been doing with Chanel is delightful, isn't it? Adding new touches without changing the traditional charm one bit."

"Ah, yes. Yes, of course. . . ." And finally, "Well, I suppose you're available to start soon?"

"That would be wonderful."

"Then we can go over the formalities in the office. Social Security and the rest."

So it was settled, an auspicious start on the third day in this vast, energetic city. It would be pleasant to work surrounded by beautiful, rich things. Granted, it would be still more pleasant to have the beautiful, rich things for oneself, Connie reflected, to own these silks and velvets before the wrinkles appeared on one's neck and the flab on one's upper arms. But one day at a time.

Next she must find a place to live.

Studio apartment, walking distance downtown.

Downtown meant very likely a dreary view like the one in this hotel, and streets abandoned after five o'clock.

18

TREASURES

Two young women will share apartment with third, share all expenses.

That meant, most probably, a sofa bed in the front hall and a parade of arriving or departing boyfriends all through the night.

Retired business couple have large room with kitchen privileges in suburban condominium for respectable single woman. Garden view.

That, now, sounded more like it, especially the "garden view." To live in the suburbs, however, she would need a car. But then, she would need one no matter where she lived in Houston unless she were to camp out in the mall. You have to spend money to make money, Eddy said. And Connie's mind began rapidly to click like an efficient small machine: Take some of Eddy's money for a down payment on a used car; then put aside a fixed sum out of her weekly salary to pay off the balance. Like Lara, but unlike Eddy, Connie feared debt. So, back to the newspaper for the used-car advertisements and then to see the room with the garden view.

Late in the afternoon she stopped her little red car in front of a neat brick building shaded by five oaks that had three stories height against the building's two. For a moment before climbing the steps to the front door, she looked back at the car. It had been a good buy, only two years old. Davey had once said, she remembered, that he always tried to get a demonstration car, and so she had shopped about and found one. This further success now gave her confidence.

A heavy woman with short, blue-gray curls answered her ring. "Mrs. Raymond?" asked Connie.

"Yes. Are you the person who telephoned this morning?"

"Yes. Consuelo Osborne. I'd like to see the room."

"You sounded older on the telephone."

"Did I?" She needn't be so independent, Connie was thinking as she smiled, because I might not even like the room.

"Is that your car?" Mrs. Raymond inquired.

And Connie replied, still smiling, "All mine."

"Well, come in. I'll show you the room."

At the rear of the house, which gave it a feeling of privacy, was an ample bedroom furnished with a Grand Rapids bed and dresser, a comfortable chair, and ugly maroon cretonne curtains. It was unmistakably clean. Connie's fastidious nose detected the very freshness of the air.

"It's lovely," she said.

"You're not a Texan."

"I'm from Ohio."

"What made you leave?"

"I can't stand the cold winters."

"Not sick, are you?"

"No, no," Connie corrected herself. You had to think fast in this world, or you'd be tripped up. "I'm perfectly healthy."

"Because I wouldn't want the responsibility of somebody getting sick in the house."

"Of course not. I understand."

"Because I would feel the responsibility, you know. We're churchgoing people."

"Oh, yes." An answer was expected. "I am too," Connie said piously. This was not exactly true, not exactly untrue either.

"To tell you the truth, we were looking for a more settled woman, someone older. But I can see you're a lady, and we do have to give youth a chance, don't we?"

Connie smiled.

"Osborne? English stock."

Connie nodded. "With a touch of Dutch on my mother's side."

Mrs. Raymond seemed satisfied. "Would you like a cold drink? I keep iced tea ready all the time in this weather."

The two sat down at the table in the immaculate kitchen. And Connie saw that the woman, now that her suspicions had been dispelled, was lonesome. It was sad to be fat, aging, and lonesome.

"So you said there was Dutch on your mother's side?"

"Yes, Mom always said we were cousins"—Connie laughed—"very distant cousins, of the Vanderbilts. That's how I got the name Consuelo." The story unfolded, rolling easily from her lips. Who knew, there might even be something to it. "I suppose if we had lived in New York, there would have been some contact, but Ohio's not next door. Dad was in the furniture business. He died just when I was about to leave for the University of Michigan, so I couldn't leave my mother alone. Not that there wasn't plenty of money, it was a question of caring for her."

"Poor dear, losing your mother so young." Mrs. Raymond was fascinated.

The afternoon wore on. At the end of it Consuelo got up, drove back to the hotel for her luggage, and by nightfall was comfortably established in the room with the garden view.

Houston was *rich*. In spite of all she had ever read, Connie had not been able to imagine how so much money could be so lavishly, so gorgeously, spent. Women bought without even asking the price: ski clothes for Vail or Gstaad, beach garb for the Caribbean or Hawaii, suede coats, cashmeres, British tweeds, Italian suits, French silks and ballgowns. The very feel of the fabrics, their softness, fluffy or crisp under the hand, was a pleasure to Connie and was communicated to her customers, bringing more sales and more commissions.

The owner was delighted with her. "You deserve a little something for your good work," she said one day. "Look in the back and pick out a couple of dresses for yourself. I'll let you have them at cost. We don't sell that many size fours, anyway," she added, "so I can spare them. Besides, you're good publicity. Just be sure to mention us when you're out on the town."

Connie, however, wasn't going out on the town at all. After four months in the city she still knew almost no one. To begin with, her working hours were long, leaving little time for anything but work. The other saleswomen were either middle aged or married or both. And the two who were neither had taken a dislike to the newcomer whose sales were bigger than their own.

How did you get to know people? Especially, how could you get to know the kind of people who came into the shop and talked about the Hermitage in Leningrad and hearing Placido Domingo at the Metropolitan in New York? Those were the people she wanted to know. The truth was, Connie was feeling more deprived here in Houston than she had felt back home.

Pride wouldn't let her admit it, however. Whenever she called Eddy, reversing the charges at his insistence, he was so full of his own enthusiasm that she was almost forced to respond in kind. When she talked to Lara, which she often did, especially on Sunday's creeping afternoons, she dared not even hint at anything less than perfect satisfaction, for Lara would only urge her, and ultimately even nag her, to come home.

One Sunday she got into the car and drove, idling along with no purpose except to pass the time. In the Memorial section the big, substantial houses spread their wings under the shade. On quiet streets nursemaids pushed perambulators while little boys and girls on their tricycles peddled alongside. Blue pools glistened, and people sat together under gay umbrellas.

In River Oaks the houses were even larger and farther apart, Jaguars and Mercedes stood before impressive entrances, and unmarred lawns were green as a billiard table. A group of young people—about Connie's own age—wearing tennis whites crossed the road and ran behind a house. One of the girls had a black ponytail tied with a red ribbon. It bobbed as she ran. There was something happy in the way it bobbed. And a feeling of desolation came over Connie; it felt as if, while she was standing in a crowd, everyone had suddenly turned his back to ostracize her.

She drove around the block, sped through the bleak downtown, and emerged upon a wide avenue on which stood great hotels among brilliant flowers, blazing in the sunlight. People, always people, in groups and pairs, were going in and coming out.

Back in her own room she could either read or turn on the television. Or else she could sit in the yard with the Raymonds and the family from the upstairs condo, two tired parents and two quarrelsome children. Or, she could stop off somewhere for a hamburger and a shake. . . . Instead, she swung the car into a hotel driveway and got out.

In spite of all the people who came and went, the lofty lobby was uncrowded. And she recognized a touch of amusement at herself for acting as if she had walked into a palace. It was only a hotel, and she was a hick, a rube, a bumpkin, staring at the chandeliers, the silk tapestries, the leather luggage on the carts, the diamond-studded watches in the jeweler's display window—staring at everything.

Presently, she went farther in, sat down, ordered tea, and watched the parade. She had been sitting long enough to have a second cup when a young woman on the banquette beside her spoke up.

"I hope you won't think me awfully rude, but I've been admiring your dress. I always love black and white, and I've been looking all over without finding a thing."

Obviously, she was hoping that Connie would say where she had bought the dress, and so, mindful of her employer's injunction, Connie did so.

"I might have guessed. Well, that place is far too rich for my blood."

The honest admission brought forth an honest response. "For

mine too. I only work there, and sometimes they let me get something at cost."

"Lucky you! I've just given notice on my job. I'm getting married and moving to Dallas."

"And lucky you! Getting married, I mean."

"I know. He's wonderful. By the way, my name's Margaret Ames."

"Connie Osborne."

A dialogue was now begun. Connie was starved for talk and the other, being euphoric, was also eager for it. By the end of half an hour intimate opinions, about clothes and hair and life in general, were being exchanged.

"I hope I can find a job in Dallas as good as the one I've had," said Margaret Ames.

"Oh? What do you do?"

"I'm at a country club, in charge of parties, lunches, weddings, dinners, stuff like that. I go over menus with people. I do it all. It's really great."

"Well, my job's pretty good, but I wouldn't call it great." And Connie confided, "The problem is, I don't meet anybody. It's hard, being in a strange city."

"I know. It's tough."

Both women sighed, Connie more deeply, and the other in sympathy.

"If I could make a change I wouldn't mind," Connie said tentatively, thinking, A job like hers at a club, perhaps? And she struck out boldly. "I suppose your work must be very complicated. Don't you have to know a lot about food and serving and—"

"Not really. I didn't know a thing when I started. You pick it up from the help, the cooks and the waitresses, as you go along. Actually, all you need is to be friendly, have a good memory, and be good looking."

Connie felt the stirring of serious interest.

TREASURES

"And you do meet a top class of people. The best. As a matter of fact, I met my fiancé there—well, not exactly, it was sort of roundabout, when his company sent him to do an estimate for a new roof."

"It sounds wonderful."

"Hey! Would you be interested? Because if you would, I'd be glad to recommend you to take my place."

"Really? You're an angel!"

"Good heavens, it's no trouble at all. And, you know, I have a feeling you'd just fit."

"I can't thank you enough!"

"Glad to do it. You know, you'd find it a whole lot easier than trying clothes on a bunch of finicky women all day. And the pay is close to double, I'll bet."

"Really? You're an angel," repeated Connie.

Every day, in the beginning, was magical. True, she was still on her feet as she had been in her only two previous jobs, and the hours were even longer. But to Connie the atmosphere of this place was compensation enough for tiredness. To look out every morning on acres and acres of green, over the golf course and the low hills beyond, then down where the pool and the tennis courts lay in a grove of cool trees! All was peace and ease; everything was beautiful. The gardens were brilliant. The airy rooms were shaded restfully against the glare of the afternoons. At dinnertime the blue-and-white dining room sparkled. At night on the terrace, candles flickered in hurricane globes and lanterns hung among the trees. One could imagine that nothing ugly or drab or worrisome had ever touched the lives of the people who played and danced here; it was as if they were all floating through their days and nights in a perpetual celebration.

Her heart expanded. Her normally high spirits soared higher. People liked her. She had a dependable memory for names and faces, which was exactly what the job required. The guests were pleased when she remembered where they liked to be seated and what they liked to drink. The staff, many of them older women who had been there for years, were almost motherly, surprising her by their total absence of resentment that someone so much younger than they had been placed over them. Apparently, to them, this was simply the natural order of things.

"Don't put the Darnley table near to the Exeters. Mrs. Exeter was Darnley's first wife, and the two women hate each other."

"If Mr. Tory says seven-thirty, he means seven twenty-eight. That man's so prompt, he'll be early to his own funeral. And you'd better have everything ready, too, because he's a crank."

Celia Mapes, who was handy with such advice, was kindly but could be meddlesome too.

"I've got a daughter about your age overseas with the army in Germany. Living with some guy she says she'll probably marry. I suppose you are, too, aren't you?"

"Living with some guy? No, I live by myself."

"What happened? Did you break up?"

"I've never had anybody to break up with."

"Never had a real boyfriend? Don't tell me. A girl like you."

"It's true, though."

"I don't believe it. You mean you've never—you're a virgin?"

"Well, believe it or not, I am."

"There's nothing wrong with you, is there?"

"Not that I know of." Connie laughed. "Maybe I'm funny, but I've just never really wanted anybody that way. Never met anybody. There was an awfully nice guy once, but he had acne, and it turned me off."

And there had been others, like the floor manager in the store back home. That one had been good to look at. But he was flat, without ambition. And all he could talk about was sports.

The older woman warned, with a shake of her head, "Well, my dear, it's no good being so fussy, or you'll find yourself left behind one of these days. Now, I've got a nephew I could introduce you to. Big guy, like a football player, and a real gentleman. He drives for an oil company. For real good pay too."

The offer was touching, and Connie felt mean to refuse it. I'm not a snob, she thought. It's not that. I'm not stupid enough for that. It's just that I'm not going to waste myself. So she lied.

"Thanks. Maybe some other time, but not now. My landlady's fixing me up with someone this weekend."

Celia Mapes looked at Connie with quizzical eyes as though she had recognized the lie. "You're pretty as a picture," she said bluntly, "but if you're thinking of teaming up with any of the members here, forget it. Money sticks to money, you know."

There were a good many young couples among the club's membership. She wondered how people so young could afford to live as lavishly as this. Had they all inherited their wealth? Her eyes and ears were curious and alert now as she passed among them, observing and catching phrases.

"There's really no difference between a Bentley and a Rolls."

"Oh, Charlie got these in Athens on my birthday. I adore Greek gold."

Connie's glance went to the brilliant, heavy necklace and the bracelets. Their owner's flat chest and protruding shoulder blades did nothing, either for them or for her glorious white dress. And the woman's voice, nasal and raucous, made you shudder.

Connie's glance flicked over a suntanned comely face and briefly met frank male compliment in a pair of dark, mischievous eyes. But she had long ago become accustomed to such fleeting admiration. Nothing ever came of it.

As the months passed, the job's first glamor inevitably began to dwindle. And she seemed to be looking down a long, long road with a dead end.

At the same time in New York, Eddy had been climbing with no shortness of breath, a long, easy hill. He and his partner, Pete

Brock, bolstered by Pete's uncle, had been advancing steadily, amassing both brokerage accounts and social contacts.

"It's a case," Pete said as the two young men sat in their office late one Friday afternoon, "of which comes first, the chicken or the egg. The guy you meet on the tennis court becomes your customer, and your satisfied customer invites you to play at his club. Not bad for a pair of immigrants from Ohio, is it?"

"Not bad at all," Eddy replied.

But not remarkably good either. Leaning back in the swivel chair, he surveyed the office, which consisted of four decently furnished rooms in a mediocre 1920s building, on a dingy street halfway between the garment district and the theater district. Pete's uncle owned the building, and so the rent was cheap. There was nothing wrong at all with the setup if one was content with security and a modest living. Obviously, Pete Brock was.

"I have to tell you something," Eddy said. "It's something I've been waiting to say and putting off because I feel a certain guilt about it."

"Why? What have you done? Been sleeping with my secretary?"

"I'm not kidding, Pete. The fact is, I want to leave, I want to leave you. I want to strike out on my own."

The other sat up straight. "Hey! I thought we were going along like a house afire! What is it? Anything you don't like about me? Give me the truth, Eddy. On the level."

"On the level. You're my friend, Pete, and I don't want you to think for one split second that I don't appreciate a thousand times over, that I'm not completely grateful, that I don't know how lucky I am that you and your uncle—what a fine, generous man!—chose me for your partner. Gosh, after all our college years, you've got to believe me, and—"

Pete waved his hand. "All right, all right, I believe you, but get to the point. What's the complaint?"

"It's not a complaint. It's that you and I go at different speeds, and—"

Again Pete interrupted. "Oh, because I don't want to take money out of the firm and invest, because I don't want a fancier office, because I'm satisfied with—"

"You're satisfied with less than I want out of life. That's about the size of it, Pete."

"More out of life! You've got a regular income, an apartment, friends, this whole fantastic city to play in. What's the more that you want out of life?"

The *more*. It was almost impossible to explain. It would sound absurd to say that this fantastic city had overwhelmed him with desire. What good was it to walk on Fifth Avenue or Madison or Fifty-seventh Street, gazing at the shops and the galleries filled with paintings of such beauty that you could hardly tear yourself away; what good to look at the airlines' posters of Paris, Hawaii, and Morocco, to stare at splendid women as they stared into the windows of splendid jewelers' shops, when every one of these was beyond one's reach? What Pete called an "apartment" was a remodeled flat on the top floor of a walk-up. A real "apartment" was on the Upper East Side on a wide avenue, Fifth or Park, or on a quiet side street with a doorman standing under a green awning. There was no use in trying to explain.

So he simplified his thoughts. "I'd like to expand, that's all. You remember how I talked to you about tax shelters? You said no. Positively no."

"And I still do. We're stockbrokers, Eddy."

"We're not limited to that, though. That's the way I see it. And you don't. But that's okay. Friends don't always have to see things the same way."

"Eddy, you're a gambler at heart." The tone was mildly reproachful. "You've got a gambling streak, and it's dangerous."

"Who, me? A gambler? You're all wrong, Pete. I've saved all my earnings. Built a nice fat nest egg. That's why I'm in a position to go out on my own. After I repay your uncle's loan and my half of the office expenses, I'll still be solid."

"Taking in a partner?"

"No, no. I'm setting up by myself. Osborne and Company. I'm the 'Company.' Brokerage and tax shelters. There's a tremendous call for them. Perfectly legal. But you have to know just how to structure them for big write-offs. Customers will come flocking if you can."

Pete shook his head. "Big. It looks like big trouble to me."

Eddy laughed. "No, no, no. But you know what's wonderful? That we can part with no hard feelings. Not on my part, at least."

Pete stood up and put out his hand. "Nor on mine. I wish you all the luck in the world, Eddy."

You had to spend money to make money. That was axiomatic. The decoration of the new office in a well-kept building on Madison Avenue had cost somewhat more than he had intended, but the result, as the decorating firm had promised, was totally pleasing.

"It's foolish to skimp on the quality of carpeting," the man had told Eddy. "You can actually feel the richness of good carpet underfoot. It conveys an unmistakable impression."

And it was true, he thought as he glanced about the new domain, from the dark green carpet to the elegantly framed etchings of classical Rome. What a relief after that dump of Pete's!

It was also true that a man's suit conveyed an unmistakable impression. One of the older men whom he had met at Pete's uncle's tennis club had recommended a tailor. What a difference a custom-made suit could make! And he stroked his arm, now encased in the best British worsted. What a difference!

At three he had an appointment with a builder. And hastening up Madison Avenue—someday he, too, would like a really distinguished office farther up the Avenue—he reflected upon the nice way things could mesh. This builder, the same man who had recommended the tailor, was planning a shopping center on Long Island and needed investors. At the same time some of the brokerage accounts who had left Pete to follow Eddy were looking for investments, shelters by which to cut their income taxes. It was encouraging to note how many customers had chosen him over Pete. And he hadn't by even the slightest hint lured any one of them away; he would never have done that. No, they had followed him of their own volition, proving that a good part of the business had come through him and not through Pete in the first place. But Pete had never been especially sociable. You had to be upbeat, you had to smile, if you wanted to attract people.

He was smiling when he entered Mr. Hartman's mahogany office.

"I want to thank you for recommending your tailor, Mr. Hartman. How do you like the suit?"

"You look like a million dollars, Eddy. If I had a son, I'd want him to look like you. So, let's get down to business. I'm swamped today, so let's waste no time. I hope you haven't come empty-handed."

"No, sir, I definitely have not. I've got five names, and I'll have two more by Wednesday sure."

The two men sat down with papers spread out between them.

"These are all responsible people, Mr. Hartman, as you can see. I'm about through checking their references, and they're all top drawer."

"I see they are. Always stick with the top drawer, young man." The older man placed Eddy's papers in a tidy pile. "And speaking of that, how would you like me to put you up for membership in my tennis club on the Island?"

"That sounds great, Mr. Hartman!"

"They've got nice accommodations. You can spend the weekend there next summer whenever you want. Get out of the city, play tennis, have a swim. It's all there. The fee's pretty steep, but it'll be worth it to you."

"I know it will, Mr. Hartman. I'm honored that you'll endorse me."

"No problem, Eddy. My pleasure."

They shook hands, and Eddy went down onto the street. It was all he could do not to whistle. This was the way you got ahead, step by step. An entrée like this one at the club would mean the opening of more new doors. He saw a long vista, a bright corridor lined with opening doors.

In such a mood, walking uptown for no reason other than that he felt like doing it, he stopped before the window of an art gallery. There, all by itself, hung a small watercolor of a pond, with catkins along the shore. Neo-Impressionist, he decided as he regarded it, set probably in New England. He had been buying art books, teaching himself against the day when he would be a buyer of art. And he went inside to inquire of a rather distinguished gentleman the price of the painting.

"Twelve thousand dollars. The artist has been doing very well. His prices are rising."

The distinguished gentleman spoke defensively, as if, Eddy realized at once, he had mistaken Eddy's expression for disapproval. Actually, Eddy's attention had been suddenly attracted by another watercolor on the wall.

"This one's better," Eddy said.

He moved closer to it. Here, too, was water, a cove or inlet where sailboats were at anchor in the evening; so deft, so real, was it that one could almost hear the soft lapping of the water and feel the cool air. Yet for all its realness it was no picture postcard; there was something—something else that the artist had put there. He couldn't have defined what the something was, he only knew that it was there, and it was art. A marvelous, unfamiliar excitement rose in him.

"Yes," he said. "Much the better of the two."

"You're right, of course. Quite right. He's a finer artist than the other."

"Naturally, it must be more expensive?"

"Actually, it's two thousand less. The man's just coming up, you see. The other has a bigger name. That's why his work's in the window."

"Ah, I see." He knew that he had spent an awful lot on the office, and he was due to move out of the walk-up flat next month, and would need to furnish the new place, but he wanted this picture.

"I'm going to buy it," he said. Then, bluntly, although it was no one's business, he added, "The price is a bit high for me at present, but this will be the first picture I'll have bought, and I really want it."

"I congratulate you on your taste. You have a fine eye. And you will not be sorry. In a few years' time I predict you'll get twice the price back should you ever decide to sell it."

After identifying himself Eddy wrote a check and carried his happy purchase home, where he hung it on the wall opposite his bed. It was a good investment, the man had said, so it was nice to know he might someday sell it and get something more valuable in its place. So much the better. That was not why he had bought it, though, and he did not believe he would ever want to sell it.

At night his room, because of the streetlamps, was only gray-dark. He lay for a while with open eyes, gazing at his purchase and smiling to himself. The artist had made magic in his ordinary little room; the purest starlight streamed from the picture on the wall and quivered, touching the very air with silver.

And this beautiful thing was his. I'm really moving up, he thought, before he fell asleep. I'm moving up.

In the service wing of the building Connie had a little office, not much larger than a cubby, with a desk and two wooden chairs. One morning a young man knocked at the open door and introduced himself. "I'm Richard Tory, and I understand you're the person to see about a surprise luncheon for my mother. You are Miss Osborne, aren't you?"

"I am, but I'm always called 'Connie' here."

"I didn't know. I hardly ever come to the club, although my family's been here since before I was born."

His was, indeed, an unfamiliar face. If she had seen him before, she would have remembered him, for he had a distinctive crown of light, very curly hair, fair skin, and aquiline features that one would more readily expect to find on a dark Roman aristocrat. Nor would she have expected him to be the son of a "crank."

He gave her a smile that was almost shy. "I've never done anything like this before. I hope you'll help me."

"No problem at all. You want to give a luncheon."

"Yes. It's my mother's fiftieth birthday, and I thought of assembling her best friends, about fifty in all. I'd love to have it at home, only then it wouldn't be a surprise. You'll be sure not to give it away?"

"No, no, don't worry."

"I suppose you know my folks?"

"Yes, they've been here quite often."

"My mother likes things simple. What I mean is, no favors or balloons, nothing like that. It wouldn't be her style."

"I shouldn't think so." The words had come out unbidden, with a ring that gave Connie a shock, for he might well have heard a sardonic tone that she had not intended.

But his eyes held humor. "Well, then, I'll leave it to you. Plenty of flowers on the tables—she loves flowers. In wicker baskets, do you think?"

"That's always pretty. Any special color?"

He considered. "She likes blue. Cornflowers, maybe? Cornflowers and white daisies?"

"You have good taste. I can get blue-and-white checked table-cloths, a country-garden-party effect. How does that sound?"

"Good, good! And you'll know what ladies like to eat at these lunches?"

"Oh, most of them are dieting. Why don't you let me talk to the chef and make up a menu? Then I can phone you for your approval, and we can go over more details."

"Of course. Be sure not to call me at home, though. I live with my parents. Here's my office number. And thanks a lot."

What a nice person, Connie thought when he left. *Nice.* She looked at his business card. McQueen-Bartlett Advertising. The telephone directory listed it at a prestigious address downtown. Then, turning pages to the residential listings, she found Roger Tory at a River Oaks address and Richard Tory with a separate number at the same address.

River Oaks. The grand stone houses under the grand old trees. Sighing, she put the directory back on the shelf.

The party went well. Fifty middle-aged ladies in silks and linens came bearing gifts, drank champagne, sang 'Happy Birthday,' and went home satisfied. At the end Mrs. Tory summoned Connie to compliment her cordially on the arrangements.

"Your son had as much to do with it as I did," Connie told her, which of course was not true. Yet something compelled her to bring his name into the conversation.

"Really? Well, Richard has always had an instinct for doing things right," his mother replied as she departed.

It had occurred to Connie that he might perhaps drop in at the party to see how things were going. But since he had not done so, it was hardly likely that she would be seeing him again —although it was absurd to think it would make any difference in her life even if she were to. So it was with some surprise that she looked up from her desk one morning in the following week to find him at the door. He was wearing tennis whites and carrying a racket.

"I hear the party was a great success, so I thought I'd come by to thank you."

"It was a pleasure to do it," she replied.

He stood in the doorway as if uncertain whether to say more, to come farther or to retreat.

"I haven't played tennis here in a couple of years," he said then. "It's handier to play at home. But I thought I'd give this a try for a change to see whether I could beat the pro."

"And did you?"

"No, but I gave him a run for his money."

"You must be pretty good."

"Well, I'm not bad."

His face was open, with a wide forehead and a friendly mouth. He had a vital look. Wholesome, she thought.

"I'm not bad either," she said immodestly. "My brother taught me, and he's marvelous."

"Then would you like to have a game sometime?"

"I'd love to, but don't forget I'm a working girl."

"And I'm a working man. This is my three-week vacation. Otherwise, I'd be in the office at ten-thirty in the morning. Ten-thirty at night, too, often enough."

How could this be happening? It seemed as if she was delicately balancing, teetering on a narrow plank, placing one foot softly ahead of the other with arms out, fearful of a fall. The wrong word, either too eager or too indifferent, could bring about the fall.

She said carefully, "I have Sundays and usually Mondays, unless there's a wedding or something, and—well, it's flexible time, depending on the schedule. They're very considerate of me here."

"They should be. So, when are you free? Anytime this week?"

TREASURES

"It happens that I've got this afternoon off. But you won't want any more tennis today, will you?"

"No, it's gotten beastly hot. I will want lunch, though, won't you?"

"Oh, I never miss lunch. Sorry to say, I've got a healthy appetite."

He smiled. "So have I. There's a great place down the road. I'll go change, and then how about meeting in the parking lot at half past twelve?"

I can't believe this, Connie kept thinking. He's so easy to talk to. He reminds me of Davey. Lara would like him. He's not at all what I'd expect from anyone who lives in River Oaks. But what do I know about anyone who lives there? I do know he doesn't seem like the men I've been watching at this club with their skeptical, suave faces. The restaurant was emptying out, and they were still settled in a booth with a second order of iced coffee before them.

"I usually like to travel someplace for my vacation," Richard was saying, "even if it's only up to New York. The company has me spending so much time there that I've got myself a small apartment near the U.N. building. My parents like to fly up for theater weekends, so they can use it too. Do you like New York?"

"I've never been there. I've never been anywhere, actually." Then, because that sounded pathetic, Connie fell back upon the explanation she had devised and now knew by heart. "First my father always said he couldn't leave his business. A large furniture business. He was a real workaholic—you know the type. Then when he got sick, naturally . . ." she made a pretty gesture with her hands. "After that Mom got sick, too, and we couldn't leave her, wouldn't leave her." She did not finish.

"It must have been awful for you," he said kindly. "Well, I'm sure you'll get to see the world. If you want to, you will, you know."

"I'd especially love to see England. My family was always so aware of roots, and they were all in England except for a bit of Dutch way back. Distant relatives of the Vanderbilts—or maybe not so distant. And then there's a Catholic branch," she added, suddenly remembering a fact from American history class. "Some ancestor came to Maryland with Lord Baltimore."

"Gosh, I'm a plebeian compared with you. Most of my folks were Irish who came over during the potato famine. And I've got a Polish great-grandfather who worked in the coal mines."

Connie spoke lightly. "What difference does it all make? People are people."

"Right you are. When shall I see you again? Saturday? Sunday?"

"Sunday would be lovely."

"Okay. Write down your address, and I'll pick you up. And bring your swimsuit. We'll want a swim before lunch."

She had to tell Celia Mapes. "Can you believe it? Richard Tory's asked me out. And to his house, no less."

Celia looked doubtful. "I believe it if you say so."

"Well, it's true. He's really sweet. The only thing is, I hate the idea of being there with the family. They look like people who won't be too thrilled about having me either."

"You can bet they won't be, honey. I've known them for twenty years, and I can tell you they don't improve with age."

"Oh, Lord, I'm scared to death already."

"You'll do all right, I'm thinking. You must have given that fellow some come-on."

"I swear I did nothing of the sort. I didn't do a thing."

There was a new respect, almost comical, in Celia's head-to-foot examination of Connie. "You'll do all right," she repeated then, with a wise nod.

* * *

TREASURES

In back of a long white brick house with symmetrical wings and a classical facade lay the perfect lawn, the tennis court, and the pool that one would expect to find there.

"We have the place to ourselves today," Richard said. "My parents won't be back till tonight."

It seemed quite clear what these words meant. And something occurred in Connie's head, a self-analysis swift as a computer printout: My heart's excited. My first time, and it's past time. I'm twenty years old. But should . . . ? Does he expect it . . . ? The day would unfold and end then, either in a bed upstairs or in the poolhouse.

At the moment, he was leading her to the tennis court. She had bought something new, a short Wimbledon skirt; it looked traditional, as shorts did not, and instinct had told her that a conservative effect would be a good thing to have today. Now that the parents were not here, she was sorry she hadn't bought the shorts. However, this tiny flounce was becoming, too, as it whipped above long, tanned legs. She played well, feeling grateful to Eddy for all those mornings when he had made her rise early to get to the town courts before they were taken.

"Hey, you're a great player. You didn't tell me how good you were," Richard called over the net.

He won the set, although not easily. But even if she had been able to beat him, she would not have done so. Never mind women's liberation; certainly she was in full accord with it, yet there were basic truths that common sense wouldn't let one deny, and one of them was that men didn't like to be beaten.

Next in the pool, where she dove and raced with ease, she was thankful again for Eddy's tough, insistent training.

"The more skills you have, the farther they'll take you." That had been his constant admonition, and she saw now that it had been worth heeding, for Richard was a graceful athlete and he was plainly admiring her skills.

"You're terrific," he kept saying. "Terrific!"

39

He had an enthusiastic way of speaking, with superlatives and exclamations, so that she had to wonder how old he might be; his manner seemed extraordinarily young.

So she asked him, and he told her. "Twenty-four. Why?"

"No reason, really."

"Were you wondering why I'm still living here at home?"

He was more keen than she'd thought! And before she could reply, he said, "Actually, I'm planning to leave. I've applied for transfer to the New York office. I have to break the news gradually. It'll be a real disruption in my parents' lives because I'm the only child they have, and naturally, they hate to let go." He added, smiling, "Not that it's been any real hardship for me to live here."

"I wouldn't think so," Connie said, looking around the terrace with its white wrought-iron furniture, its cobalt-blue awnings, and its petunias trailing out of stone urns. One would want to think it over more than once before departing from such a pleasure island, such a comfortable world as this.

"Come on, I'll show you the house," Richard offered. "Women always like to see houses, don't they?"

"This one certainly does."

One large cool room, dimmed by drawn blinds against the noon heat, opened onto another. They had walked into the eighteenth century. She might have foreseen that Mrs. Tory would belong here. She could have predicted that chairs would be Sheraton, sofas Chippendale, and that the dining room would be papered with Chinese peonies.

At the center of the table stood a crystal swan. And Connie smiled to herself, pleased to have recognized it as Lalique.

"It's lovely," she said now. "A lovely house."

In the hall Richard paused, and the thought raced through her mind: Now he will suggest going upstairs.

Instead, he said, "The cook's left lunch for us in the refrigerator. I thought we might take it outside."

TREASURES

Not sure whether or not to be relieved, she helped him carry the lunch: a seafood salad, strawberry tarts, and a bottle of white wine, properly chilled.

The umbrella and the surrounding shrubbery gave shade. If a pair of mourning doves had not been cooing at the feeder, the garden would have been completely still, and Connie sighed with pleasure.

"I think I know what you're feeling," Richard said, remarking on the sigh. "Sometimes I think I'm crazy to give this up for a couple of rooms thirty-three floors above the New York sidewalks. And yet I want to." He mused. "New York's the origin, the fount, of good things. Not that we haven't got plenty of them here, too, music, art— But then I guess you've found them for yourself."

"I'm ashamed to say I haven't."

"Really? Well, then, we'll have to do something about it, won't we?"

So today was to be only a beginning! Connie's heart acknowledged this with a small, eager leap. But her reply was calm.

"I'd like that very much."

"There's an exhibit of Western art on right now. I went last week, but I wouldn't mind going again. Southwestern things are especially good. Red rocks and canyons and Indian faces—some people find them trite by now, but I never do."

"Do you collect art?"

He shook his head. "I'm not a collector of anything except books. I feel that great art belongs in museums where thousands of people can see it. Besides, I couldn't afford great art even if I wanted to."

"I agree with you—about art belonging in museums, I mean."

Richard responded quickly, "Do you? I'm glad. Most people around here use paintings for status. The higher the price you paid, the higher your status. And some of the stuff they buy is

41

nothing but fad stuff. Why, I was at a house last week when the funniest thing—oh, I shouldn't bore you."

"Please. I want to hear it."

"But you don't know the people I'm talking about. You don't know the way they think, and if you don't, my story loses its point."

"No names, but just tell me. Do they belong to the club?"

"Yes. Most of the people I know belong to it."

"Then I have a pretty good idea how they think."

She met his glance, and in the same instant they both laughed. Oh, I like him, I like him, she thought. He's smart and funny, and honest, and I like him.

The afternoon went fast. "I've had a great day," he said when they arrived at her door. "I hope you did too."

"It was wonderful," she answered. His good-bye kiss was gentle, a chaste kiss.

They saw each other every day that remained in his vacation. When she had to go to work early, he called for her and returned to bring her home. On late nights he waited for her. It was remarkable how easily one could fall into dependence on such attentions, could assume that the face with the good smile would be there on the other side of the door.

He took her to the exhibit of Western art, to some concerts, and a ballet. All of these were enchantments for Connie. Certainly she had known they existed, and yet she was astonished when they materialized before her eyes and ears, as if they were a kind of lovely magic.

She thought about Richard almost all the time, while she was working or falling asleep or after restless sleep, waking too early in the morning. Who could tell whether anything more was to follow these few bright days? Nothing was sure, she told herself, with the remembrance of her mother's misguided optimism to warn her.

He hadn't taken her to bed. He hadn't brought her to his

house since that first day, which meant quite obviously that his parents had already disapproved, or that he knew they would disapprove if they were told. Subtleties, things spoken and unspoken, were making clear to her acute mind that Richard feared their disapproval.

This insight by no means lessened her respect for him. Was she falling in love with him? There flashed before her a picture of Lara at her wedding, of her face turned toward Davey, of the trust, the adoration, and the joy in that face. And Davey had had nothing to give Lara except himself.

However, I am not like Lara . . . for a moment she felt guilty. Suppose that Richard worked in a gas station and lived in a two-room flat, would he be just as desirable? No, of course he wouldn't. Yet that wasn't a fair supposition either. One might just as easily ask whether, if she herself had bad skin and were fifty pounds overweight, Richard would want her! Of course he wouldn't, even though she'd be the same person inside. The facts were simple: You can't separate a person from externals. They're all part of the person.

Days passed. They went on picnics. They spent a day in San Antonio. They danced at country barbecues and dined at sumptuous French restaurants in town. By the third week they were still what they had been in the first week, a congenial couple having a wonderful time, who ended their pleasant hours with a rather tender kiss. When, sometimes, Richard stroked her breasts, Connie felt intense excitement and anticipation, but he never sought more.

On this night, however, there came a difference. Suddenly over the *coquilles Saint-Jacques* and the wine, he fell into silence. Over the candle tips and the *bavaroise au chocolat*, his eyes, empty of their customary humor, fixed themselves on Connie with an almost stricken gaze. Then she, too, not knowing what to say, fell silent.

"You're the most beautiful woman I've ever seen," he said.

She responded lightly, "Beauty is in the eyes of the beholder."

"Ah, don't be flippant, Connie. Let's get out of here. Can't talk in this place."

When they were in the car, he commanded, "Now listen to me." He grasped her two hands. "Listen. They're finally transferring me to the New York office, and I can leave next week. But I don't want—I can't go without you, Connie. I'm in love with you. I never thought—I mean, you read about these things, but they never made sense, at least to me, they didn't. That a person could feel the way I do now, and be so sure of wanting to spend the rest of his life with someone! And yet I'm more sure about this than I've ever been about anything. What about you, Connie? Can you love me? Can you marry me?"

How could she not love a man who looked at her, who touched her, as if she were the most precious object ever made? The moment was brilliant, exquisite, and filled with a kind of awe. Her heartbeat thundered in her ears.

"Oh, yes," she said. "Oh, yes."

After a few minutes he released her and turned on the motor. "I want to get you home because I'm going to pick you up early tomorrow morning. You've got to meet my parents."

"Have you said anything to them?"

"No. There wasn't anything to say without knowing your answer."

She felt a small chill of dismay. "What if," she asked, speaking carefully, "they don't like me?"

"Oh, they will. When they see you—"

"Maybe I'm not what they expected for you."

"But you are. Connie darling, you're a beautiful lady. So fine —it shows in everything you do."

"But if they still shouldn't want me?"

"Then no matter. I want you."

In front of Connie's house they kissed again. The night was

calm and bright. When, still held against his warm chest and shoulder, she opened her eyes, she saw that the sky was filled with stars. It seemed as if she had never seen so many before. Surely they were a good omen.

"I hate to leave you like this," Richard whispered. "I wish I could walk in that door with you right now and stay."

She giggled. "The Raymonds would probably drop dead of shock if they found you in my room in the morning."

"That's not the only reason. We could have had my house all to ourselves and done anything. But somehow I couldn't ask you, and I wouldn't ask you now. I guess I knew from the start that you weren't going to be any one-night stand or anything temporary. I guess I'm just old-fashioned, Connie."

She giggled again. "You're from another century, darling."

"As long as you approve of me."

"I approve of you."

"Then I'll be here early. Nine-thirty? That'll give me time to tell my folks first."

She was too overwhelmed to sleep. Consuelo Tory, she thought. She sat down on the bench before the dressing table and stared into the mirror. Astonished eyes stared back at her. Why me? they asked. How can it be possible to get what one wants so easily, so soon? People always tell me life isn't like that.

On the back of the envelope that lay there she wrote, *Consuelo Osborne Tory*, reflecting on the elegance of that name engraved in navy-blue script on a pale-blue paper. Then, after tearing the paper into pieces too small for Mrs. Raymond to decipher, she threw them into the wastebasket and prepared for bed.

Disconnected shreds and fragments floated through her head. Tomorrow's dress: a white silk shirt and pleated skirt with black-and-white shoes and a flat black taffeta bow at the nape of her neck would be right, refined and demure. The wedding ring: Dare she ask for a diamond band? No, ask for nothing; just be delighted with anything you get. That day at his house the dessert plates were lovely, a single dark blue flower on a pale yellow ground. Lovely. I wish I knew where to get them. Eddy will be amazed when he hears. We'll be seeing each other in New York. . . . Eddy will be pleased with Richard . . . happy for me.

The air conditioner's sleep-inducing hum took hold. Still, in her dreams, the shreds and fragments floated, in dreams such as children have through the long impatient night before Christmas.

By eight o'clock she had already been on the telephone with Lara for half an hour.

"But you can't do this," Lara kept crying. "You hardly know him."

"Peg knew Pop six weeks before she married him, and they'd still be together if they'd lived. You know that." When no reply was made, Connie persisted, "I can tell what you're thinking. But Richard is not an alcoholic any more than Davey is."

After a moment Lara asked what he did for a living.

"He's in the advertising business, and we're moving to New York." Hastily she added, "But he's not at all what you think of when you hear 'Madison Avenue,' sharp and competitive—you know? Richard's got a kind of innocence, almost, that's very appealing. And he must have a lot of talent, or they wouldn't be promoting him. Lara, he's wonderful, he's everything you'd want for me, and I love him."

"Well, if you're sure . . ."

"Darling, I'm sure. Aren't you sure about Davey?"

"When shall I meet him?"

"He wants to be married next week. Can you get down here?"

"Honey, I can't possibly do it on such short notice. Davey's having trouble with his father, another stroke and—can't you wait a little?"

"Richard doesn't want to. But it's okay. Obviously, we're not having a big wedding. So we'll come visit you afterward instead."

And suddenly a picture printed itself in Connie's head: the

peeling paint on the two-family house, the scruffy weeds in the yard, Richard climbing the stairs . . . Not that he would ever care; he was too decent, too intelligent, for such snobbery; wouldn't he care, though, that she had lied to him?

There was time enough, however, to think about that later.

"So will you tell Eddy? I tried to get him on the phone just now, but there was no answer."

"He's probably at his club for the weekend. Our Eddy seems to have made contact in high places."

Not as high as mine, I'll bet, Connie thought, but did not say.

Later, in the car, Richard said, "I've told them, and they're expecting you."

"And?"

"Well, they were surprised, of course. It is a little sudden, after all."

"Just surprised? No objections?"

"They're only worried about whether I was sure, and I told them I was and that you were too. So," he said, "you haven't the slightest reason for being nervous. Just be yourself."

The Torys were standing at the front door when Richard stopped the car. In the second before recognition and greetings Connie had an illusion of Grant Wood's "American Gothic," the farm couple in overalls and housedress, standing stone faced and rigid together. The illusion dissolved into brass-buttoned blazer and printed silk as they all shook hands.

"I'm sorry, you'll have to get back into the car," Mr. Tory said, "and drive your mother to your Aunt May's. She's sick again. Miss Osborne can stay here with me."

"But that'll take all morning," Richard said.

"I know, but it can't be helped. I'd go myself, except for an important call that I'm expecting."

"I'm really sorry," Mrs. Tory explained. "Miss Osborne, make yourself at home. You'll have lunch with my husband and Richard will be back by two o'clock, I'm sure."

Connie looked sympathetic. "I do hope your aunt—"

"My sister."

"Your sister will be all right. And do please call me Connie."

Richard seemed flustered. "I don't know whether I told you, her real name is Consuelo."

"Consuelo? As in Vanderbilt?"

Connie smiled. Her closed-lip smile, she knew, was charmingly modest. "As a matter of fact, there is a relationship. Cousins, way, way back."

"Really? How interesting."

"You'd best be going," Mr. Tory said.

"I'm awfully sorry, Connie," Richard apologized.

She put up her hand. "Please! If your aunt's ill, family comes first. Always. I'll be fine. I'll have a quiet time reading."

The library to which Mr. Tory conducted her and where he left her was a handsome, rather masculine room furnished with leather chairs and dark red walls. She had expected to find that the books on the shelves were uniform, expensive sets of the classics, put there by a decorator, not to be read but to harmonize with the furnishings. On the contrary the books were a collection to delight a browser. And then she remembered that Richard had said books were the only things he collected. Finding a copy of the *Pickwick Papers,* she sat down to pass the time.

She hadn't been fooled by this ruse. Richard had been whipped away so that his father could talk to her alone. After a decent interval Mr. Tory would come in, probably to fetch her to lunch, and the interrogation, no doubt a diplomatic one, would begin.

And that was exactly what happened, so that by half past twelve Connie found herself in the dining room sitting across from Richard's father with the Lalique swan between them.

"You're very well thought of at the club," he began. "You're much more efficient than anyone that we've had there for quite a while. I thought you might like to know."

48

"I'm very glad," she answered simply. "Thank you for telling me."

"Have you had jobs like this before?"

"No, never. I'm quite inexperienced, I'm afraid."

"Indeed! Richard says you're a newcomer to Texas."

"Yes, I'd always wanted to see it. Such an exciting place, especially for someone who grew up in a small town."

Tory's hooded eyes were keen and all Connie could see were ugly gleaming slits.

"Didn't your family object to your going so far all alone?"

You're polite enough in your searching, Connie thought, but you're surely getting right to the point, aren't you?

Softly, she replied, "My parents are dead. And I'm sure they wouldn't have let me. I was very strictly brought up. My father's parents were British, and he had their ways." She sighed. The sigh and the words came easily now. "But they'd both been sick so long. I just had to get away from all the sadness."

"Are you an only child?"

"No, I have a married sister at home. Her husband's in business there. And I have a brother on Wall Street."

"I see. Then what would you call this? Rather a lark, what you're doing?"

Connie gave a small laugh. "You could call it that. Rather a lark."

"Richard told us this morning that he wants to marry you. We told him it seemed rather hasty."

The maid came and Tory stopped talking. During the brief, uncomfortable silence Connie's mind divided itself between tension over Mr. Tory's possible questions and observation of her surroundings. The spoons and forks had been laid facedown on the table, probably because the chased and monogrammed backs were meant to be seen. The girl's spring-green uniform matched the background of the wallpaper. She knows something is afoot,

Connie thought. Back in the kitchen she'll be reporting to the cook.

"Times have changed. I can still remember," Mr. Tory resumed, "at least here in our group, people usually married within the group, people they knew, or certainly that the families knew for a long time. Now it seems that total strangers get together after a few meetings."

Connie tried a coy comment. "Like Romeo and Juliet."

Tory said dryly, "They came to a rather unfortunate end, if you remember." When she made no answer, he continued, "Like them, too, you're both rather young."

"Richard is twenty-four."

"Richard is twenty-four going on eighteen. Oh, he's well educated, he's traveled, he's talented—all that's obvious, but we who know him best know that he's also ignorant of life. He's totally inexperienced."

She understood what the man was thinking. This girl's looking for money, and Richard doesn't see it.

Now she had to wonder and weigh how best to win the man over. To adopt a virtuous, almost a humble posture, or to show strength by standing up to him? If she made the wrong move, he could ruin everything, regardless of what Richard said. She might ruin it all, anyway. . . . When she'd come so far . . . Well, she wasn't going to let him.

"Richard is an idealist," his father said, sounding the admirable noun as if it were "embezzler."

Not having made up her mind yet as to which manner to adopt, the shy or the independent, Connie spoke a noncommittal truth. "Richard is one of the kindest people I've ever known, honest and trusting."

"Oh, yes, trusting. And that ties right into his lack of experience."

Tory met Connie's eyes with some severity, but she did not flinch.

"Now, I have the impression that you, on the other hand, are rather more experienced."

The implication was abruptly clear. She followed Tory's thought: They've been sleeping together, the girl's going to get herself pregnant, and Richard will naturally take on his responsibility.

And now she was ready for Tory. "You're implying, I think, that I'm experienced with men, Mr. Tory. That I pull tricks. No double meaning intended." Her little laugh was bitter, and Tory flushed. "You might like to know that, believe it or not, at not quite twenty-one, I'm still a virgin." She was working herself into such righteous indignation that tears began to blur her eyes. "I come of a very fine family—"

Tory was disconcerted. "Oh, I have nothing against you personally. It's plain that you're a fine young lady, and—"

"I understand that you're looking out for your son's best interest, and you should. If my father were living, he would be looking out for mine. He always did, he protected us against the world, he died too young—" By now her tears were overflowing her eyelids.

Tory stood up and laid a hand on her shoulder. And she saw that, stone face or no, he was sentimental. He thought her tears were for her dead father. Was it the tears or the indignation that had won for her? No matter; the tide of battle had definitely turned in her favor.

"Come, come, don't cry. Let's talk things over sensibly. No need to cry."

She took the handkerchief that he offered and stood up. "I'll be a good wife to Richard, Mr. Tory. You don't have to worry about that. I know the value of a dollar. I get along with people, and I'll be a help to him. And I love him with all my heart."

There came the sound of tires crunching gravel.

"Richard's back," said his father. "Come, now. He mustn't see you crying."

*   *   *

The Torys' minister performed the marriage at their house with Mr. and Mrs. Tory as the witnesses. Richard had asked Connie to invite someone on her side, but she had declined. The only people whom she knew well enough here to care about were Celia Mapes, the head waitress, and Mrs. Raymond, the landlady, who in many little ways had shown a fondness for her tenant. These two simple women were utterly bewildered by Connie's Prince Charming story, and truly glad for her as well. So she would have liked to invite them, but at the same time she knew that would only be rubbing salt into the Torys' open wound. Quite obviously, they wanted this wedding to attract as little attention as possible.

The five participants stood before a small table within the semicircle of the bow window. Connie was thinking: This is the high peak of my life, and it will be over in ten minutes. I have to remember everything. The sonorous words coming out of the mouth above the clean-shaven chin, which is above the reversed collar. Richard's parents. They're probably not such awful people, since Richard loves them. The light is streaming through the curtains, turning his face pink. Now he's smiling at me. I don't know him at all, and it scares me. Yes, of course I know him. He's everything that's good. And here's the ring, a diamond band after all. Is this happening to me? To me? I love him. I'm not scared at all. I love him. . . .

"Richard, I love you," she said the moment it was over.

Thirty-three floors beneath the windows of the New York apartment, lights moved along the East River Drive. All around in every direction the lights of the great city glimmered and gleamed, dazzling in Connie's astounded eyes. Tomorrow Richard was going to start her education in the city's ways and by-ways: the museums, Broadway, Lincoln Center, Fifth Avenue . . . No end! My God, no words, no pictures, had ever begun to realize the marvel of it all! For long minutes she stood and gazed.

It was still some time before midnight, and Richard had gone to sleep, but she, wakeful, sat down at the dinette table and drank a cup of hot milk. Her mind spun back over the hours since yesterday, living and reliving this beginning of her new life.

It had seemed fitting, like closing a circle, to spend their first night at the Houston hotel where she had learned of the position at the country club. Events had made an orderly pattern: the farewell to the parents who seemed to be so numbed by events that one had to feel compassion for them; then the entrance into the hotel wearing the unmistakable bride's going-away suit. The new luggage. The deluxe suite with the champagne in the bucket and the roses on the table. The light dimmed down to the faintest glow from the lamp in the corner. The white lace nightgown. The groom's removal of the nightgown. The bodies intertwined on the wide, soft bed.

She had thought—had not all the books, magazines, and movies taught her?—that the night would be long and slow, a dream of repeated delight. It had been neither long nor slow. To be sure, Richard had been eager enough, but it had all been over in no more minutes than the marriage ceremony had needed, after which he had immediately fallen asleep. And she had been left alone and wide awake.

She had grown up knowing about every possible variation in the sex act. One had only to pick up a magazine at the dentist's office or at the hairdresser's to read about male impotence, nonorgasmic women, lesbian women, marital incompatibility—everything you wanted to know about sex. On television, in the movies, and in most current fiction, sex was the central theme. So it seemed, excited as she was by long anticipation and stifled desire, that she knew precisely what to expect. What she expected and had been led to expect by all the above was some version of Hemingway's moving earth. It hadn't happened.

Still, that was the first night, she told herself. As she had also read, sex is not always an automatic triumph. It often requires long adjustment. And Richard was really a darling. They had had breakfast in their room before taking the plane to New York, and there, in a tiny box between the folds of her napkin, she had found diamond studs for her ears.

"I saw you once admiring them on someone," he had told her.

On the plane her conscience did a queer thing: It rose up and hit her. There were things she had to say to this good man, and she had fumbled for a way to begin.

"Richard, I don't think your parents believed me about my job being a lark, and—"

There again had come that twinkle of humor in his eyes. "They probably didn't."

"What makes you say that?"

"Because I didn't either."

She had felt humiliated and ridiculous. But having begun, she would finish.

"Richard, I lied. I lied to you."

"I know that."

"Then why—why weren't you disgusted?"

"I was only sorry that you felt it necessary."

She felt oddly unclean. "Let me tell you the truth," she had said. "My father was an alcoholic. We grew up dirt poor and miserable all the time."

"I don't need to hear that," Richard had interrupted gently. "You are you, and I don't care about another soul."

"Not your parents? Will you tell them?"

"No. Better not to. They're good people, Connie, but they have their ways."

So that had ended the subject, and she had felt a certain relief. Now she could take him to visit Lara without further explanation. There was, after all, nothing to be ashamed of.

She stretched out her hand now to observe the sparkle on her finger. Then she got up and went into the living room, which, furnished in modern chrome, steel, and glass, had a sparkle of its own. In the mirror over the console table she regarded herself in her pink baby-doll robe with the diamonds in her ears, and was satisfied with what she saw. She was young and loved. The future had arrived, and it was good.

CHAPTER
THREE

∞⌇∞

The round little table in the dining ell had been pushed toward the window so that Davey and Lara might have a view of Manhattan at night. Connie, who had found to her surprise that she liked to cook, had made a fine, festive dinner, crown roast of lamb, vegetables cut like flowers, and dessert out of Julia Child's book of French cooking.

Richard raised his wineglass and touched the others' glasses each in turn.

"To celebrate our first dinner all together," he said. And, with a bright glance about him, added then, "To celebrate life."

All five of the faces became serious, and Connie's red mouth trembled. It was such a beautiful moment! These dear people gathered here in this gleaming apartment where everything was in its place and belonged to her!

A few new touches had modified its ultramodern chill. In Third Avenue antique shops they had bought a scarlet lacquer screen to conceal the tiny kitchen. The smoky Venetian mirror that hung between the opposite windows now reflected the screen and the group at the table.

"Such a pretty table," observed Lara. "You're going to be a good housewife," she said almost tenderly.

"She is already," Richard said. "Connie's a perfectionist."

"She always was. She was the neatest little girl in school. I had to redo her hair ribbons every day at lunchtime."

Richard was amused. "Hair ribbons? Tell me everything about her."

"Oh, yes, Connie had braids until she reached fourth grade and became sophisticated."

"And now you're a shining bride," said Eddy. "Positively shining."

"Am I? Well, I'm happy. And who wouldn't be in this wonderful, brand-new city?"

"With your wonderful, brand-new husband," Lara said.

Richard laughed. "I get a kick out of her enthusiasm. She's walked my feet off every weekend, and by herself she's gone everywhere from the Bronx Zoo to the Botanical Gardens to the Statue of Liberty."

"And I took the tourist trip on the boat around Manhattan Island," Connie reminded him.

"I've been here over a year now," Eddy said, "and I haven't seen any of those except the statue."

"But you've been working," Connie said.

Eddy's sigh was satisfied. "Damn hard. It's been well worth it, though."

Davey was interested. "Tell us."

"Okay. Well, as you know, I've been on my own for a while now and loving it. I've got more business than I can handle by myself. I've hired a bright young MBA, and I'm thinking of taking on a second. When I double the business—no, when I redouble it, which should take another couple of years—I'll have to move again to a real spread, done right, my final move."

Richard was leaning with an elbow on the table and a look of genuine interest on his face, prepared to hear more.

It pleased Connie that he liked her brother. Probably, she thought, recalling the strict faces and the noiseless house in

River Oaks, he's glad to be part of a new, active family of young people.

Eddy was giving an exuberant description of Wall Street. He raised his hand, revealing fine gold cuff links.

"It's like rockets to Mars. A guy like Kramden of Kramden Jessup is worth three hundred million, can you imagine! That's not to say what the firm is worth. A couple of billion, for sure. Returns on leveraged buyouts can go as high as fifty percent— you know, it's fantastic. They're not for me, though. Not yet. Maybe I'll work up to them someday, but right now I'm doing what I want."

"Another language for me," Richard said. "My work is words and pictures. Persuasion. That's what advertising is."

"Well, I have to use a little persuasion too. Only, I use numbers instead of words." And Eddy gave his familiar grin. "Connie can tell you, I've always loved numbers. I can feel them in my fingers. I can feel the market. I dream about it." He paused a moment and resumed, "Oh, hell, we're family, so I can tell you. I'm worth almost nine hundred thousand dollars." He turned to Davey and the two sisters. "You all know what I started with when I left home too. And I guarantee that I'll have doubled that within six months."

Richard was impressed. "You're way out of my league, Eddy. Oh, I get a good salary, but I'm conservative. I put everything into treasuries and tax exempts and watch it slowly grow."

"That's fine enough if you feel comfortable that way."

"Right now I do. I'm still paying off the mortgage on this co-op."

"You've made a good investment. This is a great location down here near the U.N. I'm thinking of a co-op myself. I'm tired of paying rent. And I'd like a view, something near the East River or, better yet of course, Fifth Avenue so I can see the Park."

"That'd cost you a fortune," Richard said.

"I know. Well, I can wait."

"The way you're going, you won't have to wait long." Richard stood up. "Will you excuse me? I'm watching out for Texas time. I have to make a call to a Houston client."

"Very, very likable," Eddy said when Richard had closed the bedroom door. "He's very modest, isn't he?"

"Richard's a gentleman," Connie said.

"He must make a fortune, even at his age."

"I guess so. We don't talk about money."

"McQueen is an international firm, you know."

"I didn't. I never thought about it."

"A love match, then! Just like Lara and Davey here. But it's nice to have a few luxuries thrown in, too, like that watch you're wearing."

"You see everything, Eddy."

"Eddy always did," said Lara.

"We were passing Bulgari's on Fifth Avenue last Saturday, and Richard saw this in the window. He said I needed a decent watch."

Eddy laughed. "Decent? I'd say so. Hold out your arm."

Connie pulled her sleeve back to reveal a wide glitter of gold and diamonds on her wrist.

"Beautiful," Eddy said. "You know what? I think you're going to lead a charmed life from now on."

For an instant Connie felt discomfiture. It was as if Eddy was showing off on her behalf in front of Davey and Lara, boasting as a child might: See? See this? Perhaps she should not have worn the watch. Yet one couldn't hide facts, could one? But it was terribly common to call attention to possessions. Just having them was enough.

"Speaking of love matches," Lara asked now, "what about girls, Eddy? Anything serious?"

Eddy laughed. "Don't rush me. It's too soon for a love match."

"It's never too soon when it's real," Lara said.

Eddy shrugged. "Time will tell. Meanwhile, I've no problem meeting girls, especially at that fancy club on Long Island—uh, in the country—that I joined."

Curious, Connie asked how that had come about. Eddy explained. "One of my clients got me in. I guess it took some doing on his part, because it's not easy to get into these clubs. But then, I've gotten over a million dollars' worth of investors in his real estate for him, so I guess he wanted to do me a favor—or keep the money coming in, either one."

And again Connie felt a twinge of embarrassment, especially before Richard, who had come back into the room. She would have liked to advise Eddy very gently, without humiliating him, that he should not crow quite so triumphantly over his successes. But seeing the sheer happiness in those sea-blue eyes, she could not bring herself to do it, however gently.

Presently, though, Eddy himself seemed to become aware that he had been attracting too much attention, for he turned to Davey and Lara asking, "So, what have you two been doing since I saw you?"

"Just more of the same," Davey replied quietly.

Lara corrected him. "Not so. Davey's working on something new that looks very important. Not that I know anything about machinery, but he showed it to a doctor in town who thought it was—"

"No, no," Davey interrupted. "Don't make a big deal out of it."

"You never talk about yourself," his wife countered. "Dr. Lewis was impressed. You know he was. If you don't tell them, I will."

Davey gave in. "Oh, all right. It's a funny thing how ideas come. I'd been working half a year on something entirely different, something to do with credit cards, and wasn't getting anywhere. Then one day at a gas station I saw a kid pumping up his bike tires, and for no reason at all this thing popped into my head."

"The moment he explained it, I had a feeling—I know it sounds ridiculous to talk about feelings when I don't even understand facts—but I knew, I just knew, that Davey had something important." Lara's face was vivid with excitement.

"My wife," Davey said, looking not unpleased, "always thinks I'm a genius. All it is is a kind of improvement, a little gimmick for a heart pump. The balloons that push blood through the arteries, you know? Here, I'll show you."

The five heads leaning across the table almost touched each other as Davey drew a rough sketch on the back of a scrap of paper.

"What I've done is figure out a timing device. It's like a computer really, you set it and"—he crumpled the paper—"I can't make it clear this way, but it's really a fairly simple concept."

"For people who know about machinery or computers, maybe it is," Richard said, "but not for people like me."

"So you showed it to a doctor and he thinks it makes sense?" Eddy asked, rather sharply.

"Yes, but he's not a heart specialist. I've been thinking I ought to take my model—I've built a complete working model—to one of the big university research centers and let them see what they can do with it."

"Now, wait a minute! Hold it," Eddy cried. "You don't mean you'd just hand it over and let somebody else get all the benefit?"

"Benefit?" Davey's tone was puzzled. "If the idea's really any good, heart patients will be the ones to get the benefit, I hope."

"Of course," Eddy agreed impatiently. "My question was whether you intend to give the idea away and let other people take the credit for it."

"Oh, I'd like to have my name attached to it, of course I would."

"And money? Don't you understand those people would take your idea and make a fortune out of it? Money. Everything comes down to money. At your age you should know that."

"That doesn't sound like you, Eddy," Lara said. "You've always been a giver."

"Yes, when I've had something to give. First you have to have. Then, give to your heart's content." Eddy paused a moment, frowning. "Take care of yourself first. Why, you shouldn't even have let that doctor look at your model for five seconds. You have no patent. Hell, I can't make head or tail out of that sketch, but if there's the least chance of its being worth something, you have to protect yourself, Davey."

"I'm not thinking of it that way." Davey's voice, always low, was even lower than usual as he made his point. "I'm not looking to make money. I only want to do something worthwhile, if I can."

At that, with an expression of mock despair, Eddy rolled his eyes. "Davey, Davey. Don't you think that a person who does something worthwhile should be rewarded? Did Thomas Edison take a vow of poverty?"

"He's right," Richard said gently. "I can admire your ideals, but Eddy's right. You can do something good for the world and for yourself too."

Babes in the woods, Connie was thinking. Lara is Peg's daughter. And Davey is Lara's opposite number. You could leave your life's savings on the table, and they wouldn't touch a cent of it if they were starving.

"Listen to me. I'm taking charge of this," Eddy said. "You keep this idea under your hat, hear me? No talking about it to anyone, you understand? I'm going to find the best patent lawyer in Ohio."

Connie had to smile. Here was the familiar brother again, taking control as he had used to do when Pop had drunk too much or when Peg was sick, breezing into the house, absorbing the situation in a second and immediately organizing everybody.

"After you get the patent," Eddy went on, "you'll need financing to set up a small plant and start producing. There are a lot of defunct buildings in town, I remember, but you'll need plenty of cash to modernize. You'll need bank credit. You'll need collateral." He began to pace up and down the room. "I can take care of that. I can lend you whatever you need. A pure loan, mind you. I don't want to muscle in on your business, Davey. I only want to see you two get ahead, that's all." He stopped in front of Lara. "And if this thing is really good, I'm thinking you ought to quit teaching and help Davey. He's the dreamer who dreams things up, and you've got the head for figures. You're every bit as good as I am. Now's your chance to help Davey's brainchild get born." Next Eddy turned to Richard. "And you're in one of the world's biggest ad agencies. We'll need you, too, when the time comes."

"I feel sort of numb," Davey said, "as if I'd been gone over with a steamroller. I don't know why I don't just say no to the whole business."

"Because this steamroller is painless," Connie replied. "Go sit down," she commanded Lara, who had begun to clear the table. "You're company."

"No, I haven't had a chance to be alone with you."

There was barely room for two in the kitchen. Lara perched on a stool while Connie stacked the dishwasher. It crossed Connie's mind that most of their conversations since they had grown up had been held in kitchens after an evening meal.

"Oh, I do like Richard," Lara exclaimed now. "I know what you meant. He's delightful. And what's more important, you feel that he's good. A true good person."

"You see? You didn't trust me, did you?"

Lara laughed. "Oh, you're as smart as they come, Connie, but even smart people can make horrendous mistakes."

"Well, Richard's no mistake, as you see. Everyone likes him wherever we go."

"Tell me what you do all day," Lara said, glancing around the kitchen.

"I know what you're thinking, that there isn't enough to do in this little place and that I ought to go to work. Well, I will, but right now I'm feeling my way and enjoying it. Richard has married friends, and I've been going around with some of the wives to the art galleries and places, and oh, frankly, spending money for the first time in my life. Not on junk either; I've bought clothes and loads of books—remember how Pop used to buy books even though he couldn't afford them? Well, now I can afford them, and it's a good feeling, let me tell you."

"Guess it must be."

"Lara, I hope you'll keep after Davey and make him listen to Eddy. If Davey's really onto something, this may be your chance to get up in the world."

"We're all right. We have enough. But for Davey's sake I hope something does come of his idea. He's worked so hard on so many things that came to nothing, and I don't want him to get discouraged."

"You're an angel, Lara."

"Of course I'm not. People aren't meant to be angels."

"Well, whatever you are, you're not like me."

Connie was feeling a subtle alteration in the bond between herself and her sister. Here now in this home of her own, a prosperous home with her young, achieving husband—unlike Lara's husband—it seemed almost as if there had been a reversal of roles, as if she, who had always been the recipient of advice and counsel, were now the one to be giving them. But Lara's manner was unchanged.

"I'm so glad you have someone to love you," she said with her tender look. "Nothing else really matters very much in the end."

"I suppose not," Connie replied. Lara's cliché was irritating.

TREASURES

At the same time it troubled her that a harmless cliché could annoy her that much.

An odd silence came momentarily between the sisters, so that Connie was relieved when the men appeared to remind them that it was time to go home.

"Next time at our house," Davey said. "And make it soon. You should show Richard where your roots are, Connie."

"Not for a couple of months," replied Richard. "Connie and I are going to Europe for six weeks."

"We are?" cried Connie. "We are?"

"Yes, I was going to keep the surprise a little longer, but it just won't keep. We haven't had a honeymoon, and this will be it. Besides, I'm turning twenty-five." And at the corners of Richard's smiling eyes, fine crinkles rayed.

Connie's astonishment, Richard's satisfaction, and the others' generous pleasure on their behalf warmed the little space in which they stood together. And this warmth seemed to linger in the rooms even after all questions had been asked and answered and the guests had gone home.

"But can you afford to take six weeks off?" asked Connie while they were undressing.

"I've got some time owed to me, and besides, one's entitled to a honeymoon."

"I meant the cost. It'll be frightfully expensive, won't it?"

"I get the money from my grandmother's trust next month, and I'm going to use a small slice for this trip."

"Is that what you meant when you said you were turning twenty-five?"

"I did. And I meant that we're going to do this in grand style too. Fly over, see a bit of Italy and France, maybe Belgium, finish in England, and come back on the *Queen Elizabeth*. How does that sound?"

"Like heaven," she said dreamily.

Of course, she had hoped for such good things somewhere in a future, vague but not too far off. That they should be coming so soon was a marvel. "A small slice of the trust," he'd said. So then, the trust must be a very large one.

Richard was stretched out on the bed while she still had to remove makeup and brush her hair. This routine had already formed itself: He watched her prepare for bed while they talked over the day. There was already something very comfortable about the custom, as though they had been following it for years.

"Nice people tonight," he said. "I like your family."

"I'm glad."

It was good to have some cause for pride before him, and she had been very proud of her family on this evening. Eddy's bravado was a little overdone, to be sure, but after all, nobody was perfect, and one could only have respect for Davey's and Lara's quiet dignity.

She thought aloud, "Lara's a sweet, simple soul."

"Not that simple. She's smart and strong. It's only her manner that fools you."

"Do you think so? Yes, I guess you're right."

And Connie became aware of how perceptive Richard was; it was only *his* own manner that fooled you. People were made in layers, she reflected, and as you peeled them away one by one, you could be astonished by what you found each time. She wondered whether he could be peeling her away, layer by layer. It might be that he would learn more about her than she knew, or would ever know, about herself. The thought was forbidding. She began vigorously to brush her hair.

"Something crossed your mind just now," Richard observed.

"What makes you say that?"

"A shadow crossed your face."

"Really? I was only thinking how beautiful Lara is."

"You're more so."

"No, no. Look again at the bone structure. Hers is flawless."

TREASURES

"I've looked. Bones or no, you're the one with the energy and the life. Stand up and let me look at you. Take off your robe."

Pink silk slithered to the floor, leaving her naked before him. Turning her head toward the mirror on the open closet door, she could see herself, very white and very curved, with narrow sloping shoulders like the women in *Godey's Ladies Book*, with high, small breasts like the ones on ancient statues and with round hips like those on Renoir's rosy nudes.

"No one would ever guess what's underneath your clothes," Richard said.

"As long as you like it."

The sight of her own body, combined with the sight of his languorous sprawl on the bed, aroused excitement and a little shiver of anticipation.

"Beautiful," he murmured, his eyes shining. "Beautiful."

In the lamplight his skin was dark gold against his white silk pajamas. And through a moment that seemed very long, she waited for him to take off the pajamas, or at least to make a move. When he did move, it was to stretch his arms above his head, sigh, and yawn, showing his perfect teeth.

"It's been a long day, darling, and I'll be leaving early in the morning. I expect to be up to my ears in work for the next few weeks. It's always like that before you go on vacation."

The message was clear. She put on a nightgown and got into the bed, where Richard had fallen almost instantly asleep.

Her restless mind roamed back over the evening, to Eddy, who was fitting out a place for himself in this bewildering city as if he had been born to it . . . to Lara and Davey, who had their own very different place . . . And she wondered about them. They never changed. She thought of gestures she had seen in passing, their standing embraces in the kitchen, Davey's kisses on the back of Lara's neck when she sat reading. What pleasures must they not have in their bed? But of course one could never even

67

hint about such things to Lara, no matter how tactfully, how delicately; to Lara "such things" would be sacrosanct.

In the quiet, so high above the ground that the only sound was the soft rustle of the sheets whenever Richard turned, Connie lay thinking. How ironic it was that when she finally desired a man, he seemed not to desire her. It was too confusing.

Then she began to argue with herself. Use your head, Connie. It's obvious that he adores you. He'll do anything for you. You've been married just two months. These things take time, everybody says they do. And who knows, anyway, how often other people make love or how? What do you really know about Lara and Davey? Richard adores you. Remember that.

And we're going to Europe.

CHAPTER
FOUR

~∞~

T hey stayed on the forward deck all afternoon as the *Queen* slid from The Solent into the Channel and out to sea. Richard had gotten a deck chair, a blanket against the raw wind, and a book, but Connie stood at the railing until the coast receded into a line of gray clouds.

Behind her lay all the quaint and ancient places, the castles, lakes, and gardens, the cobblestoned alleys and the marbled palace-hotels of Europe, all of them as far removed from the thirty-third-floor apartment in Manhattan as was that apartment from Peg's flat in the Perry Building. No, farther, farther. Willingly she would turn the ship around and go back. She was already feeling the ache of nostalgia, an urgent restlessness; it was the same feeling that had swept over her when, in Houston, she had seen her first ballet and felt the world so filled with wonders. A sense of haste now overwhelmed her.

Travel with Richard was certainly rewarding, but also frustrating; knowledge emphasized her ignorance. After a morning at the Jeu de Paume and the Rodin Museum, she was envious. I must learn about art, she told herself, and I know almost nothing of European history. I know almost nothing at all.

They did very little shopping, their time being too precious, Richard declared, to waste it in stores. He did, however, buy a suit and two dresses for Connie, since, he said earnestly, no woman should come home from Paris without something Parisian to wear. Always competent about such things, he assured her that the dark red velvet and the emerald satin would be right for dinner on the ship.

In England Connie fell in love with country antiques and old landscapes. After seeing flowery Cotswold inns and burnished London shops, she began to envision old mahogany and old paintings, a library with leather chairs and animal portraits. She had a new awareness that the rooms overlooking the East River were not so grand after all, that, as a matter of fact, they were ordinary.

So, again, on the homeward voyage that compelling sense of haste came sweeping back.

Richard had wanted to ask for a table for two in the dining salon. "You won't like it if you're put with the wrong people," he warned. "I've had that experience on ships."

But Connie wanted to take the risk, and so it was that they found themselves at a large table seated next to Mrs. Dennison Maxwell. A gaunt lady well into her sixties, she gave a prim appearance that made her blunt speech all the more surprising. By the final night she was on intimate terms with the young Torys.

"It's a pleasure to see a pretty young woman with a good-looking young man for a change. In New York these days the prettiest young women all seem to be married to dreadful old men. You haven't said, but this is your honeymoon, isn't it?" And when informed that it was, she continued, "I had mine on the *Queen Mary*. There's no comparison. Of course, this ship has all the comforts. But it's so dreadfully vulgar. All this chrome and glitter. Of course, I suppose you're both too young to remember the old *Queens*, but your parents must have told you about them, I'm sure. Now, *they* had elegance."

70

TREASURES

Connie, remembering something she had once read, answered quickly, "Oh, yes, the life-sized portraits of Queen Mary and Queen Elizabeth—King George's wife, I mean. Oh, yes, it must have been wonderful. So Old World."

"I do love your Texas accent," Mrs. Maxwell told her.

"Oh, do you? I thought I'd lost it."

"But Connie doesn't—" began Richard, and stopped when her foot brushed his.

"You must meet my granddaughter-in-law. She's practically a bride like you, only married last year. You'd like each other. I have a sixth sense about people, and I'm sure you would."

"That's so kind of you, Mrs. Maxwell."

"She's terribly busy, Bitsy is. She raises more money for her charities than any three women. I don't know where she gets the energy. Or the time to keep herself so well put together. She never looks frazzled. Twice a year she flies to Paris, buys everything for the season, and then forgets about herself." Mrs. Maxwell took a small pad and small silver pen from her bag. "Do write your name and phone number here, dear. I'll tell Bitsy to be sure to call and introduce you around town. But you'll have no trouble making friends. People always adore Texans."

"Why on earth did you want her to think you came from Texas?" asked Richard when they were alone.

"Because. You heard what she said. People adore Texans."

He laughed. "Maxwell. I wonder whether that can be Maxwell Knox International. We do their advertising. She might be. That emerald has to be five carats. And anyway, without the emerald, she has that *air*. Couldn't you smell it?"

"I smelled the very good perfume. That's all."

"Not the disgusting smell of snobbery?"

"Not at all. She was interesting." An exaggerated version of his own mother, Connie thought, and wondered whether that could possibly be what he was thinking.

"You don't really want to meet the granddaughter, do you?"

71

"Why not? It might be a look into another world. What's there to lose?"

It was indeed another world, as Connie had supposed that it might be. And, to her surprise, it accepted her at once. But then, people had always taken a liking to Connie. She was bright and quick, friendly and obliging. Her zest for all the things that were new to her refreshed young women to whom everything was old and too familiar.

Sondra Maxwell, called Bitsy, was known for her independence. She wore a mink coat over a woolen skirt and sweater, sneakers, and on her wrist a gold bracelet whose value Connie, having seen enough by now to know, estimated at ten thousand dollars. Her hair, which was marvelous but no more so than Connie's own, hung long enough to be tossed as she walked. She owned a small poodle of a rare red color and persuaded Connie to buy its sister, named Delphine. The two young women with the two small dogs soon made a striking pair as they moved along the opulent streets of the Upper East Side. And Connie was no longer a stranger in the city.

Now, with Bitsy's group, she went to exercise classes, played tennis, went shopping, took art appreciation classes, had lunch at Le Cirque, and eventually even came to see her picture in a popular magazine. At Bitsy's birthday luncheon at the Pierre the group was photographed for the society page; at the bottom of a long list of names came Connie's, and at the rear of the group, barely visible behind a shoulder, appeared her face. She bought half a dozen copies and sent one to Lara.

Toward the end of the winter the Torys were invited to the Maxwell house. They lived in five spacious rooms in a solid old building on Park Avenue.

"Don't blame me for the furnishings," said Bitsy. "They're all my grandmother's, foisted on us by the family when she died.

72

But we won't have to put up with them much longer. We've outgrown this place, and as soon as we move, we'll refurnish."

This apology astonished Connie, who had been about to remark, and now did not, how handsome the apartment was.

The evening ended early, for all the young men had to get up early to appear in court, at the bank, the investment office, or wherever else it was that they had to appear within the immense stone forest of Manhattan.

Connie and Richard were reading in bed when presently she laid down her book.

"Imagine saying they've outgrown that place. Can you imagine it, Richard?"

"I could if I had the Maxwell money. The company's stock is still held in the family."

"It's hard to believe how quickly everything's happened," she murmured.

"What's happened?"

"Their taking us up as friends, especially me, when I think of where I came from."

Now Richard put his book down. "I'm amazed at you. You feeling inferior? With your brains and your personality? And besides, you were the prettiest woman there tonight."

"Was I really?"

He laid his hand over hers. "Yes, really. Oh, your friend Bitsy —ridiculous name—is good looking, but that's all she is. They were pleasant people tonight, very affable, but don't let yourself be too impressed by them, Connie."

For a moment she was silent, reflecting on the evening. "I've been thinking," she said then, "that we really need to do some serious entertaining. It's part of getting ahead, as you just saw tonight."

"Those people didn't need to get ahead by entertaining. They were born ahead."

"I know, but I was thinking. . . . We really should be able to have a dinner party, or at the very least, give a big brunch, and we can't do it here. Don't you think we need a larger apartment, Richard? One farther uptown?"

"Hey, I'm not the president of McQueen, you know."

"Of course I know. I don't mean anything outrageous." And very carefully, very delicately, she proceeded. "This place doesn't look like you, anyway. It doesn't do justice to your taste."

"Well, it isn't my taste. You know I bought it furnished."

"It's served its purpose very nicely, I realize." She sighed. It was so difficult, so unpleasant, having to press for something. "It's just that it's complicated, having always to say no to friends and make excuses. For instance, Bitsy's asked me to be on the committee for the hospital ball. It's really a prestigious thing, but the problem is one has to make a sizable donation, or better still, take a whole table. And I really don't know how to keep on refusing all the time. It's almost insulting to her when we've become such good friends."

Richard was silent.

"I'm really very fond of Bitsy. She's been so nice to me."

"Those people go to three or four affairs like that every month during the season, Connie. I told you, we don't belong with them. It makes no sense for us to try keeping up."

There was a long pause during which Richard appeared to be waiting for some acknowledgment, while she was inwardly coming to terms with her expanding knowledge of the world. The Torys were not rich, not really. They were what sociologists call the "upper middle class," very comfortable, very prosperous, but not rich. The house in River Oaks, she saw now, had had good furniture, but no rare antiques; the paintings had not been of museum quality; there had been no collections of anything, just enough silver and some fine china for use. Only what was needed for use, and no more.

Taking her hand again, Richard said softly, "You're very disappointed, aren't you?"

TREASURES

"A little."

"What's the least you'd need to give?"

"Well, fifteen hundred would do. I think maybe it would."

"Okay. I'll write a check in the morning. I'll stretch my year's budget for charity for your sake."

"Oh, you're sweet! Thanks so much. You're so sweet."

He reached across to turn off the lamp, and then reaching back, put his arm around her. His lips brushed her neck.

"Feel happier now, do you?"

"Oh, yes, oh, yes."

For the present she was satisfied. But what of the next time? It would have been easier, in a way, if these people hadn't taken her to themselves. But they had done so, and because of them, she could feel for the first time in her life that life was *fun*.

Richard was tightening his hold. He wanted sex. She wanted to go to sleep. And it crossed her mind that her original desire for him, which had been so disappointed so often and had slowly been cooling toward indifference, might possibly be turning into active rejection. His three minutes, or maybe it was a minute and a half, of pleasure, were worse than nothing for her, far worse. . . .

We have to have a new apartment, she was thinking while he lay upon her. This place is impossible. Richard gave a final shudder, sighed, brushed her ear with his lips, and rolled over to sleep.

Silver bowls, jugs, candlesticks, and platters gleamed on the shelves behind the counter.

"So you were just as pleased with the teapot after you got it home?" the proprietor inquired pleasantly.

"Oh, yes. I've got the collecting bug, and that's why I'm back," Eddy replied. And added with confidence, "I've decided to buy nothing more recent than 1900."

"Well, that's not a bad decision." The man hefted a bowl. "They didn't used to stint on weight, that's for sure."

"I like the little repoussé dish. I think I'll make that my purchase of the day."

"A precious old piece. You won't be sorry about it, either, Mr. Osborne."

Outdoors again in the bright afternoon with the package tucked under his arm, Eddy strolled along, feeling the marvelous sense of well-being that so often accompanied him these days. He was flying in blue skies, sailing over blue seas.

Little more than a year ago he had predicted how long it would take him to double his income. He had expected it to take a few years, but it had already happened. He positively astonished himself! Business was big now, really, really big; it swelled like a balloon. One client, more than satisfied, recommended another. From real estate czars came theater people, a big-time boxer, a rock-and-roll singer, rich Park Avenue widows—anybody and everybody. He kept their money growing and his own with it.

Heading into the spring sunshine and filled with such thoughts, he almost bumped into Connie on Fifty-seventh Street.

"Whatever are you doing here in the middle of the afternoon?" she demanded. "And with that twinkle on your face? You look like the cat who swallowed a canary."

"Shopping. You don't think women are the only ones who can take an hour off to go shopping, do you?"

"What are you buying?"

"Silver. I'm collecting."

"For investment, I take it."

"Well, it is an investment, but I'm doing it for pleasure too. I'm also collecting ivory carvings."

"And where do you plan to put all this stuff?"

"Come on with me and I'll tell you. I'll take you to tea at the Plaza. I worked right through lunch, and I'm starved."

TREASURES

Having settled himself into the restful shelter of the Palm Court, from which the hectic streets seemed to be miles removed, he explained, "I'm still waiting for the right co-op to come along, but in the meantime my new place isn't all bad."

"I should think not." Connie sounded almost indignant, he thought.

"But I'll need more money than I want to spend now if I want the perfect place on Fifth with a view of Central Park."

"Very wise of you, as always."

Eddy squeezed lemon into his cup, raised it, and studied his sister over the rim. Then, aware that, for some inexplicable reason, she was angry, he gave her his most appealing smile and set the cup down.

"There's something wrong with you. You're either mad, or sad, or both."

"Nothing's wrong."

"I'm inclined to say sad."

"No, I said."

"Yes. I've sensed something different these last few weeks. You've lost your glow. I'm used to seeing you glow."

"Glow!" she mocked.

"Maybe," he said gently, "you need a job. You're too smart to be doing nothing."

"Shall I go back to selling dresses? No thanks! I want to qualify for something in the art world, a gallery or auction room. That's why I'm taking art courses. But that'll take time, a lot of time, and even then I'll need to be lucky."

She fell into silence, a silence all the more glum because of the surrounding low-voiced chatter, the pleasant animation, of the teatime gathering. He could not know that she was regretting the caustic tone she had taken and was ashamed to be envious of her beloved brother. He had succeeded at everything he had ever tried. If there were pleasures to be had anywhere, Eddy would have them. If there were things to be known, he would know them. Yet nothing could have induced her to reveal herself to him, and this was the first time in her life that she had been unable to ask Eddy about anything at all. But he could not know that.

Still very gently, he ventured a tentative question. "Is there anything wrong between Richard and you?"

"No, no, what makes you think that?"

"I only asked. I like Richard. He's bright and interesting and certainly seems to be kind."

"He is kind." And then she blurted her complaint. "It's so expensive living here! I didn't expect it to be like this."

"It surely is. But it also depends on the way you want to live. Who your friends are has a lot to do with what you expect."

"Well, I want a decent apartment, that's all. I hate being cooped up in that cramped little box. You should understand. You got something better for yourself, didn't you?"

"Don't forget I'm making money, not living on a fixed salary. Even a good one like Richard's doesn't go far after taxes. The thing is, you have to know how to manage your money and make it grow."

"And just how am I to do anything about that?" she asked impatiently.

"You know," he said, "I've been doing great things for strangers. Tax shelters, arbitrage, futures, whatever. So why shouldn't I be doing something for Richard too? I've suggested it, but he's not interested, which doesn't make any sense."

"He's keeping his grandmother's trust with the same bank that the family's been with for three generations, that's why. You'd think they were married to the bank."

"One can be too conservative, letting the money lie there doing next to nothing. I never can get over how you have to prod people to do things for their own good. Take Davey. Now, thanks to me, he's got his patent approved, and I've made him a loan so he can establish credit for a mortgage. He tells me he's found a neat little building in good condition and he's begun to hire help to get started. They should be in production by fall. If I hadn't pushed, he'd be just where he's always been, doing absolutely nothing with his great idea. And Lara would be wasting a very good business head, which I've always told her to use. But I had to push, literally push. The two of them always think they have enough. And somehow, they do! You know," he mused, "when I think back to the way we lived at home, the way Peg managed, I don't understand how she did it. It's funny how fast you get used to having more and then how the more never seems to be enough either. Almost, but not quite, enough. Funny."

"Yes," Connie said soberly. "Funny." And she looked down at the skirt of her violet wool suit and at the spring-green silk cuffs of her blouse.

Eddy followed her glance. "That's a good-looking outfit."

"Thank you. Richard saw it in a window and brought it home."

"He has good taste. Listen. I'm going to call him. There's no sense in his creeping along when it's possible to fly."

"You're a good soul, Eddy. With all your faults you're a good soul."

Connie patted his hand, and he knew that her anger had vented itself.

"Well, I try. I'll have my little talk with Richard next week."

"This is a nice office you've got here," Richard said.

"But it's getting way too small. Look out there." Eddy indicated the rooms beyond his private office. "We're falling all over each other."

"Out there" was a vista of four rooms packed with desks edge to edge and piled with a jumble of telephones and computer terminals, all under the care of various young men and women in a harried hurry.

"Not that I'm complaining, by any means," Eddy assured

Richard. "We'll just have to move. But between ourselves, I sometimes marvel at the growth. Where does it all come from?"

"You're a likable person, Eddy. You're open and frank. People have confidence in you."

"Thank you, brother-in-law."

"You and Connie—you're the same. Full of energy. Full of life."

"Well, life's exciting, isn't it? I never think I'll live long enough to see everything I want to see or do everything I want to do, especially in this business. Sometimes I think I actually feel the adrenaline pouring." Eddy riffled through the documents that lay before him. "Let's see, have you signed all these? Yes, you have. I'm glad you've finally cut your ties to that stuffy bank. Steady growth, my foot! Eight percent, and what's left after taxes? Wait till you see your tax bill at this year's end! You won't recognize yourself, Richard."

"I was wondering whether you might do something like this for some cousins of mine. There's one in particular in Florida. He's got five children, and it's a struggle. I don't believe he's ever invested in a limited partnership. It might be just what he needs."

"By all means. Call him up. Want to use the phone now? I'll leave the room."

"No, no, Eddy. I'll do it at home tonight. Come to think of it, I could get up a whole list of people, friends in Texas and people in my office too. You'd be helping them, and I guess they'd be helping you. That's the way it works, isn't it?"

"The way it works." Eddy was pleased. "And I'll appreciate the new business very much. It's awfully generous of you to go to so much trouble."

"What trouble? Anyway, people in families are supposed to do for each other, aren't they? At least in Texas they are."

"In Ohio too," Eddy said cheerfully.

TREASURES

Richard stood up. "Well, it's been a good day. I feel I've made a good start. Now I'm off for home."

"And I'm off to the country. Spending the week at the club. I give myself a week's vacation twice a year. I need it."

"Great. Have fun. You deserve it." The men shook hands, and Richard left.

"What a decent guy," Eddy thought. "There's something innocent about him. You wouldn't think he came from Houston. You'd think he came from a two-horse town like mine."

The club had quickly assumed the feel of home. When a young man, a not bad-looking young man, has a sense of humor, plays excellent tennis, is a good dancer, is friendly, and has some money, he can be at home anywhere, Eddy reflected as he lay alongside the pool.

On his left the golf course, a glaze of summer green, undulated toward some distant bushy hills. On his right below the terrace stood the line of umbrella tables, brightly orange. A lively chatter surrounded him.

"Gosh, it's beautiful!" he exclaimed.

His friend and favorite tennis partner answered with a deprecation.

"You think this place is? I can show you a club that makes this look like a dump."

"Not possible!"

"Oh, yes, it is. This place is vulgar, if you want to know. Nouveau riche, and it shows."

Eddy set his cold beer aside and came to attention. "If it's that bad, how come you're a member?"

"Frankly, because they wouldn't take me into Buttonwood. I'm nouveau riche." Terry laughed. "And not all that 'riche' either."

Now Eddy wanted to know more. "What are the differences between the two? Give me an example."

"Oh, I don't know. It's the people, I guess, the way they look, who they are."

"How do you know all this?"

"My sister married a member of Buttonwood." Terry laughed again. "She married up. I'll tell you what, I'll ask her to get two girls for us and invite us to their Saturday dinner dance. It'll be a change, it'll be fun, and you'll see for yourself what I mean. All right with you?"

"It's fine with me," said Eddy.

Buttonwood really was different. Age and elegance, a slightly sober elegance, registered their immediate impression upon Eddy's sharp eyes. The house had very likely been the summer mansion of some railroad, oil, or banking tycoon back in the 1890s. No contemporary decorator had had anything to do with this dark, carved paneling or these gently faded English chintzes.

Apparently, no contemporary fashion dictator had had contact with the women either. They looked, he thought at once as he followed Terry through the crowd on the porch, they looked— well, underdressed, might one say? At his club on Saturday night the women glittered in jewels and dresses fit for an opera ball, jewels and dresses such as one saw in the Sunday papers' society photographs.

Terry, having found their party, was making introductions.

"And this is my good friend, Eddy Osborne."

The sister was a cordial older feminine copy of Terry. Her husband, whose name Eddy had not quite caught—it sounded like "Truscott"—was thin and bald; he had a lordly manner and cold eyes. He dislikes me, Eddy thought at once. To hell with him.

The two young ladies, Marjorie Somebody and Pamela Somebody, were both tall; they had attractive faces and straight hair fastened with barrettes. Preppie types; one saw their photographs shining in the newspapers and glossy magazines, taken at garden weddings, dog shows, and gymkhanas. One wore white linen, and the other yellow.

Since Terry, who was after all entitled to first choice, had immediately opened conversation with the yellow one, Eddy was left with the white one.

"I'm Pamela," she said, giving him a quick smile, "in case you've gotten the names mixed, for which I wouldn't blame you."

That was nice of her. He had indeed thought that the other one was Pamela.

"You have no drink," she said.

Truscott—or was Truscott the last name?—overheard. "There's not much time for drinks. You're late as usual, Terry."

"I know. I'm sorry, but I come here so seldom that I forget the way."

Touché! There's no love lost between those two, Eddy thought. Unexpectedly, he met Pam's eyes. They were laughing. *Old prude. Icicle.* Her lips formed the words silently. He winked, she winked back, and he went in to dinner feeling rather happy.

An older couple, almost certainly the Truscotts' original guests before Terry had invited himself, was at the table. This other gentleman, whose name mumbled by Truscott sounded like "Ripley" or "Brearley," was apparently a stockbroker, because Truscott and he launched at once into an informed discussion of the market. Eddy was torn between the attractions of Pamela and the attractions of that discussion. "Federal Reserve," "gross national product," and "earnings ratio" kept crossing the table to meet his ears.

Finally, he had to express an opinion. There had been a moment's pause between the two men, and he took advantage of it.

"I couldn't help but hear," he said. "You're right, there's no doubt about hotel stocks or limited partnerships in hotels. This is the new age of travel."

Truscott's cold eyes stared at Eddy's striped tie. "It's good to know you agree with us," he said.

"Are you in the market these days?" asked Ripley, or Brearley. His tone was kindly, as if, Eddy sensed, he wanted to atone for the other man's sarcasm.

Terry gave a boom of a laugh. "Oh, slightly, just slightly!" Shaking with his delight, he turned to his brother-in-law. "Osborne and Company? You've never heard of Osborne and Company?"

"Certainly I have," Truscott answered stiffly. "Is—"

"He is. Vernon Edward Osborne himself."

Truscott flushed. "You didn't say—"

"I know. I introduced him as Eddy, which is what he's called."

"Well, I'm certainly happy to know you," said Truscott, recovering. "I had no idea—"

No, Eddy said to himself. If you hadn't assumed I was just one of Terry's insignificant friends, you son of a bitch, you'd have looked at me very differently. But aloud, in his most gracious manner, he replied that he was happy to be here this evening and to meet Terry's family and friends.

Money, money, he thought as he turned back to Pamela. Eddy Osborne without it is nothing. But I knew that, didn't I? And that's why I left Ohio.

"What's Osborne and Company? Is it stupid of me not to know?" asked Pamela.

"Finance. Investments. And it's not stupid of you. Why should you know? You probably know a hundred things that that old fossil doesn't know."

"Well . . . horses, dogs, animals, the environment. All that stuff. That's what I'm involved with. But he hurt you, didn't he? You shouldn't let people like him hurt you."

"Thanks. I won't." He looked into the clear gaze of long, almond-shaped gray eyes under a rosy-tanned low forehead. "Dogs and horses, you said? Tell me about them."

"Well, I love horses. I teach at a riding school—"

"How old are you? Where do you live? Do you mind my questions?"

"I'm twenty-two, and I live with my mother not far from here, and no, I don't mind your questions."

"I'm twenty-seven, and I live and work in New York. I live alone. I'd like to get the hell out of here so we can talk, Pamela. That is, if you'd like to," he added quickly.

"I would, but obviously we can't. And I'm called Pam."

"How about tomorrow? May I take you to dinner?" When she nodded, he gave her a pen and a scrap of paper. "Write down your phone number and some directions to your house. Six-thirty all right?"

"Fine. And now we'd better join the general conversation," she said very properly. "We're being rude."

He understood the propriety. She had breeding and manners. The Eastern Establishment, that was the expression. She had that air. And heart too. The way she'd seen through the old snob.

She's something new, he thought when he left her that night.

The back road was not far from the Sound. He had driven through here before and knew his way. The houses were far apart, most of them the bulky, brown-shingled summer "cottages," secluded at the end of a lane and built by New York families in the early years of the century. Turning into such a lane, he passed through a tunnel of overgrown, dark shrubbery and stopped in front of a wraparound porch from which the paint was peeling. The place had seen better days.

Pam, with a shining smile, came down the steps. Looking at her, he felt curiously lighthearted.

"I hope you're hungry," he said, "because I've made a reservation at what I'm told is the best French restaurant within fifty miles."

"I'm always hungry."

"It certainly doesn't show," he answered with another quick appraisal of her body, which was lean, well curved, and taut.

"Exercise. I'm a sports freak, but mostly, as I told you, I ride. Do you?"

"Ride?" Eddy, having never been on a horse, hesitated. "I haven't ridden in years, but I've been thinking that I'd like to start doing it again."

"Oh, do! It's marvelous. There's nothing like getting up early, while the world's still asleep, except for yourself, the horse, and the birds. What I like best is riding along the beach."

She had a pleasing, animated way of speaking, so he encouraged her with his comments and questions. He had insisted upon having a very private table at a corner window overlooking the twilight garden, and there they sat undisturbed until long after black darkness fell. By that time he had learned many things, among them that she had been a debutante, that her father had died, and that her mother had given up their New York apartment to economize.

"Mother gave a dance for me at the Pierre. She really couldn't afford it, and I wouldn't have cared if I hadn't had it, but tradition means a lot to her. Our family has lots of traditions. It used to have money, too, a couple of generations ago, but somehow the money just ebbed away, got less and less. I never understand how that can happen."

"Oh, it happens very easily," Eddy said. "Takes no effort at all."

They both laughed. "I really don't mind," Pam said. "I like my life here. The riding lessons pay well enough, and what can be better than getting paid for doing what you love to do?"

"What about the winters out here?"

"We have indoor rings when we can't go out on the trails."

"And what do you do when—" He broke off. "Please excuse me. I suddenly realize I've been asking too many questions. It's a failing of mine. When I meet a person I like, I always want to know everything about him right away. I'm sorry."

"No, please! You were asking me what I do when . . . ?"

"When you're not busy around horses."

"Oh, I'm a volunteer. My mother calls me a professional volunteer. I work at the animal shelter, and I'm on a committee to save the wetlands, and the Sierra Club, and stuff like that. I get really enraged when I see developers tearing into this earth. They'll rip it apart until there'll be nothing green left. We people who live here all year round love this place. It's not just a vacation spot to us."

In his daily travels between the office tower and the apartment tower, Eddy had to confess that he had been giving very little thought of late to whether the earth was green or not. He tried to think of another woman or man he had ever met who was worried about wetlands or stray animals, and could not. These must be chiefly the concerns of people who have owned land in the same place for years and cherished it, he thought. Interesting. Another world, not like any world he had ever known. And he wondered what she might be thinking about him. . . .

Driving back to his club, he reviewed the evening. Should he try to see her again? It was a long way out there from his club, and he certainly had no dearth of women who were more conveniently situated. She wasn't a tremendous beauty. As to the possibilities of sex, in spite of the fact that she obviously had a splendid body, he had a feeling that she would be rather cool in that respect. And yet there was something about her. . . .

He was still in this state of mild concern when he walked into the club. There in the lobby someone hailed him.

"Osborne?" An elderly man, one of Mr. Hartman's friends, went up to Eddy. "I'm Julian Jasper. You've met me at the Hartmans', in case you don't remember me."

Eddy held out his hand. "Of course I remember you, Mr. Jasper."

Anyone would, anyone who was at all in the know. Having made his fortune years ago in Bolivian tin, Jasper, now retired, had become one of the city's prominent philanthropists, with a seat on the boards of a dozen charities.

"I've been wanting to talk to you. Can we sit down for a minute?"

A request for a donation was sure to follow, but that was all right. There was enough coming in, and it was only right that some of it should go out. So Eddy waited.

"You may have heard that I'm to be the new chairman of Mount Mercy's board."

"Yes, I read about it in the *Times*, Mr. Jasper."

"Well, I have a big job ahead, Osborne. It's an old hospital, its needs are tremendous, and I need help to meet them."

"I understand." Twenty-five thousand? Eddy was thinking. Fifty?

"The board is too old. What I mean is, most of us have been on it for years, we've gotten no new blood for ten years at least, and I intend to bring some in. New blood and young blood with fresh ideas. Would you be interested?"

Eddy was unsure that he had heard correctly. "I'm afraid I don't quite understand," he said.

"I'm offering you a place on Mount Mercy's board."

He was flabbergasted. Membership in this most distinguished body, he who had come as a nobody to this city? Naturally, a very large donation would be expected; a hundred thousand, he quickly guessed; but it would be worth it ten times over in honor and prestige.

"I'm overwhelmed, Mr. Jasper. Of course I accept. Who wouldn't? Yes, I'm overwhelmed. There's no other word for it."

The other was pleased. "You'll be a great asset to us, Osborne. Hartman's said fine things about you, and of course, I've heard your name mentioned most favorably on Wall Street. Yes, yes, young blood. I'd like to introduce you to the other members someday soon. Lunch at the Harvard Club, perhaps?"

"Wonderful. Any day. I'm delighted, Mr. Jasper. Delighted."

As always, he had to keep himself from whistling all the way up to his room. Well, well, Vernon Edward Osborne, you're moving ahead.

Then, all of a sudden, his thoughts went back to Pam Granger, and he made a connection. He could almost hear the connection click in his head. The real reason for his hesitation about calling her again was a very simple one: He had been afraid of rejection. He had been afraid that she was, after all, too different, too far out of his reach. A strange insecurity for Eddy Osborne, who would have said that insecurity was one feeling from which he rarely suffered! But this brief encounter downstairs just now had lofted his place in the world to a new height. And he reached for the telephone.

"Pam? I hope I didn't wake you."

"No, I'm reading in bed."

In bed. Long hair loose on the pillow. White nightgown sheer enough to see through to the rosy flesh.

"I don't know about you, Pam, but I had a great time tonight. Would you care to repeat it?"

"Why, I'd love to, Eddy."

"Tomorrow?"

"Wonderful."

"Fine. Shall I pick you up at six?"

"I have a thought," she said. "It's going to be another beautiful day, so how would you like to meet me at the stables and go riding? I'm free all afternoon."

Whatever had he told her? He seemed to remember having given the impression that he knew all about horsemanship but had simply been away from it for a time. What a fix! He had a vague recollection of having read that one mounted on the animal's left and rose and sank in the saddle as the creature moved. That was called "posting." And that was all he knew.

"Eddy? Are you there?"

"Yes. Oh, yes. Pam, I was only thinking, my riding clothes are at home."

"Oh, dear!"

He thought quickly: Buy an outfit the first thing in the morning, then wing it. You've always been athletic, and it can't be that hard.

"I'll buy some stuff in the morning. My old stuff's probably moth-eaten, anyway. I haven't had it on in so long. And be prepared. I'll be stiff as a board, I'm sure."

"Don't worry, it'll all come back to you. Besides, don't forget, I'm an instructor."

He felt so eager, so excited, that he sang in the shower that night. A man didn't often have two triumphs in one day.

So began a memorable week. Because he had assured himself that his first attempt to ride a horse would be successful, so it was. At least, it was no failure. Smart in the new habit and armed beforehand with an hour's worth of study from a paperback book of instructions, Eddy managed to give a fair performance.

"Am I too awful?" he asked Pam as, carefully, they walked their horses past low-hanging branches.

"For somebody who hasn't ridden in years, you're doing well," she assured him. "All you need is practice."

Actually, he was enjoying himself. Tomorrow he would certainly have a sore rear, but that was unimportant. One could get hooked on this sport, he felt. It was a whole lot better than golf, which had always seemed too slow for him.

The city, in the days that followed, might as well have been on another planet for all the differences between its noisy, melting streets and the bliss of fresh winds and airy lawns. Pam and Eddy went exploring. They sailed, swam, sat on a dock eating lobster sandwiches, played tennis, and laughed a good deal. To Pam's surprise Eddy wanted to take a tour of historic houses; she was even more surprised at how much he knew about furniture periods and architectural styles.

"I like to have beautiful things around me," he said simply, "so I need to learn about them."

She took him then to an antique shop, where they both browsed and he bought a pair of Staffordshire figures, authentic and charming, but modestly priced. In the same shop he saw a pair of Dresden figurines, which were naturally expensive; those he would have liked to buy, but did not do so for fear of seeming ostentatious before Pam, whom after all he scarcely knew. One evening they went to an Italian movie, on another to an outdoor concert, and on one had a backyard supper at Pam's house, then sat on the porch with her mother, who went upstairs after a proper interval.

On the sixth night, under a bright moon, they came back to the porch. The house was already dark, and there was no sound as they came up the steps but for the thumping of the old dog's tail.

"I haven't seen him before," said Eddy. "Where are the poodles?"

"They sleep in my mother's room. This is Buster. He's mine. I rescued him from the pound. His owners left him there after twelve years. Can you believe it? It could have broken your heart to see the look in his eyes. He couldn't understand why they were walking away without him. So I took him, and I think he's getting over his loss. Poor guy."

I really like her. I really do, he said to himself. And curiously, he asked, "Tell me. Do you ever look far ahead? Plan what you want to do with your life, I mean?"

"Oh, I'd like to live pretty much as I'm living now. And someday have a husband and children, but not for a long time."

That seemed strange, since she wasn't one of the competitive career women who filled the banks and the law offices these days. Most other women had "marriage" written on their faces after the first half-dozen meetings.

He pressed her. "You don't feel that you're missing anything?"

"No. I like being independent. What should I miss?"

He hesitated and then took a chance. "Well, sex, for instance."

She laughed. "I don't deprive myself. Not when I meet the right person."

He pressed again. "How do you recognize when you've met him?"

And she, laughing again, replied, "Now, you know better than to ask a silly question like that!"

Their chairs were so close that their knees almost touched. The sweetest, most alluring fragrance lay on the air: her perfume or that flowering vine that climbed the railing? He stood up and took both her hands. Her body, yielding easily, rose up to meet his.

"Where shall we go?" he whispered.

"Here, in the swing. Don't worry, it doesn't creak."

His head swam with an explosion of fire that came from the very depth of him, from the racing of his blood. Clothes dropped in an instant to the floor; an instant later he lay with her in the swing. He had heard about sex on a water bed, about its soft, erotic sway; he had heard, too, about sex outdoors on a summer night, and had never tried either until now. Those were his quick thoughts, and then there was no thought, only that fire exploding, and afterward, the sweetness. The sweetness.

"And I thought—I thought you would be cool," he said.

"Cold? Frigid?"

"No, not that. Far from that. But—it's hard to explain. I just didn't think you would be like this."

She had been lying with her head on his shoulder and now sat up.

"Like what? What am I like?"

TREASURES

He sat up, too, shaking himself. Never, never had he had such sex. "You won't believe me. You'll think it's just a line that a man hands out. But the truth is that I've never felt anything quite like this. I don't know what you did, but—"

"And if I tell you that I don't make a habit of sex with a practical stranger, will you believe me? You're probably thinking, Oh, they all say that, and you're right, I suppose, but in this case it happens to be the truth. I need to have real feeling, real and quick and deep. And that happens very, very rarely." Pam took his hand. "So. Do you believe me or not?"

He looked into her eyes, which shone now in a sudden shaft of light from the sky.

"I do believe you," he answered.

After that he knew he could not forget her. All the way back to New York when the vacation week was over, he thought about her. He would have liked to give her a present, not flowers, chocolates, or books, but something beautiful, like a pendant or a bracelet. Just as a remembrance of seven wonderful days. But he remembered that she had once spoken with scorn of some girls who accepted expensive presents from men. She had standards, Pam had. Having learned that much about her, he decided on flowers, the most lavish roses that could be ordered.

One other thing he knew about her: She was not a fortune hunter, like so many of the women to whom he had been introduced of late. He had learned to recognize and to expect their lingering, hungry look whenever they passed a jewelry store.

Still another thing: She had said quite plainly that she was not ready for marriage, which was perfect because he was not either. Not yet.

But when I am ready, he thought, it will be Pam, or if she won't have me, which is possible, then somebody just like her.

About six months later Richard Tory was able to say, "He's a financial whiz, your brother is. Do you know, with those futures he bought, I added ten percent to my capital? It's incredible. I think," he proposed cautiously, "I think we're in a position now to look for that apartment you've been wanting."

Warmth like a glow from liquor surged through Connie's chest, and she took a last look at the common little box, adorned with cheap chrome and steel, the little box that had once been a delight.

"How large can we go?"

"Well, four rooms, perhaps?"

She thought of Bitsy's ten new rooms. "How about five, so we can spread out some? You said you wanted to bring all your books from Houston."

"Well, all right. It'll come high, especially where Eddy's looking, and I guess that's where you want to be too. Not that we can plan anything on his scale." Richard got out a pad and pencil, and she waited, looking over his shoulder, with an anxious tilt to her head. "Let's see. I can go as high with my salary as five or six hundred. I can handle the mortgage. And I'll pay it off as fast as Eddy can make my money grow. After all, property's always the best investment. You can't lose on a New York co-op."

"What about furniture? The only things we own are the screen and the mirror."

"We'll shop carefully on Third Avenue where we found those. We'll go gradually, step by step, take our time."

Not too much time, Connie thought. Richard was so slow, deliberate and slow. Not like Eddy, who went right after what he wanted and got things done.

CHAPTER
FIVE

❧

Eddy and Connie had flown out to see Davey's brand-new plant. It was a day for celebration.

"Before we go see the plant," Lara said, "we'll have a big lunch—I've got a turkey in the oven. Then we can go later."

"But not too late. Eddy and I are taking a six o'clock plane home."

"I thought you were staying over Sunday," Lara said, sounding plaintive. "Such a flying visit—"

"I know. But Eddy changed his mind. You know he's a workaholic, and as for me, I do have a husband. By the way, Richard said to tell you he's terribly sorry he couldn't make it. He's bogged down with evening meetings, but we will definitely both come during Christmas. A promise."

Connie looks extraordinarily pretty today, Lara thought. Her hair was lighter, almost ash-blond, and she was wearing a mink jacket. One didn't have to be experienced in the wearing of mink to know that this was no ordinary department-store bargain, nor were the claret-colored shoes and the matching woolen dress.

"You look lovely," she said. "And happy too."

"Do I?" Connie replied lightly. "It's probably the new apartment."

"Is that all?"

"All? That's plenty."

"Tell me about it."

"Well, it's between Madison and Park. You wouldn't know where that is, but it's a prime neighborhood. The whole thing isn't exactly what I wanted, because two of the rooms at the rear are rather dark. Still, it's a dream compared with the old dump. All we have to do now is furnish it." Connie sighed. "We've got the bedroom finished and a lot of other stuff on order. English country things, mostly, mahogany and oak, lots of chintz and linen. I sort of fell in love with all that when we were in England."

There was a casual air of authority in her tone, a subtle change of which she was probably not even aware, from the last time Lara had seen her in the place she now described as a dump. It had always seemed strange to Lara that money changed people so abruptly. Although, she reflected, if Davey's new enterprise works out, it won't make any change in him. That she knew. And yet she felt no disapproval of Connie, but only a vague doubt.

Then she said shyly, "I'm rather happy today. Happy and hopeful. I missed this month. I might be pregnant, I think."

Connie got up and hugged her. "Oh, darling, I hope so! A person really ought to get something she wants so much!"

"And you? Or shouldn't I ask?"

"All in good time. I'm in no rush."

"It looks as if Eddy's in no rush either. I wish he'd get married, at least."

"Why? He couldn't be happier than he is now, although I do think he has a girl he sees a lot."

"Really? Who is she?"

"All I know is that her name is Pam. She likes horses." Connie laughed. "So he's taken up riding in a big way. I think she's in the *Social Register* or something."

"Well, Eddy always had big ideas." Lara was amused.

When the men came in they all had lunch, and right afterward got into Davey's new Jeep to drive to the far side of town where the plant was situated. It was a neat, low building that had been a small warehouse, behind a wire fence. The spacious parking lot was empty.

"Room for five hundred cars, I'd estimate," said Eddy, "wouldn't you say so, Davey?"

Davey grinned. "More than I'll ever need, that's for sure."

Eddy corrected him. "More than you'll need for a while, you mean."

Above the white-painted entrance was a dignified sign, saying only THE DAVIS COMPANY. The open warehouse space had been divided into various work areas, where sundry pieces of machinery, some still disconnected and others still uncrated, had been placed.

Lara made a proud comment. "A little different from the workbench in the shed out back."

Offices had been partitioned off at the far end of the building. Davey pointed them out.

"This one's mine, and that's Lara's. She takes a load of paperwork off my shoulders, let me tell you."

"You've got a first-class accountant, I hope," Eddy continued. "You've got to watch those taxes, watch those dollars."

Davey nodded. Lara, standing between them, could not help but feel, regardless of her own independent strength and confidence, a certain sense of being protected by the two men. I suppose that's from generations of brainwashing, she told herself with some amusement.

"I watch them," Davey said.

"You've got to make them grow faster and bigger."

"What do you mean?"

"Listen to me, Davey. You can't afford to lag behind. You've got a good thing here, a growing child, and it needs to be fed. You've got to nourish its growth."

"What do you mean?" Davey repeated.

"What I mean is, it's time to go public, to issue stock. You need capital so you can expand. Listen to me, Davey. I know what I'm talking about."

"I'm comfortable with the size we are. Lara and I—well, she really manages the office, the wages, and the orders, while I get my hands black in the machine shop. And three salesman are out traveling. I have been thinking of adding salesmen, it's true, but—"

"If you were to get as few as twelve stockholders, each with fifty thousand dollars, for example, you'd have over half a million for improvements."

"I don't want to get involved with strangers and give them a vote in the running of my affairs. I'm a small-town guy, Eddy, I admit it."

"Listen to me. You wouldn't have to sell stock to strangers. There must be a dozen well-heeled people in this town, maybe even friends of yours, who would jump at a chance to invest in a growing company." Eddy looked around and up at the ceiling. "This place is nice, yes, but it can use a lot of fixing up. And you'd have cash to buy machinery. I'm sure you'll be needing some."

"Well, yes," Davey acknowledged. "I was hoping to get a loan for it."

"Then you'd be saddled with interest payments. Will you please do it my way, Davey? I can set up the whole thing for you. Finance is my business, isn't it, for God's sake? All you need is to keep on with what you're doing and leave the rest to me. Have I ever steered you wrong?"

"No. No, you haven't."

"All right, then. Go home and start thinking about whom you can approach to buy shares."

Davey and Lara looked hesitantly at one another. After a moment Lara spoke.

"Dr. Donnelly? He's been Davey's family doctor since Davey

was a baby," she explained to Eddy. "And Tony? What do you think, Davey? His aunt Alma left him a pile of money." Again she explained, "He's been Davey's best friend from kindergarten through college."

"That's great! Those are the kinds of contacts you need."

Davey spoke. "I could ask Ben at Levy's Dry Goods. He'd probably be interested."

Eddy's enthusiasm mounted. "There. You see? That's three already, so keep it up." He glanced at the clock. "I'm in a rush. Got to get back. Listen. I'll get working on this, talk to my lawyers, and get back to you by the end of the week. I see a big future here, Davey. Bigger than you probably realize. But you've got to put it on the road, and not in a horse and buggy either. You understand?"

"I guess I do," Davey said. "You are convincing, I must say."

"Okay! We'll be talking."

They took a roundabout route to the airport. Connie said she felt as though she had been away forever and if there was time she would like a tour of the old places. Davey told her that there was nothing really new in town except a strip mall and a housing development on the south end that they could pass.

When they came to it, a scattering of unoriginal, yet pleasing, shingled colonials on a huge, sloping field that had been denuded of trees, Eddy insisted on seeing the model house. So they all trooped through empty rooms that had the fresh smell of new wood, through picture-book bathrooms and a magnificent kitchen with a barbecue and a view of the autumn sky at the top of the slope.

"This," Eddy declared, "is what you two should buy."

"This isn't the time," Davey said. "We need to put money back into the business."

"This is exactly the time, Davey. I always tell you people should enjoy life as they go along. Today won't come again. It's now that you're young." Eddy pointed toward the window.

"Look at the space out there. Fence it in, make a hedge of evergreens. You'd have room for a garden, maybe even a pool eventually. What have you got now? A dingy yard and a shabby screened-in porch."

"He's right," asserted Connie. "After all, he's not talking about a mansion, just a pretty simple house."

Lara considered the lemon-yellow appliances, the European cabinets, the butcher-block island, and the brass chandelier. In her estimation these were hardly simple, and she said so.

With slight impatience in her voice Connie rebuked her. "You never want anything!"

Just so had Connie used to speak, with that frown, when she was in grade school. And Lara, countering that impatience with the patience she had used back then, replied, "It's no use wanting what you can't afford."

Eddy clapped Davey on the back. "Go for it! You can afford it. I'll be your mortgagor. I'm flooded with cash right now."

"Thanks, Eddy, but the answer is no. I owe you enough already," Davey said.

"Okay, brother-in-law. You're a stubborn customer and always were. But I don't have to tell you that I never give up either." He looked at his watch. "We don't have a lot of time. Let's go, folks."

At the local airport the Davises watched Eddy and Connie climb the steps to board the plane. At the top of the steps they both turned and waved, Connie's newly bright hair streaming out in the wind. And Lara, along with a sense of loss at this departure, had a curious sense of relaxation. They were both so —so energetic. The two of them were alike, people in a hurry, bright and lovable and quick to fill every hour, with no rest. It made you tired just to think of living like that.

"It was a nice visit," Davey said. "I'm surely fond of them both, but I'm glad—"

"Glad of what, dear?"

"Well, glad you're different."

"It was a nice visit," Eddy said as the taxi turned into Connie's street. "They both looked well and happy. It goes to show you what happens to people when things start looking up for them."

"They always did look well, Eddy. But that flat—it's even dingier than I remembered."

"Oh, it's not that bad. She keeps it clean as a whistle."

"Yes, and if you don't think it's hard work to keep that place clean! Especially if she has a baby. She told me this morning that she thinks she's pregnant. They really ought to buy that house."

"They will. But Davey's so damn slow to make a decision! I have to prod him, push him, and pull at him before he'll finally come around. Gosh, I hope she really is pregnant! It'll be fun to see her with a kid at last."

Fun for her, not for me, Connie said to herself. All the work and the tugging at you, literally, for fourteen hours a day.

It felt good to be home even after that short time. Tomorrow there was the art class at the museum, and after that an appointment with the rug people about the dining room. Richard wanted to make do with carpeting, but Bitsy Maxwell had just bought an Oriental, and there was no possible comparison between the two effects. Her Oriental had the muted shimmer of stained glass. Richard would just have to be convinced.

The taxi stopped at the door and went on with Eddy. The old doorman saluted her. His posture, still erect as a soldier's in the pseudomilitary uniform, was pathetic. Imagine a lifetime spent in opening doors and greeting people as if you really cared whether they came or went. And then to travel home late, maybe for an hour on the subway, to some dreary dwelling on a dreary street. Sad.

"Good evening, Higgins. Mr. Tory home?"

"Yes, ma'am. He came in a couple of hours ago."

It was only ten-thirty. The big meeting must have broken up very early, then. There was no light in the foyer when she opened the door of the apartment, and no light anywhere else. He must be already asleep. He was a great sleeper. She sighed and suddenly became aware that this sigh of hers, resigned and exasperated, was becoming a habit that must be broken.

The poodle whimpered in its basket. She turned on a lamp, picked up the dog, kissed it, and urged it to be quiet. Then, removing her shoes so as not to disturb Richard, she crossed the bare floor to the bedroom. The door was open. A weak shaft of light from the lamp fell directly on the bed, where Richard lay naked and facedown.

She felt a shock, as though her hand had touched a spark. The thought sparked: He's *dead*, and her hand went to her heart.

She must have made a sound. Afterward, in her countless recapitulations of the scene, she remembered only that she turned on the switch at the door, illuminating the room with rosy lamplight, that he started up, that she saw his horrified face, all eyes, and that there were not one, but two men on the bed.

During the fraction of time when she stood there absorbing the total truth of what was before her, she was to remember what is said about drowning people, how in seconds a whole life flashes; that might well be true, although to her, it was not a whole life, but rather sporadic incidents out of that life, her mother's face, dead in the satin coffin-bed, and Richard in tennis whites on that first morning, and Lara talking about having a baby . . .

Richard was cowering behind the blanket, absurd as a prudish old woman covering her nakedness. The other man slid beneath the far side of the blanket, absurd as an ostrich hiding its head. And Connie's laugh was a shrill falsetto shriek that ended in a gasp. Still Richard had not spoken.

Then she fled. She sat down at the kitchen table, the kitchen being the only other room that was complete, and put her head down on it.

"Oh, my God," she wailed. "Oh, my God!"

After a long while she sat up and rocked her body back and forth, bent over, with her hands on her elbows, rubbing and rubbing her arms. Her head was empty, numb.

When the deep, shaking sobs subsided, she swung around in the chair and looked out of the window across the courtyard at a checkerboard of lighted windows and then into the opposite kitchen, where a maid was putting dishes away. The people must have had a party for someone to be still cleaning up this late.

And behind all those windows, all those trivial, ordinary, daily routines, extraordinary things were happening, or could be happening. Anniversaries and terminal sickness, feuds, crimes, reunions, deaths, bankruptcies, and weddings. Who among the tenants who nodded greeting in the elevator to young Mr. and Mrs. Tory could imagine what had occurred in their bedroom just now?

Presently, she heard whispers at the outer door and the soft thud of its closing. Without turning she knew when Richard came to the kitchen door. He would be wondering, in his desperation, what to say to her. Although, after her first shock, she was beginning to feel the rise of fury—she, desirable and young, to be so cheated, so tricked—she could not help but feel pity for him, too, in his utter humiliation.

As he approached, she had to look at him. He had put on pajamas and a bathrobe, but they were loosely fastened, and his bare flesh was repugnant to her. His voice was barely audible.

"I guess I don't know how to start, what to say."

"I don't know what to say either." And again her tears welled. "What is there to say? A thousand things or maybe nothing at all."

"Listen. Please listen to me. This was my first time, I swear it. And I can't explain it, except that we had a business meeting, then it was a nice night so we walked uptown together, and I asked him in for a drink. A perfectly natural thing to do."

She could not answer. This is unreal, she was thinking. This isn't happening to me. To me, Connie Osborne. Osborne. That's my name.

"The thing is, I guess—I knew we had too much to drink. On an empty stomach," he finished lamely, standing before her still with that imploring look upon his face.

"Who is he?" she murmured. "Anyone I might know?"

"He works in the office."

She said bitterly, "How nice for you. How convenient."

"Connie, I told you I don't make a practice of this. I'm sorry. I'll spend the rest of my life being sorry."

"Your being sorry doesn't help very much. Oh!" she cried. "I should have had some inkling, I should have been smarter!" And she bent over again in pain, rubbing her arms.

He asked softly, "Why should you have? There was no reason."

That was true. What possible reason could there have been to suspect this blooming young man, this vivacious, enthusiastic athlete? That he was too shy, too cowed by his parents, perhaps? Not necessarily. That he had waited until marriage before taking her to bed? Not necessarily. That he had been lacking in desire after marriage? And desperately, soundlessly, she asked herself: What do I know? He's my first. I can only guess. . . .

Richard had, perhaps unconsciously, clasped his hands before him. The gesture was so pathetic that she had to close her eyes.

"We've been so happy together," she heard him say. "Traveling, listening to music, making a home. We've been so happy together."

Yes, she thought, in all those ways we were. He's shown me so much and taught me so much. And given me so much besides. Oh, it's rotten! Everything's rotten!

TREASURES

He moved closer, looming tall above where she still huddled, so close that she smelled the fresh scent of his cologne.

"Connie . . . you're not going to leave me, are you?"

She looked up then, straight into his eyes, which were pleading and pained as those of a dog that had been harshly treated.

"Is it true, will you swear that you never did this before?"

"Connie, I swear it. And I never will again. Never."

She sighed. It was as if her heart were crying, heavy with its confusion of anger, shame, and pity for him. Poor man. Poor, foolish young man.

"You're shivering." He fetched a shawl from the closet. "I don't know how the wind manages to seep into these buildings."

"I don't want it," she said, shaking it off when he tried to place it around her shoulders.

His gesture was a plea; she understood that; yet, imagining where an hour ago those hands and that body had been, she could not bear to feel him close to her. Not yet.

Possibly he understood, because he let the shawl drop and went back to the chair. For a long time they sat, not speaking. An hour passed, and the silence, like a heavy sea, swelled over them both. Once Richard opened his mouth, made a slight sound, and closed it again. On the second attempt Connie questioned him.

"Is there something else you want to tell me?"

He looked past her, out toward the nighttime sky stained rusty pink by the city's million lights. Sweat dampened his forehead, and tears stood in his eyes.

"I wanted to ask—I mean, I hope you won't tell anyone about tonight."

"Of course not, Richard."

"Not even Lara and Eddy?"

"No one, Richard."

"Because I don't want to lose their regard."

"I know."

"And you will give me another chance? Will you? Will you?"

"Yes, I will." How could she not? How could she just throw him away?

"Oh, bless you, Connie. Bless us both." He got up then, saying gently, "You're worn out. Go on in to bed. I'll sleep on the folding cot out here."

"No, I'll take the cot."

Did he really think she could lie down in that bed after what she had just seen there? For a man who was so sensitive, so perceptive, this was incredible. He must, however, have realized immediately how obtuse he had been, because he gave no argument, but pulled out the cot instead and set it up for her.

When she lay down on it, she could see, high at the top of the window, an oblong of sky. Pink, obscuring what should have been deep, soothing black, looked dirty now, like a silky blot on the enormous world and on her own small life.

In the morning things look different. Troubles are smaller, Peg used to say. Well, perhaps not all that different, but possibly a little smaller, she thought, more manageable. She had slept so heavily, in such deep exhaustion, that she had not even heard Richard leave the house. Meticulous as always, he had rinsed his coffee cup and juice glass and left them in the dish drainer. Now Connie sat musing over her own coffee.

Something in her deepest heart, her clearest mind, wanted to make sense of things. This was, after all, his first time. He had sworn so, and he was truthful. He had been drinking, he wasn't much of a drinker, and whiskey had probably turned his head inside out. Quite probably, too, he hadn't even known what was happening. The other man had instigated the business, while Richard, in a fog, had been led along. As she sat there puzzling, reconstructing the event, she became more and more certain that this was the only reasonable explanation.

Yes, of course it was. Poor Richard, she thought again. He

must be cringing inside. He must be longing for a hole to hide in. She imagined him now downtown, trying to concentrate on his work, holding to his dignity while the ugly memory of last night filled his head.

Later that afternoon an impulse struck her. "I'll phone him," she said aloud to herself. "It may encourage him, may help him through the day. It'll help me too. It's the only right thing to do, isn't it? Maybe I'll suggest a weekend away at some peaceful New England inn. We'll take a few books, go on country walks, and have dinner by an open fire. A quiet time like that is cleansing and strengthening. What happened is rotten, but you have to excise rot wherever you find it. Cut it out like an abscess. Yes, I'll phone him and then make reservations. I should be able to get something within the next few weeks. We'll start fresh."

The little old white inn on a dirt road just beyond the little old white village was framed with autumn reds and yellows. In a mild, warm wind leaves sank slowly onto the still-green grass. In the orchards yellow jackets swarmed over rotting fallen apples, whose sweet, fruity fragrance tinged the air. There were tennis courts at the inn, there were canoes, and there was a section of the Appalachian Trail to hike on.

The two had tacitly agreed to put the sorry episode away forever, so nothing was said to impede a return to normal living. On the third night Connie was even able to shut out that appalling scene in their beautiful bed at home, and to respond to Richard's wish for sex. In the morning at breakfast he reached suddenly across the table and clasped her hand; she was sure she read gratitude in the clasp and the smile.

An elderly couple at the next table, catching the gesture, gave one another an endearing look of recognition that said plainly, We were young, too, honeymooners, so in love, and wasn't it wonderful?

And Connie, responding inside her head, said, Well, it isn't quite like that over here, you know, but it's been good in many ways and worth preserving.

They drove back to the city feeling both reconciled and refreshed. Their pleasant routines were waiting for them: Richard's at the office and Connie's, for the next few months at any rate, at the shops acquiring possessions for the new apartment.

They had begun afresh.

And then, on a fair Saturday afternoon in the following month, on her way home Connie entered Central Park near the Mall to enjoy the short remaining walk away from the traffic on the streets. The day was closing, perambulators, bicycles, and dog-walkers were all heading for home, but here and there in sheltered spots a few people still sat on benches in the warm sun. Connie was smiling; she felt the smile on her cheeks. What a wonderful city in all its variety! How wonderful to be young here, to have some money in one's pocket, and to be able to buy such heavenly Chinese blue lamps as she had just found today!

This was the moment at which time was arrested, so that ever afterward she would associate those lamps with what she saw sometime between three-thirty and four o'clock. What she saw were two men on a bench, only partly hidden in a cluster of long-needled pines, two men in an embrace, arms encircling and lips joined. . . . How disgusting, here without caring who saw, or perhaps so engrossed as to be unaware that people were able to see. . . . One of the men was Richard.

She froze. Her heart made such a frantic leap that for an instant she thought it would stop. But her legs kept moving. It was as if her legs knew enough to carry her away from there as fast as they could go. It was as if they understood that she must get home to shelter and safety. Get home. Get home.

Shut the door and sit down, still with coat on, sit gasping, numb. You tried, you did what you should. How could he have lied to you? Rotten. Rotten.

After a while she got up and made a cup of coffee. She was

drinking it, warming her cold, shaking hands around the cup, when the key turned in the lock and Richard came in, looking as cheerful as always.

"How was your day? I had more to do at my desk than I'd thought, or I'd have been home by noon."

"At your desk?" she said. "Try Central Park."

He stared. "What do you mean?"

"Richard, I saw you, so don't try to lie your way out. You've lied enough already."

He looked away from her. A flush like a sore disease swept over his forehead and down to his collar.

"It wasn't your first time, that night." She waited and, as anger mounted, cried out fiercely, "Answer me! It wasn't, was it?"

"Well, not quite. But truly, truly, there haven't been a lot of times. I mean—"

He floundered. The strength drained from him. It was visible in the sag of his shoulders and the helpless droop of his hands. And within Connie's chest hung the heavy weight of disillusionment.

Her voice was thick in her throat. "I believed you. How could you have done this to me? To a person who trusted you?"

His reply was so low, so strained, that she barely heard it. "I guess—I guess I couldn't help it. It just happens sometimes."

"That's all the explanation you can give me?"

He sighed and dropped down onto the other chair, facing her across the table.

She thought, what a waste! But he couldn't help it, so it wasn't his fault. Except for the outrage of the lies, from the very beginning.

"You should never have married me. Can you tell me why you did?"

"I wanted to love a woman," he answered simply.

"It was an experiment, then? Some sort of therapy?"

"No. I can—I can do both."

"You prefer that way, though."

"I don't know. But I loved you, Connie. I still do."

"I can't imagine why."

"Your beauty, your intelligence and curiosity, your drive that I don't have. My spirit loves you, and my body does too." At her scornful stare he insisted, "Yes, it does."

Connie shook her head. Tears stung, but she did not want to let them fall. In crises one must keep one's control. And this was crisis. This was the end of the road that had begun that morning when he had walked in, sun-bronzed and tall in his tennis whites. Then a tear fell.

And Richard cried out, "Oh, my God, I'm so sorry, Connie! What can I do? Can I ask you again to give me another chance?"

She wiped the tear with the back of her hand. "It wouldn't do any good. It wouldn't work, and you know that well."

"What then? Divorce?"

"I have no choice, the way things are."

Divorce? And then? This misery would be over. But the friendly, everyday routines of life with him would be over too. Until that instant, in this tense and hopeless silence, she had not realized just how friendly, in spite of its disappointments, that life had been, with his comical anecdotes at supper, or their evening walks to window-shop or to see a foreign movie or to go dancing or just to sit reading together.

Presently Richard, clearing his throat, began with difficulty to speak.

"Whatever you do, whatever, just please . . . If there were some way my father could be kept from knowing your reason. I don't think I could face that."

"Do you mean that in this day and age he wouldn't accept what you are?"

"Not everybody's out of the closet, Connie."

"And your mother?"

"If they had always known, maybe they'd be used to it by now. I don't know." He gave a weak, apologetic laugh. "But this would be quite a surprise, to say the least."

The Grant Wood couple in front of their imposing house, faces without smiles, cold courtesy.

"Yes," she said, "I can see. They'd take it out on you. They would."

"I don't know about 'taking it out.' Their silence can be rather awesome too."

"Have you ever thought maybe that's got something to do with the way you are?"

He became suddenly, ruefully defensive. "I'm happy. And I would have continued to be happy if you hadn't seen me today. I've accepted the way I am, and I won't fight it anymore."

"You would have gone on doing this to me?"

"I said I was sorry, Connie."

"All right, I won't say anything to your parents, or to anyone except my brother. You can depend on my word."

"I know I can."

"Blame the divorce on me. They never liked me anyway, so they'll no doubt be pleased."

He did not deny it, but said only, "You can keep this apartment. It's paid for, free and clear. It cleaned out almost all my cash. What's left is invested with Eddy."

This unexpected offer made Connie feel cheap, and guilty, too, as if he had read her mind and seen there how painful it could be to give up this home.

"I don't want blood money," she said stiffly.

"You won't have to fight me for anything."

"I don't want to fight you at all, Richard. I just want to talk to Eddy. He'll know what to do. Now I can't talk anymore. I'm exhausted. Wrung out."

* * *

"I'm in no mood for explanations or for commiserations from friends like Bitsy Maxwell," Connie said. "They'll all just have to wait. I'll tell Lara myself, so don't you tell her, Eddy. She'll be heartbroken for me, but other people will ask only out of curiosity, you know that."

They were in Eddy's office, waiting for Richard to arrive. Laid in readiness on the otherwise immaculate desk was a tidy stack of papers like a white island on a mahogany sea; this was Richard's portfolio of securities.

Now Richard entered. He had been sleeping for the last week at a hotel, or very likely had been lying awake there; gray pouches made semicircles beneath his eyes.

Eddy rose, offered his hand, and smiled. "Come in, Richard. I'm glad to see you, but awfully sorry about the reason."

Connie twirled a ring around her little finger and did not look up. Richard, stifling a quiver in his throat, rushed to begin.

"I suppose Connie's told you everything. I don't know how you will regard me now, Eddy. This is hardly what you expected for your sister. I feel—"

"She's told me. As to how I regard you—well, I'm not here to judge anything or anybody. All I can say is, people make mistakes. What can you do? You're both decent and honorable, so there's no reason why this business shouldn't be agreeably settled. Those are my sentiments."

He was in a hurry to finish this business as fast as possible. It was certainly not that he was wanting in sympathy; it was precisely because he had so much of it that he shrank from contact with sadness; he must strike at the cause of sadness and eradicate it, accept the fact as accomplished and get down to practicalities.

"I never meant to cheat Connie. I realize now that I should have told her. It wasn't honest."

"Well, that's water over the dam. The thing is now to look

ahead. I've already put Connie in touch with a lawyer. I assume you have one too?"

"I don't need one. I've told Connie I've no plan to fight her. She can have the apartment. She can have everything."

It was painful to hear Richard sound so beaten. And Eddy saw by his sister's woebegone expression that she was feeling the same pain. Then she spoke.

"I told you, Richard, that I don't want to rob you. I don't want to hurt you."

"But you'll take the apartment," Eddy said quickly.

"What will I do with a lot of big, empty rooms?" Connie's voice was bleak.

"They won't be empty," Richard said. "I'll pay for everything we ordered."

Eddy had a strange impulse. He wanted to cry out to Richard: Why are you so damned good? The world is contemptuous of such goodness! It's weak, this goodness of yours. It would be easier for us if you'd put up a little fight for yourself. He looked at the man sitting uncomfortably and looking small—however could Richard manage to look small?—in the oxblood leather wing chair. Richard looked back with a faint, tentative smile, to which Eddy responded with compassion, until abruptly there flashed into his mind a picture of two men in a bed, and he felt anger. He'd had no right to marry her, no right!

That this marrying business can end in such a mess was appalling. Connie, poor girl, had been in such a rush to get married too. Pam, now, was just the opposite, he reflected thankfully. A modern woman, she was happy enough to be on her own, earning her own few dollars, taking each day as she found it without anxiety. She was a perfect complement to himself—and not just sexually—because that was exactly his own style of living. He saw hardly any other women but her; rarely he found himself roped into a "date" by some business connection whom he did not want to offend by refusal, and he never liked the "dates" because, as he always put it, they usually had "marriage" beaming from their eyes.

Freedom. Freedom was the ticket, and no binding ties, only loose ones that can be dropped when the time for dropping comes. One had only to look at this poor pair of mismatched—

"As to alimony," Richard was saying, addressing Eddy now, "well, you know what I own. I'll make no trouble over any amount you think is justified. Just give me the figures. And remember, Connie's got expensive tastes."

"You make me feel disgusting when you talk like that!" Connie gasped. "We have no children and I don't need alimony. Just make some sort of fair settlement."

Eddy put up a hand before Richard could answer. "Enough. Enough. Let me settle this by saying there's plenty for you both. Richard, your shelters got you a four-to-one write-off this year, remember? And they'll do the same next year. Connie, why don't you read a magazine in the waiting room while we run over some figures? It won't take all that long."

Unable to concentrate on a page, Connie laid the magazine aside and allowed her mind to wander about among disconnected places and faces. The conclusion of the wandering was that you can depend on nothing. Why should Peg, still in her forties, have died of cancer? Why should Richard have turned out like this? The only thing you can depend on is money. That's tangible. It doesn't die young or disillusion you. Take care of it and it lasts. It's there to keep you warm and safe and give you honor, besides. That girl at the reception desk thinks I don't know that she's looking me over, envying my mink and my alligator shoes. I used to do that, too, when I worked at Richard's club; I used to see the rings on their hands when I gave out the menus. I know. . . . So I'm to have the apartment completed, warm and safe in spite of it all. Well, it could be worse, a lot worse. And it won't ruin Richard.

TREASURES

The receptionist was speaking to her. "Mr. Osborne just buzzed. You can go back in."

As she opened the door to the private office, Eddy's cheerful voice rang out, too loud.

"I give her two years at the outside before she'll be married again. And thank goodness you have no kids."

Some six weeks later Connie stood on the sidewalk in the cold, white winter sunshine with a slip of paper in her hand. It's not possible, she thought. Given the way I lived with Richard and careful as I always was, especially after that awful night, how can this be? Yet there was no denying the fact. It must have been that weekend in the country. . . .

"You're not happy about it," the doctor had said, observing Connie's face.

"My marriage just broke up. This is absurd. I can't have a baby."

The doctor, a quiet elderly woman, kept a neutral manner, saying calmly, "You mean you don't want to."

Although her mind was quite made up, Connie's heart had begun to flutter in a small panic of its own.

"It's nothing to look forward to, is it?" she said. "An abortion, I mean."

"True enough," the other woman said. "That's why I told you to go home and think it over for a couple of days. No longer than that, though."

"I don't have to think it over. I'm not in a position to have a child. I don't want it!" she cried, twisting her damp hands in the strap of her pocketbook. "I particularly don't want this child. I wouldn't welcome it, and would that be fair to it? Would it? I don't even know where my own life is going, let alone somebody else's life. No, no, I can't."

The doctor stood up. "Well, then, you can make your appointment at the desk. They'll give you your instructions."

So Connie folded the instruction sheet and started home. It was midafternoon, darkening, and children were being brought back from the park. Three baby carriages passed on her block alone. A few months from now she could be pushing one too. It was unthinkable.

Her heart was still fluttering when she opened her apartment door. For a minute or two she stood still in the foyer and just looked around as if to orient herself. Then, still wearing her coat, she picked up the patient little dog and walked around the rooms.

It was almost impossible to believe that a life was growing in her body. Surely birth was as common as death, and yet was death not incomprehensible too? She did not feel any different, but the life was there, a minute heart already throbbing. And she was about to let them rip it out! A violent shaking overcame her. And as she clasped Delphine, she felt the little dog's heart beating, beating. . . .

What to do? What to do? No, I can't. I'm not ready for a child, I didn't want one before I knew about Richard, at least not yet, I didn't, and I certainly don't want one now. I wouldn't welcome his child. I would have to pretend I did, and the child would feel it. We would both be so wounded and unhappy. . . . She sat down and cried. The dog in her lap looked up at her face and licked her hand.

Presently, cried out, she got up and looked around. Much progress had been made during these last few weeks. The living room was almost complete, an English oak stretcher table stood in the dining room and the cabinets that were to have held Richard's books in the den were finished. She would simply have to fill them one by one with books of her own. A new bed stood in the bedroom now, which was a pity because the original bed had been a handsome piece. But she could never have slept in it, and this one, covered in yellow quilted chintz, was pretty enough. The sight of these accumulating possessions began to

116

soothe her. They were curiously comforting, enfolding her and reassuring her that she was, after all, safe.

There was no reason for any panic. If you just kept your head, you could get through almost anything. By tomorrow at this time the simple operation would be over. And after that go forward, she told herself.

Thus Connie passed the evening, slept through the night, and in the morning, was calm.

On that same afternoon Lara, too, had been seeing a doctor. She said wanly, "I felt so sure this time. I can't explain, but I was so sure when I missed that this was it."

Through the window behind the doctor's head she could see the parking lot, in which a young woman, carrying a baby and holding with the other hand a little boy in a yellow slicker, was hurrying through the rain.

"I don't know," she said again. "I just don't know."

"And I—I don't know anything much either. Only that we've tried everything possible, Mrs. Davis." The man had a kindly manner, he was genuinely sorry for her, but that did not help. And he said so. "Sometimes we doctors run up against problems that won't let themselves be solved. That doesn't help you, does it?"

Lara shook her head and wiped her eyes.

"Adoption?" queried the doctor. "It can work out beautifully, you know."

"It takes years to get a baby, Doctor. There aren't nearly enough for all the people who want them."

"That's true of infants. But if you would take an older child who needs parents, and there are many such, shunted from one foster home to another, and it tears your heart to think about them—you might be very happy, I think. You and your husband would make wonderful parents."

I wanted Davey's baby, our baby, she was saying to herself.

117

Not a child who remembers her own mother. But she said nothing, except that Davey had said the same thing himself.

"Well, think about it," the doctor said. "Go home and talk it over."

So all that evening they talked it over, sitting together on the sofa. Davey had his arm around Lara when finally he said, "There comes a time, no matter what the problem, when one has to face the hard truth. And I think we've come to it. As a matter of fact, at the last stockholders' meeting, Don Schultz happened to mention that a cousin of his adopted a boy from a home somewhere in Minnesota, I think it was. It's a church-run place, and they give you the child's history and the background and everything. I really believe we should try it, Lara. It's time we stopped fooling around and made a decision."

Of course, he was right. She knew that. And she said, "I'm ready. Yes, I'm ready. Will you get the name of the place tomorrow?"

"I will. And Lara darling, listen to me. Things aren't all bad. We'll find a child in need of love, and we have a lot of love to give, you and I. Think of poor Connie, married three years and finished. That's a trouble we don't have."

"I know. She's pretty shaken by it too."

"Why don't you go to her? You haven't seen her since it happened, so why not get on a plane tomorrow and surprise her? Stay for a couple of days and cheer her up. See a few shows, go to a French restaurant, have fun together. Meanwhile, I'll talk to the people in Minnesota or wherever it is, and we'll drive out there first thing for our baby—our child."

Well, I'm hardly alone, Connie thought, as she waited her turn, and passed the time in speculation about the others in the room. There were a dozen women and almost as many men. Two very young girls, unmistakably sisters, held hands; it was impossible to guess who of the two was to have the abortion, for they were both frightened and suppressing tears. A tired woman, nearing fifty, wore a wedding band and a shabby coat. One had the impression that she had already reared a houseful of children. A tough young woman wearing false eyelashes, false nails like bloody pins, and pants that revealed every smallest line of her body tried to encourage the sisters.

"Nothing to it, girls. Honest. This is my fourth go-around."

In the white room with its rows of flashing instruments, the doctor and nurse in white and its cold, white light, Connie remembered that: nothing to it. Lie back. Be confident. Remember the infected and impacted wisdom tooth? It was just like this, the whiteness, the bareness, and the low commanding voices; the stab of pain, the quick stab; clench your fists and hold on. The room whirled. You're not here. You're far away on a beach, under a tree. You're sweating under your arms, but you haven't made a sound. Brace your feet. Almost finished, someone says. Now vast relief. . . . It's over.

They led her to a cot and told her to rest. They gave her a long, cool drink, and she fell asleep. When she awoke, the short winter day was ending, and they came to tell her she might go home.

So there really was nothing to it.

The first person she saw in the lobby at home was Lara, sitting on a bench near the elevator.

"Oh," Lara said, rushing to Connie, "I've been here for hours! They wouldn't let me into your apartment."

"Why didn't you say you were coming? Is anything wrong?"

"No, not with us. But you—oh, Connie, I just couldn't stay away. I've been thinking and thinking about you and Richard." Lara's voice rose, plaintive and troubled, so that a couple emerging from the elevator turned to stare.

Lara was like that sometimes, naive and artless. Of all times for her to come here! Connie said to herself. Any other day I

119

would have been overjoyed to see her. Now there'll be a long talk going on half the night, I suppose, with explanations and regrets.

"Come up," she said, almost peremptorily.

She switched on the lights, bringing to life the living room and the den beyond, all thickly carpeted, the furniture waxed and gleaming, and the air scented with potpourri.

"Oh, how beautiful!" Lara cried, clasping her hands like a child beholding a Christmas tree.

The gesture irritated Connie, whose legs were suddenly going weak. There had perhaps been something to "it" after all, because she wanted only to lie down again. But then Lara put her arms around her.

"Darling, I would have come to you if I had known you and Richard were having problems. I might even have helped straighten things out between you. Who knows?"

Connie gave a brittle laugh. "You don't know what you're talking about. It was not preventable. I never told you the whole story. I planned to do it soon, but I just haven't felt like talking. Eddy is the only one who knows. Not another soul." That was true. She had not even told Bitsy yet, although she spoke to her almost every day.

Lara looked stricken. "I'm so very sorry. I can't tell you how sorry. We were shocked, Davey and I. We liked Richard. We really liked him so much."

"He's likable." Connie spoke dryly, without energy.

Lara gave her a quick look. "You don't look well, darling. Are you terribly unhappy?"

"As a matter of fact, no. Not terribly, that is." Her legs were shaking now. "Why are we standing here? Sit down. I'm awfully tired."

She remembered then that Lara would want dinner. There were vegetables and chops in the refrigerator, but the thought of getting up to prepare them daunted her.

"Actually, I'm not feeling well. Maybe I'm coming down with something."

"No," Lara said decisively. "It's your nerves, and no wonder. You're going through a crisis. Shall I make you some tea?"

"It's dinnertime. You must be starved. Wait a few minutes, and I'll go get it ready."

"You'll do nothing of the sort. Stay right there. I can find my way around your kitchen."

Like Peg, Connie thought.

"What a sumptuous kitchen!" Lara called.

She heard the slam of the refrigerator door and the clink of a pot, cheerful, domestic sounds, reminding her again of Peg. And she was ashamed of having been so unwelcoming to Lara. I really am wrung out, she thought again, and closed her eyes.

When she opened them, Lara was standing in front of her holding a tray with a lamb chop, a salad, and a cup of tea.

"You look too weary to sit at the table, so I've brought the tray. But maybe you should have it in bed."

"No, I'm fine here. It's lovely. You're too nice to me," Connie said. The kindness made her eyes tear. "You always were."

"Come on, come on. Now, I'll sit here with you, and if you feel like talking, do. And if you don't, don't."

"You made the salad dressing, didn't you? It's good. I don't bother with meals much anymore."

Lara reproached her gently. "You should. You mustn't neglect yourself."

And seating herself with a tray on her lap, Lara began to eat, while at the same time, with anxious concern, observing Connie. "Do you want me to talk, Connie? I don't mean about your troubles either. If you want quiet, just say so."

"Talk, of course. And as to my divorce, I'll tell you tomorrow. It's a long story."

"All right, then, I'll tell you something about myself. First,

121

we've decided to buy that house. Eddy convinced us that we can afford it."

"Really? Oh, I'm glad! It's a lovely house."

"Wait. There's bigger news. I almost don't want to talk about it until it comes true. And you're the only one I'm telling. But we think—we expect to have a child."

"You *are* pregnant, then! Oh, my God, how wonderful! You've wanted it so. But you don't look it, you don't show. When will it be?"

Lara shook her head. "No, darling. I'm not pregnant, and I never will be. We've finally made up our minds to adopt, that's all."

"Oh. Well. That's wonderful, too, isn't it? Tell me about it. I've heard one has to be on a waiting list for years, though. Is that true?"

"Well, I hope not. It's much easier if one agrees to take an older child. So it won't be a baby. But we don't mind."

"Oh." The brief vision of Lara holding an infant, a miniature edition of herself, had vanished. "Boy or girl?" Connie inquired brightly.

"Whichever we find first. In the meantime we're getting the spare bedroom ready until we can move."

Connie had a swift double vision: the sterile glare of that room this morning when something had been taken away, and the bright clutter of another room which Lara would be filling now with toys and noise and—

"I hope it won't take too long to leave that dreadful flat behind," she said.

Lara said, smiling, "I've never found it so dreadful," and Connie smiled back. "You wouldn't. You never complain."

It was pleasant to be there in the quiet with her sister, and she was glad, after all, that Lara had come. The food and the hot tea began to revive her. Then she remembered that she had eaten nothing since that morning and said so.

"Whatever made you go all day without eating?"

An odd thought, possibly induced by Lara's concerned expression, that tenderness of eyes and voice, crossed Connie's mind: I have always been cared for. First, there was my mother—father, too, in his way, but mostly Peg—then Lara and then Richard. From this thought came a sudden desire to tell everything to Lara now. And starting at the end of her tale she said, "The reason I'm weak is that I've just come back from having an abortion."

Lara's fork clattered onto the plate. "You what?"

"I had an abortion."

"I can't believe what I'm hearing!"

Lara's body seemed to go limp. Her lips parted, and her head bent forward. She had been instantly, totally stunned. And Connie's heart began that panicked fluttering again.

"I didn't know I was pregnant when I left him, not that it would have made any difference," she explained. "You don't know about Richard. He wasn't a bad person, he was very good, but I couldn't stay because he was—"

Lara flung up her hand. "What does Richard matter? I don't care what he was or what he did, but you—you killed your baby!"

Of course. This was how Lara would see it! And Connie reproached herself: I should have kept my mouth shut. Her eyes are absolutely fierce.

"I didn't exactly love doing it," she said as quietly as she was able. "But it was necessary, Lara. I had to. . . . And anyway, it wasn't even a baby yet. It was the size of my little finger." In the face of those eyes, gone dark with horror, she stammered, "Or something like that."

"You're lying to yourself. The size! The size! It was alive, breathing and growing, and you murdered it. I—damn you, Connie! I'd have given years of my life to have a child of my own, and I still would give them. Is it fair? God, is it fair?"

Lara jumped up, knocking over her tray; blue Wedgwood

123

broke, and meat gravy splashed brown on Connie's new beige carpet.

"The carpet!" gasped Connie. "It's ruined! Ruined! And it was just laid last week."

She rushed to the kitchen for club soda and rags. Lara picked up the broken dishes. For a few minutes nothing was said while the two women, on their knees, worked to repair the damage.

"It's almost out," Lara said at last, as she rose to her feet.

Connie, burning, assessed the destruction. " 'Almost.' That's a big help! A light brown stain instead of a dark one." And it seemed to her that this accident, minor and trivial as it might be, was just the last straw on her pile of woe.

"I'll buy you another carpet," Lara said.

Connie, sure she had heard scorn in Lara's voice, flashed back, "You? You can't afford what this cost."

"Well, I'm sorry. People have accidents. I guess it's not my day."

"It certainly isn't mine. I should be having a quiet evening, pulling myself together, instead of this."

"It should take some pulling together after what you did to-day."

Through bitter tears Connie cried, "I'm not psychologically prepared to have a child right now! Can't you understand that? I'm in the middle of a divorce. What kind of a home could I offer it?"

"*I* would have given it a home. That baby—that baby was a part of Peg, a part of her that would have gone on, and you destroyed it. God knows whether Eddy will ever have children. *I* certainly won't. I'll never get over this. Never."

"That's your problem! I'm going to *make* myself get over it. *I* have no choice."

Lara's flushed face was mottled. Her nose dripped while she fumbled for a handkerchief. She seemed to have crumbled into complete disarray, like a heartsick, tired old woman.

TREASURES

And Connie pleaded, "Why are we quarreling over this, Lara? If you think I was wrong, well, it's your privilege to think so. Let's understand each other. But I can't undo what's done, can I? And anyway," she finished gently enough, "it really was my business, my decision, my sorrow."

Lara shook her head. "I can't help thinking over and over, What would Peg say? Can you believe she would ever have done it?"

This new reference to their mother stung. It was too painful, it was irrelevant and did not belong here in this room on this night. So Connie's answer was sharper than she had perhaps intended.

"Peg was never in my circumstances. Furthermore, Peg did things I wouldn't do, like staying on with a lovable drunkard, for instance."

"Oh, my God, how can you say such a thing about her?" Lara wailed.

"Because it's true. It hurts me to say it, but you know very well she never wanted to face facts. Don't you be like that too. Please, Lara."

"I faced them well enough all those years when I brought you up. And I'm the one who did bring you up, remember?"

"Oh, I remember." Lara's kind hands doing her hair. Lara's kind face in the schoolyard at three o'clock . . . "But I'm not the little sister now, taking advice at your knee. Sometimes I wish I were. Life was easier then."

"Advice like this you never got at my knee. If I thought you had I would never forgive myself."

"Lara, let's stop this before it goes too far. You mustn't try to run my life anymore."

"I never tried to run your life, Connie."

"You're trying now."

"That's what you think of me? Well, I've heard everything." Lara sobbed. "I came here to help you, came out of love, and this is what I get for it. This."

Suddenly Connie felt hot. She could feel the heat rising from the very central pit of her body. And terror rose with it. Emotion and conflict could be the cause, but infection also could be the cause. And the sight of Lara's futile tears infuriated her. She lashed out.

"If there's anything I despise to see, it's people feeling sorry for themselves."

"I'm not sorry for myself. I'm sorry for you, Connie."

"Well, don't be! I'll get along all right. In fact, I'll get along just fine," she said, not meaning it.

"This is what you call 'just fine'? You're a terrible disappointment, Connie. Terrible. I can only hope that somehow you'll straighten out your life. I can only hope."

"Sanctimonious. Holy . . ." Connie muttered under her breath.

"I heard you. I heard you!"

"So you heard me! Will you just please let me alone? I can't stand any more preaching or moaning. Just let me alone!"

"Oh, I'll let you alone. Indeed I will. I'll bother you no more." Lara ran to the closet. "Where's my coat? I'm leaving, Connie. You just go ahead and run your life your own way. And good luck to you."

This violence, this rupture, was too ugly to bear. Again Connie's legs went weak. She had to sit down.

"Wait, Lara. What are you doing?"

"Taking the first plane home," said Lara, fastening her coat.

"You won't get one at this hour. Wait."

"Then I'll sleep at the airport."

The door clicked shut.

For a while Connie sat staring at the door's blank face. Presently she got up, walked past the pathetic stain that would exist as a reminder of this day as long as the carpet lasted, and lay down on the sofa in the den. Never, never had such stormy anger come between her sister and herself, or for that matter, among any of the family! Anger simply wasn't their way. This sense of outrage must have come up from deep within Lara, from a deeper place than she herself knew existed, perhaps so deep that she would be lost to Connie forever. And the pain within Connie was now palpable, a knot, a clenched fist in her chest.

The room was absolutely still, the charming room that she had planned, with the English-country-home effect that she had desired. The curtains were drawn for the night, shutting out the world, accentuating the stillness. She sprang up and pulled them open onto the city, onto the street below where life moved.

Life. Only this morning, a few hours ago, she had been accompanied by another life, now gone. A strange thought came fleeting: We would have loved one another. I would have loved you, even though I didn't want you. A strange, lonely thought.

Tomorrow she would tell Eddy what had happened. Or maybe she wouldn't, just yet. He had his own affairs, he was a busy man, and he had already done so much for her. Maybe, though, she might just ask him for some advice. It would be long before the art courses could materialize into a really important job. So in the meantime, should she think of going back to work in a boutique? There had to be something to fill the days. She needed advice.

The little dog crept around her feet, and she bent to stroke it. Its love was pure and simple. It, unlike the human animal, neither judged nor disappointed.

"Without you, Delphine," she whispered aloud, "I don't know how I'd get through this night."

127

CHAPTER
SIX

‰

L ara looked across the small parlor to where Davey was
sitting, as if to find affirmation. This was the final moment, the climax, the arrival after some months' journey
through time and some miles' journey through a fading autumn
countryside to this plain clapboard house in a plain clapboard
town. Now here they were. And she was suddenly conscious of
her thundering heart.

Mrs. Elmer was an unpretentious gray-haired woman of the
type often described as "motherly." And for the last half hour
she had been relating a sad, simple story.

"Susanna is a very intelligent little girl, but she's lived through
what I call a war. Her father died in a factory accident while her
mother was pregnant. The mother, an immigrant from eastern
Europe without family, was so devastated that, although she did
take good care of the child, she was not able to provide the
happiest environment. Then, when she herself fell ill with leuke-
mia—well, you can imagine."

Lara's eyes never left Mrs. Elmer's face. "Who took care of
Susanna then?" she asked.

"Neighbors. First one family and then another. When, after
the mother died, they weren't prepared to keep her, the state
took charge and she went to a foster home."

TREASURES

"A good home?" asked Lara.

Mrs. Elmer shrugged. "Let's say, not a bad one. Now I've had her here for the last two weeks, after your telephone call prepared the path for a possible adoption. I'm sort of a way station. They come and they go."

Davey spoke. "Is she a very, very frightened child, would you say?"

"Actually, I think she's been remarkably brave in the circumstances. Nothing's ever lasted for her. Nothing. She's in first grade, and has already changed schools three times. What she needs is permanence and a lot of patient love."

When Davey asked, "Are there no relatives on the father's side either?" Lara knew he was concerned lest some stranger arrive in years to come to claim her.

Mrs. Elmer understood immediately. "No, not a soul. If you adopt Sue—she likes to be called that—she'll be your child without question. Now, would you like to see her?"

Davey smiled. "I think we're ready, Mrs. Elmer," he said.

"I'll go get her. They're all playing in the yard."

He came over and laid his hand on Lara's shoulder. Feeling the tremble of the hand, she thought, This is how he would be if I were giving birth, only it would last longer and he would be walking the length of the corridor getting in people's way, lighting and relighting his pipe with these trembling hands—

At that moment the door opened, and the woman returned, urging a small girl ahead of her, a thin child with extraordinary blue-black eyes in a narrow, delicate face, and a long brown ponytail. And Lara's immediate reaction was a kind of shock: She doesn't look at all like either of us. I'll never have the quiet joy of seeing Davey or part of myself in her. Then, swiftly, she admonished herself: There is no perfect joy, Lara.

"Sue," said Mrs. Elmer, "these are Mr. and Mrs. Davis. Will you shake hands with them?"

Fearfully, the child raised her gaze from her own scuffed shoes

129

and looked down at Lara's shoes. A small, cold hand was held out, and an almost indistinguishable word was murmured.

I mustn't cry, Lara told herself. And softly she said, "Sue . . . We've heard so much about you, about what a lovely girl you are. So we wanted to bring a present for you, a surprise. It's in this box. Do you want to open it, or shall I?"

As if unsure what answer would be the right one, Sue waited, and Lara said quickly, "Here, we'll do it together. You hold one end of the bow, and I'll pull it open."

Under layers of tissue paper lay the most extravagant, the most beautiful doll that could ever be imagined, a perfect little girl with real blond hair, an expressive face, and a party dress of white lace and pink ribbons.

The child stared, not touching it.

"Take it, pick her up," urged Lara.

Still the child just stared.

Mrs. Elmer spoke almost pridefully, "You see how well behaved Sue is."

Lara and Davey glanced at one another with a common thought between them: *She's well behaved because she's terrified.* And lifting the doll out of the box, Lara placed it in Sue's arms.

"She's yours, dear. She wants you to love her. What would you like to name her?"

This time a reply came promptly and clearly. "Lily."

"Oh, I like that name," Lara said, while above Sue's head Mrs. Elmer's lips moved silently to say, "That was her mother's name."

I can't bear this, Lara said to herself.

Suddenly, passionately, Sue clutched the doll to her chest and ran with it to the armchair at the other end of the room.

Davey's raised eyebrows, furrowing his forehead, asked a question of his wife, a question similar to her own: Should we? Will this child's problems be more than we want to undertake?

And yet, what child brought to live among strangers, wrested from whatever home it once knew, did not carry problems in its baggage? Some baggage was heavier than other kinds, that was all. Only an infant could come without memories.

Mrs. Elmer drew her chair close to Davey's and Lara's, out of Sue's hearing.

"Well, what do you think?" she asked. "Do you think you want her? She's really a sweet child."

The question was an eager endorsement, too much like salesmanship. As if they were buying a new car: *Do you want it? It's really a good buy.*

"She has good manners for a six year old, hasn't she? She's really been no bother. I've seen children who haven't gone through as much as she has, who cry and have tantrums, which is surely understandable, heaven knows, but it's hard to deal with."

Davey was paying no attention to Mrs. Elmer. And Lara, following his look, saw that Sue was rocking the doll in her arms and smiling. The smile, most feminine and most endearing, would, Lara saw, go straight to Davey's heart, obliterating there any last regret he might have over not getting a boy.

That smile, unselfconscious, as if Sue were alone in the room, went straight to Lara's heart too. She had a sudden revelation: I can make happiness bloom again in this child. The result will be worth the effort. Almost gaily, she thought—silly, frivolous, happy vision—oh, I will braid her hair when it grows longer, I'll make one thick braid with a ribbon bow at the tip, I will—

"Of course," Mrs. Elmer was saying very low, "your taking her depends on whether she wants to go. I will not send an unwilling child away from here. You wouldn't want it either." She raised her voice. "Sue, will you come over here? We want to ask you something. Would you like to go home with Mr. and Mrs. Davis?"

Lara made a correction. "Aunt Lara and Uncle Davey. That's what we'd be if you would come to live with us." And yet she felt a pang of regret that she would very likely never be called "Mother."

But those eyes, so black and lustrous! The piteous plea as they were raised to Lara, studying Lara's face. Were they saying, Take me! Take me! Or were they saying, I don't want you. Let me alone.

"We've been wanting a little girl like you," Lara said, trying not to coax too blatantly, wanting just to seem friendly. "We have no children in our house. You'd have your own room. It's painted yellow and white, and the shelves have wonderful toys, a carriage for Lily, a little kitchen—"

And still, wasn't this talk merely bribery? On the other hand, why not? What other way to lure a six year old?

"And if you'd like to have a puppy—" Davey began.

"A real live puppy?"

"A real one."

Solemn again, the child said, "I'd like that."

"You'll go to school," said Lara, "and have lots of friends. I know some nice girls for you to play with."

"What are their names?"

"Well, there's Betty and Jennifer and Lisa. Oh, lots more."

Careful now to do nothing abrupt or alarming, Lara put her arm very loosely around Sue's waist.

"We shall love you very much," she said.

There was no answer. Yet, what answer might she have expected?

"Will you come with us, Sue? It will be a nice long ride home. I think we'll stop for ice cream cones on the way." More bribery. "So will you come?"

Sue paused. The pause seemed very, very long. Oh, I want this child! Lara cried to herself. There's something about her. . . . I want this child.

"Will you?" she asked once more.

"All right," said Sue.

And Davey, almost tearful himself, spoke with a catch in his throat. "How fast can we get the basic legal preliminaries over with so we can get back to Ohio?"

"It won't take long," said Mrs. Elmer.

And so it was that Susanna Davis went to her new home.

All was not to go easily, nor had the Davises expected it to. True, the first hours went well enough. The drive home was enlivened by many stops for food, a sailboat ride on Lake Michigan, and shopping in Chicago, which was most necessary, since Sue's entire shabby wardrobe fitted into one suitcase.

Trying on a winter jacket, she pranced in front of the mirror. A wholesome, greedy pleasure in the total new experience of receiving things lessened her shyness so that at one point, behaving like any normally secure young girl, Sue actually rejected one of Lara's suggestions. This touch of spirit encouraged Lara.

"But I like the red one. I want the red one."

"The red one it shall be then, Miss Sue."

Then, saying so, an echo sounded in Lara's head, an echo of her own voice years before saying something like that to another little girl who always had such decided ideas about her wants.

"Whatever you say, Miss Consuelo."

It was a year since that tragic night in New York. After it weeks had passed during which the hurt and smart of Connie's words had increased. "Ruining my life"—how cruel and untrue! And as to what Connie had done . . . To take a life that could have grown to stand in front of a mirror like this skinny little thing here preening herself in the red jacket . . .

If Connie could be standing here now, with us—Lara thought. She should have called me. All these months . . . She should have. And I know Eddy told her we were going to fetch this child. At least she could have called to wish us luck. For an instant Lara's throat was choked; then the lump receded, leaving an ache of grieving resignation. And she turned back to the moment, to her new little girl.

Arriving home, they found Eddy in a rented car parked at the driveway.

"For Pete's sake," cried Davey, "look who's here!"

"I figured you'd be arriving about now, so I grabbed a plane, rented a car, and here I am. I didn't want to miss the homecoming."

There he was, the old familiar Eddy, breezing in as always with his glad enthusiasm, filling the air with welcome and rejoicing.

"Look at this pretty kid! So you're Susanna! I'm your Uncle Eddy, so do I get a kiss?"

Lara looked dubious. She wanted to caution him: Not so fast. Don't frighten her. But Eddy had already lifted the little girl up above his head, and now, hugging her to his chest, was kissing her cheeks. And Sue was actually laughing.

Eddy had magic in his very fingertips. Was there ever a human being who could resist him?

"I stopped in town," he said, setting Sue down, "and bought a little something for Sue."

The little something was a small two-wheeler, bright blue with a bell and a basket.

"I'll bet you haven't learned to ride one of these, so we're going to show you how this minute."

"Wait, wait!" protested Davey. "We just got here, and we haven't even opened the front door yet."

"Okay, okay, I just want to make sure this fits her." And lifting her onto the seat, Eddy directed her. "Listen to Uncle Eddy. Put your feet there. No, keep them there. Fine. Now I'll push you. I won't let you fall. Fine. That's the idea. It won't take you long to learn."

So the first few hours passed. Sue was shown to her room; the new clothes were put away, and Lily went to sit on the doll's chair by the bed. Lara made a quick dinner. Eddy, invited to spend the night, declined.

"No, I took a room near the airport so I can leave first thing in the morning. Anyway, this first night is for you three to spend together."

"Eddy, you're a prince," Davey said.

Eddy laughed. "Call me Wales. Hey, the next time I come, you'll be in the new house!"

"Thanks again to the prince," Davey said.

Eddy jingled the car keys. "Well, I have to be going. Be happy, all of you." He kissed them and, leaving, was heard trotting swiftly down the outer stairs.

"I never realized he was so wonderful with children," remarked Lara. "He should be married."

"He still has a steady, hasn't he? That girl on Long Island? The one with the horses?"

"I think so. But he may have ten steadies for all I know. He keeps his private life to himself."

After dinner, which Sue ate hungrily, Lara gave her a bath, observing that she was none too clean and that her ribs stuck out. She had had minimal care, poor little girl. When Lara had washed, dried, and powdered her, brushed her hair and teeth, and put on a new white nightgown, she put her into the bed and drew up the pink comforter.

"Would you like me to read a story, Sue? This is a lovely book. *Winnie-the-Pooh*, it's called. Let's begin," said Lara confidently.

"I don't want a story, Mrs.—I forgot your name."

"Mrs. Davis. But to you, I'm Aunt. Aunt Lara. Don't you remember?"

And again the thought, the hope, crossed Lara's mind that someday, perhaps, she would be called "Mother." Perhaps, too, that would never happen.

"Will you say 'Aunt Lara'?"

"Aunt Lara." The girl yawned.

"You're sleepy." The delicate face was so white, so wan, in the beam of the nightlight. "It's been a long day," Lara said softly, "and we've lots to do tomorrow. We have to get you registered at school, ride the new bike if you want to—oh, lots of things. Let me hug you good-night."

"How is she doing?" Davey asked.

"Very well, I think. So far, so good."

But deep in the middle of the night loud crying awakened Davey and Lara in their room across the hall. Lara ran. Sitting up in the little yellow bed, Susanna was shaking with deep sobs. Lara took her into her arms.

"There, there," was all she could say. The banal words, without meaning in themselves, yet had the utmost meaning when warm arms and a warm voice went with them.

Anxious, Davey asked from the doorway, "Does anything hurt her, do you think?"

"Everything does," Lara answered, and comprehending, he nodded.

For long minutes she sat with the child's tears wetting her shoulders, her own tears brimming. No questions were asked, no answers given. There was no need. The child cried because the world was fearsome; she wanted her lost mother; the place was strange; the night was dark. The woman wept because this was not the baby she wanted; she was sick with pity; yet she knew she was going to love this child and longed for the child to return that love.

So they stayed together holding each other until the sobbing ceased and Sue was laid back under the quilt to fall asleep. But Lara, not leaving her, sat dozing, crumpled and cold, in the rocking chair until the morning.

Patience, patience was all. It hurt when Sue, defying a command, cried out, "You're not my mother!"

Very quietly, Lara answered, "I know that. But since your

mother's gone, I'm the one who will take care of you as mothers do."

It hurt when Sue cried at night and clung, hurt to imagine the nightmare that had awakened her. So patience, patience was all.

Still, little by little, day after day, small changes, almost imperceptible, began to occur.

Lara's friends brought their children to play. At first when Sue was invited back, she refused to go. She's afraid that I'll leave her there, and she'll be given away again, Lara knew. It's not that she loves us, of course not. It's only that she's afraid of another change. And something told her that it would be a good thing to speak openly about that fear and about everything, school and all the foster homes and the dead mother too.

"Tell me, Sue, is that why you won't go to Jennifer's house? That you're afraid you'll be kept there?"

Sue's silence was the answer.

"Will you go if I stay there with you?"

A nod of the head was the answer.

After half a dozen trials of this sort one day Lara left her to go down to her office, which, Davey and she had agreed, must be turned over temporarily to someone else while Sue got adjusted and while they made the move into the new home. When she returned to the friend's house, Sue was playing in the yard. She hadn't missed Lara at all.

"Now," Lara said, hugging her tightly, "now you see that I always come back to you. Uncle Davey and I will never let you go. Why, even if you wanted to leave us, we wouldn't let you. We'd find you no matter where you went—even to the moon! And do you know why? Because you belong to us, and we belong to you, forever and ever. That's why."

Fortunately, the first-grade teacher was especially understanding. "In the beginning, Mrs. Davis, I did see tears starting, but always held back, hidden from the other children. She's a proud little girl. But—let's see, it's six months since she came—the improvement in attitude is really wonderful."

"She's very bright," Lara said. "When my husband and I talk at dinner, we notice that Sue pays close attention. When we use a new word, she wants to know what it means."

"And she's pretty. That means acceptance. You'd be surprised at the way young children gravitate toward good looks."

"Thank goodness for Sue's good looks, anyway."

"She's going to be fine, Mrs. Davis. She's still unsure of herself socially, she has a way to go yet, but I'm not worried about her. You people are obviously doing something right."

Then Lara felt a flood of beaming warmth from head to foot. At least once every day as the months passed and Sue grew closer, she had been feeling that warmth, so that she had to remind herself sometimes to hide it, not to sing out for fear of boring people with the repetition of her hope and joy.

Bozo Clark, the rock star, wore jeans and ten thousand dollars' worth of gold chains. He regarded Eddy solemnly from the other side of Eddy's desk.

"You're a winner, Osborne. This is the first year I paid no income tax, not one cent. God damn, I can't get over it! Can't really understand it. I know you explained about deducting losses on the partnerships and—"

Smiling, Eddy interrupted. "You don't have to understand, Bozo. Just keep making records, and I'll preserve your millions for you."

"Good enough. I'll be in touch. And one thing," Clark said on the way out, "that offer stands. As many tickets as you want for any concert, anytime."

The last thing Eddy wanted was to be squeezed into a crowd of crazed teenagers while Bozo swiveled his hips and yawped. Bozo would be amazed to know that he preferred the Metropolitan Opera and the Philharmonic. But his reply was enthusiastic.

TREASURES

"I'll get a couple of friends together and one of these days soon, I'll take you up on it. Thanks, Bozo."

As soon as the door had closed on Bozo Clark, Mrs. Evans appeared with a silver tray upon which stood a plate of thin-sliced whole wheat sandwiches and a little pot of coffee, also silver.

"Do you realize, Mr. Osborne, that you had no lunch and it's after four o'clock?"

Eddy, smiling, was aware that the smile was sheepish, as if he were a boy being reprimanded by a loving mother. He enjoyed this little byplay, enjoyed having a dignified, gray-haired widow with an upper-class British accent in his service. Most men looked for a secretary who was curved in the right places, who knew how to display the curves, and was on the right side of thirty. But Eddy had a different sense of the suitable.

"You take too good care of me, Mrs. Evans."

"Well, if I didn't keep after you the little bit that I do, you'd work yourself to death. Now, I'll put this down on the coffee table and you can relax in the wing chair. Relax and unwind."

"I'm starting to do it right now. As soon as I eat, I'm heading out to the country. It's worth the Friday traffic to have two grand summer days when you get there. And you go home, too, Mrs. Evans. You could do with some unwinding yourself."

"Thank you, Mr. Osborne. I believe I will. And I'm leaving orders that you're not to be disturbed."

Eddy stretched, uncramping the legs that had been tucked under the desk since morning. It had been a wearying day, and yet as always, he was exhilarated by this very weariness. If that was a contradiction, an oxymoron, let it be; it was the truth. No doubt a mountain climber grasping his pitons at ten thousand feet knew exhaustion, but he pressed on to eleven thousand feet nevertheless, and felt joy when he reached it.

"I'm climbing my mountain," he said aloud into the quiet room.

Or he might even say that he had already climbed it to the peak. For here he was, established at last in this, his third and final office, the perfect place he had dreamed about. It filled a floor and a half of the building. He had an able staff of forty, not counting secretaries. The business hummed like a dynamo, making money. Every minute, every second, counted, making money. Phones rang, the ticker rolled. Computers wrote, while the bright young men and women conferred at their desks. Oh, these were the exciting eighties, and Eddy Osborne was at the very center of the excitement!

When he looked out the window, westward to the Trump Tower, southward to Rockefeller Center and the Empire State, eastward to Sutton Place, northward to the Park and the Museum, it resembled a diorama; the gray-white towers were neat miniatures, so that leaving this private oasis to plunge down in the elevator, and emerge onto the pavement into enormity and a cacophony of horns and fire sirens, was total shock. Yet he loved that shock.

This room is marvelous, he thought. Even the Royal Worcester sandwich plate caught the right note. The decorator was a genius; he had read Eddy's mind. At the demolition of a nineteenth-century hotel downtown, he had salvaged the mahogany paneling that now burnished these walls. It had the warmth of age, with a few dents to validate it, such as one would find in a London club. In such a club, too, the enormous Oriental rug would be richly dark, faded in areas where daylight had touched it for half a century or more. From a corner a tall clock would strike the hours with a rattle and chime; Eddy's tall clock, bought last year at auction, was an authentic piece out of the seventeen hundreds, and it had cost him almost two hundred thousand dollars. There were, of course, even better specimens to be had; very likely he would get rid of this one sometime and replace it with a better.

His affairs were going well enough, he reflected, to warrant his buying almost anything he might want. Anything at all. Often when he woke up in the middle of the night, or when suddenly passing a mirror or a plate glass window while hurrying along the street, he felt himself startled by a brief, flashing sense of unreality. Then, feeling the air on his face above the blanket or, as the case might be, feeling the ground firm beneath his shoes, or recognizing his own young face, newly shaved and nicely tanned under his healthy thatch of hair, he admitted the astonishing reality.

He was worth, he calculated, not quite nineteen million dollars, and this after just seven years. His income had reached eleven million a year. The firm's securities portfolio now topped six billion. And he mused over the old cliché: Nothing succeeds like success. How true it was! His feel for the market had not failed him yet. Even in a rising market there were plenty of investors who, snaillike, got almost nowhere; even in such a market you had to know when and where to move. But the firm's chief business was still tax shelters, in real estate, oil, cattle, anything to produce losses that would reduce one's taxable income. That was where the real money lay, in the ability to keep hold of what one had. And that was why people were flocking to Osborne and Company.

He had done quite right, he thought now, to go it alone. Who needed partners with their inevitable disagreements, repetitious consultations, and compromises to slow the action, and drag at you, when you were so able to soar by yourself? What he did need and what he now possessed were quick brains to feed him the information he required, to comprehend his instructions, and to carry them out. He paid high salaries to attract the brightest MBAs out of Harvard or Wharton. When they did well, he gave a huge bonus, and when they did poorly, they were dismissed. He was demanding, but he was respected for being so.

It still surprised him to be so easily accepted everywhere. To be sure, there were in the world of finance plenty of successful young newcomers with whom the social establishment was ever willing to do business if need be. But it was definitely not willing to accept them in its homes and clubs, while Eddy was invited everywhere.

As if to bear witness to his thought the phone rang.

"Eddy, are you in town tonight? A couple of the fellows are getting together for dinner and backgammon at the Yale Club. Want to join us?"

"Sorry, Doug, I'd like to, but I'm going out to the country. Thanks for thinking of me, though."

"Then how about Tuesday?"

"Tuesday's great. I'll see you around six. Okay?"

Once or twice a week he met with a group at the Yale Club. Swinging into Vanderbilt Avenue, he'd look back at the view up Park; sometimes he'd stand on the corner for a minute, just gazing, feeling the thrill before going on to the game.

Being adept at games, he often came away with a few thousand dollars in winnings, but he was wise enough not to win too often. It was better to be known as a man who lost casually and gave easily. By now he was on the boards of half a dozen philanthropies, all important, all entailing lavish donations, but Eddy, far from begrudging these, actually welcomed making grand gestures. Even making loans to friends, which he frequently did, made him content with himself. It made him feel in charge.

The tall clock chimed. Calculating swiftly, he allotted his time: an hour to go home, shower, and throw some clothes into a bag, then two hours, if he was lucky, out to Pam's place. But first came the Friday call to Lara that he never missed. And he reached for the telephone.

When Sue's treble voice answered, he played the expected game with her.

"Hi. This is Uncle Eddy. Is this you, Davey? No, let me guess. You're the boy next door."

TREASURES

There came a giggle and a protest. "Uncle Eddy! You know who it is!"

"Oh, of course. You're Sue. I should have recognized you by your pink shirt, anyway."

"Not today! I'm wearing my Snoopy shirt. Can't you see?"

"I can't see so well. I left my glasses somewhere."

Lara's voice cut in. "My turn, Susie. Uncle Eddy's probably in a hurry. Hang up, dear."

"I can't get over the way that child can kid me right back. She's got real wit."

"I know it. And she's such a joy! To think that in the beginning we were worried that she'd never be happy again!"

"Where are you this minute?"

"Where am I? What do you mean?"

"What room are you in?"

"In the kitchen, getting dinner. Why?"

"Because. I just like to imagine you in the house, cooking up a storm in that picture-book kitchen or having a crowd in the den on Saturday night."

He had an instant picture of her standing at the island where the copper pots hung; the last time he had been there, she had a row of African violets up on the windowsill.

"I'm using the barbecue right now. It's marvelous."

"Aren't you glad I made you buy that house?" he demanded. "Don't you love it?"

"Of course I do. Who wouldn't?"

And again he felt that glow of pure pleasure, a physical glow that spread, tingling as it rose up into his throat, to end with a chuckle of laughter. Here again he had been "in charge"; because of him Lara and her little family were in the home they deserved, modest as it was. It was not that he had paid for the house; he had not; he had only lent Davey enough for the down payment, a sum that Davey, in the healthy growth of his new prosperity, had already repaid. But the impetus had come from, and the seed had been sown by, Eddy Osborne.

"Is Davey home yet?" he asked now.

"He just came in. He's upstairs getting the grease from his hands."

"A new invention in the offing?"

"An instrument for bone surgery. He just came back from seeing an orthopedic man in Cleveland. Here he is. Davey, it's Eddy."

"Hi."

"Hi, Davey! Lara says there's a new gadget in the works."

"Well, I hope so. It looks promising, but I can't tell yet." That was Davey, prudent and cautious.

"I looked over that copy of your accountant's report yesterday, and it looks mighty good."

"Yes, things are going well. The orders keep coming in, and I took in five new men just last week. Even at that we can barely keep up with the work."

"Do you still not want to talk about investments with me? I can make you rich, Davey, if you let me."

"Eddy, again I tell you, we're not interested in what you call 'being rich.'"

"Okay, okay. Some other time. I'm in the usual rush. Kiss Lara and the kid for me. How's the kid doing?"

"We've got ups and downs, but mostly ups, happy ups. We're all pretty well used to each other by now."

"That's great! Give Sue an extra hug from Uncle Eddy."

When he hung up, he felt good. He always felt good after his call to Ohio, anyway, knowing that Lara was solidly placed for the first time in her life. She would always be secure, with a tidy interest in a steady, flourishing business. Davey could be a typical nineteenth-century small-town manufacturer, he reflected, and thought again: If he would only let me invest for him, I could make him rich. He's the finest guy in the world, but he's got a stubborn, puritanical streak, and Lara's the same. Not to want, actually not to want to have money, real money, with all the liberty and power and delight it gave! And Eddy shrugged, smiling to himself at the thought.

A short time later he was in his car, heading toward the Queens Midtown Tunnel. Halfway there, he changed his mind abruptly and turned up Madison Avenue instead. He hadn't seen Connie in at least two weeks. It wasn't five o'clock yet, so he would probably just catch her before closing time.

The little shop took up a narrow slice of space between a large corner store and an art gallery. Its single window contained a mannequin wearing a smart black-and-white knitted suit and a red hat. A life-sized stuffed Dalmatian pulled on a red leash.

"Very clever," Eddy said as he entered.

Connie was alone in the shop. "What is?"

"The window. Did you design it yourself?"

"Of course not. One hires a window designer."

"I didn't know. What does he charge? An arm and a leg, I suppose."

"Just about. Between the rent here, which will undoubtedly be raised next time around, and the wages for the two salesgirls, I just about break even. You need to sell a lot of handknits to make the expenses. It's a worry." Connie sighed.

"Fortunately, you don't depend on this for a living. And you look wonderful, so the work must agree with you."

Connie shrugged. He didn't like to see her like this, disgruntled and abrupt. Besides, since he himself was in a cheerful mood, he wanted her to match him.

"I guess I didn't tell you that I flew out to Lara's over the Fourth. She's got a really nice little kid. Really nice. Or did I tell you?"

"No, you didn't, Eddy," she answered, a trifle sharply, he thought.

And he said, "Well, if I didn't, it was because I didn't know whether you wanted to hear."

"Why shouldn't I want to hear about a child? What can I have against a child?"

"What can you have against Lara for so long?" he countered.

"It seems to me that it's the other way around."

"I'm stumped by each of you! She thinks you should have called her to congratulate them on getting Sue. You think—"

"I think that after she accused me of murder and stormed out of my house, the burden is on her. That's what I think."

"Oh, I give up," Eddy said. "It's beyond me."

Connie's expression softened. "Dear Eddy! You do mean well. You always want to straighten things out, don't you? But some things just won't be straightened. You don't think I'm happy about Lara and myself, do you? My only sister . . . Do you?"

At the break in her voice and the sight of springing tears, he shook his head.

"I shouldn't have mentioned it again. God knows I never mean to upset you. Lara breaks up, too, whenever I say anything to her, so I've stopped. I'm sorry, Connie."

She kissed his cheek. "It's okay, Eddy. I'm closing up. Want to have some dinner with me?"

"Thanks, I'm on my way to the country. But I'll see you on Monday, if you're free."

"I'm free. Have a good time, dear."

It was a fair, cool evening, and the air rushed softly through the open windows of the new gray Mercedes two-seater; he had considered buying a red car, but then had decided that a bright red toy was inconsistent with dignity. Anyway, the car was superb. It responded like a living thing, like a fine horse. As he drove, maneuvering fleetly through the traffic, his mind kept clicking; his mental processes were as finely tuned as was the piece of machinery beneath him.

If only those two would get together again! It wasn't in his

146

nature to comprehend how pain could be nurtured for so long. They were both anguished, he knew, anguished and angry. The words they had spoken to each other had apparently cut as harshly as knives. It was a pity, a sad, sad, pity.

At least, though, he had seen Connie out of a profound slump. At least, now with that sorry divorce out of the way—poor Richard!—she had the boutique to keep her busy. It puzzled him that she wasn't married yet. She was the marrying kind if any woman ever was. He seemed to remember betting Richard that she would be married within two years at least, but it was already two years, with no one in sight. Connie was critical, of course, and having been burned once, would be more so than ever. Moreover, she had a right to be highly selective; she was a stunning young woman, and she had a brain, a pair of qualities that didn't always, or even frequently, go together.

Now further thought slid naturally to Eddy's own most private affair, the Pamela affair. For the last few weeks he had sensed a growing impatience within himself, a feeling that things had been drifting for too long. What the reason was, or whose fault it might be, if fault there was, was difficult to know, probably because both of them, Pam and he alike, were responsible. Neither had been in a hurry to marry.

Undoubtedly, there was substance in what she always said, that she wanted some years of independence before making a commitment. Good enough. But there were too many attractive men hanging around her. . . . He both knew it and didn't want to know it.

He had very quick perceptions. Too often he saw men's glances at her quickly turned away when Eddy intercepted them. And then there were all those casual invitations, like the one last Sunday when they were coming from the movies.

"Hi, Pam! Can you make a fourth at tennis tomorrow?"

The man had had a supercilious look on his dark, vivid face. He'd had a swagger, and his arrogant eyes would appeal to

147

women. Mean men attracted some women, absurd as it seemed. Eddy recognized the type. He probably crawled out of one soft bed into another, a different one every night. A man like him wouldn't stop at tennis. . . .

To think that on first meeting her he had thought she was "cool"! Under the correct, the "preppie," exterior, she smoldered. How Pam loved sex! Sex, the imponderable and unexplainable. Who could say what she might do or might not do during the long week while he was working in the city? Suddenly, he was furious.

The sight of a police car pulling a motorist over to the side of the road sobered him, and he slowed down. Ah, but I am probably making a mountain out of a molehill, he began to assure himself. I'm imagining. I'm exaggerating. Pam cares about me. There can't be any mistake about that, about the way we are together, and not only in bed. . . .

As he turned into the long gravel drive, past shaggy bushes that brushed his fenders, he thought with a secret smile how Pam's mother was dying for him to marry Pam. Oh, in the beginning it had been different! He wasn't in the *Social Register*; he might well have been just another Wall Street fly-by-night, spending everything he made and as likely as not to lose his job with the toss of a coin. By now, she knew otherwise.

He parked the car and got out, reaching for a magazine on the seat. It was a popular business weekly. This issue, which had come out only yesterday, contained the long-anticipated article about himself, the "Young Prince of Wall Street." A few years ago he would have bounded into this house waving it in his hand, but now he thought carefully before acting. Yes, he decided, there would be far greater impact if people were to discover the article for themselves, as they were sure to do. He walked up the porch steps without it and knocked on the screen door.

When Mrs. Granger's cool voice called, "Come in," he followed it to the dining room, where he found her on a step-stool changing bulbs in the chandelier.

"Oh, Eddy! It's good to see you, Pam's upstairs showering, and I'm struggling here. If only I were three inches taller, it wouldn't be so impossible—"

"Here, let me." He took off his jacket, revealing smartly striped braces and a shirt pocket with a small, tasteful monogram.

"What three extra inches can do!" he said gaily as Mrs. Granger handed up the bulbs.

"A good deal more than three. Oh, I don't care what women's lib people say, a woman needs to have a man around. A husband." The tone was wistful.

Deciding to keep the talk light, he answered with a laugh, "What for? To change light bulbs?"

She was shrewd. At once her retort became equally light. "Oh, to mix drinks and cope with the plumber. All that sort of thing."

They were onto each other. Yet he liked the woman. Her prattle, while it was so obvious, was both amusing and interesting to him.

"It must seem foolish to you that two women live alone surrounded by so much empty space. But my great-grandfather built this house, and the best parts of my life were lived here. The house was always filled with cousins and guests; we used every inch of it. It would crush me to walk away from it. Besides, Pam loves it as much as I do. She's got her horses just down the road and, well, you know."

He knew. He could imagine the house in its heyday. The wicker chairs on the porch would have been newly cushioned and the greenhouse, now fallen into neglect, would have provided flowers enough to fill every nook and bay window. Even now the place had its charm and dignity.

He looked over to the sideboard—original Sheraton, he was pretty sure. On it stood a George II tea service. Old silver acquired a special soft gleam, and it felt like silk in the hands. These pieces must have been in the family for five generations. It would feel nice to be part of such a family, he was thinking while he screwed in the last of the bulbs. It would make you feel solid, rooted, as if you really belonged somewhere.

"Hey!" Pam came clattering down the stairs and into the dining room, waving a magazine. "You there with your secrets! Mom, look what they've written about Eddy!"

The two women leaned over the magazine, reading the double-page spread. Evening light sifted through the screen and passed through Pam's pink silk housecoat, outlining her long legs to the hips, and giving rise in Eddy to certain very warm anticipations and recollections. He stood waiting modestly until they had finished reading and then modestly listened to their astonished praise.

"Eddy!" Pam cried. "I never dreamed what really big things you were doing. You never talk about yourself."

"Because Eddy is a gentleman," said her mother.

"All these articles exaggerate," he said. "Writers have to make them startling, sensational. It's their livelihood, after all, so I suppose one can't fault them. Anyway, everybody has a talent for something and should try to live up to it. And that's all I do, for whatever it's worth, and it's the whole story," he concluded with an easy smile.

Mrs. Granger complained, "If I'd only known, I'd have had a celebration for you. Now we're just having hamburgers and salad."

"Sounds great enough to me, Mrs. Granger."

"I think you two had better eat without me. I'm invited to my cousin Mona's, and I'm not dressed yet. I'm running late." At the foot of the stairs she turned around. "As a matter of fact, I'm going to spend the night there. It's too far to be driving home by myself. Just don't forget to turn on the burglar alarm, Pam."

TREASURES

"I'll be staying at the club," Eddy said, "but I'll make sure to see that she does before I leave her."

So, he had just been handed a nice little present, a welcome comfort for the night instead of the porch swing or the blankets in the rear of Pam's station wagon, which were their only choices in between her infrequent stays in the city.

Pam's eyes beamed straight toward his. "Let's eat and then go change. Have you brought your riding stuff? On second thought, you won't need it. We'll ride Western, in jeans."

"How come?"

"Somebody's boarding a pair of pintos, and I thought it would be fun to ride along the beach tonight. They need exercising, anyway. Are you game?"

"Sure am."

"There's a moon, and it'll be gorgeous."

Night riding was one of the exhilarating pleasures she had taught him. The beach was usually deserted, and the quiet, except for the sound of waves and horses' hooves slapping the hard sand or splashing in the shallows, was an amazement to a New Yorker's ears.

"Okay, I'm for it," he said.

This time, however, they were not to have the night all to themselves. In the paddock were two young men getting ready to mount.

"Hi, Pam, what's up?" one called.

"We're going to take the pintos out. These are my friends, Alex and Marty. They're horse crazy like me. This is Eddy, Eddy Osborne."

"Know how to put on a Western saddle?" inquired the man called Alex.

"I think I do," Pam said.

"I think you don't. Come on, I'll show you."

Don't do us any favors. Eddy felt another twinge of anger. He despised the man's very walk, the nonchalant sway of his shoulders.

The stable was fragrant with hay and the natural smell of clean, well-tended animals. In two stalls, facing each other, stood a pair of identical brown-and-white mares. Pam stroked their long cheeks.

"Aren't they lovely? The owner's starting a Western ranch upstate."

"Take this one," Alex advised. "She's a might narrower in the seat."

Standing behind Pam, he had laid a familiar hand on her shoulder, while Eddy watched. He watched while the other man adjusted the Western saddle on Pam's animal and then copied him. They led the mares outside and mounted.

"There's something funny about this stirrup. It doesn't feel right," Pam said.

Eddy moved to dismount and help her, but Marty, still on the ground, got there first. And again, Eddy watched a man's familiar touch, this time on Pam's leg.

Who the hell did they think they were? Damn their hands, damn both of them! But Eddy knew he had to smother his anger. The night was too wonderful, the opportunity too splendid, to ruin it. Later, later he would solve this, find out once and for all whether—

They rode. A wind came up, blowing the sounds of speech away off over the water, and they rode without talking. They rode in single file with Pam at the head. When she put the mare into a gallop, her hair flew out behind her. The total effect of girl and animal, both of them so lean and agile, was as graceful as any spectacular ballet at Lincoln Center. Pam's strength and beauty fired Eddy. Then he tried self-analysis. He knew he was the most competitive of men; he knew he was affected by the rivalry, real or fancied, of every other male. But he had never before been so bothered, so possessed.

He said nothing until they were back home and having coffee in the kitchen. There, more abruptly than he had planned, his words came out.

"Have you ever slept—seriously and steadily, I mean—with anybody but me?"

What he wanted to ask and could not bring himself to ask was: *Do you ever sleep with anybody now when I'm not here?*

"What makes you ask such a question?"

He hesitated. "Don't take this the wrong way, but sometimes I get the feeling that men are too intimate with you. Like tonight, for instance. The way those guys had their hands on you."

"Oh, Eddy, that's ridiculous."

"No it isn't. You're a very, very sexy lady."

"Putting a hand on a woman doesn't mean anything."

"That depends on how it's done. It often means that the man wants a lot more from the woman."

"Well, if I'm as sexy as you say I am, it's not strange that men would want to. For goodness' sake, Eddy, are you going to be jealous?"

"I don't like to see men so intimate with you. Is that jealousy? I don't know. I've never been jealous before. But I sense something when men are around you, that's all. Frankly, I sense that you enjoy it."

"I'll be frank too. It's fun to be admired, Eddy, especially when a whole week goes by sometimes without my seeing you."

There was a pause before he brought forth another bold question. "How many men have you had besides me? If you don't want to tell me, I'll understand that I don't matter to you, and that will be that."

Pam stood up and laid her face against his. "You matter very much to me, and I'll tell you whatever you want to know. I've had two men, only a few times each, and they were before I met you. Of course, I was afraid of pregnancy and disease. But even if there were no such thing, I'd never be promiscuous. Why bring all this up now, Eddy?"

He felt that she was being truthful and, moved, reached up and took her hand.

"We've never talked seriously about things, have we? I just felt that the time had come for us to do so."

She smiled. "I'll talk about anything you want."

He smiled back. "Later. I'd rather go upstairs. Shall we?"

"Just let me get ready. I'll call you."

He had never seen her room or even been upstairs in the house. When he heard her call to him, he entered a blue-and-white bedchamber, all summer sky and silk clouds. On a little couch at the foot of the canopy bed, Pam sat naked among white lace pillows. Her expression as she looked up at him was absolutely serious in a way that was different from anything he had ever seen upon her face before. Startling impressions and sensations raced across his mind in seconds. Even this room of hers was something he would not have imagined, it was so soft and womanly; it might well be the place where Lara slept with Davey. It was matrimonial. *Our bedroom is the most important room in the house*, Lara said when they moved into the new home. And a queer yearning ran now through Eddy's veins and through his very bones at the recollection. He had never felt such a yearning. To come home every night to a lovely woman, to share this bed with her, to belong to each other in a total trust!

He felt a little catch in his throat, a little stab near his heart, and he held out his arms.

"Would you—" he almost stammered. "Could you make this permanent, do you think? What I mean is—marry me?"

"Oh," she said. "Oh, oh, yes, I could. Yes, yes, I will. I want to."

She was laughing, she was crying. She was live and perfect. Almost as tall as he, she fitted into his arms. She was right for him.

TREASURES

Laughter, their familiar mood, took over again in the morning.

"Do you suppose you'd better clear out before my mother comes home?" asked Pam.

"Lord no, she knew I was going to stay here. She practically invited me. She's probably figuring out the wedding date."

Pam looked out over the lawn where sprinklers were showering drops as bright as sparks.

"Whenever I thought about it," she said slowly, "and not being in a hurry, I never thought about it often, but whenever I did, I pictured a huge reception on that lawn. A dance floor under a marquee. The ceremony at St. John's of Lattingtown. A marvelous dress, six bridesmaids, the works. You know."

"Fine with me."

"Darling, my mother couldn't possibly afford it."

"I'll pay! What's the difference?"

"A lot of difference. She wouldn't hear of it, a matter of pride, much, much pride, darling."

"I think it's silly, if you want to know."

"Maybe so, but that's the way it is."

"So what shall we do?"

"We could elope."

Disappointed, Eddy replied, "That's not very festive."

"I know. Well, let me think a little."

"Okay, think. But I want you to meet me in the city this week. Somebody was telling me about a grand apartment for sale, twelve rooms, prewar with high ceilings, a beauty. Let's take a look."

"I can't believe it! You talk as if money didn't matter. Are you really that rich, Eddy?"

He grinned. "I do all right. Enough for you not to worry about money. Enough for you to have anything you want."

Wonderingly, she said, "I don't want a lot, Eddy. I never have. This seems so strange. I can't get used to it."

The grin turned into a laugh. "You will. You'll love it too."

Eddy's plans developed as rapidly as a roll of film unwinds. The apartment was magnificent, with paneled walls, marble fireplaces that worked, a far view of the East River, and a near view of private gardens. Pam, looking down at this green enclave, found it hard to understand how anyone could part with a place like this one.

"Divorced," Eddy told her.

She gave a small mock shudder. "I don't like the omen."

"Don't be an idiot. Divorce isn't contagious. Besides, I've seen the woman. She's fat and homely, so no wonder." He surveyed the long drawing room.

"They want to sell the furniture, but we surely don't want it. It's garbage. Expensive garbage. Now, I'd have a cabinet, a pair maybe, on either side of the fireplace to house my silver. The collection's grown so that I've even got boxes under my bed."

"That's a handsome piano, though. I think it's rosewood."

"Hey, you're right! You want to buy it?"

"I don't play."

"That doesn't matter. It looks wonderful where it is. Enormous rooms need a piano. It'll be a showpiece. Next to you. You'll be the real showpiece."

Sometime later he said thoughtfully, "You know, maybe it's not such a bad idea after all for us to get married by ourselves. I've been thinking that a big wedding, even a small one, would be a problem for me too. I've told you about my sisters' feud, and I don't know how I could— It would be awkward, painful, to have them together. The whole thing hurts my heart, Pam. And they're both such good people. You'll see when you meet them. I want to fly out to Ohio with you soon to see Lara. You'll fall in love with her. Everybody does."

"Still, she's being awfully stubborn, isn't she?"

"Well, they both are. Neither one wants to give in or take back the rotten things she apparently said." Eddy sighed. "Well, let's get back to you and me. I just had a brainstorm. What about an elopement to Paris? Your mother's pride is intact, my family problem is solved, and we have a great vacation. What do you say?"

"Why, I say yes," Pam answered promptly. "Double yes."

They were married at the American Church, attended by a young lawyer, a client of Eddy's who with his wife happened to be in Paris that week. Afterward, they had dinner at the Grand Véfour and returned to their suite at the Hotel Ritz. In the morning they walked out onto the Place Vendôme and in wonderful, slow leisure, at Van Cleef and Arpels, bought the diamond ring that, in their general haste, they had not gotten around to buying at home.

Pam knew Paris rather well, having been there frequently with her parents during the good times before her father's death, and she led Eddy easily to all the sights from the Eiffel Tower to the Louvre. The fall season had begun, restoring the beautiful city after the summer lull to a thrilling life of concerts, theater, restaurants, gallery openings, and discotheques. Eddy and Pam were out every night at one or another of these.

Then they began to shop. She remembered where to look for antiques; they bought a Louis XVI cabinet, an ormolu clock, and some chairs. Eddy knew what he was buying, surprising the antiquarians in the shops and surprising himself also by the extent of his own knowledge, acquired in a relatively short few years. On the Île St. Louis at a small art gallery, they bought a Postimpressionist seascape of a beach at dusk with a group of young women sitting on the sand. It was Pam's choice.

"It's nice," Eddy agreed, "but it's the kind of thing you put in a bedroom or some little sitting room to enjoy in private. Frankly, in public rooms like the drawing or dining room, I want important art, things of museum quality."

In total companionship the two of them rollicked through

three splendid weeks. They walked, danced, laughed, and thought in identical rhythms. And he was proud, swelling within, when men turned to glance at the healthy, tall young woman so unmistakably American, even in her new French clothes, with her long hair so casually worn, her confident, long stride, and her white, perfect teeth.

Occasionally, he caught the tail end of a question that trailed across his mind and as quickly vanished: Is this love, then? The thing they tell of? *Till death do us part . . . I can't live without you. . . .* Well, yes, he decided, this must be it. But whatever it is, it's wonderful.

He was supremely happy.

CHAPTER SEVEN

❧

"Pam's going to a bridal shower, so I thought I'd spend the evening with you," said Eddy, and added as he looked around Connie's library, "The place looks beautiful. That's a new lamp."

"I treated myself. Can I fix you a drink?"

"A cup of hot coffee. I fought a real wind walking over here."

His eyes followed his sister across the hall toward the kitchen. She wore a dark red velvet housecoat embroidered in gold thread, along with a pair of magnificent earrings. Greek, he knew, and handmade. There was no mistaking either the design or the dark gleam of twenty-two-carat gold. They were most likely another "treat," and Eddy had to smile. Connie took good care of herself. But shouldn't she, after all? Thanks to him the settlement that Richard had given to her was growing ten times over; it was no fortune, but certainly it was more than enough to maintain a little place like this one in good style, and to dress Connie in high style.

Pam would never think to buy a housecoat like that. She was most comfortable in a sweater and skirt. Any treasures Pam possessed had been brought home by him, as almost the entire contents of the new apartment had been. Pam's two interests were horses and sex. Well, that was all right. He liked horses well

159

enough, and as for sex, just let her keep on loving it the way she did, as long as she never used her wiles on anybody else. But ever since that conversation in her mother's house, she had given him not one moment's unquiet. Some other young wives indulged in mild, harmless flirting even when their husbands were present, but not Pam. All that sort of thing she saved for him. Eddy's smile, broadening at certain recollections, turned into a rather joyous grin.

"You look like a Cheshire cat," said Connie, coming back with a tray. "What are you smirking at?"

"Thinking of my wife. Being happy. She leaves me at loose ends when she goes out."

"For one night? Lucky you! Loose ends is where I am most nights."

The disconsolate tone fitted ill with Connie's physical brilliance, the sheen of hair and skin, the scarlet mouth, the scarlet tips of the long white fingers. But the fingers were tensely clasped together on her knee, Eddy saw, and there were two vertical trouble lines between her eyes.

"Where are all your friends?" he asked. "You had so many."

"Bitsy and her crowd? They'd have lunch with me if I had time, which I don't because I'm in the shop, but they're all married, and they don't want an extra woman around at night."

"Not when she looks like you, that's for sure. You're a menace, you are."

"Well, thank you. Oh, I've been going out some, you know that, but there's really been nobody who amounts to anything. They all just want to sleep with you, and what I want, plainly speaking, is to be married."

"It's too bad—" Eddy began, and stopped before completing a remark that would be both tactless and pointless.

"Too bad about Richard, you meant to say? Yes, it was nice living with him. We really had everything except a good love life." And with a candor she had never shown before, she said,

160

"And if it hadn't been for the other thing—the men—I guess I could have put up with that too. The fact is, I'm not very passionate."

In spite of himself Eddy was embarrassed. A pity! He wondered whether she knew, whether it was even possible for her to know, what she was missing.

"Yes," she continued, "he was good to me, and I feel sorry for him. He still remembers my birthday. Isn't that sort of sad? Birthday and Christmas cards. Never misses. And I do the same."

"Well, that's nice. Civilized. But there's no reason not to be, is there?"

It occurred to him as always that it would also be civilized if she and Lara were to do something about their sorry situation, when Connie inquired whether he ever saw Richard.

"I handle his investments by telephone. But I did happen to run into him on Madison Avenue a week or two ago, and we had a quick lunch together. He looked the same as always."

"What did you talk about?"

"He asked about you, and I told him you were doing very well. That's all. Then we got onto money. I'm getting him eleven percent on his investments, four to one on his tax shelters, deductions, and taxes deferred to infinity. So naturally, he's happy. He got a big bonus this year and handed me the whole thing to take care of."

"It all sounds terribly complicated."

"Not really. Someday, if you're really interested, I'll explain it to you."

Connie laughed. "Except for the bottom line you know I'm not really interested."

"I thought not."

Her laugh was delightful, and the gesture that went with it, the uplifted chin, was charming. Really it was too bad that such

161

a woman should still be alone. And suddenly, for no logical reason, he had an idea.

"Pam and I should have a housewarming," he said. "A real party, a real smash. What do you think?"

"That's up to Pam. It's a lot of work, and you haven't been there six months. Your living room isn't even furnished except for the piano."

"All the more space for dancing. When it's finished, we won't be able to dance."

Eddy was already planning. He ought to get up a whole list of clients and potential clients. But the main thing was to gather a few eligibles for Connie. Off the top of his head he couldn't think of any, but with a little effort he surely would, and Pam would have some ideas too. She liked Connie. Of course, Pam liked most people. But Connie was more than likable, and they got along very well.

"Yes," he said, "we'll have a party. Will you help Pam with invitations and stuff?"

"Of course I will. And I'm awfully glad that everything's going so well for you, Eddy." Connie laid an affectionate hand on her brother's knee.

It was sleeting outdoors, and the cold was intense, so that in contrast, the apartment was a southern garden, fragrant and warm. Connie arrived early just as preparations for the party were being completed. In the foyer, which was as large as her own living room, the walls were lined with flowering trees in marble tubs. The staircase leading to the second floor of the duplex was decked with smilax, hung in ropes and garlands. Casual, overflowing bouquets of roses and freesia stood on tables and mantels in the library and the dining room, in Pamela's sitting room and Eddy's den. Back in the immense drawing room, still unfurnished except for the white silk curtains on the tall windows, the caterers had arranged their gilt chairs and tables in a circle, leaving space for those who wanted to dance.

Connie stood contemplating this magnificence. She felt awestruck. That was the only way to describe her feelings. Richard had been generous to her, there could be no doubt of that, but you could fit her apartment five times over into this one and still have space left. She walked back into the library. Its walls of French boiserie were precious. The needlepoint rug was handmade. Above the fireplace a new painting had been hung: a Sargent? Connie had taken her courses at the museum very seriously and knew what she was looking at. The pearllike flesh, the dusky velvet, the woman's very pose, were unmistakable. This was what you could do when you had *real* money. How ever had Eddy managed to achieve it all? Again, she was overcome with awe and a profound respect for his intelligence and energy.

"Admiring the lady?" Eddy inquired from the doorway.

"Of course. When did she arrive?"

"Just in time for tonight. Isn't she a beauty?"

"You don't have an art adviser? So many people do."

"Why? What for?"

"Well, to keep his eyes open for prospects all over the world. You surely don't have the time or the contacts."

"I read," Eddy said. "I read everything. Right now I'm learning about Orientals. I never knew there was so much to know about rugs. Sarouk, Ispahan—" He threw up his hands. "My God, the world is full of so many kinds of art! Books—I bought a set of Dickens first editions the other day with illustrations by Phiz. And how do you like this lamp?" he asked, pointing out a bronze flower on a thin bronze stem. "Art Nouveau."

"I know. It's very lovely."

"Cost me almost two hundred thousand," he whispered. "Don't worry, I know it's vulgar to talk prices, but I'm only telling you and no one else. Now come look at this—" he began when Pam interrupted him.

"Darling, do leave your sister alone. When Eddy gets enthusiasms, I don't have to tell you how he throws himself into them with all his strength. I'm afraid he'll be worn out before he has these twelve rooms filled up. Connie, you look beautiful as always."

Connie's sheer apricot silk dress was a column of Fortuny pleats in the style of ancient Greece.

"And how smart of you to wear no jewelry except those gorgeous earrings!"

"Thank you." I've learned, Connie thought. The sumptuous diamond tassels, an extravagance she had not resisted, were made to dazzle by themselves, without competition. "You look lovely too. Like a bride," she said, returning the compliment.

Without appearing to do so she studied Pam, who looked aristocratic in heavy white satin. You had to be very tall and reared in the right environment to possess the *air* that let you dress so plainly, to wear your hair caught back with a barrette and still have such elegance.

"A bride! Well, it's white, anyway, the nearest I could get to wedding regalia. I suppose I'll always be a trifle sorry that we didn't have a big wedding."

"I know. I didn't have one either. Not that there's any comparison." There was not, and the unthinking, somewhat pathetic remark left Connie feeling foolish and tactless.

Then the doorbell rang and Eddy said quickly, "We're having a varied crowd here tonight, Connie. There should be some interesting people for you."

It was difficult to tell who was "interesting" and who was not while one was drifting from group to group and room to room, with the buzz of chatter in one's ears, a drink in one hand and a canapé on a napkin in the other. There were the usual elderly married men wanting to strike up a conversation apart from their wives, whom they had left on the other side of the room; there were the usual hunters, some of them very, very attractive, jostling each other for a chance to take a young woman home and spend the night; there was the usual interior decorator—Eddy's and Pam's this time—intelligent, refined, and homosexual; there was a promising young man with whom Connie was having a promising discussion about the newest Woody Allen movie, when he revealed that he'd been married three weeks before, and "There she is, the beautiful redhead in the blue dress."

Mostly, she found herself standing on the fringe of some group that had gathered around her brother as he passed among his guests. Eddy was to be marveled at, she thought, as men, some of them twice his age, showed their regard for him.

"I hear you've brought in six million dollars' worth of pledges for the cardiac unit at Mount Mercy."

"We're having our own open house at our new place in Nassau, and we expect you to be there, Eddy. My wife's going to get in touch with Pam."

"My law partner wants to meet you, Eddy. I thought maybe we might have lunch next week at the Travers Guaranty in their private dining room. His cousin's the president, you remember."

Eddy's blue eyes were sparkling in contrast to his perpetual tan. He reveled in every word, and why should he not? All that he was, secure, admired, and sought after, he had accomplished by himself. And Connie's heart swelled with joy for her brother.

She was making conversational remarks to strangers when dinner was announced. Finding her place card on one of the overflow tables in the library, she wondered why she had been seated in such a quiet backwater. However, she was not in a mood for dancing, so perhaps it was just as well. Except for Connie's, all the other places were filled, and a quick glance showed that the occupants were chiefly married couples in early middle age.

The unaccompanied man seated next to her stood up and pulled out her chair. As always, it took her only a few seconds to appraise him, to take, as it were, a mental photograph of his person. He was not young, nor was he old. His dark, wavy hair was flecked with gray, he had remarkably fine brown eyes, watchful eyes, and a strong frame marred by a slight paunch.

"Martin Berg," he said, introducing himself.

"Connie Osborne. I'm Eddy's sister."

"Ah! Somebody said he had a beautiful sister. I had no idea I'd be lucky enough to have you as my dinner partner."

The conventional remark was one that might easily be dismissed, either as meaningless or else as a minor, perfunctory flirtation. Beyond that, the man had little to say. When the first course came, a lobster bisque, he announced that he was hungry and began to eat. Connie, assuming that this meant she would do better to keep silence herself, did just that. Again she wondered why she had been seated here.

The others apparently all knew each other. A voluble conversation sprang up around the table and across the table, or rather, several conversations sprang, concurrently and interrupting.

"Oh, were you at their Southampton affair? I hear they had flowers flown in from Europe. . . . Well, you can't get those old roses in this country. . . . I heard Charlene spends ten thousand a month on flowers."

". . . speaks French like a native. They all went to school in Switzerland."

"The Côte d'Azur is ruined. When I remember how it used to be . . . that marvelous house in Cap Estel . . ."

"Of course, it's all the thing to have a *mas* on some isolate hillside in Provence. She had the decorator come down from Paris to do it."

Beneath this trivial, loud prattle about things French came a soft voice, just above a whisper, at Connie's right.

"You look far away," said Martin Berg.

"Do I? I didn't mean to."

"I think you're bored. I think it's your nature to be friendly, to be lively."

"How can you tell?"

TREASURES

"I saw you before dinner in the other room. Am I right?"

"Well, I usually do more talking than I've done here, but—"

"But these people are boring as hell, and you wouldn't have had a chance to break in if you'd wanted to. So talk to me—if you want to, that is."

The mellow bass of the voice was, curiously, both appealing and demanding. So she answered readily, "I'd like to. What shall I talk about?"

"About yourself. Are you married?"

"Divorced. And you?"

"Soon to be. We've been a long time separated, but there've been complications. Two children. Have you got babies?"

"Fortunately, no."

"You notice I said 'babies,' not 'children.' You can't be long out of school yourself."

"Thank you, but I'm not all that young, I'm twenty-seven."

"I'm forty-seven. My son's in college at the Sorbonne. And I have a little girl, a dear little girl whom I miss most terribly."

Such a candid, pained admission from a stranger seemed unusual. He was either a timid, lonely soul in need of sympathetic contact, or else a person so sure of himself that he could afford to say whatever he pleased, whenever and wherever his mood moved him. And, glancing again from his face with its firm, narrow lips to his fine, tasteful tie, to the equally tasteful gold cuff links and watch, she concluded that very definitely he was the latter.

"Where does your girl live?" she asked.

"In Paris, with her mother. Divorce is a wound, no matter what the circumstances."

Connie, nodding, remembered Richard standing in the kitchen saying over and over, I'm so sorry I've hurt you, Connie.

Berg's manner turned brisk. "Let's talk about something cheerful. About your brother," he said deliberately. "Of course, you know they're all calling him the 'young prince.' And he really is a wonder. I know it took me years to get even a footing on Wall Street, and look where he's gotten almost overnight."

"Oh, you're in finance too?"

"Yes. Stocks and bonds." An odd smile passed across his face. Had the question been so amusing? And for a moment he toyed with his dessert, a baked Alaska with a mound of meringue and a thick chocolate sauce. "I shouldn't eat this stuff, although sweets are my weakness. How do you manage to keep so thin?" he asked, for Connie had not left a particle on her plate.

"Exercise, daily workout."

"I should do it, too, but I hate exercise. The only kind I like is dancing. Would you like to dance now?"

They stood up, excused themselves, and went to the drawing room. A little alcove in the semicircle of palms near the piano had been prepared for the musicians; their pulsing music had brought almost everybody to the dance floor, whirling and gyrating to the tom-tom rhythm.

Berg danced well. Older people so often looked absurd when they attempted rock and roll, but he was adept, and she saw by his smile that he was enjoying himself. Then, at somebody's request, the music changed, surprisingly, to another genre: show tunes from *My Fair Lady*. Now Connie had to move into Berg's arms. She was almost as tall as he, so that their cheeks met. And when she moved her head, their eyes met. There were minute green flecks in his brown irises. They were friendly eyes, she decided, like Richard's except that there was no humor in them, or shyness, either, nor was there shyness in his firm hold around her waist.

People were watching them. A man called pleasantly, "Great performance, Martin!" as they swung past. The admiration was palpable, pouring like warm water over their perfect steps and over Connie, who could not help but know that she was the best-looking woman in the room.

When the music switched back to the tom-tom rhythm, Martin paused. "I've had enough of that for tonight, haven't you? How about going somewhere else for some real old-fashioned dancing? To the St. Regis Roof, maybe? A dress like yours should be shown off. Or would you rather just go someplace after the party for a quiet drink?"

He was obviously very, very interested. And with a difference. What it was that made his interest different from the usual none-too-subtle bid for a night in bed she could not have said. So she told him that a quiet drink would be very nice.

"I'm glad you chose that, Connie. I was hoping you would. Where shall it be?"

"My place," she told him.

"This is a pleasing room," said Martin, looking around the library.

"No Sargent over the fireplace. No fireplace, for that matter."

He shrugged. "What's the difference? Your brother's a rich man. He can afford a Sargent. And this is very nice. In good taste."

They were on their second glass of champagne. She had learned that it was smart to keep a chilled bottle ready for unexpected occasions like this one. But now she was beginning to feel the wine's potency; her blood ran hot and her words were coming too slowly. It became absolutely necessary to keep from falling asleep.

"We could put some music on and roll up the rug in the hall," she suggested.

"A great idea. Let's."

Firmly held again, she followed in perfect rhythm. Coming face to face, they regarded each other rather solemnly; then he placed a light kiss on her lips. His mouth was pleasing with its fragrance of fruity wine, mingled with a trace of mint. He kissed her again; her head spun; they pressed more closely to each other. Presently, they stopped dancing and stood still where they were, pressed together from mouth to knee. The tape stopped. And still they stood together in a quiet so thick and deep that she could hear the throbbing of his heart. There was no question about what must follow.

"Connie? Say where."

In the bedroom they undressed slowly, not taking their eyes away from one another. At last she stood naked of everything except the long diamond earrings.

"God, you're beautiful!" he cried.

Expertly, he unscrewed the earrings, laid them on the night table, and drew her down onto the bed.

He knew how to please, how to prolong pleasure. Indeed, Connie had never had as much pleasure with anyone before. It was not ecstatic—she knew by now that she was one of those for whom it never would reach the ultimate, just as there are people for whom food is never a real delight—but it was good enough. Quickly she grasped the fact that Berg was passionate and would want a passionate response from her. Not getting it, he might probably never come back. She hoped he would, for he was unmistakably a man, and she had had her fill of boys.

Things she had read and been told by other women, all sorts of tricks and variations, now came to mind. Sex was an art. Very well then, she would practice it.

"You are," Martin said in the morning, "the best I've ever known." His eyes were bright with happiness and admiration. "You're marvelous, Connie."

It was late on a dark gray Sunday. But the kitchen where they were having breakfast was cheerful, and the feeling was companionable.

"So you're from Ohio?"

"A small-town girl."

"You surely don't look it. You look like Fifth Avenue. Or Paris.

170

As for me, I'm from Flatbush. Originally, that is. That's Brooklyn, in case you don't know."

"I've heard, but I've never been there."

"You haven't missed anything. It's pretty awful."

"Then shall I say you don't look it either?"

Martin laughed. "As a matter of fact, I do. My parents were Polish immigrants. My father drove a taxi. He's dead now. My mother too." He stopped. "That's enough. It's of no interest to you."

"Oh, but it is." And it was, for in a startling instant she became aware that this man was the first person she had met since leaving Texas who had made his own way, and that he had come, as she herself had, from the class that is called "working."

"Go on. What about the rest of the family?"

"I'm the youngest of seven, one of the only two born here and who speak English without an accent. The other one, my brother Ben, teaches economics in a community college. The eldest brother was killed in the Korean War, one sister died, two brothers are in the wholesale millinery business in Chicago, and the other sister is married to a doctor in Houston." He gave her a modest, rather touching smile and concluded, "So the taxi driver's children have done pretty well, all considered."

"You've left yourself out."

"Me? There's nothing unusual to tell. I worked hard. I've been a waiter, and I've pushed a handcart in the garment district. But I was also lucky, I know that. I got a scholarship to Yale and after that to the Wharton School."

"That's hardly the result of luck, Martin."

He shrugged. She saw that the shrug was a characteristic gesture for him. And he continued, "Ben is the remarkable one. You'd expect him to be a free thinker, he's such a 'liberated' man in other ways, satisfied to live on next to nothing, so antibourgeoisie and all that business, and yet he's religious, practically Orthodox. We're Jews, of course."

He wasn't concealing his origins; he was, in fact, being prideful about them, while the memory of hers was so repugnant to her that she must hide it not only from others but from herself as well. This became clear to her for the first time, and she heard herself saying to this stranger, "I always lie about myself. I let people think I'm from a Texas family connected with oil. If I could tell you what my life was really like—"

Martin put up his hand to halt her admission. "You don't need to tell me anything. I'm only curious about why you're not lying to *me*."

"I don't really know." She played with the bacon and egg on her plate. Why? Perhaps because he created confidence, because he was so calm and composed and confident himself, even in that absurd unisex Turkish towel bathrobe.

She amended her reply. "I suppose I feel that you won't care about backgrounds and families and all that stuff the way other people do. And I trust you."

"Don't worry. I'll never betray your little secret, since it means that much to you."

"You think it's stupid of me, don't you?"

Again he shrugged. "Probably. Anyway, it's not important. What's important is that you trust me. I hope you don't trust everybody as quickly. It can be dangerous."

"I know that. But I'm pretty good at judging people, except," she added ruefully, "except when I married. The one time I should have judged well, I didn't."

"You have plenty of company, if that's any help. And as you said last night, you're lucky there are no children."

There was a silence so prolonged that Connie, feeling uneasy, broke it by suggesting that they move out of the kitchen onto more comfortable chairs in the library.

A small stack of books lay on a table next to a bowl of early tulips. Martin examined them.

TREASURES

"You're reading history?" he asked, with the emphasis of surprise on the word *history*. "Napoleon? The French Revolution?"

"I'm trying, a little at a time. Actually, they're Richard's books. He read everything he could about France. He has a remarkable mind, curious about everything, history, art, music, everything."

"It's nice that you're not bitter," Martin said.

"Well, the truth is the truth."

He nodded. "My wife is crazy about France too. She's gone off to live permanently in Paris. In the winter she takes an apartment in Cannes, though I don't know why. It can be damn chilly in the winter, and the beach is awful, anyway."

Connie was curious. "Does she—did she come from Brooklyn too?"

"No, Doris's people were a couple of steps higher on the ladder. They lived on the Upper West Side. She was a social worker when I met her. She's a fine person, very sensible, very serious. A high-quality woman. I still respect her. So I suppose," he said, "the natural question is why, then, are we ending with divorce?" Two dark furrows cut Martin's forehead, and his eyes looked weary so that, quite suddenly, he resembled the man he would someday be. "It's insidious, this process of growing apart. Hard to analyze, because there are so many ways you can blame each other. But mainly, since I've been living alone—I moved out of the apartment, although I still own it, and took two rooms in a hotel, a far more cheerful place—I've come to a conclusion: She was too serious. All those deep discussions, those 'political' friends of hers . . . There was never anything easy or light-hearted. I get enough heavy stuff all day. I want some *fun*, just plain fun. I love to dance. She hated to. Things like that." He broke off. "But I miss my little girl. Let me show you her picture." He got up and returned with his wallet. "Here she is. Melissa."

A plain child, a homely child with Martin's dark eyes, looked up at Connie while he waited for a comment.

173

"She's sweet. She doesn't look like you, though, does she? except for her eyes."

"She looks like Doris. But she's *like* me. Her mind, her ways . . . she's like me. She was here for Christmas vacation, and we had a great time. It broke my heart when I had to take her to Kennedy and put her on the plane back."

Connie felt the man's pain. "I'm sorry, Martin," she said gently. "I wish I could say something to make you feel better."

He caught her hand and held it between both of his. "You've done other things to make me feel better, Connie. I never expected—honestly, I swear I never expected what happened last night. But you're a beautiful, vibrant woman, and a passionate one, so it happened, that's all."

"I don't make a habit of things like this, I assure you."

"Nor do I. I was never a man for one-night stands. I want a relationship, a feeling for each other, with no holding back. I lived for too long with prudishness—it's strange, my telling you so many personal things about myself! But I suppose you might as well hear it now, because we're going to be seeing a whole lot of each other, I think."

When Eddy telephoned that evening, Connie said, "You beat me to it. I was just going to call and tell you both what a marvelous party that was."

"You left early."

"I didn't really want to, but Martin Berg—"

"I saw. You must have made a hit with him."

"He's very nice. He reminded me of you, in a way. Started out poor like you—"

"Like me? Don't I wish it."

"What do you mean? Does he do any better than you do?"

"Can you possibly mean that you don't know who he is?"

"Finance? Securities—isn't that what he does?"

"Oh, my God. He's Frazier, DeWitt, Berg! They've got five

thousand employees and branch offices all over the world. It's one of the oldest white-shoe firms on the Street."

"And just what, pray tell, is a 'white-shoe firm'?"

"Old-line aristocrats. Firms that go back a couple of generations. In this case Frazier's dead, but they keep the name. DeWitt took Berg in twenty years ago in spite of the Brooklyn background because he had a lot of business to bring along and because he happens to be damn brilliant. They deal in billions. Hostile takeovers. Big, big fees, whichever side of the deal they happen to take. Where did you two go?"

"To my house. We sat and talked awhile, then he went home. He's nice to talk to, very modest. You'd never think he was what you've told me."

"The man's worth about five hundred million. And he's given millions away to charity over the years."

Five hundred million. It was unreal. That was why people were watching them as they danced. Five hundred million.

"You think you'll see him again?"

"Maybe. You never can tell about men, can you?"

Eddy laughed. "You'll see him. You looked gorgeous last night. Pam said I should tell you that dress was a dream."

"Thank her. She looked lovely herself."

"She always does, my preppie lady. You're more to Berg's taste, though."

"What does that mean?"

"It means that I have a hunch you'll be seeing a lot of him. And you know how good I am at hunches."

"Well, I don't know," Connie said cautiously, "but he's a sweet man. Really sweet."

The months unfolded. He was an extraordinary man. He had prodigious energy, at work for eighteen hours out of the twenty-four. Every morning at half past six his chauffeur drove him to a seven o'clock breakfast meeting at his own office, at some other office, or at a hotel.

"Breakfast is the most convenient time to get people to-gether," he explained. "Lawyers, bankers, accountants, and prin-cipals."

"I don't know where you get your energy," she would whisper when, still half asleep, she heard him moving through the room on tiptoe so as not to wake her.

"As long as I have enough left for you," he would answer.

He had that too. She would have been satisfied had he been much less ardent, but he did not know that and never would know it, for her purpose was to please. His kindness, intelligence, and immaculate appearance made it easy to do the pleasing.

Sometimes, when she had spent the night in his rooms, she would walk around examining, without prying, the possessions that always tell so much about their owner: the twenty-five-hun-dred-dollar suits and London-made shirts behind the open closet door, the silver-backed brushes on the chest, the leather-bound books and photographs of his houses, the Palm Beach house and the house in Vail. One time as she picked up a book, a snapshot fell out, and she saw in a family group the woman who must be his wife, a tall woman wearing a blouse and skirt; she had a dour face like Melissa's. Connie wondered then about the divorce.

"It will involve a settlement, a pretty big one," Martin had told her, "as high as a hundred million, maybe. Who knows? It's vengeance, of course." And when Connie had gasped at the sum, he had added, "There have been larger settlements than that. It's funny, too, because Doris was never a spender, never wanted much. We started out in an apartment on Long Island, next we had a small ranch house, and it was only at my insistence that we graduated to a good-sized colonial. Then when we decided to move to the city because of my night meetings and late hours, it was I who chose the apartment; she thought it was too big and too expensive. The only thing she ever really loved is the house in Paris; it's small, but it's a gem, and now it's all hers." He grunted. "It's not too far from the Sorbonne, where she takes courses. She likes to be thought of as an intellectual. Never even wanted to wear jewelry. Middle-class ostentation, you know."

Joyously, Martin bought and bought for Connie. "I feel like a hick," he complained on the Saturday afternoon when they got the sable coat. "It's so many years since I've bought anything like this, that I can't believe how prices have gone up. Not that I mind," he said quickly. "Far from it."

From Harry Winston on the same day came a Burmese ruby, and from David Webb, a pair of diamond-studded bracelets.

"We're going to a hospital benefit ball next week," he explained, "and I want you to wear the coat, the ruby, and the bracelets."

She understood how very much it meant to this man to make an entrance with a splendidly dressed young woman on his arm. What she did not understand were his ultimate intentions; was she to be a cherished mistress, or finally a wife?

Often all that year, when Martin attended breakfast meetings at the Regency Hotel, Connie would wait in the marble-and-velvet lobby, observing the flow of people at the door. They came, quite naturally, in every age and size, but out of proportion to their numbers, or so it seemed to her, were couples consisting of a paunchy, balding man with a young woman half a head taller than he. These expensive young women wore anything from jogging outfits or anoraks with skin-tight black pants to ankle-length black mink. Often they had proud, sulky faces. Mistresses, they were, or second wives, acquired for their youth. Martin and she must look like that. . . . She didn't want to think about it.

Then he would appear at the top of the steps, striding briskly and smiling toward her. Under her guidance he had lost ten pounds, and along with them as many years. He was unmistakably a powerful man and unmistakably an attractive man. No, they did not resemble the others. . . . And it would hurt to lose him. . . . A little shiver of fear would run down Connie's back, while the essential question trembled, waiting to be asked. But she dared not ask it.

In early spring they went to Vail, traveling on the private jet that belonged to Martin's firm. Connie was a warm-weather person, and Vail was still deep in winter. But the mountains were magnificent, and so was the house, with its handmade furniture, bright Indian fabrics, and photographs of the Old West. Martin was an expert on skis, while she had never had a pair on her feet and was wary of trying.

"You're not afraid, are you?" he asked, and she, remembering that he had happened once to mention that Doris had refused to learn, assured him she was not.

A private instructor came to teach her, and mastering both her fear and the cold, she made good progress; mastering, too, the language of the slopes, she began to talk like an enthusiast around the various fireplaces where Martin's friends, of whom he had incredibly many, spent the evenings. And so she pleased him.

The seasons flowed. In the summer the city had a different air. Their favorite restaurants were relatively uncrowded, there were open air concerts, and delightful sidewalk cafés. Sometimes on weekends they met Eddy and Pam in the country. But most of the time Connie was busy, having kept her boutique open. Because her future was uncertain, it seemed more prudent to retain it; besides, to be idle all day in expectation of the night was to be nothing but a courtesan, which was, in spite of being an old-fashioned word, an apt one.

The fall brought parties again, charity benefits and balls. Martin bought tickets and took tables for everything. Through her experiences with Bitsy Maxwell, Connie was able to calculate how much money all these cost him. Generous as were Martin's gifts, they were commensurate with his wealth; she wondered whether Eddy gave in the same proportion and rather thought not. Eddy liked the personal pleasure that came with actually seeing the person to whom he gave, and perhaps, she thought, too, of controlling that person along with the gift.

A second Christmas approached. Martin announced that his daughter was coming to spend the week with him. She loved the ocean and was to fly directly to Florida.

"I haven't used the house in two years. But I've been letting my friends use it whenever they want to. I've invited my brother Ben this time too. He's had the flu, and a rest will do him good." Martin chuckled. "Ben doesn't approve of the house there, you know. Says it's outrageous, and from his point of view, I guess it is. He doesn't approve of me either. But we get along fine, anyway."

These last words held a sting for Connie. Although she mentioned Eddy quite freely and happily, she had never told Martin anything about Lara, except to say that she had a sister in Ohio, for she could not have mentioned the separation without tears. There was too much pain for her to enter into explanations.

In Palm Beach, at the end of the vast lawn stretching up from the ocean, immured by gates and flourishing shrubbery from public view or trespass, lay a long pink stuccoed house with a red tile Spanish roof. Striped awnings shaded the tall windows. Hibiscus and oleander blazed in the sunshine. Enormous rooms led from one to another and out through loggias, terraces, and a Mediterranean courtyard where a fountain splashed. In an oval conservatory Martin displayed his orchid collection.

"I thought it would be a good hobby," he explained. "I even bought books to learn about orchids. You'd be surprised how much there is to know about all the varieties. But I've given it up and let the gardeners do it. I never have enough time to fool around with things like that."

179

Connie was looking over his shoulder toward the pool and the guest wing.

"How many rooms are there?" she inquired.

"Sixty-four. Not counting the quarters for gardeners and chauffeur, which are separate."

Ben Berg and Melissa arrived from New York and Paris within an hour of each other, and shortly afterward were seated at a little table in the courtyard having dinner. Three pairs of identical dark, heavy eyes surrounded Connie. All three Bergs had the same thick hair; the girl's was just a tangle of coarse black silk. The two brothers had the same alert and vigilant face, but Melissa's expression seemed either worried or perhaps just absent-minded. At any rate, she looked like one of those children who have been born old. She was badly dressed in sallow green with a loose wide collar, out of which rose a long neck and a pointed chin. Her mother ought to know better or to care more, Connie thought pityingly.

The fountain trickled. Whenever the voices ceased, this music alone filled the night. No air stirred a leaf. The candle flames were steady.

"A perfect night," Martin murmured. He reached across the table for his daughter's hand and held it while she held her fork in the other hand.

Connie smiled. "How can you eat like that?" she asked.

"I'm left handed," replied Melissa, not letting go.

They loved each other, Connie saw. The girl, suffering, was the ultimate victim of the crumbling marriage. As always. And again, she was moved to pity.

Long after the dessert was cleared away, the men were still talking to each other. Inattentively, Connie heard that they were having a mild argument, Ben, faintly sardonic, saying something about industry: *It should be making jobs and products, not paying off debt.* And Martin emphatically responding. Melissa did not speak, but Connie felt her furtive glances. She was wondering, probably, what Connie's position here might be, and could not know that Connie was wondering the same about herself.

The melancholy began to weigh too heavily, and Connie stood abruptly, saying, "We're forgetting about jet lag. For Melissa it's already past midnight."

"Of course," Martin said at once. "Go to bed. You, too, Connie. Maybe you ladies might want to do some shopping tomorrow. I think Melissa needs some summer clothes."

So he had noticed the awful dress. Naturally. He noticed everything.

With Melissa in the house Martin would of course stay in his own bed. So Connie lay awake in a room that was too large for one person to occupy alone. Her memory spun.

"How are things between Martin and you?" Eddy had recently inquired, meaning, *You're starting the second year. When is he going to marry you??* To which she had answered only, *Things are fine*, and left him uninformed.

The divorce proceedings were taking their time, it was true. Still, there was no guarantee that Martin had anything else in mind but to continue as they were, even after the divorce should become final. There were no guarantees of anything in this world, and nothing lasted forever. She ought to have learned that by now. She should not be taking for granted this protected life, this voluptuous nest, this gold-lined cocoon. Indeed, she should not have let herself grow fond of the man. And as she lay looking up at the dim ceiling, a tightness came to her throat, as though she were about to cry.

The day's purchases were spread on Melissa's bed, were hung in the closet and laid over chairs. There were swimsuits and sundresses, clothes for every possible occasion in the life of an eleven-year-old girl. Regarding herself in the mirror, Melissa allowed a timid smile to spread from her lips and brighten her sober eyes. Peach-colored linen brought becoming color to her pale cheeks. Her thick hair had been smoothed back with a bandeau above her forehead.

Connie, from her seat on the chaise longue, observing the change, remarked, "You like yourself. That's good."

"I've never had things like this before. My mother . . ." And Melissa stopped.

"Well. Now you know you must always wear lively colors, pretty colors, don't you?"

"I'm going to wear this tonight. Daddy will like it."

"I'm sure he will."

Melissa is my heart, Martin had said.

The girl sat down on the edge of the bed and began to fold sweaters. Connie looked at her, round shouldered and ungainly still, in spite of the improvements. It was absurd that this child should be able to make her feel awkward. Never before, no matter where she had gone with Martin, no matter whom she had met, had she felt the slightest uncertainty or discomfiture. Yet here in this house, in the presence of his child and his earnest, ironic brother, who would surely be as disapproving of Connie as he was of the house itself, she was displaced. She was the outsider.

She was thinking of a way to make a smooth exit when Melissa spoke.

"Are you a special friend of Daddy's?"

"I'm a friend. I don't know what you mean by 'special.' "

"Oh, special. A lady who lives here."

Connie flushed; she had a sense that some unwelcome information might be forthcoming. Nevertheless, she pursued the subject.

"Why, do special friends usually live here?"

"Not always. But Daisy did. She was very pretty. But you're even prettier, I think."

The remark, and the girl's frank look, were absolutely ingenu-

182

ous. She was too timid, too unworldly, to be malicious, so this then must be the truth.

"So Daisy was a special friend, was she?"

"Oh, yes. When we left Daddy and went to live in Paris, I guess Daddy was lonesome, so Daisy moved in. But then I think he stopped liking her after a while."

"What makes you think that?" asked Connie, keeping her voice careless, although her heart began to race.

"She didn't want to go away, but Daddy told her to. I was here and I heard them."

"I see. He told her to."

"Yes. I think I'll take this dress off and go swimming. Want to come?"

"Not just now. Maybe later I will."

For long minutes Connie stood in the bathroom staring at herself in the mirror. The flush had receded, leaving her face pale and shocked. *He told her to go.* And holding her hand to her cheek, she contemplated the delicate fingers spread like a fan, the well-kept nails, and the darkly glowing ruby. Had that other woman, called Daisy, also worn a Harry Winston jewel? And had she stood here before the mirror, too, contemplating herself and her future? Had she, too, been "fond" of Martin Berg before she was cast out?

Outside a wind had risen, rattling the royal palms that stood about the lawn. She went to the window to watch them lash and struggle against the coming rain. For a long time she stood, absorbed half by the approaching storm and half by the storm of her own deliberations.

Finally, she fetched her cosmetic carrying case from the closet in the bedroom, took out the birth control pills, and poured them down the toilet.

CHAPTER EIGHT

~~~~~~~~

Midway through the spring the doctor confirmed Connie's guess.

"You'll have a December baby," he said.

Having heard tales of women who, after an abortion, had never again conceived, she was reassured. She thought how ironic it was that, pregnant for the second time in uncertain circumstances, she should now find herself in the opposite position. But it still remained for her to inform Martin, who might very well not be pleased at having fatherhood thrust publicly upon him by his unmarried lover. On the other hand, might not a man nearing fifty be delighted with such a reenactment and confirmation of his youth?

As it turned out, he was neither displeased nor delighted, but rather more astonished than anything else.

"But you were using the pill!" he exclaimed.

"I'm afraid it's not infallible."

A disturbing possibility came to her, that he might suggest an abortion. He looked thoughtful, while she endured an ominous silence and studied his face.

He asked then, "When will it be?"

"December."

Martin nodded. "At least the timing is convenient."

"The timing?"

"My divorce will be final in thirty days. I found out this morning. That's why I picked this place for dinner. To celebrate."

They were at La Grenouille, one of their favorite choices for dining out. She looked past his shoulders at a mass of yellow hyacinths, and beyond them to a family of voluble teenagers with their youthful, handsome parents. A solid family. A *young* family.

"We can be married over the Memorial Day weekend. We'll have a seventh- or eighth-month baby."

She understood. He had his dignified position to maintain. Modern times or no, the world of finance was not the world of the theater or the arts. And she had to ask herself now what he would have said or done if the divorce had not yet come to a final solution, or what would be happening if his desire for her had already waned, as apparently his desire for another—or others—had done.

But those were useless speculations. Those dangers were past.

"You look troubled," he said.

"I guess I'm still in shock."

"Well, so was I a moment ago." He smiled. "But now that I've absorbed the shock, it's really rather nice, you know. Let's order champagne."

They toasted each other. Martin became talkative; once he had accepted a reality, he always began to organize projects around it, jumping from one thought to the next.

"We'll have to move into my apartment. Wait till you see it. It's spectacular, a whole floor overlooking Fifth Avenue. Of course, it needs to be completely done over. I never liked the way it was done in the first place. Doris wanted her own way, but she knew nothing. And Melissa needs a proper room, no matter how seldom she uses it. Bear in mind a room for my son. Make it suitable for a young man. He may never sleep in it. He's his mother's boy, and he probably hates me. But do it, anyway. And guest rooms. I suppose now your sister will want to bring her family sometimes."

"Perhaps not. She's a country girl. And they're so busy building up the business, anyway."

Pictures flashed as a camera clicks through one view after another: Lara as she must look standing in the doorway of the new white house, standing with Davey in front of the proud facade of the Davis Company, Lara bringing her supper tray on the last night, Lara . . . The trouble was that the longer one waited to make a healing move, to write a letter or to pick up the telephone, the more difficult it became to do, until finally it became impossible, and one buried the grief at the bottom of one's mind.

"Well, I'll be having people fly in now and then. It's nice, when a man comes in from Australia, not to have to put him up at a hotel."

Still Connie's thoughts went wandering. She was acutely conscious of the life that she was nurturing within her. It seemed of a sudden so remarkable that such a thing could be happening to her, so remarkable that she ought to stand up and announce it. And she thought again of what Lara would say if she knew. She thought of Peg. And, strangely, she thought of Richard. For a few fleeting moments a dark melancholy passed through her.

"We'll have the wedding, a garden wedding at the place in Westchester. It will need a little freshening up, that's all. Otherwise, it's in good shape."

"I wondered why you've never shown it to me, or the apartment either."

"Because I didn't remember much joy in either one of those places. But now you'll bring joy. And beauty. And life."

There were twenty-seven rooms in the apartment. Past piles of furniture draped in sheets Connie followed Martin into a gymnasium, a poolroom, a music room, a restaurant-sized kitchen, and more. The dining-room floor was marble, but the Victorian chairs were ugly, as was a dark, gigantic painting of men and horses whirling in battle among half-naked women pinned to the ground and ready to be raped. Connie wrinkled her nose in distaste.

Martin laughed. "Yes, it's awful. Get rid of it. I want you to hire the best decorator in town and give him carte blanche. It'll take a few million to do this up right, but it's our home. His home." He poked her gently in the stomach.

"Or hers."

"The corner bedroom will be fine for it. The sun's there for hours."

"All right. It."

And Connie felt again the excitement and acute awareness of the growing life. She looked about at the grand rooms. The new life, as yet unknowing, would enter the world in possession of all this, the safety and the grandeur.

The top decorator was an elegant young man with a faintly disdainful manner who moved rapidly through the apartment, approving and discarding, most often the latter. At Connie's house, to her surprise, the only item that he found worth keeping was the old mirror that Richard had bought on Third Avenue.

"Whoever bought that knew what he was doing," the man remarked.

Nor was he impressed by the words *carte blanche*. Carte blanche apparently was, in these lofty neighborhoods, merely to be expected.

"I shall of course be bidding for you myself at the important auctions," he informed Connie, "but I'll also keep my eyes open for things you can bid on. You'll find that auctions are entertaining even when you don't buy." And then he cautioned, "Keep to the French. Important houses don't furnish English." So vanished Connie's English country look, of which she had been so proud.

Now began a friendly rivalry between Connie and Eddy, who had long since discovered the lure of the galleries, "Although," Martin grumbled good-naturedly, "I don't understand how your brother finds time for such stuff." And then he added, "I hope he's on firm ground, Connie. He's soared like a Roman candle."

"Don't worry about Eddy. He's always known exactly what he's doing and where he's going."

Often the brother and sister went together, seeking treasures. Connie bought a pair of Tang horses, eighth century. Eddy bought a Tiffany desk. She bought a Chinese vase for twelve thousand dollars. He bought a pair of Empire *bibliothèque* cabinets at forty thousand dollars each. She bought two jewel-studded Fabergé eggs, and he bought a Berthe Morisot painting of children in a garden. She also bought portraits, to be represented as ancestral, and, shamefaced, laughed a little at the intended deception.

"You have to help me with art, Eddy. I have to admit that unless something has a name that everybody recognizes or it's frightfully expensive, I'm not sure whether it's great art or not."

"Great isn't always what you need," Eddy said gently. "I've learned that. Loving is the thing. Last week I bought for a few dollars a watercolor from a student in the Village. Maybe he'll be great someday and maybe he won't. But I don't necessarily care. I can always buy 'great' things, and I do. This was a fine little piece, a cat drinking out of a puddle in the rain. You can tell it has just stopped raining, and it's hot because there's a mist rising from the pavement. The feeling is extraordinary."

Eddy had always had a sense of rightness. When he sent flowers, he specified what he wanted. Once, long ago, she had watched him buying flowers for their mother's birthday, scarlet peonies with purple iris; the florist had said they didn't go together, but Eddy had insisted, and they did go together, very beautifully too.

"You're spending a fortune," he said. "Berg doesn't mind?"

"He told me to."

The brother and sister stared at each other. "Can you believe what we're doing? That it's really us?"

"And that you're going to be Mrs. Martin Berg?" cried Eddy.

Things changed. From having lived, albeit luxuriously, in the background of Martin's life as an almost anonymous feminine companion, now Connie was made visible.

Early one morning she accompanied him to his office.

"Wall Street," Martin said. "Do you know how it got its name? Because it ran inside the wall that the first Dutch settlers built around the city. Hard to imagine that now, isn't it?"

They entered a long, wide hall leading to a private elevator. At intervals on the walls hung portraits of solemn gentlemen, smooth shaven or bearded, but all white collared, with some wing collared in the fashion of the nineties. The eighteen nineties. And now the nineteen nineties were approaching.

"The founding fathers. Look pompous, don't they?" Martin remarked with some amusement. "But they were smart old birds. That one's Frazier."

"Where's DeWitt?"

"You'll meet him. He's alive and well upstairs. We don't put pictures up until people die. Come, I'll show you the 'bullpen.' That's the trading floor."

Row upon row of desks faced a large electronic board across which numbers flickered in a continuous march. More lights blinked from telephones on the desks, at each of which sat a man with piles of papers in front of him.

"Block trading." Martin spoke just above a whisper. "Huge blocks for institutions and pension funds. They can move millions of dollars in a couple of minutes. Fascinating, don't you think so?"

He had a way of making a statement and then asking one to agree with it; she had to tell herself that, really, she had caught on to his ways remarkably fast. She also knew that he expected her to agree that block trading was fascinating, and so, although she thought it more static than fascinating to watch a man sit like a zombie with a telephone stuck in his ear, she agreed.

"When all is said and done, Connie, this is the core of the business. Trading, I mean. Mergers and acquisitions are the big thing these days, of course, and I'm in the midst of them, from Zurich to Tokyo, but I never forget that right here is where I began. Okay, let's go on to mergers and acquisitions.

"Behind every one of these doors," Martin continued as they walked through the floor above, "sits some bright young MBA working on a deal that can either earn millions for the firm or go bust. If too many of his deals go bust, he goes too. He's got to produce, to earn his six hundred thousand a year, let me tell you. These fellows work, and I mean *work*. Twenty-four hours at a stretch sometimes when they're near to a closing. Kids," he said almost affectionately, "and think how they've changed the country's face! Think of the ripple effect of their prosperity! Houses and condos, theater tickets, antiques and boats, restaurants, travel—it's amazing. Well, here's my lair."

The room was modern, neat, and spare. It was utilitarian, with its own electric quote-board at one end. The only decoration was a ficus tree. This was strictly a workroom. It bore no resemblance to Eddy's plush London club.

She walked to the bank of windows and looked out. She saw the narrow stretch of Manhattan from river to river, saw the harbor, the twin towers of the World Trade Center, and, small in contrast, the Statue of Liberty. Turning from these, her eyes fell upon the moving numbers on the screen; they seemed to be pulsing with a meticulous beat, like a heartbeat, as though they were in command of this body, this city with all its towers, and all its life. And she said so.

Martin smiled. "You speak more truly than you know. Well. Come meet my partner. He's across the hall."

Preston DeWitt stood up at his desk when they came in. He was very tall and thin; his well-shaven narrow cheeks were pink, and his lavish white hair sprang crisply on either side of the parting.

Martin, having made the introduction, announced, "I'm playing hookey this noon, Preston. Taking Connie to lunch at Twenty-One in honor of our engagement."

"Splendid." The accent was crisp, too, verging on the British, or more accurately, Connie thought, on the speech of Franklin Roosevelt that one heard in documentaries. "And when's the wedding?"

"Memorial Day weekend in the country," Martin said.

"You can bet I'll be there, and so will Caroline if she's up to it. It's all just splendid."

In these few moments Connie and Preston had appraised each other. Of his impression she could know only what she saw in his clever, keen black eyes, so odd in contrast to the fair skin; the eyes were calculating. Most probably he liked what he was seeing, since there was no reason not to like a young blond woman wearing a quiet, elegant beige broadcloth suit. Connie's own impression was positive: He's handsome, he's really startling. His suit looked absolutely starched, as if he never sat down. Martin, on the other hand, was wrinkled an hour after putting on fresh clothes. The two men were the same age, although one would never guess it. Preston seemed fifteen years younger.

"He looks young," she remarked when they were in the elevator.

"He takes care of himself. Riding, tennis, sailing, everything. He learned all that when he was a kid, he grew up with it. In

Brooklyn, where I grew up, I didn't have a sailboat, or a horse either."

"What's the matter with his wife? Is she sick?"

"Only when it's convenient. She's never sick when there's a *Social Register* function, which our wedding isn't, so we'll see. Anyway, she's a pill, and I don't blame him for having a roving eye. Oh, how it roves!"

"So you don't see each other socially."

"Rarely. But don't get me wrong, we like each other. I have a lot of respect for Preston. He works hard, and he doesn't even have to. He inherited this firm, but he's also got independent wealth from his mother's family. Mines and lumber for at least three generations. Maybe he's the fourth, I'm not sure."

"It's remarkable that you fit so well together, being so different."

"Hey, I've quadrupled this firm's assets since I came in! It was purely and simply a brokerage firm, and I'm the one who's turned it into a powerful investment bank. I'm the one, and Preston knows it."

"I'm sure."

Once in the car, Martin kept talking. "That's the stock exchange over there. I'll take you to see it one day. You'll think it's a madhouse. Hundreds of traders shrieking and waving their arms, right up to the three-thirty closing bell. What an industry! Little guys gambling, big guys in risk arbitrage. Your brother does some of that, I'm told. Not me. I don't like risk."

The car rolled along Wall Street. On either side were walls of windows and behind all the windows, Connie now knew, were rows of desks, telephones, and people talking. The fantastic wealth that talk produced! Of course, she corrected herself immediately, there was more to it than talk. To think otherwise was to oversimplify. It was naive. And yet, for an instant, a totally irrelevant picture came to mind, an image of Davey, bustling in his little factory, making something with his grimy hands.

TREASURES

A cold April rainstorm had arisen, a brief return of winter. People were hurrying along the windy streets, crowding the subway entrances, pushing through the crowds, clutching the collars of their coats and their shabby parcels. But inside the car as it rolled uptown to Twenty-One, it was warm and dry. There was even a folded lap robe if you wanted one, dark blue woolen with a monogram. Connie sighed and stretched her legs in comfort.

"Feeling all right?" Martin asked, as always.

"Wonderful."

To be so safe, and so removed from the poor souls in the streets and in the subways, was bliss.

Forty-three acres surrounded this residence among the low hills of northern Westchester County. From the window where Connie stood, she could see the tennis courts, the heated pool, the stables, and the riding trail curving toward the woods. When the door opened, she turned toward Martin.

His eyes grew wide. "My God," he said, "my God, but you're perfection itself!"

"I don't look three months pregnant?"

"No one could possibly guess."

"I've gained eight pounds. And all where it shows. Or it would if this skirt weren't so full." She smoothed the diaphanous pink silk.

From behind he put his arm around her waist. Through the mirror that faced them, she could see the white carnation in his buttonhole; she could see his happiness.

"Are you sure you feel all right?" he asked.

"I feel absolutely wonderful."

"The judge is already here, but we've got half an hour yet. People are still arriving. And Eddy just came with a surprise for us. Shall I send him up?"

"Do. I'm getting nervous up here all by myself."

One could hear Eddy's approach even on carpeted stairs and

floors. His running steps thudded; he rattled keys, cleared his throat, made *noises*. It was as if his vigor, like Martin's, were too much to contain. Now he almost leapt into the room, shouting at Connie.

"Were you wondering why you haven't gotten my wedding present yet?"

"What a question! What am I supposed to answer?"

"Don't answer. Just go to the window."

Cars were lined up in the big graveled circle and all down the driveway as far as she could see.

"Where am I supposed to look?"

"Down on your right. Behind the Rolls where the chauffeur's standing. What do you see?"

"A station wagon."

He corrected her. "A Mercedes station wagon. Like it?"

"Of course. It's stunning."

"Well, it's yours. From Pam and me."

"Eddy! You're a darling! I love it. Love it!"

"Well, it was Pam's idea. We thought it would be just right for you and your offspring to go tooling about the countryside in. There's room for Delphine and the rest of the dogs in the back too."

"Oh, you're both darlings," Connie repeated. "Why doesn't Pam come up so I can thank her?"

"You can thank her later." Eddy hesitated, grew grave, and exclaimed softly, "What a pity that you never invited Lara!"

Connie drew a sharp breath. There was a fluttering in her heart, and she had to sit down. "Oh, Eddy! How can you do this to me today? I can't start crying, smudging my eyes now! I did invite her. I wrote a lovely letter last week and sent it with such hope, and such fears, I can't tell you! I didn't know how she would take it. I thought probably she would be angry that I even asked her. And you see, I was right, I haven't heard a word. Not a word. I knew she wouldn't come."

TREASURES

Eddy threw his head back in delighted laughter. "Oh, but you're wrong! She's here! They've even brought Sue, all dressed up like a wedding cake. She didn't answer because she wanted to surprise you. She's waiting in the hall at the top of the stairs."

"Oh, my God! Oh, Eddy, where is she? Bring her in!"

Connie's eyes, brimming with tears all mingled with mascara, stung so sharply that Lara seemed to be wavering in the doorway. She's grown older, Connie thought; her waist is thick, she's thirty-five. And she held out her arms.

Lara cried. Then, murmuring, "I mustn't crush your dress," she let go of Connie, saying over and over, "But I am so glad, so glad."

"You didn't answer me, so I thought you weren't coming."

"Oh, I was hoping you would invite us. Davey said, and Eddy said so many times, long before this, that I should call you. And I wanted to, but I dreaded a rejection." Lara's eyebrows drew together, giving her a painful, almost an imploring expression. In that instant Connie recognized their mother.

"I wish Peg were here," she said.

Eddy, who, like a proud, tender parent, was watching them, said quickly, "If she were, she'd say, 'Get on with the party.'" He looked at his watch. "I'm going to leave you two now, but in twenty minutes I'll be back to take the bride downstairs and give her away."

"When you come back, will you bring Davey and Sue for just a minute? I want Connie to see my Sue."

The sisters were left with more than two years' worth of living to disclose.

"Eddy tells me your little girl is darling," Connie began.

"Oh, she is. I am so grateful for the way she's growing."

"And he tells me that Davey and you have a fabulous business."

"Well, he ought to know. He's had enough to do with it. But *fabulous* is a big word."

"Doesn't Eddy always use big words? Big, that's Eddy. But I'm impressed, anyway. When I think of that shed in your backyard, when I think of so many things we lived through together, and of all the changes now . . ."

"Sometimes it doesn't do to remember too much. I wish I could forget, and maybe I will yet, the things I said to you. I was too harsh, Connie. I guess it was just that, after all those years of wanting a baby, I went crazy because you could have one and didn't want it."

"Don't," Connie said gently, "it's past, it's over. Don't spoil this happiness."

"You're right." Lara glanced around the room. "This house! I've never seen anything like it. Why, you're living like a princess, Connie."

On the floor near the door stood a pile of brass-bound luggage ready to be taken downstairs. The matching pieces were made of maroon leather, the softest, most perishable kind that is used for expensive handbags.

"Such beautiful suitcases," Lara said.

"My birthday present. Martin selected them."

"I hope they don't bang them all up at the airport. Just flying from home to New York, they made a dent in my brand-new case. But Davey says it can be fixed."

A careful, frugal housekeeper had spoken. *Use it up, make it do, wear it out.* That was the way Lara had been taught and the way she would follow. And Connie could barely imagine Lara's shock if she knew that Martin had paid twelve thousand dollars for those six pieces.

"You must be going far. Or is your honeymoon a secret?"

"We're going around the world." Connie hesitated, trying to decide whether to minimize the truth or to reveal it all, and decided to reveal it; they had never hidden things from one another in the past, and there was no good reason to start now. "Martin's firm has bought a new jet. It's got everything, even a grand piano. Isn't that fantastic? We'll be seeing such fairy-tale places too. Bora Bora and Kashmir and Madagascar. I've been trying desperately to learn something about them before we get there. Martin admires me when I know things. Did you meet him when you came in?"

"Briefly. Eddy introduced us."

"Martin's very sweet. And he's a man, not—" She had been about to say, "not a Richard," but was stopped by the recall of last week's affecting note from Richard, wishing her every happiness with Martin, and said instead, "When you get to know him, you'll see. You'll really like him."

"If you love him, of course I will." The conversation then came to a stop. It was as if they had both at the same moment been struck by the reality of each other's presence. They were examining each other. She is sturdy and comforting, Connie said to herself. She copes, and will be the same if she lives to be ninety.

"What are you seeing when you look at me so gravely?" asked Lara.

Connie shook her head. "No, no, I was only seeing your dress. I like the color, the blue."

"I bought it on the run as soon as I knew we were coming. Does it make me look fat?"

"Not really. But you have put on some weight."

"Fifteen pounds."

"As much as that! How did you let it happen?"

"I suppose you can't guess." Lara's eyes were very bright, as if still tearful, although now she was smiling. "I'm pregnant."

Could she be? No, not after all those years.

"Are you shocked? Yes, it's true. I'm in my sixth month, so you see, I'm really not all that fat."

Connie got up and put her arms around Lara. Moved to the heart, she could find nothing to say.

"Connie, no tears," Lara protested gently. "Your makeup. Here, let me wipe it."

"Did Eddy tell you I was pregnant too?"

Eddy, appearing just then at the door, denied that. "Definitely not. I considered that your secret if you wanted to keep it. Now, take a look at who's here."

"Davey!" There he stood, almost shyly, with a twinkling smile, immediately so familiar that she felt with a shock how much she must have missed him too.

"Come in and let me hug you. You look surprised. . . . You heard what I said."

"It seems as if an awful lot's happening at once, that's why."

"When is it to be?" asked Lara.

"Not till December. Are you shocked?"

"Of course not, darling."

And Davey added, "Why should we be? We're only happy for you."

"Yes, both of them making an uncle out of me," Eddy said. "Or I should say 'again,' because I am one already. Where is she? Where are you, Sue?"

"Here." And from behind Davey stepped a dark-haired little girl in a party dress.

"This is Aunt Connie," Lara announced. "Isn't she pretty in her bride dress?"

Great, solemn eyes stared at Connie. "She's not as big as you are, Aunt Lara."

"Her baby's not as near to being born as ours is, that's why." And as Connie's confusion must have been evident, Lara explained, "Sue's known for a long time that she's going to have a sister. The doctor told us."

"So we'd know what color to make the baby's room," Sue interposed. "The room's right next to mine. It's pink, and I'm giving her a pink cat when she comes. I bought it with my allowance."

TREASURES

They've worked some sort of miracle here, Connie thought, recollecting Eddy's first accounts of a frightened, orphaned waif and Lara's patient struggles. Bending to kiss this little chatterer on either cheek, she said, "I think your baby will be the luckiest baby in the world to have a sister like you."

Connie's eyes met Lara's over Sue's head. The emotion inside the four walls of the room was tangible, almost too much to be borne.

"This is something like it, you two together again," said Eddy. Then he, too, must suddenly have sensed the need to lighten the moment, for with mock brusqueness he gave orders: "Go on out, everybody, hurry down. I'm giving the bride away, and we're ready to make our grand entrance."

Connie floated. In her long pink dress, the color of evening clouds, she floated down the spiral stairs into the drawing room and down the aisle between the guests on their little gilt chairs, to where Martin stood waiting.

Beside her there hovered a singular creature, her own spirit, disembodied, cannily observing the event and everyone in it, including herself.

The judge is wizened; his voice is as dry as his words; there is no poetry in them as there was that other time in Houston when the minister began: *Dearly beloved, we are gathered here.* Connie likes poetry in stately ceremony, but it's better this way after all, less complicated than choosing either minister or rabbi. As long as they are safely married and the baby safely growing, nothing else is important.

In a few minutes the ring is given, and it is all over. Martin bends down and kisses Connie; it is a long kiss on the mouth, and she is a little embarrassed before all these people. She catches Bitsy's eye. Now she is infinitely richer than Bitsy, which is what counts, even though Bitsy may well sniff at Martin Berg for being nouveau.

They are walking back down the aisle between two rows of smiles. Martin's brother Ben thinks Connie is a trophy wife, and perhaps she is, for she's Martin's prize today, and he treats her like a prize. But his Chicago sisters-in-law, elderly and bedecked with jewelry, have kind, sentimental faces; *Oh, Martin, she's beautiful*, they whisper as she passes. Eddy winks, and Pam blows a kiss. Pam is a sport. She has a good time everywhere. There's Preston's white patrician head. His eyes, with a canny twinkle in them, meet Connie's and linger a second too long. His wife looks about old enough to be his mother, although they met when they were both in college. Martin's son is sullen. He came unwillingly and will fly back to Paris tomorrow. There's Melissa in bottle-green with real lace, a beautiful French dress, but green again. Her mother must not like her. Connie will help her. Connie will be good to Martin's children, will remember their favorite foods and do everything right.

Now they stand in the receiving line to be kissed and congratulated. Having passed through the line, the guests disperse themselves among the airy rooms and out into the gardens. Music strikes up, music for happiness.

How Connie's mother would have loved all this! How Connie loves it! She is glowing.

Tables were set up under flowered umbrellas on the terraces and lawns. Waiters bearing silver trays in their white-gloved hands moved about among the tables and followed guests along paths between high banks of laurel, offering a variety of hors d'oeuvres so lavish as to make superfluous the dinner that was to follow inside the great house.

So large and so diverse was the crowd that friends had a hard time finding each other. Some husbands and wives had to stand apart with no one else to talk to, while other people, weary of wandering, glass in hand, took the first available seat and started some sort of courteous conversation with total strangers.

"Twenty-three years and then a divorce," remarked Caroline DeWitt. "The man ought to be ashamed, that's all I have to say."

"This is hardly the place in which to say it," her husband replied. "You're talking about my partner."

"I'm not in the habit of embarrassing you, Preston. I was practically whispering. And it is shameful, no matter what you think. Doris was a much more suitable wife. Not that I ever knew her that well, but you could just look at her and see she was more suitable."

"Apparently, he doesn't think so," Preston answered dryly.

"Just look at the dress this one's wearing. These people are terribly overdressed. The whole thing is overdone. Ostentatious. Too much food, too many flowers. Ah! Now, there's a well-dressed young woman. The tall one in the black-and-white print over there."

"She's the bride's sister-in-law. Married to the Young Prince."

"Not that Osborne they talk about?"

"Yes, Osborne. I've been in this business a long, long time and my father before me, but I still don't know how he does it."

"He knew enough to marry a lady, anyway. There's no mistaking quality. Even to the way she sits. You see what I mean?"

Pam was saying, "This must be a wonderful country for horses. We ought to buy a place like this, Eddy, don't you think so? I'm getting tired of Long Island. It's gotten too crowded, even in the best parts of it."

"Kentucky? I can't live there, honey. It's too far."

"I visited my school roommate there one summer, and I love it, loved all the space." Pam spoke wistfully.

"All right. When I retire. But I'm hardly ready to retire yet! Things are going too well for that."

Hopefully now, Pam regarded Eddy. "It could be an investment. Horses can make a lot of money for you."

"You'd really like it?"

"I'd adore it."

"Then I promise I'll keep it in mind for the future."

And why not? Make her happy. That's what life is all about, what money is for, he thought, feeling again the nice glow of ample generosity. And he imagined himself saying someday, "Our place in Kentucky"; he imagined himself walking—no, riding—over hundreds of acres, all his own; he imagined, too, the people who would be their friends and neighbors, the southern gentry. Pam would fit there to perfection. He had noticed that sourpuss wife of DeWitt's admiring her a few minutes ago. Like seeks out like, he told himself. Old wealth, even when, as in Pam's case, it had been lost, left its aura.

"Your sister's done well for herself," Pam remarked now, "taking a big step farther up with each marriage."

"Oh, this will be the last, no question about it."

"You think so?"

"Positively," replied Eddy, feeling at the same time a jolt of memory. For Richard had come to his office only a month before to make another large investment. "Positively," he repeated.

"It's strange how different your two sisters are."

"Why? They're both pregnant," Eddy joked.

"Well, good for them!"

"Not good for you? For us?"

"Sometime, of course. People all do if they can, don't they? But the time has to be right."

He agreed. There was too much going on right now; their days were filled with work, social contacts that led to more work, genuine friends, sports, theater, music, and travel; short, quick trips to see a client somewhere in Europe; longer sojourns to see the horse shows in Ireland, or to La Scala to hear a fine voice; and surely, always, to Paris, his first love, where a permanent hotel suite was always waiting. As soon as he could manage to fit it into his schedule, New Zealand and Australia would be next. In such a life there was indeed no room for a baby. Not yet.

Pam mused, repeating herself, "It's remarkable how different they are. I don't mean physically, I mean temperamentally. Lara's so strong, much more so than Connie."

"I wouldn't say that."

"I would." She nodded. "And you'll see sometime that I'm right."

At that moment Lara was not feeling especially strong. Her feet, in the new shoes bought for this occasion, had begun to hurt. And the baby under her skirt's flounce had been doing some vigorous exercise. So Davey and she had scurried for two vacant seats in the shade of the laurel hedge, while Sue, who had found a boy about her own age, went wandering off with him.

The other two chairs were filled by two men. One was soberly middle aged, while the other, not much older than thirty, was distinguished by a head of copper-colored hair and a freckled face. The two, apparently strangers to each other, were already involved in conversation.

"Things are out of proportion," the older man was saying. "I read the other day about some tycoon who owns seven houses. One was in Morocco, one in the Fiji Islands—the Fiji Islands, by God! Can you make any sense of that?" The man's earnest tone almost verged upon anger.

"If I were a left-winger, I wouldn't. Of course, the right-winger would say that if a man earns it, he's entitled to spend it as he wishes. But then, I'm not a right-winger either." And the young man, as if he wanted to lighten the atmosphere, turned toward Davey. "What's your opinion?"

Davey, never a voluble speaker, especially on abstract subjects, hesitated a moment as if embarrassed before replying, "It's a matter of proportion, isn't it? I know I'm not against wealth." Then he laughed. "I'm even trying to accumulate a little of it for myself."

The sober one seized on these words. "Good enough. But I

wasn't talking about a little of it. I was talking about hundreds of millions. May I ask what you do?"

"I own a small plant. We manufacture electronic parts for medical uses, arterial surgery and—"

"Well. Then you're a producer. You make things that people need. You're earning honorable dollars. What I'm looking at are manipulations, junk bonds, and takeovers that end in debt." And with a dark frown he warned, "That debt will wreck the economy in the end."

"I have to agree with much of what you say," said the redhead, adding with some reluctance, "Unfortunately for me, I have to."

"Why do you say unfortunately?"

"Because I earn my living from takeovers. I work for Frazier, DeWitt, Berg."

There was a silence until, after a moment, the first man gave an embarrassed laugh. "I seem to have put my foot in it again. Old as I am, I never seem to learn." He motioned toward the animated crowd, the spring-green lawn and the house with its spreading terraces and yellow awnings. "This was hardly the place or the time for my remarks, was it?"

"No harm done, I assure you." The freckled face and the tone were both amiable. "By the way, my name's McClintock, Allen McClintock."

"I might as well put both feet in my mouth while I'm at it. My name's Berg. I'm Martin's brother."

The three others looked their astonishment. And Davey, suppressing a laugh, said quietly, "I'd better round out the story. We're the Davises, Davey and Lara. Lara is Connie's sister." But when he saw the two men's dismay, he added quickly, "Don't let it bother you. It's not important. We've forgotten it already, Lara and I."

They all stood up as if to separate, yet waited awkwardly as if not knowing how to do so. It was Allen McClintock who broke the pause.

"It looks as if they might be serving dinner, and I'm starved," he said.

So the odd-met group dispersed, joining the movement up the rise toward the house.

"Interesting and amusing," remarked Davey.

"More uncomfortable than amusing," answered Lara.

By the time they reached the house and had found Pam and Eddy, the bride and groom were already alone on the dance floor. Connie's pale dress floated, and her pale hair tumbled as they whirled. Frankly exuberant and frankly triumphant, "I could have danced all night," she sang into the faces of the smiling crowd.

To Eddy, as he watched, came the recollection of the night when those two had met at his house, and he had had a premonition of today. Charming Connie, Consuelo, he thought, their mother's darling. Well, Martin Berg might not be the Duke of Marlborough, but probably commanded greater wealth than the duke had. And Eddy's tender heart swelled with pride.

To Lara there came other memories, first of the small, demanding sister, then of the young woman leaving home because "there had to be more to life," and because "I'm not like you, Lara."

She took her husband's hand. "Isn't she beautiful? I hope she'll be happy this time, Davey!"

"Oh, Connie gets what Connie wants. But happy? That's something else," he replied.

CHAPTER
NINE

◈

T he week-old baby lay sleeping in a bassinet beside the bed
on which Lara rested. Afternoon sunlight touched her little round head and glinted on a soft, red-gold fuzz.

Eddy observed, "She's going to have Peg's hair."

Pam asked, "Are you going to call her Peggy, or will you be
formal and stay with Margaret?"

Lara laughed. "Whatever comes naturally, I guess, though we
seem to have begun with Peggy."

Martin Berg had provided his private plane for this visit, and
so there had been plenty of room to carry gifts. They had come
laden. The bassinet, a froth of white point d'esprit and pink satin
rosettes, was Pam's choice. A handsome British perambulator
with a dark blue monogrammed cover came from the Bergs,
along with a silver feeding set and an embroidered lace christen-
ing dress and, most thoughtfully, presents for Sue as well.

Eddy focused his Polaroid camera on the baby. "Connie said
to take some pictures. She was so angry that her doctor doesn't
want her to fly." He looked at his watch. "What time is that
stockholders' meeting again?"

"Half past three. Davey's picking Sue up at school, and then
you and he can go on to the plant. We're all off our schedules

this week on account of Miss Peggy." And Lara felt a smiling warmth from head to toe.

Pam wanted to know about Sue. "I don't know much about child psychology, but I know that a new arrival can cause a lot of trouble in a family."

"Well, we've tried from the very start to prepare her, and so far, so good. But of course, one has to be lucky, I'm aware of that. Oh, there they are. I hear the car."

A moment later came a clattering on the stairs. Sue and another little girl, followed more quietly by Davey, tore into the bedroom.

"Mom! Mom! I've brought my friend to see our baby. She didn't believe we have one, so I brought her."

The two children glanced briefly into the bassinet.

"Can we touch her hand?" asked Sue.

"If you're very gentle. Babies are very soft. You haven't told me your friend's name, Sue. Remember what I said about introductions?"

"Oh, yes. This is Marcy. And this is my mom. And my sister's name is Peggy. Are there any Popsicles in the freezer?"

"Yes, darling. Daddy will reach up and get them for you."

When the little group had clattered back downstairs, Lara reached for a handkerchief and blew her nose. "Excuse me, I feel a bit teary."

"Why, what's the matter?" asked Pam.

"You didn't notice, of course. But this was the first time she called me Mom." Lara looked toward the bassinet. "I'm so happy that I'm in a daze. Nothing seems quite real. How can happiness like this last?"

"Good heavens," said Pam, "I thought you were an optimist like Eddy."

"She is," Eddy said, declaring heartily, "it's real, and it will last. There's no reason why it won't."

With that he went downstairs to join Davey.

* * *

"So you've got friendly stockholders," Eddy said on the way into town. "That's one of the nice things about a small community. Sometimes I miss it."

"The hell you do!" Davey laughed. "You couldn't wait to get away from here, you know that. But it's a matter of temperament. I happen to be comfortable with smallness. Now, take my stockholders. I've told you, I've known every one of them practically from the cradle up. Doc Donnelly and Henry Baker, he's the superintendent of schools, and he was a friend of my father's, and my best friend Tony—gosh, he and his wife rushed over at two in the morning last week when I had to take Lara to the hospital. They slept on the sofa, got Sue up and ready for school, had Sue and me over for dinner—gosh, you don't make friends like them on every street corner."

He's normally so silent, Eddy thought; today he's positively euphoric. And why not, with everything finally coming together for them?

"They have total confidence in me. They know that I can run this business. This stockholders' meeting is just a formality, you might say. No one ever questions a thing I do. It's a good feeling, Eddy. Sometimes I think I'm the luckiest man in the world."

"I wonder," Eddy said, an idea having that very minute occurred to him, "whether after your meeting—incidentally, it's very nice of you to let me listen in, and I'd just as soon walk around the plant and see all your great new machines—"

"Whatever you want to do, Eddy. I only thought you might get a kick out of hearing the financial report."

"Oh, I certainly would. What I was thinking was, would you have any objection to my presenting, after the meeting, a few of my ideas about personal finances? Some of your people might be interested. Of course, this is totally apart from your company. It has nothing to do with you."

"Sure. Go ahead. It's fine with me if anybody wants to stay late."

This, Eddy reflected as he watched the proceedings, is unlike any stockholders' meeting I've ever attended. It was not a matter of numbers, but a matter of attitude that made the striking difference. Here were no challenges, no arguments, no hostile questions. This handful of men, and one decorous middle-aged lady, a prosperous widow, he guessed, were all friends. He saw distinctly what Davey had described. He recognized the honest, forthright personalities.

To introduce Eddy, Davey in his plain, frank way had made a little speech.

"This is the man who is really responsible for the birth of the company. Without him I wouldn't have gotten started. He made me put my ideas to work."

One wouldn't find many men willing to give such abundant credit to another for their success. Not in New York, not in my business, Eddy thought, reminded of the inflated egos that he so often encountered.

"And now Mr. Vernon Osborne, whom we all call Eddy, would like to say a few words."

To begin with, naturally, must come thanks and a few enthusiastic remarks about Davey and the Davis Company. After that he would come quickly to the point.

"I can't tell you how happy I was just now to learn of your fine big dividend. And I'm sure you were mighty glad to find your money working so successfully for you. However"—and here Eddy made a significant pause—"however, let's just take a second look, a look at your personal income tax returns. Oh, my! Oh, my, how many of those beautiful dollars will be yours to keep and how many belong to Uncle Sam? Now I would like to explain to you a way in which, by buying a limited partnership, you can keep a larger part of that income, or even keep the whole of it. No tax at all! Oh, yes," Eddy said in response to some expressions of surprise, "it's legal, it's simply a matter of investing in limited partnerships. You are all sophisticated investors, I'm sure, and so you understand how losses generate tax deductions. But possibly you're not familiar with ten-to-one write-offs and tax deferrals."

He was about to illustrate further when a hand went up, and the lone woman had a question.

"I'm Carol Robinson. I've been a bank vice-president, so I'm familiar with limited partnerships. In fact, I am a limited partner in a garden apartment development. But I never heard of ten-to-one. It's incredible."

"It's incredible, all right. But it's done all the time."

"You mean you invest one dollar and deduct ten dollars' worth of losses?"

Eddy nodded. "I do mean that. The write-offs in some investments can be tremendous, and not just in oil and real estate. Cattle, movies, lithographs—"

He was holding their attention. He was in his usual top form, and it was easy for him because he knew what he was doing; it was what he did every day, and he had never had a failure.

His presentation, to which he had mentally allotted less than half an hour, extended into the second hour. By the end of it he had convinced all ten of his listeners, who agreed to invest sums ranging from fifteen thousand to seventy-five. Addresses and phone numbers were exchanged, hands were shaken, and a very satisfactory meeting came to a close.

"What about you, Davey?" Eddy asked on the way home.

"I don't think so. I'd rather pay my taxes and sleep nights."

"Oh, for God's sake, Davey! Would I steer you wrong? Again I have to ask."

"It's not that. It's just—oh, you know how I am."

Eddy did not answer. Best to drop the subject instead of using one's valuable energy trying to move this—this *mule*. Sometimes Davey could be infuriating.

TREASURES

When Pam and Eddy had gone home that night, Davey sat on the edge of the bed and talked.

"I feel that he's a little sore at me, although he's too nice to show it, but I wouldn't touch that stuff with a ten-foot pole." He snorted. "Marlboro Capital Formation! Ten-to-one write-offs! Why, it's not even moral. The losses are fabricated, they're artificial, it's just a gimmick, the whole thing!"

Lara spoke mildly. "It's apparently a legal gimmick, Davey. I don't see why you're so upset."

"I don't care whether it's legal or not. It's indecent. I'm going to advise everybody who was there today not to send his check in, to steer clear of it."

"You're not!" Lara, who had been standing beside the bassinet, put her hands on her hips in defiance. "You can't be going to tell them you don't trust Eddy!"

"Of course I wouldn't say that. I'll say I don't believe in the deal, and I'm not having any part in it myself. Cattle, lithographs —good Lord!"

"I'm astonished, Davey. How can you do that to Eddy?"

"Because these people are my friends, Lara. My friends."

"But he's my brother! How can you go behind his back, how can you? Especially after all he's done for us, after all his goodness. All right, if you personally don't want to invest, but to tell other people not to is unconscionable, that's what it is."

The argument went on for a long time that night. In the end Davey agreed to keep silent.

"Maybe I am making a mountain out of a molehill," he conceded. "Maybe I am."

Connie, too, had a daughter before the year was out. She came into the world with little fuss on a blustering December afternoon shortly after the stock market's closing bell. Martin rushed uptown to the hospital, tore into Connie's room, and tore down the hall to see the baby through the nursery window.

211

When he returned his eyes were wet. "Oh," he cried, "she's lovely! Little Tessie. She's beautiful!"

Tessie, thought Connie angrily, oh, no. But she spoke calmly. "I know I promised to name her after your mother, and I will, but Tessie is really only short for Thérèse, and I do want her to be called by her full name. Also, I want it to be spelled with accents, Thérèse. That's what I really want, Martin."

"All right, all right. Tessie. Thérèse. What's the difference?"

"Thérèse. That's the French pronunciation, and it's much prettier."

"You," he teased. "My fancy French lady. And to think that your sister named her child just plain Peggy." And he chuckled. "Thérèse. What a wonderful baby! She looks a bit like Melissa."

Good Lord, I hope not, Connie thought.

Martin leaned over the bed to adjust the embroidered pillow that had been brought from home, and kissed his wife lightly as though he feared to hurt her by pressing too hard. He exulted.

"Oh, I've had more joy in my short time with you than in all the rest of my years put together!"

PART TWO
1981-1990

CHAPTER
TEN

❧

G olden times these were, not the golden years of age, but of youth spent in health and comfort. The sisters, in spite of living so far apart, were closer than ever. If Peg could know, Connie thought, she would be so thankful to see us, and to see another generation growing up. Even the two husbands got along well. Their backgrounds and experiences were surely different enough, yet because both were busy men with many interests, they were compatible. Martin's charities were on a colossal scale that frequently were front-page news, but Davey, too, could take pride, and did, in his contributions to the life of his town: a Little Theater Group, a day-care plan for his workers, a fund drive to enlarge the town library, and more.

Sometimes on a weekend when Davey was free to get away, Martin would send the company plane to pick up the Davises and bring them to Westchester for country sports or to New York for the theater, to which he was always able at the very last minute to procure the best seats. He loved putting his ample houses to use, and they were rarely empty of guests.

One fall afternoon during Thanksgiving vacation, while Davey and Sue were at the Central Park Zoo, the little girls, now three, were playing in Connie's Fifth Avenue drawing room while their mothers, along with Thérèse's Scottish nurse, watched over them. Martin had been right. Thérèse was like Melissa, pale, small sized, and serious. The child looked up at her now out of Martin's brown-gold eyes, but unlike his, hers were wistful. And within Connie two feelings struggled with each other, resentment and also a fierce, determined love. She must protect Thérèse, although against what, she could not really say, except that she would teach her how to take care of herself.

Lara's child was chuckling over a ball that kept rolling out of reach. Two large dimples appeared in her cheeks; her red-gold hair curved loosely about her charming face. And Connie wondered what Lara would be feeling if Thérèse were hers. . . . . A sudden restlessness came over her. Lara could sit all afternoon with the children, but Connie needed to move.

"Do you still feel like going to the galleries with me?"

"I wouldn't mind. What are you looking for?"

"There are a few things I've had my eye on. I'd like to see them again before the bidding tomorrow."

"I can't see where you have room for one more thing in here."

"These are for the country place. Or maybe for Palm Beach. We've gotten rid of a few awful things that Doris put there, and now we need replacements. I'll tell you something," Connie said, "half the fun is in the doing. I'm really sorry that this apartment's finally finished."

After four million dollars' worth of improvements it was magnificent. And she looked around at the moss-green antique tapestries, the gilded moldings, and the coral silk that festooned the windows. There was no drawing room in the city, none that she had been in, and she had been in the best, that could surpass it.

"There's a Cézanne that I love," she said. "But I'm not sure about it. Of course, it's a fortune, so Martin will have to see it first. Who knows? He just might not like it." She stood up. "Shall we go? Mrs. Dodd's going to take these girls for their naps, anyway."

Sculpture on pedestals and paintings on walls filled the long

216

galleries. Furniture and bibelots, antique treasures from every continent, filled lofty rooms. Lara followed Connie, who was examining and making notes.

"My decorator told me to look at a table for the Westchester house. It's to stand behind the sofa in the yellow sitting room. Here it is. Chippendale. It should go for about a hundred thousand, he says. That's quite a lot, isn't it?"

Lara was silent.

"Of course, it is a marvelous piece. Look at the pierced fretwork, Lara. Well, I'm not going higher than ninety. These decorators always exaggerate. Still, maybe I ought to consider—oh, for goodness' sake, what are you doing here?" she cried to Eddy, who had just appeared around the corner.

"Same thing you're doing here," he replied. "Looking to buy."

"Buy what?"

"A Corot. A jewel. I've been wanting one, and this one is a treasure. Want to see it?"

Eddy had become a connoisseur, and not of art only. He knew about wines and horses. He knew where the finest chefs were to be found, where to get the best pedigreed Shar Pei, and how to choose a diamond. Connie was sometimes in awe of his accomplishments.

"Lara," she said, "are you aware that our brother is a Renaissance man?"

The three went back to where the paintings were ranged. Two or three separate estates had been assembled for this sale, so that the display was varied. When they passed a wall of buttocks, of various other naked organs, and unattractive bodies of both sexes in bold embrace, Eddy grimaced.

"What they do is their business, and I don't care, but I sure as hell wouldn't pay to look at them on my walls!"

Connie peered at the name. "He's one of the rising stars. You could buy one as an investment and keep it turned to the wall in your attic until the right time to sell."

"You're laughing, but I'll tell you, I've been reading Barron's charts of auction prices, and there seems to be no limit, even for stuff like this. Maybe especially for stuff like this. Seriously, I've been going in for something new—to me, at any rate. Russian antiques. You can mix them with practically anything, and they add sparkle. What do you say, Lara?"

"I don't know anything much about art," Lara answered. "We don't see much where we live, do we? We were at the National Gallery last year when we went to Washington for Davey's birthday. I think it's so wonderful to have those precious things in museums where everybody can look at them." Then she flushed, as if she had become aware of the unintended rebuke. And making quick amends, she said, "Do let's see the Corot. Where is it?"

"I've changed my mind. And I don't want to go near it, or I'll weaken again and buy it."

"But if you wanted it so badly, why not get it?" Connie said.

Eddy's eyes wandered, searching the room. He looked vague. "I don't know. I'm sort of cutting back a little. A temporary blip in the cash flow."

Connie was astonished. "You? Cutting back?"

"Not really. Just temporary, I said. No room for a Corot this particular month, that's all." He brightened and flashed a smile, showing his fine teeth. "There'll be other things coming along next month." He looked at his watch. "I'll have to be going. Got an appointment. But say, why don't we all get together and make a date for a long weekend in Bermuda, or anywhere?"

"Not a long weekend," Lara told him, "but a short one sounds possible. Davey's got to work, you know."

"He works too hard. He should get away more often before he tires himself out."

"You look tired yourself, Eddy," Lara said.

He straightened up. He puffed his tie and smiled again. "Do I?

Well, it's nothing that a good night's sleep won't fix. Hey, I'm late. Be in touch."

"He really doesn't look well," Lara insisted as soon as he was out of hearing.

Connie shrugged. "I don't know. The other night Martin thought that he looked harried. But Martin can't figure him out, anyway. He likes Eddy, although he can't understand how he's made money so fast. Of course, Martin came up the long road himself."

"I'm worried about Eddy. The way he acted just now—"

"He's probably been up all night. They live a kind of crazy life, if you ask me. Disco half the night, horseback riding—they've got a thing about dawn riding on the beach. Now Pam says he wants to buy a sloop, wants to get into the Bermuda races. He thinks Martin should get one too." Connie giggled. "Can you imagine Martin tugging on ropes in a rough sea? Goodness knows what Eddy will think up next. I can't imagine. Can you?"

No, Lara could not. So much of what she saw, in both Connie's and Eddy's lives, was far outside of her ken. And it always seemed excessive, regardless of its propriety. However, to each his own, and she would not judge.

"I can't imagine, either, Connie," she said. "It's all foreign to me."

Eddy strode rapidly across Madison Avenue to his office. He had dawdled too long at the gallery. Damn, he'd had his heart set on that Corot! It was such a beautiful thing. But he wasn't in the mood. Face it, he told himself, you wouldn't have any real joy in it, the way you feel right now.

Bad luck, that's all it was. It had always worked before. Or almost always. And it would have to be those folks out in Ohio who got caught. You never knew with the IRS. Dealing with them was like sticking your hand into a grab bag. You could come across a commonsense, reasonable examiner, or, just as easily, some troublemaking nitpicker. The law was whatever the person who happened to be interpreting it said it was.

Well, but Abner Saville would know. Abner was one of the smartest accountants in the city. And Eddy hastened his steps toward his office, where Abner, in his calm, rational way, would surely quiet his jangling nerves.

"You sounded awfully upset when you asked me to come over," Abner began as soon as he entered the room. "You worried me."

"Did I? Well, I guess I was a little upset. It's not like me, is it? But I've had a couple of nasty telephone calls in these last few days, that's why, and I'm not used to stuff like that."

Abner's black eyebrows rose in mild surprise. "Nasty? What about?"

"I sold a bunch of tax shelters a few years back when I was in Ohio. My sister's husband has a business with ten or twelve stockholders, all his friends. And they all bought limited partnerships from me. Now it seems the IRS is going to disallow the deductions." Eddy sighed. "God damn, the deal was beautiful too. Ten to one."

The black eyebrows rose higher into a troubled, puckered forehead. A low whistle came from Saville's lips.

"Ten to one, Eddy! What the devil! They can't have been real estate partnerships."

"No. Lithographs."

"Oh, for God's sake! I could have told you that would never wash."

"It has washed."

"Yes? How many times."

"Well, once. It's been five years, and not a word from the government."

"So it slipped by once. A fluke. You should never have inveigled people into buying such garbage. I have to tell you so."

220

TREASURES

"*Garbage* isn't a nice word, Abner." Eddy's tone was sorrowful. "And *inveigled* isn't either."

"Maybe not, but you're a most persuasive salesman, Eddy. And you're also a keen investor. You should have known that deductions like those make no financial sense and that the government was bound to catch up with them."

This was not the comfort that he had expected to receive from Abner.

Next Abner said, "I note that you don't personally invest in such stuff."

"No. I make my profits from the commissions." And as Abner offered no comment, he protested, "Nobody's done as much successful business in shelters as I have, and the whole city knows it."

"I'm afraid the government knows it too."

"What do you mean by that?"

"Eddy, the IRS is starting to go after fake losses in a big, big way. And you are a most conspicuous purveyor of fake losses."

"They're not 'fake' losses!"

"Eddy, you know better. You've been my client for a long time, a very important one, and a very good friend besides. It's no pleasure for me, I assure you, to disagree with you."

"Yes," Eddy grumbled, "everything's fine when it's fine. Then everybody loves you. But let something go wrong once, and it's another story."

"Tell me about the phone calls."

"Oh, these people are in a frenzy. One woman called me a fraud and started to cry, another said his accountant told him he would never have let him buy in if he had been consulted and that it was a disgrace, and so on and so on. A bunch of hysterics. And as I said, unfortunately, they're all friends of my sister and her husband. It's a small-town affair—they know each other inside out, they know what everybody had for breakfast yesterday."

221

There was a silence, during which Eddy felt the pounding of his heart; then the prime question burst.

"All I want to know is: Can they sue me for anything?"

Abner grimaced. "No, it wasn't fraud on your part. You just gave them terrible, terrible advice. But it surely doesn't do much for your reputation, Eddy, when you go peddling stuff like that."

"Fortunately, they're all far away in Ohio. No, come, I don't mean that. I'm really sorry for them all, sorry it turned out badly."

"It will be bad, all right. Back taxes, penalties, and interest besides. No fun."

"But they can't sue me, you're sure."

"I'm sure." Abner stood up. "But before I leave, I'd like to give you some advice, Eddy."

Momentarily more cheerful, Eddy managed a smile. "What? Again?"

"Yes, again. I'm not happy about your tax deferrals. Some of your figures puzzle me. They're on the edge. I need to go over your books very, very carefully during the next few months. I advise you to stop playing at brinkmanship, Eddy. You know what I mean. A word to the wise, and all that."

Saville gave with one hand and took away with the other. It was a vast relief to know that he wasn't going to be sued. But the talk of "brinkmanship" left him with a feeling of insecurity, compounded with a certain resentment at being challenged. Arriving in the outer hall at home, he did not announce himself with his customary signal whistle.

Pam greeted him with a kiss. "Smell the paella? That's your dinner. Crabs, chicken, ham, fish, and plenty of garlic. I think we've got ourselves a marvelous cook at last. Why, what's the matter? You look bushed."

He wished people wouldn't always comment on his appearance, so he answered merely, "I'm fine, but it was a long day."

A man didn't bring his troubles home with him, especially

when there was nothing a wife could do about them. It would be like Pop's thumping heavily up the stairs with yet another burden of bad news. Remembering, Eddy shuddered.

They were having their after-dinner coffee when the telephone rang. Pam answered.

"It's Davey. He wants to talk to you."

Eddy stifled a sigh. "I'll take it in the den. Please hang up."

Anticipating another long, defensive explanation, he settled into an armchair and cheerfully covering his dread, began, "Hello, Davey. How's everything?"

Davey's answer was glum. "Bad. Very bad."

"Bad? What's happened?"

"Eddy, let's not play games. You know what's happened."

"About the partnerships, you mean? The tax examiners?"

"Every single person who bought one has been called for an audit. And every one has been told by his accountant that he doesn't stand a chance. Not a chance."

"Wait, hold on! I think you're jumping at conclusions. The principals here in New York, the guys who produce the lithographs—I know they'll put up a fight, you can bet on that. They've got more to lose, after all, and—"

"That's bunk, Eddy. I myself went up to Cleveland to check with a friend, a fellow I knew at school, who works for the IRS, and that's bunk."

Eddy's first thought was: He went to Cleveland before he even talked to me; he has no confidence in me. His next thought was: What does he want of me now?

The accusing voice grew louder as Davey resumed. "My friend Tony will lose the whole inheritance from his aunt and more besides because, to make things worse, he borrowed from his cousin—hell, the details don't matter. But his cousin's not speaking to him, and Tony's not speaking to me."

"That's ridiculous. Why should he be sore at you?"

"I'm the one who recommended your judgment, remember?"

What does he want of me? An apology? Well, all right, he's entitled to one, if that's what he wants.

"Davey, I'm sorry as hell," Eddy said softly. "God knows my intentions were of the best. But that doesn't do anyone much good, I know. And still you have to admit that there are risks in any investment, whether it's a horse, or a house, or—anything." He finished stumbling, pushed as he was into an unfamiliar defensiveness and resenting it.

"It seems that this was less an investment than it was a gamble. The deal was so badly structured that every man who looked at it was dumbfounded."

"That's a matter of opinion. I don't happen to agree. I've built a reputation in this city doing deals for hundreds of millions of dollars, deals that your people, I don't care who they are, never saw and never dreamed of."

"I don't think you should be resentful, Eddy. If anyone should be, I should. And I am resentful. Every one of my stockholders, my trusting friends, is my enemy now because of this."

"That's ridiculous," Eddy repeated.

"You may think so, but that's how it is. Lara can't even walk into Levy's to buy socks for the kids, she's so ashamed to face Ben."

Never in all their years had he known Davey to be so agitated. Davey, gone over to the attack! This thing was escalating. . . .

"I'm sorry. I've said I am. What more do you want me to do? I don't know what else to do."

The reply was cold. "Don't you?"

"No, I don't."

"I know what I would do if I were in your position."

"Suppose you tell me, then."

"If I had the wealth you are reputed to have, I would make it up to those people."

Eddy jumped in the chair. "What? You can't mean that."

"I mean it. I most surely do."

TREASURES

"Well, if you do, that's the most goddamned stupid thing I've heard in a long time. You expect me to reach into my own pocket? For God's sake, Davey! Look here, they made an investment, it went sour, and that's too bad. I have no legal obligation to any of those people, and if they have any such ideas—"

"I'm talking about a moral obligation. When a widow puts her trust in you, and at my recommendation—"

"Don't preach, Davey. Get real. I've always admired your principles, but there comes a point when they become unreal. Do you think I have no principles? It's naive to—"

"So you don't intend to do anything. Just let them all down. That's it, is it? You led them to the water, and you're going to let them drown."

Oh, my God, what a day! That weepy widow, and Abner, and now Davey's loud complaints ringing in his ears. Eddy's nerves, those steady, healthy nerves that so seldom even made their presence known to his body, were quivering.

"Look, Davey, I don't know what to make of you. I've never known you to be so unreasonable. Frankly, you're driving me to my wits' end over this sorry business, which I regret, I deeply regret, how many times do I have to tell you, so will you kindly let me alone, just let me alone tonight, for God's sake, will you—"

"Oh, I'll let you alone, all right. You can bet I'll do that. I'll let you so alone that you'll forget I exist."

Who of the two first hung up the telephone it was impossible to say. For a long minute, needing to collect himself, Eddy sat still. He was completely frustrated. He was angry, he was humiliated, and he was sad. How could this have happened to Eddy Osborne, the conciliator, who avoided argument, above all in his family?

But it had happened, and how it was to be resolved he did not know.

*　　*　　*

225

These were dark days in Ohio, miserable days under the wintry sky.

"Is this to be another wasteful feud like the one between Connie and me?" demanded Lara. "Every time I talk to Pam, it looks more hopeless, and we feel terrible about it. She can't get anywhere with Eddy, and I can't get anywhere with you."

"I'm tired of talking about it," Davey answered wearily. "And I have to think you don't really understand my position."

"Well, I'm not the only one. Connie says that Martin's position is: Let the buyer beware."

"Oh, beautiful! I wonder how Martin would like to come up against the faces that I'll confront at the next stockholders' meeting. Standing there at the head of the table, feeling the outrage directed straight at me!"

As soon as the business of the meeting had been dispensed with, and as the shuffle of departure began, Davey called for attention. His heart beat almost painfully, yet he knew he must speak from that heart if only to relieve it of its burden.

"I want to say something to all of you. I'll only be a minute. I find it hard to breathe these days. The atmosphere has been very heavy. You avoid me. You, my friends." For a moment he had to stop. "Oh, I know you've been hurt in the pocketbook, some of you badly hurt. Joe, I know you bought in to provide for your boy's education. Doc Donnelly, I know you were planning to help your retirement. Dick, you were my coach in Little League. . . . Would I hurt you?" Here Davey had to stop again. Then he threw his hands out toward the whole assemblage in a gesture of appeal. "Tell me, do you think I would deliberately hurt you?"

A silence that Davey found extraordinary, even ominous, then followed. He looked around the table, but no eyes were raised to his.

Then someone spoke. It was Henry Baker, the superintendent of schools, a man known for his sharp, outspoken tongue.

226

"You should have advised us against the investment. But he's your brother-in-law, so you didn't. That sums it up, I think."

"Why should I have, Henry? I had no reason to think it wasn't a sound investment."

"Not true, Davey. You had your doubts, and now you're cornered. No, Davey. You must have suspected something, or else you would have gone in too. Mighty strange that you didn't."

At this ten pairs of eyes came to rest on Davey's face.

"I'm well aware that it doesn't sound convincing, yet the truth is simply that I—I personally don't invest in anything but this company of ours."

"You're right, it doesn't sound convincing," said Henry Baker.

"Of what are you accusing me? I don't understand. Did I make a profit out of this fiasco, for God's sake?"

"No, but your brother-in-law did."

"So is this going to go on till the end of time? Am I to be shunned like a leper because of my wife's brother?"

"You can't expect us all to have the same respect for your judgment that we once had. That's putting it plainly. But you asked for it, so there it is. The plain, harsh truth."

Dr. Donnelly said quietly, "Time. Time will ease things. Now I suggest that we call it a day, shall we?"

I am as bruised, Davey thought driving home, as if I had been beaten. "No more respect for my judgment," the man said. And I saw by their faces that they all agreed.

The late February evening was still fairly light after supper, when Peggy, bringing her snowsuit, asked to go outside. Lara, while fastening the suit, kept talking furiously over the child's head.

"They have no right to be blaming you, or Eddy either. They were willing enough to save tax money. It looked pretty tempting to them, didn't it?"

Davey's thoughts were back at the meeting. "The air congealed. I froze in it. The hostility . . ."

"You'd think they were all going to jail! All right, the IRS disallowed it and they have to pay up. It's not fun, but it's not the worst thing in the world either. Oh," Lara said, "I saw Doc Donnelly's wife at the hardware store, and she pretended she didn't see me. It's disgusting."

He had no more heart for analyzing or explaining; this night was only a repetition of a dozen other nights. And yet he had to add something new.

"If I had invested with them, it would be different. This way it looks suspicious, as if I hadn't believed in Eddy. Or I should have advised them not to believe in the project. As I didn't believe in it! Only, damn it, you wouldn't let me, Lara, remember? You said he had done so much for us and it would be awful to undermine him, and—"

"Well, he had done for us, hadn't he?"

"Anybody in your family you'll defend. Especially Eddy."

"My memory isn't that short, if yours is. He's the salt of the earth. He's entitled to a mistake."

"Some mistake!"

"I never thought you'd be an ingrate, Davey Davis— Oh, for heaven's sake, who's at the back door?"

Someone was pounding, rattling the knob. Lara ran.

"Whatever do you want?" she began. And then, at the sight of Sue's face in the glass top-half of the door, she cried, "What? What happened?"

The child was terrified. "Peggy! She fell down the Burkes' stairs. I don't know—" she began to cry. "She won't move! Oh, Mom, she won't move!"

They flew. In the neighbor's floodlit front yard a little group had already gathered at the bottom of the long flight of stone steps. Behind a barricade of legs and stooped backs a short, limp leg in a snowsuit was all that was visible; Lara had to thrust through the barricade before she could see her baby—her baby, whose cap had fallen off, whose hair lay spread upon the snow, whose eyes were closed. She fell on her knees. No sound came out of her throat.

A voice said, "Don't move her. You're not supposed to. I took first aid."

Another voice above Lara's head kept asking, "What happened? What happened?"

More voices babbled. "The ambulance will be here in a minute. . . . They take so long. . . . Don't touch her. . . ."

Sue wept on Lara's shoulder. "Mom, Mom, I was in Amy's house next door, and Peggy must have been looking for me at the Burkes', and slipped on the ice—oh, Mom!"

But Lara still said nothing, as she knelt there staring at her child.

Davey put his head against Peggy's chest. As if one could hear a heartbeat through that thick cloth! He looked up at Lara.

"She's fainted. That's all it is. She's fainted." Then, with a queer, awkward gesture, he put his hands over his face and someone led him away.

People helped Lara climb into the ambulance, where she and Davey sat beside the stretcher. Endlessly they rode through the empty nighttime streets. The day that had begun with a thaw had turned into a bitter, angry night. Lara had never been so cold. Her teeth chattered so that she could hear them. Imploring, she looked up into the eyes of the young man in the white coat who sat at the head of the stretcher.

"She isn't dead, ma'am," he said, answering the unspoken question.

Lara nodded. Her thoughts spun, repeating themselves in some strange, determined ritual: If I keep quiet and calm, if I do everything they tell me to do, not scream or fuss or lose control, then I will be rewarded for good behavior and she will be fine again. Yes, yes, I must. I will. Her hands clasped themselves together on her lap as if in prayer. Then Davey put his hand over hers, and they sat, still without speaking, never taking their eyes away from Peggy, who had not yet moved.

Lights from the emergency wing glared into the courtyard, giving forth the only warmth and brightness in the freezing town. The light looked friendly. Once they got inside there, it would somehow be all right. People there would know at once what to do.

Such a tiny body in her overalls and T-shirt, such a small body next to such big ones all in white! Doctors, nurses, interns; who was who? Lara did not heed; Davey did the talking off in a corner. Low, hurried voices spoke and came back again to look, to touch, and listen. Peggy's labored breathing was like a snore— a dreadful sound, but at least it proved that she was alive. The man in the ambulance had said she wasn't dead, hadn't he? Pay attention to that, Lara! She isn't dead.

They were taking her blood pressure. They were listening to her heart.

"No blood in the lungs," announced a young man with a stethoscope around his neck.

But surely that was blood seeping out of her ears? Still almost speechless, Lara pointed.

"That's from the skull fracture," the young man said. "A skull fracture need not be as dreadful as it sounds."

He meant to be kind. "Need not be." What did that mean? It meant that it could be.

Now Peggy's little face began to swell. One could almost see it happening as the flesh rose, black and blue. A crust of blood had hardened on one cheek. As Lara bent to wipe it away, she was gently restrained.

"That's nothing, only a skin scrape."

"But will she wake up soon?" It was her first question, a foolish one, she knew as she was asking it.

Davey shook his head, warning: Don't distract them. They

know what they're doing. And he said aloud, "Darling, it takes time."

"But look," Lara whispered, "look, her lips are moving."

Indeed, the child was shaping her mouth into an unnatural grimace, an expression that they had never seen before.

"She's unconscious," repeated Davey.

A little more than an hour ago she had been eating banana pudding at home.

And suddenly the little body stiffened, rose into an arc, straightened, arched again with head thrown back and legs jerking while her arms flailed frantically from side to side.

"My God!" cried Lara, grasping Davey's arm.

They were putting a tongue depressor into Peggy's mouth and holding her firmly.

"A seizure," a nurse told Lara. "Look away. It will be over in a minute or two."

"But why? Why?" Lara wailed.

"Perhaps you had better take Mrs. Davis out," said the doctor, who now appeared to be the one in charge. An older man, he had just arrived, hurrying as though he had been summoned from a distance.

"No," Lara protested. "No. I'll be quiet. Please. Please."

When the seizure ended as abruptly as it had begun, the child lay back inert, and the slow, noisy breathing resumed as before. Davey was motioned aside. Again there was swift talk at the far end of the room, and again he came back to Lara.

"They'll be taking her for X rays of the chest and skull. And after that, an electroencephalogram."

So she knew. She knew enough about brain damage to understand what was happening. If she had had any thoughts—and she had had them—about swift repairs in this emergency room, after which they would take Peggy home as good as new, she now knew better.

* * *

231

Hours in the intensive care unit were to follow. Now came the specialists, the otolaryngologists, the ophthalmologists, and the neurologists to observe, to test, to prescribe, and mostly, in the end, to counsel patience. As the hours went past, they spoke more guardedly and less frequently of hope. No nuance of their voices or their glances escaped Lara and Davey. Admitting nothing to each other, they did not have to admit anything, for the fact was plain: The child was still unconscious.

Every third hour the parents were allowed to see her. And the pathetic silly sentence kept sounding in Lara's head: She was eating banana pudding, sitting on the other side of the table next to Sue.

They had almost forgotten Sue. At home, on the first night of the disaster, each had asked the other whether he had told Sue to watch Peggy in the yard, and each had answered, "No. I thought you had."

"So that's why she was at Amy's that night. Peggy left the house a bit later, I remember now. We were arguing," Lara said, and wept again. "Arguing, like fools."

On the second day Connie flew in and met Lara in the waiting room outside the intensive care unit.

"Sue phoned me. Poor child, she could hardly talk. Oh, Lara, what can I do for you?" Connie lowered her voice. Two middle-aged women, farm wives perhaps, were staring in frank curiosity at her sweeping fur coat. "And Martin says if you need anything, if you run short, Davey must let him know. You understand? I'm going to stay a few days. Davey says you haven't rested at all. You have to go home and sleep, Lara. I'll take your turn here watching."

"I can't sleep. I haven't slept. Anyway, Davey will be here."

"He needs rest too. And he has to spend some time at the plant. It can't be allowed to fall apart, he says. So I'm staying for a few days. Don't argue."

"I can't sleep, anyway. I told you."

TREASURES

"You can try. If Peggy wakes up, I'll be here. She knows me, and I'll telephone you right away and tell her you're coming. Now go home."

On the next day Eddy arrived with Pam. Pam took Lara into her arms, but Eddy went first to embrace Davey.

"Davey, Davey, there are no words for this. I take back every mean word I said to you that night. God help us all."

Davey's eyes were wet. "It's all unimportant, not worth a breath. Only our baby matters. . . . Thank you for being here, Eddy."

From everywhere came an outpouring of concern and help. Neighbors took Sue to school, watched the house, and fed the dogs. The telephone rang, the mail flowed; there were fifty names on a huge card from Peggy's nursery school. Even those who had felt so bitterly unforgiving toward Davey came through. Dr. Donnelly's wife took Sue to play with her grandchild. Ben Levy left a roasted turkey at the kitchen door. And Henry Baker, meeting Davey at the gas station, came up and took his hand.

Without animosity Davey could not refrain from asking sadly, "Still won't trust my judgment, Henry?"

The reply was not unkind, yet it was unmistakably firm. "That's entirely separate from your little girl. The one has nothing to do with the other. I pray for the child."

Later that week Lara came home to find a message on the answering machine. Sue had not gone to school that morning.

The three adults, Lara, Davey, and Connie, stared at each other. Is it possible for another disaster to strike this little family? Davey asked himself.

"She had her schoolbag," Lara said, "I remember that distinctly. I watched her go down to meet the car pool."

"Who drove today?"

"Lee Connor. I'll call her."

When she returned to the others, Lara's eyes were terrified. "Lee says Sue telephoned her this morning to say she wasn't going to school." Lara sank down on the sofa. "I don't think—I just don't think we can bear one thing more." Her voice quavered.

Davey cleared his throat. "We mustn't panic. Think clearly. Don't get excited. Think clearly."

He has to play the male role, Connie thought with pity. He's not supposed to show that he's shocked to death. Lara can show it, but he doesn't dare to.

Aloud she said, "Give me a list of her friends, and I'll make phone calls. She's probably gone with one of them to the movies or the mall."

"Sue wouldn't do that," Lara said faintly. "She's very responsible, very obedient."

"Even so. There's always a first time, and she's getting to the independent age. Give me a list, Lara."

"There's one on the bulletin board in the kitchen. I'm class mother."

After eighteen calls Connie, receiving no clue, began to feel weak in the knees herself. The world was so full of horrors! Could the child possibly have become involved with an older boy and gone to meet him someplace? Some pervert, some killer? One heard of all kinds of terrible things on the news.

When she came back from the kitchen, she found Davey and Lara still where she had left them, staring into space as if devoid of energy or the ability to think. Somebody would have to think for them.

"I have a hunch she might have gone to the movies," Connie said, trying to sound positive.

Davey frowned. "What makes you think that?"

"Because I remember once when I was about eleven or twelve I was so furious at my parents about something, I forget what, I went off to the movies all alone and sat there sulking through two double features." There was no response from anyone. "Listen," Connie said, feigning a vigor that she did not have. "I'm going to ride down to the theater and take a look, just in case. I'll want your station wagon. Maybe I should try the mall too. Kids like to hang out in malls. Are there any particular places where I should look, Lara?"

"The record shop, I guess," Lara said, still so faintly that Connie almost missed the words. "And she likes thick shakes."

The matinee was ending when Connie drew up at the theater. At once she saw that there were no children among the scanty crowd of retired oldsters; this was, after all, a school day. Next she tried the mall, which, being merely a small strip, was easily scanned from end to end. On the way back home with no success, she had a cold, sick feeling in her stomach.

Determined, nevertheless, to keep up a positive attitude, she walked briskly into the kitchen. Lara and Davey were at the kitchen table, each with a coffee cup in hand. It was after six o'clock, and no dinner was in evidence.

"What about food?" she demanded. "I know you don't feel hungry, but we have to keep our wits about us, and that's impossible when the stomach's empty."

"I can't swallow," Lara said. "But there's plenty in the refrigerator. Help yourself. There's a whole roast that the Burkes sent over."

Connie opened the refrigerator. "I don't see it," she said.

"It's right there."

"It's not."

Lara got up and looked. "That's strange. It was there this morning."

"Perhaps it's not so strange. Look and see whether any other food is missing."

Bewildered, Lara moved her gaze slowly around the kitchen, and then, as if in a daze, reported, "I'm sure I left the fruit bowl filled with apples and pears. And there was a pie that somebody gave us in the cake box."

Connie's thoughts took swift shape. "How has she been acting lately?"

Lara raised her weary eyes. "Upset, of course, like the rest of us."

Davey spoke. "She's been very quiet." And then he added, "But I guess I don't really know, Connie. We haven't been paying much attention to anything except—"

Connie interrupted. "I want to see her room."

"Oh! You're thinking she's run away! But why should she run away?" implored Lara.

Connie was already halfway up the stairs while the others followed her into Sue's room. Her immediate impression was of abandonment; it was as if these inanimate things, the four flowered walls and the bed where lay no carelessly dumped sweaters, jackets, or schoolbooks, were giving a message. Opening the closet door, she saw an even row of pretty clothes, some of which she recognized because they were her own gifts.

"Is anything missing?" she asked Lara.

"The doll. The one we gave her on the day we met. It always sits on the bed," said Lara, choking.

Davey pointed to the piggybank, whose china head had been broken open.

The pattern of Connie's thought, growing clearer, filled her with an urgent sense of haste. And she demanded, "Tell me quickly what clothes are missing and how much money was in the bank."

"Maybe seventy-five dollars. Her warm jacket's missing, and her boots." Lara opened drawers. "I think some sweaters are gone. But I don't know, I can't tell—" And she collapsed on the edge of the bed with her face in her hands.

"Darling," Connie said, "I know it's hell, but we've got to face it. So far it's plain that Sue's run away. She hasn't been waylaid and murdered on her way to school, we know that, and she hasn't been kidnapped for ransom, thank God. The job now is just to go after her."

Davey was pacing back and forth. At the end of the room, each time he turned, a loose floorboard made a maddening squeak. More to himself than to anyone he groaned, "And how am I to do that? Go after her? Where? And we have Peggy, neither dead nor alive, and the doctor wants a consultation in the morning."

The telephone rang. As if instant hope had been injected into them, all three ran to where it jangled in the bedroom across the hall. Davey picked it up. In the next instant hope receded.

"It's Martin for you," he said, handing the receiver to Connie.

"I suppose," Martin said, "that there's been no change, or you'd have let me know. So in that case you'd better come home."

"I can't." Davey and Lara had politely left her alone, so she spared no words. "Martin, there's total disaster here." And she told him about the missing child.

His low whistle carried into Connie's ear. "My God! What next? The police have been notified, of course?"

"Davey'll do that now. But there are thousands of missing children, and I personally wouldn't leave it to the police. I believe in some self-help. A little private-detective, thinking for oneself."

"Meaning what?"

"Meaning that I'm going to stay here for a while and have a try at it. These two people are in no condition to handle any more trouble."

"Listen to me," Martin said, "this is ridiculous. You are not a private detective. You're not to go playing games, Connie."

She was offended. "Games! As if this weren't deadly serious!"

"Yes, deadly. A deadly game. You don't know the whole story. The child could have been lured away by God knows whom, and you could end up—Listen to me, you have a child of your own back home here, and you can't afford to take chances with your own safety. I want you to come home tomorrow, and I'm sending the plane for you."

"Martin, I can't."

"You have been there a week, and that's long enough," he shouted.

"It would be," she persisted, "if this hadn't happened today. It would be inhuman to leave them now in this situation. So I'm not leaving. *Not*, Martin."

"That's your final word?" Martin never liked long conversations.

"It is."

She had never defied him, had never had any reason to. When he slammed the receiver down, she knew he was frustrated and furious. But he would have to get over it.

Davey had been using another telephone line downstairs to appeal to the police.

"She hasn't been gone long enough," he reported. "They can't go searching for every kid who decides to run off to his grandma's for the night, they told me."

"The difference is," observed Connie, "that she has no grandma. And I've called all her friends."

"She's taken her suitcase," Lara said.

"She's got money, food, and clothes, so she has a plan. The question is, where would she be going? Whom does she know?" Connie reflected.

"But why? Why?" Lara cried again.

"We'll find that out when we find her, Lara."

"If we find her!"

Or if, Connie thought, if some monster doesn't find her first. The darkness was black beyond the window, black and forbidding. She mused aloud. "The only people she knows outside of us are Pam and Eddy. So maybe she went there."

Lara cried out again, "Call Pam!"

TREASURES

"You're not thinking," Connie spoke gently. "If Sue had already reached there, they would have telephoned us. So why worry them? But she might be on her way. I'm going down to the bus station."

Neither Davey nor Lara objecting, she went for her coat and bag. At the door she called out, "What color is her jacket?"

"Navy blue with a red-and-white striped collar," Lara called back helplessly.

At the local bus station Connie gave a description and asked a question. Did anyone remember seeing such a child alone boarding a bus to the connecting major bus routes? No, no one did.

"She's probably—or she might be—catching a bus to New York."

"Our last bus makes the connection to the terminal. We leave in an hour," the man said.

"No, I'll drive."

The old station wagon bucked and rattled over the road. Damn kid! Connie thought in a moment of anger. As if the family hadn't enough to cope with right now! What could have been in her head? A wonderful home, plenty of love, she muttered. But Sue was an earnest child, not given to caprice. Some terrible trouble must have compelled her. She wasn't old enough to have gotten herself pregnant, was she?

It was after ten when Connie arrived at the bus station. Light from the ticket window sent a painful yellow glare into the night. A few disconsolate souls with tired faces sat with their bundles and baggage in the waiting room.

"Bus for New York?" she inquired.

"Tomorrow morning."

She stood there, then, as disconsolate as anyone in the room. What to do? Then something drove her to ask a question that, considering the daily traffic in that place, was probably foolish.

"Do you by any chance remember selling a ticket to a little girl about eleven or twelve years old today, traveling alone?"

"Lady, I'd need a memory like an elephant" was the contemptuous answer.

"Maybe," Connie persisted, seeing two other people behind the counter, "one of them remembers. Please ask, will you?"

"Hey, seen a little girl about eleven traveling alone?"

A woman came forward. "Come to think of it, I did, and I wondered about it. She bought a ticket for Chicago. Said she wanted to go to Minnesota, and I told her she'd need to make a connection in Chicago. Yes, I wondered. Lots of kids travel alone, but usually not that far. I figured she was going to be met by a relative."

"Thank you," Connie said, "thank you very much."

Now to think. In a place this size there could be a dozen little girls buying tickets every day. But not for that distance, the woman said. And Minnesota, where Sue had come from. Was it possible that she could want to return to another round of dreary foster homes? Not likely. This would most probably end as a wild goose chase. No, it wasn't Sue. And yet it might be.

Now it was cold and late, Connie was starved and tired, Martin was angry, and Thérèse missed her.

Yet, she got up and bought a ticket to Chicago. Lara's car was in the parking lot. To hell with it. If someone steals it, I'll buy her another, she thought as the bus rolled in.

The ride was miserable. On one side a man snored, while on the other a pathetic, uncomfortable infant cried. The bus rolled past bleak, sleeping towns, stopping here and there to discharge or take on passengers. One had to wonder what errands took people jolting across the country through the long, dismal night instead of lying at home under warm blankets. She wondered whether any of these people had ever gone on an errand like hers.

It was raining when they reached Chicago in the early morning. Famished by now, grimy and red-eyed because she had not slept, Connie rushed to inquire about a connection to Minneapolis.

This time there was a pleasant person at the ticket window, pleasant and also surprised.

"Yes, yes! There was a little girl here. She wanted to buy a ticket to Minneapolis, but didn't have enough money, I remember. She seemed about to cry, and I didn't know what to do, so I wrote out directions to the railroad station and told her to find Travelers' Aid there. I figured they'd help her. Afterward I thought I probably should have called the police," he finished.

Of course you should have, Connie thought with indignation at such well-meaning stupidity. But she thanked him and made her own way to consult Travelers' Aid. There the woman at the desk had just come on duty and knew nothing about the previous day's occurrences. Connie would have to wait until afternoon.

It was a long, long day. She bought a frankfurter and coffee, her first food since yesterday's lunch, and sat eating this odd breakfast within view of the Travelers' Aid desk, then managed a face and hands' wash in the rest room and rushed back to the desk. She was so tense, so charged up, that she was hardly aware now of having gone twenty-four hours without sleep.

And yet she fell into a doze, sitting straight up on the hard bench, and was awakened by someone speaking to her.

"You're the person who's looking for a little girl on the way to Minneapolis?" a woman asked.

Connie sprang up. "I'm her aunt. What can you tell me?"

"I spoke to her yesterday. She's a runaway, of course."

"Yes, yes. Where is she?"

"I don't know. She wouldn't tell me her name, and apparently I asked too many questions, because she ran from me, and I lost her in the crowd. I felt terrible. Such a well-spoken child, an attractive little blond—"

Blond? Not Sue, after all! Connie released a long, anguished sigh.

"Oh, I'm sorry, it wasn't Sue. She has dark hair. Strange, because things seemed to tie together, Minneapolis and—"

"Actually, it was a town not far from there. She was going to her grandmother's, Elmer, the name was, and she'd lost her money."

Elmer. Connie had a keen memory. Surely that was the name Lara had mentioned.

"Yes. We called information and even checked with the post office in the town. The woman has either moved away or else the post office people said they thought she'd died. So it was all a puzzle. And when I questioned the child, that's when she ran off."

It had to be Sue. . . .

"You said she was blond."

"I might be wrong about that. But I'm positively right about the name."

People hurried by, racing for trains, jostling each other, each intent on his affairs. One felt the world's indifference, standing there, not knowing where to turn.

Then Connie said aloud, "I just don't know what to do."

"You know, I have a hunch that she might come back here. It's beastly cold on the streets, she can't just wander aimlessly through the city, and this is a kind of shelter, in a way."

Connie looked into the vast space, into the crowds.

"Then you think I'd do well to wait a little."

"I do. If she doesn't return, then I'd say go home and leave it to the police."

The thought of bringing this defeat back to Lara and Davey kept Connie going for another hour, and yet another hour or two, until at last, toward evening, she had to give up. Years later, she was to tell of her panic upon finding that in her haste at Lara's house, she had forgotten to check her wallet, and now found herself in this strange city with no credit cards and not enough money to fly home. There she sat, with a Bulgari watch on her wrist, Martin's eight-carat diamond on her finger, and an alligator bag that held just about enough cash to pay for the long bus ride back to Ohio and no more.

Beaten and exhausted, she made her way to the bus station, where sat another dejected group with its burdens and baggage, ready for a long ride through the night. There was half an hour to wait, so she bought a paper to fill the time and was too tired to read it. Half dozing, she was jarred awake by a little flurry of talk, and opening her eyes, beheld—a policeman holding Sue by the hand, a bedraggled, dirty-faced, tearstained Sue.

And she would remember Sue's story, told between sobs on Connie's shoulder while the curious watched and listened.

"I thought they hated me, they never talked to me, it was my fault about Peggy, I always watched her when we went outside, and if Peggy dies, it'll be really my fault and I thought maybe Mrs. Elmer would take me back, there isn't anybody else. . . ."

"But they love you so much, Sue! And it wasn't your fault about Peggy. They never thought it was. You had nothing to do with it. It was an accident, just an awful accident. And if anything bad happens—you know what I'm thinking of—all three of you will need to be extra good to each other and help each other. Don't ever do anything like this again, Sue. Don't break all our hearts. Will you promise?"

"I wanted to call home and tell them where I was, but I was afraid they'd be angry at me. I knew it was awful, what I did. Besides, I had no money for the telephone. It dropped out of my pocket someplace. It must have dropped out when I went to buy a chocolate bar. The turkey was all gone, and I was hungry."

"Oh, poor darling!"

The policeman said, "We found her sitting on a step down near the river, and brought her to the station house. Then we called home, and her father said we might put her on the bus, and he would meet it." He put his hand on Sue's shoulder. "Listen, little girl, I have a girl just your age, and I know what your father and mother must have been going through. I think you've almost given them a heart attack. Now, you promise never to do that again, do you?"

Sue sniffed and nodded. "I slept all night in the waiting room at the station, Aunt Connie. It was awful. Nobody came. Nobody cared."

I can believe it, Connie thought. People don't even see the homeless anymore.

"How did you know I was here, Aunt Connie?"

"I didn't. I came here looking for you, but I didn't find you until now."

"I'm glad you found me."

The bus was just pulling in, and the policeman said, "Well, there'll surely be a big celebration when you get home."

Connie smiled. "That's right. And thank you, officer."

Out of exhaustion, in the night that followed Sue's return, Davey slept. But no sleep came to Lara, lying beside him. Toward dawn she got up and, with no aim, wandered through the house, not knowing what to do with herself in that dark, cold hour. After a while she sat down on the stairs and began soundlessly to weep, making the age-old human promise to God: "If Peggy gets well, I promise, I swear, I'll never ask for anything again. If we can just be together, the four of us, I'll never want anything more. I'll never complain. Oh, please, please."

At the top of the stairs above her Sue, who must have been awakened by her steps, quiet as they were, stood mute and scared. Then, comprehending and moved by an extraordinarily adult compassion, she came down to sit beside her mother, and laid her dark head on Lara's shoulder, still without speaking a word.

* * *

TREASURES

At the end of the third week Peggy was moved to the subacute floor. The threat of infection was past, the swelling had gone down, and her face looked normal. It was the face of a child asleep.

"In a way it's worse," Lara said to Davey. "When she looked so awful, we could blame everything on that and could look forward, as if as soon as she looked like herself, she would also be herself. And now there's nothing . . ." The words trailed off.

"I know," Davey said. And then, perhaps by way of giving to his wife some encouragement that he himself did not feel, he reminded her that "all the doctors say it will take time, darling. Patience."

Kindness never ceased. "It's only because you've always been like that to everybody else," a neighbor said when Lara remarked with wonder about all the kindness. "You and Davey are being paid back, that's all."

Connie flew in once or twice every week, making, without intending to, a small stir in the hospital every time.

A nurse said, "Your sister's beautiful," and then almost apologetically to Lara added, "Well, you do look alike. Her clothes are what I meant. They're so—well, you know, so New York."

And another reported, "My boyfriend drives the taxi from the airport. She comes in a private plane, he says. Is that true?"

Yes, it was true.

"Such a good sister! So devoted."

That was true too.

"Martin says you should get another opinion," Connie reported one day.

"We've had a half dozen, and they all say the same thing. Wait."

"Wait for what? Is anything happening?"

Nothing was happening. The weeks went by, the snow melted, spring came with lilac and forsythia, and still Peggy lay asleep, the sweet head quiet on the pillow.

In the beginning of the third month they were summoned together to the hospital. The doctor, obviously troubled at what he had to tell them, spoke somberly.

"We'll have to face it. There's nothing more we can do for Peggy here. I think you should be looking at a chronic care facility." He looked away at the wall over their heads. "That's about it," he concluded.

Davey let that sink in for a second or two. Then he whispered, "Chronic? She could spend the rest of her life there? Is that what you mean?"

"She could." The words were barely audible.

No longer did Lara or Davey or both of them together spend the whole day at the hospital. The house and the family had to be looked after. An anxious little girl still had to be cared for and cooked for. The Davis Company had to be looked after, too, if there was to be any food to cook. They were both aware of these realities as keenly as of the dreadful reality that waited on the fourth floor of the hospital. And so, like walking ghosts, they did what was necessary, day after day, and waited, for what they did not know.

From her window in the office wing late one afternoon, Lara looked out onto the parking lot, where a long bank of junipers hid the hard outline of the steel fences, and weeping willows that had been little more than sprouts a few years ago stood like green fountains.

Idly, because it was so hard for her tortured mind to concentrate, she wondered about the young man in the impeccable suit who had jumped so briskly from his car and gone into Davey's office. The door opened, and Davey brought him into the room.

"This is Mr. Harrison. He represents the P.T.C. Longwood Company," he told her. "And since you're an officer of the Davis Company, I think you should hear what he has to say."

"Happy to meet you," said Mr. Harrison.

TREASURES

"Mr. Harrison has brought a proposal. I've told him I'm not at all interested, but—"

"If you're not," said Lara, "then surely I won't be either."

"It won't take long," the man said. "I'd just like you to listen for five minutes, no more."

Lara felt a rise of impatience. "I'm sorry, but we have a very sick child, my brother's here to see her, and I have to get home."

"Mr. Davis has told me about your child, and I understand that you're under pressure, so I'll be quick. Here it is: My company—I'm sure you know it's one of the top hundred corporations in the country—is interested in patents that you hold for several surgical instruments, cardiac, orthopedic and—you're familiar with them, I'm sure, Mrs. Davis?"

"Very familiar. My husband invented them all."

Harrison smiled. "Of course. So that brings us to a question that I think makes a lot of sense." Spreading his hands out, he began to count on his fingers. "Here are some of our products. We are a conglomerate, as you must know. We make rubber footwear—your children may wear them, or you yourself may—hospital supplies, a medical book publishing house, electronic parts, and of course our soft drinks. Well, that's enough to give you an idea of our spread. Our hospital supply division is connected quite naturally with our electronic parts division. And that's where your patents come in. Not just the patents, actually, but your whole operation. I'm talking, of course, about an amalgamation, a merger. Two fine firms tying up together."

Davey smiled this time. "It would hardly be a tying, Mr. Harrison. It would be more like a swallowing. Ours is a small operation, as you can see."

"Many smalls make a large, especially when the small one is as fine an operation as yours is. We have a niche for you, Mr. Davis, just the right niche, and once you are a part of P.T.C. Longwood, you wouldn't be small anymore, would you?"

Lara did not like this courteous flattery. Not at all. Young Mr. Harrison, she saw, had an iron fist inside his velvet glove.

"Perhaps we like being small," she told him.

He agreed at once. "Oh, I can understand that it has its advantages. But it has disadvantages for you too. Bigness can afford to take risks, the risks that have made this country move ahead."

"I know about risk," Davey said. "This whole business was a risk. It started in my backyard."

"I'm sure it was a struggle too. And nobody knows more about struggle than we do. Our president, Franklin Bennett, started in a backyard situation himself. He didn't have a penny when he was a boy. He pulled himself up all the way to where he is today. So we do understand. But you wouldn't deny, would you, that if you had had some financial backing when you started out, you could have gone ahead faster? And with fewer headaches, fewer sleepless nights? Think how much more you could be doing even now if you had almost unlimited funds and efficient management behind you."

"We're very efficient," Davey said. "We don't need new management."

"I meant no reflection on you, Mr. Davis. Quite the contrary. You have a well-run plant and some excellent products. I wouldn't be here making this offer if that were not the case, would I?"

"True," Davey acknowledged.

Lara thought, I wouldn't let him waste our time. I wouldn't be so polite. But then, that's Davey's way.

"Handsome as this plant is, I'd like you to see our main plant in Michigan, where we would move you. You really should fly out and take a look at it for yourself. Then you'd know what I'm talking about."

Davey said, "Even if I were interested, which I'm not, Mr. Harrison, I have an obligation to my employees and to this community. They—we—don't want to move. We have roots here."

248

"You're saying we can't do business?"

"I'm afraid so." And Davey made a small move as if to rise from his chair.

Harrison stood up. "This has been sudden, I realize, but it's not fair to yourself to dismiss the whole thing without some more thought. I'd like very much to go back and tell Mr. Bennett that you're going to give it some."

"Smooth talker" was Davey's comment when Harrison had gone.

"I didn't know we were so famous, did you?"

"I could do with less fame of that sort," Davey remarked, somewhat darkly.

At home, with Eddy and Pam, that evening, he told of the day's event.

"Why do you dismiss it like that?" asked Eddy. "Leveraged buyouts are the thing now. You'd come away with a fortune."

"I don't want a fortune."

"You didn't want this house, either, and now you love it."

"All right, I was wrong about the house and you were right."

"I'm right about this, too, Davey."

Davey grumbled. "Bankers! Brokers! They trade businesses as if they were baseball cards. They only understand numbers, not people. Not the hopes and the sweat that go into a place like mine. Talks of moving to—where was it, Lara?"

"Michigan."

"Close this down and walk away from it, just like that! And who knows, after they'd bought us, what they'd do? They call it merging, but what it is is buying, so what's to say they can't sell you all over again and send you somewhere else? Vagabonding all around the country," Davey finished indignantly.

"Vagabonding? Some vagabond Bennett is! Have you any idea who he is?"

"I know, Eddy, I know who he is, and I want no part of him at any price."

249

Eddy took a mouthful of food and chewed thoughtfully. "I want to tell you something," he said then. "It's not so easy to get away from these people once they cast an eye on you. If they really want you, they'll get you. They'll either buy up the stock or reach your stockholders with such a fantastic offer that they'll vote Bennett in, no matter how you feel about it."

"I don't think they'd do that, regardless of—past events."

"I wouldn't be too sure. Thanks to me . . ." The words faded mournfully away, and for a moment nothing was said until Eddy, recovering, took up the argument again.

"You don't fool with a man like Bennett. He's got a brain like a steel trap, and he grabs you in a vise like a trap too. If I were you, I'd think this over very carefully before I said no."

To this Davey made no answer. And Lara knew that he wanted to shut out the possibility of trouble for the very reason that he *was* beginning to be troubled, albeit faintly, as was she. Almost certainly, they had not seen the last of Franklin Bennett's persuasive emissary, she told herself.

Eddy resumed his cautions. "I still don't think you people understand who Bennett is. He's a legend, one of the most powerful corporate executives in America." There was awe in his voice.

"I've read enough about him," Lara said. "As far as I can make out, he's a heartless, greedy tough guy who doesn't care whom he steps on as long as he gets his way."

"What do you care if he can improve the quality of your family's life? Money's the ticket, and always will be."

"Yes and then again, no," Lara said. "Mostly no."

"Mostly yes, Lara. Think about it. Money won't solve your problem, but it can ease a hell of a lot if things don't turn out for Peggy."

"Oh, Eddy, please!" Pam reproached him.

"I know, Pam. But the truth has to be faced."

TREASURES

From the basement where Sue and her friends were playing came shrill, rippling laughter, poignant now in the silence.

Eddy was the first to speak. "I've just mentioned the bad advice I once gave you. Now I'd like to remind you that I've also given you some of the best advice you've ever had. True?" he asked, turning to Davey.

"True."

"Well, all I'm saying is, don't write Bennett off. Think about it very seriously."

Then Pam spoke softly. "Darling, do leave these people alone tonight. They know what they want. And they've got enough to think about, God knows."

One Saturday Martin Berg arrived. Davey was at work, and Lara had just lain down for a few minutes on the sofa in the den when the doorbell rang.

"Oh, I've startled you," he said. "Were you sleeping?"

"No, I was just making a cup of tea." She lied with the first thought that came into her head, as if she were ashamed to be caught resting in the middle of the afternoon.

Martin's eyes examined her acutely. "You look beat. And why not? Go lie down and let me make the tea."

She smiled. "Heavens, no. You don't know how."

"I grew up dirt poor, you forget. I guess I know how to use a stove."

There was always something commanding about Martin Berg; one didn't disagree with him. So she returned to the sofa and was still feeling surprised at his coming, when he returned with two cups of tea. He got right to the point.

"These doctors, I'm not saying anything against them, they've done their best, but Connie's told me their verdict, and we just can't accept it, Lara. Now, there's a place not far out of New York, a famous place where they specialize in head injuries. It's small and always filled up, unfortunately, but I made some con-

251

tacts this morning, and we can get the baby in. I think we should give it a try, Lara."

She stirred her tea, watching the milk swirl in the cup as her thoughts swirled in her head. Without being willing to confess it to anyone, not even to Davey, not even really to herself, she had little hope. Ever since they had spoken of chronic care, she had known this was the end of the road. It was as if her child had died. No, it was worse.

She looked up at Martin. His eyes were filled with sadness. And he had said "we," when, after all, the child was not his.

"I suppose there isn't anything to lose, is there?" she replied.

"Nothing except money. And as Connie told you, I am ready—"

"No, no," she said quickly. "Thank you, but we have savings, and we're prepared to use every penny of them if it will help . . ." She could not go on.

"It's a very fine place. I've only passed it on the road, but it looks beautiful, and of course its reputation is the best." He paused, waiting. "Shall I talk to Davey?" he urged then.

"You needn't. If I want to try it, he'll want it too. We were both—we couldn't bear the thought of that other place, the chronic place. It would be like a—like a warehouse, Davey said."

Berg nodded. "I'll call him tonight anyway, when I get home. I won't bother him at the plant."

"You're going now?" For Martin had risen.

"Yes. I'll be flying back. I guess I could have done this on the telephone, but I didn't expect it to be so easy, or that you'd accept so promptly. I like that, though. I like quick decisions, quick action."

"That's evident," she said, and smiled. "You're a good man, Martin."

A good man, and so competent. It was a relief, in a way, to let him take over, to make this decision for them.

"By the way," Martin said as she accompanied him to the

door, "have you done any thinking about that offer of Bennett's? I know this is a terrible time to be talking about business, but I just wondered."

"Not really," she replied, and then, curious, asked how he knew about it. "Did Eddy tell you?"

He smiled. "No, not Eddy. I get around. I hear things. And rumors float fast in my business."

"Then you must have heard that we're not interested. Not at all."

"Not even enough to think it over?"

"We just dismissed the whole idea."

"But they won't just dismiss it, you may be sure. As soon as all their financing is arranged, they'll be back. I know how these things work. And—"

"Martin," she said, interrupting him, "we can't think about anything. I can tell you that. It's all too much to cope with, first our child, and then this impossible proposition. Davey's suffered too much already."

"You might welcome the money," Martin said gently, "especially if—"

So he, too, meant, if Peggy never recovers.

"Well, think it over," Martin advised again as he left.

She had been so sure of Davey's acceptance that his reply that night to Martin's offer on behalf of Peggy was no surprise. What did astonish her was his reaction to Martin's other remarks.

"Lara, I don't care anymore. If they really want the plant, let them take it. Give us some money for it and good-bye to it."

"I can't believe you're saying that!" she cried.

"Why not? What does it matter? If Peggy were well, you can darn well believe it would be a different story. But as it is, I don't give a damn."

But you will, in spite of everything, she thought. Yes, you will. Yet she said no more. Poor man. Leave him alone.

And she went outside to sit on a bench in the yard. It began to rain, although the evening sun was still shining; great, slow drops fell glinting and spattered on the stone walk. They darkened the steps next door, where the child had fallen; it seemed years since that night.

All her senses were tender, as if each had been wounded and could shrink when touched. The wet stone smelled sharp and bitter. A car went by with a blast of hideous rock music. In the house Sue and her best friend Amy were having one of their noisy, though fortunately infrequent, fights. Dear Sue. These had been dreadful months for her too, with all the gaiety gone from the family.

Then, mercifully, the silence flowed back, and she closed her eyes, feeling the soft rain on her face, not minding it.

Why us? she thought. Why me? And the answer came, as clear as the sound of the rain or the wind in the new-leaved trees: Why not you?

CHAPTER
ELEVEN

❧

They took Peggy, then, to a new place, a smaller one surrounded by pleasant, expensive trees; otherwise, nothing was different, for when at the end of the day they walked away from her, she was still lying in a bed connected to monitors and tubes. Lara asked no further questions, and Davey, too, had gone silent. It was as if they both had learned that there were no answers. Passively, they stood gazing down at their child while Connie took charge, talking in turn to doctors, to nurses, and to administrators.

"If only she were to die," Davey murmured once. And Lara knew that the words had come unbidden; he was quite probably not even aware that he had spoken the thought aloud. She took his hand and kept holding it as they walked out to Connie's car.

"You'll stay with us here, of course," said Connie, addressing Lara. "Davey can fly in weekends. We'll keep the plane available."

"Oh, but I can't. There's Sue at home."

"Bring her here," Connie said promptly.

"School isn't out yet. Besides, we can't disrupt her life any more. She's scared, she's been through enough as it is. I will accept the offer of the plane rides, though. It's a godsend, Connie. Martin and you are godsends."

So a routine began. As the plane descended toward the West-chester Airport, Lara, looking down, would see her sister, a bright red spot or blue or white, waiting and waving. Then there would be an embrace, an anxious question, and an answer.

"I went yesterday. The same."

The hospital visit would follow, and that, too, would be the same. Lunch at Cresthill would be brief so that Lara could fly home early.

One day while at the lunch table, it occurred to her that she had not seen Thérèse for weeks, and she asked why.

Connie hesitated. "I thought—to tell the truth, I thought it might be too hard for you to see her."

Lara's eyes filled. "Oh!" she cried. "Oh, the world mustn't stop because of Peggy! Do call her. I want to see her."

When Thérèse came, Lara took her on her lap. The child, wriggling, turned to look up at her.

"Where's Peggy?" she demanded.

"Peggy's sick, darling."

"When is she going to get better?"

"We're not sure yet."

"Oh. Can I have that cake?"

Lara had lost her appetite, and most of her dessert was still on the plate. "Of course," she said.

Connie was feeling a particular shame. How often on behalf of her own little girl had she not envied the beauty of her sister's child! And here sat her Thérèse, healthy and bright, on Lara's lap; what must be Lara's pain as she made the comparison?

They were to drive to the city that day, and Lara was to fly home from LaGuardia Airport instead of Westchester.

"Thérèse has to see the pediatrician for her regular checkup, and I ordered some summer things on Madison Avenue. Anyway, a little change, a little window-shopping, will do you good," Connie told Lara.

These errands accomplished, they stopped to give Thérèse an

256

ice-cream treat and then walked slowly back up Fifth Avenue, on the Park side in the shade, to the apartment. Suddenly, nearing the museum, they stopped short.

"The man on the bench," Connie whispered. "Oh, my Lord, look, it's Richard."

Her first impulse was to cross the avenue. It was one thing, strangely touching really, to receive his birthday and his Christmas cards, but another thing actually to see the man again. After her moment's hesitation it was too late to turn away, for he had recognized them and stood up.

"Well, Connie, this is a surprise."

"How are you, Richard? You remember Lara, of course? And you've never met Thérèse. Darling, say hello to Richard. He's a friend of Mommy's."

There! Hadn't she managed that smoothly? But then awkwardness set in. Since one couldn't very well just walk away now, something more had to be said, and Connie said the most obvious thing that rushed into her head.

"Lara's visiting from Ohio."

When, murmuring some politeness, he acknowledged this fact by turning toward Lara, Connie observed him and was astonished at what she saw. His shirt, which was open at the neck, was plainly dirty. He wore a cotton jacket, but no tie; the jacket, too, was soiled, and he needed a shave; an unkempt blond growth of hair, about three days' worth, glinted in the light.

Moved by concern and curiosity, she asked him what he was doing. Was he still in advertising?

"I got fed up with that place. Actually, I'm between jobs. I'm taking a vacation."

"Nothing wrong with that," she returned brightly, and was irritated by her own fatuous answer. Still, one couldn't, after all, expect to feel completely at ease in an encounter with one's former husband. She smiled; the smile also was too bright.

"But you haven't changed, Connie."

"Not in seven years?"

"Well, you do have this lovely girl. Thérèse," he mused. "You always did like anything that was French. And she could be a French child, with her dark bangs and that dress."

Indeed, the dress had been bought in Paris. He noticed everything. He always had. But what had happened to him?

Lara, too, was conscious of something very strange. And turning up her wrist to show her watch, she reminded Connie of the time.

"Oh, Lara, your plane, of course! Goodness, we have to rush! Sorry, Richard, but—"

He nodded. "Go ahead, don't be late." And giving a little wave like a salute, he sat down again on the bench.

They crossed the avenue. Connie, looking back, saw that he was still sitting there, not watching them. His head was sunk on his chest, and he was apparently just staring at the ground.

"What can be wrong with him?" she cried. "Those terribly sad eyes! He looks sick, like a sad, sick beggar." And Connie shuddered.

"Drinking, do you think? He looked as if he might be."

"He never drank. Never. But I suppose . . ." She had no idea what had happened.

They walked on without speaking anymore. Lara was pretending not to have stared quickly at Connie and then looked as quickly away. She's wondering, Connie thought, what my feelings are. Well, what are they? Disconnected memories speed through my head: those first vivid days in Texas and the euphoria; the child I destroyed would certainly be different from the one whose hand is now so tightly held in mine . . . how queerly it all unfolds . . . poor gentle Richard—what's happened to him?

The car was already waiting at the curb for Lara. When the driver opened the door, Connie laid a hand on Lara's arm, detaining her.

258

"Lara . . . try to take care of yourself. Did you ever think living could be so damned hard?"

"It's just as well we didn't think."

Connie sighed. Bad memories . . . Richard . . . Peggy on the hospital bed . . . the eerie stillness in that room . . .

She sighed again and kissed her sister, saying only, "Get home safely," then stood there watching while the car merged with traffic on Fifth Avenue.

"If by some miracle Peggy should be well again"—too often Lara had caught herself saying or thinking the words, and had reprimanded herself because sensible people didn't count on miracles. That age was past.

And yet it happened.

It was Connie who witnessed it. One afternoon in the third week when she was making her regular stop at the hospital, Connie saw Peggy open her eyes. As, still in a state of shock—"I shall be shocked for the rest of my life when I think of it"—she described the happening, the child's eyes had opened just long enough for the two pairs of eyes to meet in mutual astonishment. Then Peggy's had closed again.

"I don't know how I even had enough strength in my legs to run down the hall. I think I just screamed at the first nurse I met. And the doctors came running, and more nurses. Can you imagine what went on? The excitement? Then I telephoned you, Lara, and you know the rest."

Within the hour Martin's plane flew to Ohio. Davey left the plant where he had been discussing an order from a southern hospital, Sue left school, and Lara, trembling and laughing, joined them at the airport.

Before they arrived at the hospital in the early evening, Peggy had awakened for a second time.

"Mommy," she had whispered. Her frightened gaze had swept the room, and finding the faces all strange except for Aunt Connie's and Uncle Martin's, not finding Mommy, she had begun to cry.

Connie stroked her hair. "Mommy's coming soon. She's on the way," she whispered over and over.

And Mommy came. By now they had Peggy propped against pillows, half sitting and half lying. Lara came rushing. She saw no one, spoke to no one; the little crowd parted to let her through, and she fell on her knees beside the bed. Davey, behind her, reached down and curved Peggy's arms around the mother's neck.

Nurses standing in the background cried, too, and a young male intern on his first week of service had to turn away.

"How do you explain this?" Martin asked Dr. Bayer. "It's incredible, a miracle."

"Well, it's so rare a happening that you might well call it one," was the response. "The swellings that come with head injuries seldom take this long to subside. This coma has lasted an extraordinarily long time. Extraordinary."

"When may we take her home?" asked Davey.

The doctor shook his head. "She won't be ready for a long time yet. We can't be sure how much of her mental function has been restored, how much memory or cognition. We don't even know whether she can walk. You'll need to keep her here for extensive therapy." As the parents' faces fell, he added kindly, "However, what's very much in her favor is her age. So we don't in any way mean to sound discouraging, but only to counsel patience."

And so the families entered the next phase.

Peggy was to spend, it was estimated, another three to eight weeks in intensive care; then if all went well, she might be taken home and brought back every day for rehabilitation therapy, which would take another two to three months.

"Oh, but we live in Ohio," Lara cried out in dismay. "How can we—"

TREASURES

Davey began a proposal, "Maybe there's a place—" to which Martin at once objected.

"Davey, there's nothing like this anywhere near where you live. You know that. She'll stay with us, and Connie will drive her over here every day for her treatment."

Lara and Davey looked toward each other, she reading his mind: I hate to take favors.

"I know you think it's too much to accept," she told him in front of everyone, "but you would do it for them, Davey," and finished mentally, *absurd as it seems to think of Martin Berg's ever needing a favor.*

"Of course," Davey said.

"Good," Martin answered promptly. "And the weekend offer of the plane still stands."

The routine was established. It seemed to Lara as if the little person who was Peggy Davis was being lifted and reinjected with life through the sheer loving will of the many who were concentrating all their strength upon her. Now hope at last came pouring through Lara's very veins, to surge out in sudden bursts of happy tears or reckless laughter. Day by day came small, repeated spurts of growth. Peggy began to walk, tottering a little between the nurses' hands, then taking her first steps unaided down the hall. Memory came back, as she began to ask about Sue and her friends in school. Carefully, she printed her name on a card to her teacher, who, along with half the town—or so it seemed— had sent cards to her. As the days passed, she demanded attention, and even lost her temper when Connie refused to give her a candy bar before dinner.

Dr. Bayer, who happened to walk in on the tantrum, was amused and pleased. "An excellent sign. A return to normalcy."

He swooped down on Peggy and lifted her above his head. "My friend! Aren't you my best friend? Come on, I'll show you something. You too," he told Connie. "There's something you ought to see."

In the glass-walled sunroom at the end of the hall, he pointed outdoors.

"Look. We don't often get a chance to see this."

Blurred by the soft rain, a magnificent rainbow arched across the sky and disappeared behind a tree.

"Oh, beautiful. Beautiful," Connie whispered.

"The pot of gold must be right there in back of those trees."

"I won't even bother to look for it. We've already found its pot of gold." And Connie stroked Peggy's arm, which lay on the man's shoulder.

"You're right, of course," he said seriously.

Something in his voice, a richness or a compassion, made her look into his face. For all these weeks she had seen him in Peggy's room and had noted only that he was authoritative in a kindly way and that the child had begun to adore him. Now suddenly she saw him as if for the first time: a man about her own age, with a long, narrow face, long, narrow eyes, and a markedly cleft chin that softened the angularity of his bones.

Spontaneously, she said, "I hope you know how grateful we all are. And not only for your skill. You are so tender with Peggy! I should have told you so before this."

"You're very tender with her yourself."

"She's my niece, about as close as my own child. We're a close family."

"You're fortunate."

"You have no children?"

"I'm not married. I have no parents, brothers, or sisters. No ties." He smiled. "Still, there are always compensations. At the drop of a hat I can pick up and go wherever I want to go in the world."

"I hope you aren't planning to leave us before Peggy's all well again."

"No, I've no plans now. I've been everywhere from Vietnam to Egypt, studying head wounds and injuries, so it's time to stay put for a while. Come, Peggy, we're going back to your room. You'll have your dinner, and then you'll have your candy."

Connie, as she followed them, had a fleeting thought: He's someone I'd like to know. But their paths, their ways, were far apart, and the thought vanished.

The day came when Peggy was discharged from the hospital. A room had been prepared for her at Cresthill, a rosy shelter filled with welcoming toys that stood, sat, and lay about: a dollhouse like a Swiss chalet; a stuffed polar bear, a mother Scottie with puppies in a basket, and a panda taller than Peggy herself; dolls —a bride, a Cinderella, and a Peter Pan; a real fish-tank with real tropical fish; a shelf filled with games and a blackboard with colored chalk. It was a mirror image of Thérèse's room across the hall.

Lara gasped. "What have you done here? I can't believe it."

"Well, believe it or not, Martin bought them all," Connie said. "He goes positively berserk in toy stores." She opened a closet where hung a row of childish clothes, ruffled and flowered. "Peggy's certainly grown a size since the winter, so I thought there's no sense in your bringing old things from home."

Lara shook her head fondly. "I know. You're the one who goes berserk over clothes. Oh, Connie, they're beautiful."

Connie was pleased. "So you like your goodie packages?"

The "goodies" in their shining white boxes were numerous: a powder-blue velvet dress and pajamas hand embroidered with balloons and teddy bears for Peggy, two Norwegian hand-knitted ski sweaters for Sue, a snowsuit monogrammed in red for Peggy, and a British camel-hair coat fastened with leather buttons for Sue.

"I had such fun shopping. You know how I love to shop. Are the things really all right?"

"You're a dear, and they're all wonderful," Lara said, wondering where and when Peggy would get to wear a powder-blue velvet dress back home. "But what can I say to all this?"

"Say nothing," Martin answered as he came into the room. He smiled with satisfaction. "She ought to feel at home here for a while, I think."

"Don't you dare worry a minute about her," Connie said. "She'll be just fine. She's quite used to us already."

From the window they could see the two little girls bobbing on the seesaw while the nanny carefully watched.

Connie read Lara's mind. "Nanny's been told to be careful of her, not to let her get too tired or to fall. Although really, Lara, that child has to be made of iron. She's almost back to herself, from what I can see. Well, almost."

And indeed, compared with Thérèse, Peggy was far the sturdier and the tougher of the two. It crossed Lara's mind that if the situation were reversed, Peggy would not have been as gentle with her cousin as Thérèse was with her. Peggy had Connie's drive and energy and sparkle; maybe that was why Connie, without realizing it, had become so attached to the child. So Lara mused, as she watched them playing on the stately lawns of Martin Berg's great house.

"I think she'll be spoiled there," she frequently remarked to Davey whenever they departed for home late on Sunday afternoons.

He laughed. "It won't hurt her. She'll get back to normal soon enough when she gets home and has to help clear the table after dinner."

On the Fourth of July the Bergs gave a party, a celebration for Peggy, who now, except for the slightest hesitancy in her walk, was practically recovered from the long ordeal. Eddy and Pam came. Sue came, at Connie's suggestion, with a friend. And Peggy, to everyone's surprise, wanted Dr. Bayer to come too.

"I want Jonathan to come to my party."

"Jonathan? You mean Dr. Bayer."

"I call him Jonathan because that's his name."

"She's really in love with him," Lara said. "What do you think, Martin? Would you mind?"

"Of course not. He's a very nice guy, and we surely owe him a lot."

Connie observed, "He probably won't accept. He must have six other invitations."

But he did come, to Peggy's great delight, and proved to be a very pleasant guest, enjoying the children and tennis and a swim in the Olympic-sized pool.

At dusk they all sat down to supper on the terrace. Candles in five-armed silver candelabra flickered through the shadows, and two maids served. Sue and her friend Amy, who had expected the usual red-white-and-blue picnic of fried chicken and corn on the cob, were obviously overawed by this unfamiliar splendor. They were also not particularly appreciative of duck à *l'orange* and Grand Marnier soufflé.

The fireworks, however, went well. As darkness fell, blankets were brought to the crest of the hill from where, as they sat on the grass, they could see the rockets from the township's fireworks display go soaring through the sky.

When the last artificial stars had burst and fallen to the ground, the party broke up. Thérèse and Peggy, half asleep, were carried back to the house.

"Beautiful, isn't it?" remarked Lara as she walked beside Dr. Bayer.

Connie, within earshot, heard his reply.

"It's a palace." And then he added, "I'd never want to live like this, though."

Surprised, Lara asked why.

"I don't know. I guess it would just be too much for me." He laughed. "It's academic anyway, a problem I'm not likely to have."

"Nor I," said Lara.

There was a pause, and Connie heard the doctor say, "Your

sister's a very kind and generous woman. I've seen her with children on the floor in the hospital—in the children's wing, I mean. You'd never imagine that she lived like this, like a princess."

"Oh, Connie's very natural. She loves all this, but it's never changed the way she behaves. People all like her. Everyone does."

"Yes, I can see why." He paused. "She has great charm."

"We think so. Well, it's been a lovely day, hasn't it?"

That was typical of Lara, Connie thought, putting a proper end to the conversation lest it turn too personal. She would have liked to hear more. But that's absurd of me, she scolded, as if I were an adolescent needing to be assured that I'm admired. Absurd.

Upstairs, a short while later in one of Connie's country French guest rooms, Lara had her own odd thoughts.

Bayer was definitely attracted to Connie. . . . I caught him glancing at her all through the evening. They did look well when they stood together. . . . How ridiculous I'm being!

Davey, lying beside her, spoke into the darkness, interrupting the ridiculous thoughts. "Eddy told me something rather interesting. He said he heard somewhere that Martin's firm is involved in financing P.T.C. Longwood."

This jolted her into attention. "But that's incredible!"

"Why is it incredible? I find it perfectly plausible."

"I sort of had the idea that the deal had fallen through. I know Martin hasn't said anything in a long time about him, so Bennett couldn't be wanting it anymore."

"Maybe the reason Martin hasn't said anything is exactly that he is involved."

"Oh, Davey, think of the complications! After all Martin's done for us—what are we to do?"

"Let's not think of it unless we have to. Eddy's not even sure it's true. I shouldn't have mentioned it to you." He reached for

Lara's hand and squeezed it. "The main thing, the only thing, is that Peggy is all right again."

"I know, darling."

Nevertheless, Lara worried silently long after he had fallen asleep.

Summer was fading when they finally brought Peggy home.

Connie was very emotional about the parting. "We'll miss her so," she kept saying. "Thérèse will be an only child again."

They had all grown very close together through these last hard months, and the separation hurt. Loaded down with stuffed animals, dolls, and parting gifts, the Davises climbed aboard Martin's plane. Far below, as they rose into the air, Martin, Connie, and Thérèse were still visible, tiny figures still waving as the plane turned westward toward Ohio and home.

"Dear, wonderful people," Lara said.

At home, more dear, wonderful people waited for them. Neighbors had prepared a feast. Men from the plant had brought their marching band to parade around the yard, tooting and blowing to Peggy's huge delight. The weekly newspaper was out with an item on the editorial page about the marvelous recovery of Peggy Davis.

And on this night the Davis parents made real love for the first time since that terrible hurt so many months before. The house was quiet at last as Lara walked softly through the hall, along which every bedroom was occupied once more by a sleeping child. In her own room Davey was already in bed. A small wind stirred the curtains at the open windows and put a fresh chill in the air. She undressed quickly and sat down on the edge of the bed. Davey looked up with a kind of mischievous anticipation.

"You know what? You look young again," she said. "Those lines you had around your eyes are all gone." And she smoothed his cheeks.

"There are better places for your hands, aren't there?"

"I know."

"Well, come on. What are you waiting for?"

"Not a thing."

"Then turn out the light."

He raised the blankets, making a warm little cave, just tight enough for the two of them. Enormous gratitude, incredible joy, enveloped her as she slid into the cave.

CHAPTER
TWELVE

❧

A taxi honked, and the driver swore at Eddy. The driver was justified, for he had almost walked into the side of the cab. And he felt a chill that had nothing to do with his near accident. This meeting with Abner Saville would be one of those interminably uncomfortable ones like the last few, with reams of paper spread out before his splitting head. Besides, it was humiliating to be practically cross-examined by a man whom he paid to do a service, a man, moreover, with whom he had become so friendly after all the years of their association.

He felt like going home and telephoning with an excuse that he was coming down with the flu or something. Nevertheless, he hastened his steps toward his office.

"Mr. Hendricks has been here almost half an hour," Mrs. Evans told him somewhat reproachfully.

"Who's Hendricks? Where's Abner?"

"Mr. Hendricks is one of Mr. Saville's partners, Mr. Osborne." The tone was still respectfully reproachful, as if Eddy ought to know who Hendricks was.

And Eddy really did know who Hendricks was. So Abner had sent someone else in his place. What could that mean? Perhaps it was only because Abner had to be out of town or wasn't feeling well.

He entered his office. Mr. Hendricks was already at the conference table with papers spread out and a full leather briefcase on the floor beside him. He stood up and the two men shook hands.

"Sorry I'm late, Hendricks. The cab got caught in traffic on the way back from Wall Street. It would be a great thing if they could pick up Wall Street and move it uptown. A lot easier for people like me."

This flat attempt at a friendly relaxed approach brought no response. Hendricks sat down again and bent to open his briefcase.

Eddy went to his desk. Its glossy, broad expanse, its tidy piles of papers ready for his signature, its diagonal placement that gave him views on the one hand of Manhattan's towers and on the other of his handsome room, his control room, the command room of an army or an empire, had the effect of lightening the gloom that he had brought to this meeting.

"What happened to Abner?" he inquired pleasantly. "Not that I mind seeing you. I meant, I'm used to Abner. We've been friends for years."

"I know that. Abner thought it advisable to get another opinion. Sometimes friendship can confuse things."

These words, although delivered without emphasis, almost without inflection, were ominous. Hendricks's eyes, enlarged by thick lenses with wide black rims, made him look like a raccoon. But a raccoon was a friendly beast. Or maybe it wasn't. Eddy knew he was not thinking straight. So he pulled himself up, bracing his spine against the high-backed chair. This chair had sometimes felt a little bit like a throne when he presided over meetings and all the faces were turned up toward him. That was another ridiculous thought.

"Would you mind coming to the table," the raccoon inquired, "so we can look over these together?"

Eddy became alert. "Of course. No problem."

"I have here," Hendricks began, "our worksheets for the firm and also your personal tax returns." The glasses were bent on Eddy. "I don't like to say it, but frankly, Mr. Osborne, some of this material is very distressing."

Distressing! A two-bit number shuffler. There's a roomful of men down the hall sitting at their faxes and computers, and they all work for me, producing numbers you'll never come within a hair's breadth of—

Eddy raised his chin and met the man's somber gaze. "Well? Fire away."

"You know, of course, that we've had a rather suspicious feeling for the last few months that things are not altogether in balance here."

"Suspicious? I don't like the word, Mr. Hendricks. I don't like it at all."

"I'm sorry. Perhaps I should have said 'doubtful' instead."

"Okay. Just get to the point. Give me the bottom line." His head had begun to throb. Quick darts of pain, needle pricks, ran down his arm.

"The bottom line is this: Osborne and Company is too highly leveraged. You haven't got enough cash to tally with your investments. In short, your liabilities exceed your assets."

"All right, all right, I know that!" Eddy exclaimed. "A couple of big investors happened to take their money out a short while back, and that played a little havoc with the cash flow, that's all. Don't you think I know, every minute of every day, where I am? This is a temporary situation, and nothing to worry about."

"I wouldn't say that. If any more of your clients decide to pull out, you'll be facing disaster."

"Listen, if every depositor in the country decided to take his money out of the banks at the same time, the whole system would collapse," Eddy retorted.

The other persisted. "This is different. If these people want their money, it won't be there. What then?"

"It'll be there. You don't know what you're talking about. But

271

why should they want their money? There's no reason in the world why they should." And Eddy's mind ran through a list of names, the glittering names of stage and screen stars, artists and real estate investors; his mind recounted his whole familiar, so-often-quoted galaxy of stars. For a moment these names fortified him. "No, there's no reason in the world."

Hendricks sighed. "I don't like being the bearer of bad news, Mr. Osborne."

"What bad news?"

Hendricks hesitated and sighed again. "One thing piles up upon another. There's been a commingling of funds—"

Eddy's pains grew sharper. He should have obeyed his instincts, pretended to be sick, canceled this appointment, and given himself a few days to straighten things out before seeing this watchdog.

"What are you talking about?" he cried.

"Your personal checkbook." Hendricks looked away. "There are entries that don't match, or rather they do match up to withdrawal from general funds. For example, on June seventeenth—here, if you'll take a look—"

"I don't need to look. Just say it."

"Well, you made out a check to the Winterheim Galleries for six hundred eleven thousand dollars that you didn't have in the account on that date. But on the eighteenth you deposited an exact amount to cover the check and withdrew it from the account of Mr. Sidney—"

Eddy's heart pounded, and he jumped up. "All right! I did a damn fool thing, I'll admit it. I got in deeper than I expected to. I go a little crazy sometimes, mostly buying art. But everything I buy, securities, real estate, whatever, is all prime stuff, investment quality. I never fool with junk. You know that. That's how I've achieved what I have. Look, I know it wasn't right, but I got in a little over my head, that's all. It's not the first time this has happened to the biggest people in the country. It's just cash flow, for God's sake! I need a couple of months to straighten things out, that's all I need, and I'll take damn good care not to let this sort of thing happen again."

"It's more than a question of time. I'm afraid you'd need a good deal more than a couple of months, anyway." Hendricks's monotone was mournful. You would think he was consoling somebody at a funeral. "There are questions that have to be answered. How to explain, for instance, why you opened a separate personal account with another stockbroker, in which you deposit money that you've taken—borrowed—from your own customers?"

The floor seemed to rise and walls seemed to tilt inward. Eddy grasped the arms of his chair.

"For Christ's sake," he said, "you're talking like an IRS man or somebody from the SEC."

Hendricks said gently, almost kindly, "But this is the way they will talk when the time comes, Mr. Osborne." He picked up the briefcase and began to put papers away.

"Is that all you have to say?" asked Eddy. "What about doing my income tax? Isn't that what you came for?"

"You see, we really wanted you to look over these records so you'd understand why we can't file this return."

"Can't file? Why can't you? Who's to do it, then?"

"Please. Please think. You can't expect us to put our name to these declarations when they are not true, can you?"

And Eddy now heard, as if he were a witness to his own plight, a frantic cry. "What am I supposed to do?"

"I think you should get a lawyer. And a very good one. And waste no time about it," Hendricks said. "I'm truly sorry, Mr. Osborne," he added.

As Hendricks went to the door, Eddy called to his back, "Why didn't Abner come and tell me himself?"

And from the doorway the mournful voice replied, "He's been trying to tell you all along, but you haven't been hearing him."

Only once before in his life had he been so humiliated, when, in the first grade, after wetting his pants he had been called to the blackboard, and the whole class had seen the dark stain. He had never forgotten their laughter, or the tingle and prickle of shame as it ran up his back, as it lumped itself in his throat and stung the back of his eyes. Now, standing at the window among a forest of stone towers, he felt it all over again.

From behind him came the solicitous voice of Mrs. Evans. "Is there anything special you want me to do, Mr. Osborne?"

"No, nothing. I have a few calls to make, and then I'll go home."

"You're not feeling well?"

For the first time Eddy resented the woman's manner, which he had always admired. It occurred to him that perhaps her solicitude was not well meant after all, that this was merely prurient curiosity and that people in the outer offices were already talking.

"Just a slight cold coming on. I want to nip it in the bud," he replied with a formal smile.

Alone again, he slumped into the wing chair beside the fireplace and tried to think. There had to be a solution. There was a solution to everything, as long as you didn't panic. That little raccoon might not even have known what he was talking about. . . . He got up and went to the telephone on his desk.

"Hey, Abner, what's wrong? Sending substitutes—are you running out on me?"

"I wouldn't put it that way," Abner said.

"Well, I would. That Hendricks—I didn't like him."

"Didn't like him, or didn't like what he told you?"

"Well, what he told me, I guess. I have a sense that he was dramatizing, exaggerating the situation. Granted, I've messed up a little here and there, but—"

"Eddy, he didn't exaggerate. I've warned you before about

things I didn't like, but this now is critical. This is a very dangerous situation. Believe me."

"If you're so worried, why didn't you—"

"Why didn't I come myself? Partly because I thought a
stranger might shock you into seeing reality, and partly because
I'm cowardly. I didn't have the heart for it."

"Son of a bitch! After all these years, all the fees you've earned
through me and—and I thought we were friends! Yes, when the
going gets rough, you find out who your friends are, all right. You
sure as hell do."

"Eddy, don't be bitter. I understand that you're worried and
scared."

"Scared? You still don't know me, do you? It'll take a lot more
than this to throw a scare into me, Abner. A lot more."

"Well, good then. Will you finally, calmly, listen to me, listen
to my advice? Go home and see what you can liquidate. You've a
fortune in that apartment. Then get a top-notch lawyer and work
it out with him, plan for the day when the IRS or the SEC, or
both, come knocking."

"Liquidate? Sell the art? Everything I've worked for? You're
crazy, Abner."

"I don't think I am. Listen, Eddy. I'm still your friend, I still
like you, you're a smart man, and what's more important you're a
generous one. But you're a gambler too. Don't gamble anymore.
Straighten yourself out. That's why I'm recommending a lawyer."

"In the meantime, what about my taxes? That guy Hendricks
refused to do them for me. Will you come over tomorrow so we
can go over them?"

"Eddy, I can't. I can't risk my name. Surely you can see that,
can't you?"

Abner's patient voice was infuriating. And Eddy said stiffly,
"So if that's the case, I'll get another accountant. It'll be a nui-
sance, but not insurmountable."

The voice, still patient, came back. "You won't find any who'll take the risk either."

"Then to hell with them all. I'll go to work and prepare my own."

"You'd be signing a false return," Abner said gravely.

Eddy shouted into the telephone. "Don't worry about me, I'll solve this somehow, damned if I don't."

"I hope you can. I wish you luck, Eddy."

They had a dinner date that night with another couple at a neighborhood bistro. The four were intimate friends, accustomed to frank speech.

"You look awfully tired, Eddy," the wife said.

"Wrung out," the husband added. "You should have told us. We'd have had it another night."

This was the second time that day that he had been told how tired he looked. He must look awful. And he tried unobtrusively to glimpse himself on the mirrored wall, but caught only a blur.

"You were so silent tonight!" Pam exclaimed during their short walk home.

"They did enough yapping to make up for it," he replied.

"Why so cross?" she asked.

"I am not cross, Pam. Do you hear? I am not cross!"

In their bedroom she undressed very slowly, taking her good time to walk around in her white chiffon chemise. Then she went to a drawer and drew out the black lace nightgown that, laughing at the very vulgarity of the thing, they had once bought together in Mexico City; afterward they had gone back to the hotel room, where Pam had given a belly dance exhibition, and they had rolled on the bed, laughing some more until they had stopped laughing.

Now she stepped out of the chemise, and gave him a double view, one through the mirrored door, and the other of her long, white, tapering back. Languidly she stretched, raising her arms and lifting her small, round breasts, then with a pretty gesture shook herself like some graceful animal, just awakened from a nap. When she picked up the slithering black gown and slid it over her head, he now saw nakedness even more provocatively covered by a thin black veil. And he understood that hers was a well-meant effort to cajole him out of his mood, even more than just a signal of her usual desire. But sex was the last thing he wanted this night.

He dropped onto the bed and gave a deep groan. "I'm awfully tired!"

She got in beside him and touched his arm. "You're sure you're not sick?"

"Tired, I said."

"It's so unlike you. I thought maybe you'd seen a doctor and found out something awful."

"I'm not sick," he repeated.

"The truth, Eddy?"

"The truth. Now will you let me sleep?" he asked, not ungently.

But he was sick, truly, with a rising fear that ran like ice water through his blood and bones. All during the casual chatter at dinner he had been reliving the scene in the office. *You withdrew from the account of So-and-So and So-and-So. . . .* Actually, it had been only juggling, moving dollars that could easily be replaced, when you considered the firm's assets. Small potatoes. Cash flow, that's all it was. Sometimes the flow dried up a little, but only temporarily. His mind strove, but when you were handling so many accounts, investments, and clients, it was hard to recall each separate transaction, each in itself so relatively insignificant when one looked at the overall picture. He could recall, to be sure, the day he'd seen the Maserati in the showroom; he had always really desired a red car from the time he'd bought his first Mercedes, but all his cars had been a conservative gray or navy blue. Then Pam had said that day, "Oh, let's let our hair down! The red is gorgeous." So they'd gone tooling up to the Vineyard in it and down to Palm Beach, attracting admiration all the way. Yes, and he could recall the Fragonard, the excitement of the frenetic bidding, and then taking it home, the treasure, fine as any Fragonard in any museum anywhere. Yes, and Fifth Avenue in Christmas week when the rubies, glistening like dew on roses, had beckoned from their black velvet bed in the window. So the millions flew, millions upon millions, before you knew it. *Your separate brokerage account . . . This is a very dangerous situation, believe me. . . . The IRS, the SEC . . . A first-rate lawyer . . .*

He could hear his heart pound. That small, pathetic thudding and the rustle of the sheets as Pam turned over were the only sounds in the room. And he was conscious, as he had never been before, of the immensity of the world, or rather of his own smallness within its enormous, threatening expanse. When you were scared, when you were in a panic, you were alone. The world was indifferent at best and hostile at worst. The IRS and the SEC would tear him down and pull him apart, not knowing or caring to know that Eddy Osborne had never meant to hurt anyone. He was the kindest man alive. He was known to be, and he knew he was. He wasn't like the rest of the world, or most of it, anyway.

The first thing he would have to do in the morning was to find a new lawyer. He couldn't possibly see himself walking into the austere offices of his regular attorneys; it would be an unbearable humiliation to let those dignified poker-faces see that Vernon Edward Osborne had let himself get into a mess.

What he needed now was somebody who could grasp the situation at once, somebody to quell his fear. After all, he hadn't stolen anything, had he? A competent lawyer would know what to do. You had only to read the newspapers to see how skillful guides found paths through the jungle of the courts. The question was just where to go.

Inquire of Connie's husband? Martin Berg was a sophisticated

TREASURES

New Yorker and must have all sorts of connections. But why let the family know he was in trouble when it surely would blow over? Perhaps the best thing, after all, would be to go ask Abner, since he knew all about it anyway, to make a recommendation. Abner was one of the smartest men he had ever known.

This is very, very serious, Abner had said.

Somewhere in the apartment a clock struck. The place was full of clocks. Eddy had been collecting them: old English tall clocks, a rare eighteenth-century skeleton clock whose marvelous mechanism, functioning still, was fascinating to observe. He recognized now the C-sharp note of the little French gilt-and-marble clock in Pam's dressing room. Ten strokes. Morning was only eight or nine hours away. If he could only stay here in this dark room and not have to get up and go out or even think, but just lie here like this, sheltered and safe! If he could only tell Pam! She was his wife, and she would care about him. Yet he didn't want to pour his fears out before her. A man had pride, after all. A man wanted to be a hero in his wife's eyes. And Pam was so proud of him.

On sudden impulse he reached for her hand, whispering, "Are you asleep?" although he knew well that she was not.

"Of course I'm not. What's the trouble, Eddy? Won't you tell me?"

He sighed. "It's the rat race. I told you, I'm tired of it. It's been getting to me."

She waited.

"I've been thinking." Thoughts were forming as he spoke, thoughts that had not been there even minutes before. "You've always had that idea of buying a place in Kentucky, and I've always said, 'someday.' You know, it's come to me that maybe 'someday' should be now. I wouldn't mind living there for good, making it our home."

She was astonished. "Leave everything here? The office? The business? Just close up and leave?"

"Why not? People do it all the time."

"But whatever put it into your head right now? I don't understand."

"Oh, I don't know. I guess I've been keeping it in the back of my mind for a long while. And then the other night when those Kentucky people at our table were talking about that wonderful horse farm for sale near them, it popped to the front of my mind."

"Well, I can't say I'm not bowled over. You never said you were tired of the rat race. I thought you loved it."

"I did love it. But there's a time for everything. Time to begin and time to end. So how about our going down to look at this place? If it's as wonderful as the description, we'll buy it. Or rather, you will."

Put everything into her name. All the treasures in this apartment and the apartment itself. Sell it to her for a few dollars, five or ten thousand, make it a bona fide sale. Just in case . . . In case . . . It's the smart way. . . .

There was sudden alarm in Pam's voice. "But why, Eddy? This is too sudden. Something has to be wrong, and you don't want to frighten me. Have you found out you've heart disease or something so you have to take it easy? You look so worried."

"You always suspect that when I look a little tired."

"Well, then, if you're not sick, there has to be another reason."

No, he thought again, I will not tell her. I'm not going to frighten the life out of her when I'm sure, I have to be sure, that a good lawyer will iron the whole problem out. Smart as he is, Abner has always been unduly cautious, anyway.

Eddy's confidence swung like a pendulum. It will be all right. It will not be all right. His thoughts dashed here and there. Who's a top lawyer? Marvin and Blake? The Andrews firm? Henry Rathbone? Abner will probably recommend Rathbone, I think. . . .

TREASURES

"There has to be another reason," Pam repeated.

"Honey, I'll explain it to you, but I really am too tired now. And there's not all that much to explain, anyway, nothing to worry over. It'll be a great thing for us. We can go down and raise horses. We'll live longer and be healthier. It makes a lot of sense. Believe me."

And with that Pam had to be satisfied.

It took almost no time at all to buy a fine old house, enriched by six hundred acres of woods and fields, because they fell in love with it on sight. It stood at the end of a long drive lined with dogwoods and redbuds, a perfect picture-book house with columns, a veranda, and a fanlight over the door. Eddy's pulses beat; he was captivated. For one marvelous minute, as he rested his eyes upon that house, he forgot why he was here, forgot that this was to be a refuge, a hideout, an escape.

"Well," he said, "well, what do you think?"

"We almost don't need to see the inside, do we? I can describe it to you now, and then we'll see whether I'm right. Of course, there's a center hall, there's a dining room on the left because that has to be the kitchen wing. Let's see. . . . Six bedrooms, I estimate, and probably not enough bathrooms."

"Those can be put in," Eddy said quickly.

"And I'll bet there's a fireplace in every room. Let's go in."

In a happy kind of daze they followed the caretaker through the rooms, Pam murmuring, "Oh, it's too good to be true! I'd love to hang your Rowlandson prints in the little upstairs hall. This corner bedroom should be ours; I'd do it in pale blue, very cool, because the sun must come in most of the day."

She's thrilled, he thought. This is her rightful setting, far more than the apartment is or the suite in Paris; she'll have a dozen dogs running all over the place.

The caretaker had some comments for them when they went outside again.

"Back there's a pond, and behind it the woods. The orchard, the cornfield, and vegetables are on that side; they've been a bit neglected this last year, but there's no great harm done. Some folks might think the stables are too close to the main house, but," he added regretfully, "I sure would hate to see them torn down."

"Torn down!" Pam exclaimed. "Absolutely never!"

Two long, handsome buildings faced each other across a courtyard. On one, a clock, and on the other, a gilded weather vane twinkled in the sunlight.

"There's room for thirty horses," the man said.

On Pam's face there was an expression that could only be described as rapturous.

"So you love it, darling?" Eddy asked.

"Oh!" she said. And then anxiety passed across her face. "But are you sure it's right, what we're doing?"

"It's right," he said decisively. "Let's waste no time closing the deal and getting workmen in here to fix it up."

For time was pressing. Time was "of the essence," as lawyers say.

Lawyers . . .

CHAPTER
THIRTEEN

❧❧❧

From a stall in the ladies' room at the Metropolitan Museum, Connie overheard an indiscreet conversation.

"This is the third—no, the fourth—second wedding I've been at this year." The voice was not a young one, and the tone was indignant. "First they make their fortunes, and then they ditch their wives for these trophies. It's disgraceful."

"I know," came the response. "And all those gushing articles about what wonderful, sensitive, caring—I'm sick of that word *caring*, anyway—fathers these fifty-year-olds are to their new babies! It's ridiculous."

"Nobody mentions the first family," said the first voice. "I often think of Martin Berg's children. They say the son is alienated, and the last time I saw the daughter, she looked absolutely forlorn. A pathetic waif."

Connie emerged from the stall and stared directly into the flustered countenance of Mrs. Preston DeWitt. Then she turned her back, washed her hands, and, with a scornful laugh, left the room, banging the door behind her.

Old fools! Jealous old fools! Preston probably stayed with Caroline only because she was ill and he was decent. There hadn't been photographers waiting on the front steps of the museum for *her* tonight, as they had been when the Bergs arrived. There would be no articles about Caroline DeWitt in the society columns tomorrow, as there would be about Connie, with full description of her dress and the brand-new sapphires around her neck. They were drop-dead sapphires, too, Martin's most recent gift, presented for no reason other than "I adore you."

Connie's silver heels clicked over the stone floors through the long, dim sculpture galleries as she hurried back toward the Temple of Dendur. Round tables covered with lace cloths over turquoise petticoats surrounded the temple, which still, some thousands of years after its conception on the Nile, held a powerful, dark mystery. The shrubbery and the flowers, the gilded candelabra, the poached lobster, and the Haut Brion, all were magnificent, as befitted both the setting and the marriage of one of the most important financiers in America. Oh, it was wonderful to be among grand events at the pinnacle and in the heart of the city! These were the people who kept the city moving, and she was part of them. Often when she had given her name, Mrs. Martin Berg, in a shop, she would hear, as she turned away, the awed whispers among the salesgirls. And then, remembering her days in the Houston dress shop, she would jubilate, as now at this moment.

Nevertheless, the word *trophy* could still rankle.

Bitsy Maxwell was at the Bergs' table. "I hear," she said, "that you've just bought a marvelous house in London. What's the location?"

"Belgravia. It's one of those early-nineteenth-century terrace houses and needs a lot of work."

"I don't envy you the responsibility," said Bitsy, who could not afford more than a New York apartment and a place in Southampton.

"Oh, I don't mind it at all. I wanted the house for Martin. He goes back and forth from London so much that I really thought he should have a place of his own to relax in. The Savoy is a perfect hotel, but still a hotel isn't a home, is it?"

Bitsy shrugged. "I don't object to hotels. We stay at the Connaught."

"Well, from now on you'll have our place to stay at when you're in London." And Connie, looking about with satisfaction, caught Martin's eye just as he was rising from the table.

"I see Simmonds over there," he whispered. "He's supposed to get some more publicity on the neurology wing I'm donating. Damn, I want it known that I do something with my money besides making more of it."

"Darling, everybody knows what you do. Sit down and relax. You work too hard, anyway."

"I have to if I want to keep up with your expenditures." Martin smiled. "But I don't mind. Do you know you're the most beautiful woman in this whole room, including the bride?"

She watched him walk away, reach for a cigar, and then, remembering where he was, put it back in his breast pocket. It was a hardship for him to go more than an hour or two without a cigar. He really looked well, thanks to her unrelenting supervision of his exercise and diet. She had been good for him; his sisters had even told her so. Ben, the disapproving brother, they fortunately saw quite seldom. As to Martin's children, she was careful to be as loving to Melissa as to her own Thérèse, and Martin saw that.

Now and again, she still wondered what it was to be "in love," to feel the euphoria, the willingness to "die" for another that one read about and that sometimes, rarely and shyly, Lara talked about. Not that she needed to hear tell of it; you simply saw it between Davey and her. . . .

Well, this was all immaterial, anyway. She was here tonight in pride and splendor. Later, they would go home, and in the carved rococo bed she would practice on her husband the arts that kept him loving her and kept him feeling young.

He was standing now in the center of a cluster of men. Her first thought was that he looked awfully short, and she must watch the height of her heels. The second thought was that something had happened, for the group around him was enlarging. Men were putting their napkins aside and rising to join it.

"What's going on?" asked Bitsy.

"Oh, the prime rate's gone up or down or something," Connie answered.

Presently, Martin came back toward her and beckoned. "Come outside to the hall for a minute."

Surprised, she stood up and followed. "What is it? Is something wrong?"

Martin was glum. "I'm afraid there is, and I wanted to tell you before we go back to the table, in case anyone says something. People are generally tactful, but there might be somebody there who doesn't know your name is Osborne. It's about your brother, you see. No, no, nothing's happened to him, for God's sake! Except that there's a leak in tomorrow's papers. He's to be indicted by the United States attorney. The news is all over Wall Street. I would have heard it if I hadn't been in Boston all day."

A wave of shock swept over her. "Indicted? For what?"

"I don't know all the details. Insider trading, defrauding Internal Revenue. I'm not sure."

Eddy! But he was so clever and so good! Surely this had to be a mistake, some sort of unjust accusation. Oh, poor Eddy!

Then, after the first few seconds, came another fright. "You're not involved in anything with him, are you?"

Martin was indignant. "What a stupid question! I'm surprised at you. Me? An eighty-five-year-old firm like ours involved with a kid like him?"

"All right, it was a stupid question. I'm sorry. I'm just upset. I'm just horrified."

"Honey, don't cry here. Don't let it show."

She took a long, deep breath. Then very softly she asked, "Martin, if it's true, what's going to happen to him?"

"If it's true," Martin said grimly, "he'll go to prison."

CHAPTER
FOURTEEN

∽∾

Henry Rathbone was one of the most celebrated lawyers in the city and one of the most expensive, and he had counseled Eddy to keep calm and go to work as usual while relying on Henry to negotiate. Naturally, he had made no promises, but his general demeanor had suggested a modified optimism. And so, keeping that in mind, Eddy dressed himself that morning to his usual perfection, ate his usual breakfast, and was now seated at his desk with the usual pile of papers before him. But his gaze kept straying, first toward the sullen, dark Hudson on the one side and then back into the room, where a sullen, steely light slanted across the Sheraton bow-front chest beside the door.

Abruptly, the door opened, revealing Mrs. Evans in dismay.

"Mr. Osborne! There are two men here. They say they're United States marshals, they showed me their badges, and they're coming in, I couldn't stop them, I don't know what they want—"

Eddy stood up. "Let them in," he said, and along with immediate awareness that his heart had begun to pound, and that every pulse in his body was pounding with it, was the consciousness that this must be the moment when he must bear himself well.

Two men entered, men so ordinary as to be indescribable. They might have been selling insurance or vacuum cleaners. Eddy's thoughts went helter-skelter.

"Mr. Osborne," one said, "we have a warrant for your arrest."

Arrest. The helter-skelter thoughts focused: But Rathbone said —These were paper proceedings, weren't they? Things settled by words between lawyers, settled in offices, at desks and on telephones, not physically! Not taking your body. Arrest was *seizing*. Seizing your body.

He stammered. "What for? I mean—I don't understand. There's a mistake. My lawyer's working on it right now."

"You'll be able to call your lawyer. But you'll have to come along first." The man extended a piece of paper. "Read the warrant."

Eddy took it. Bold printed lettering and lines of typewritten sentences blurred toward a signature at the end. He handed it back unread. And a silence thrummed, rang, tingled in his ears.

"You'll have to put these on," the second man said.

Mrs. Evans was staring at the handcuffs. Her lips hung open, and her faded, neatly waved hair was rumpled.

"I'll go with you," Eddy said. "You don't have to put those on me. You don't understand, I'm not the sort of person who'll make trouble. You don't understand."

"Make it easy for yourself," the man told him. "Put out your hands."

Oh, God, Eddy thought, not through the main door! Not to be marched past all those desks and all those eyes.

"Can we go out the back door?" His voice faltered badly; he was furious at his damned voice.

You must bear yourself well, you're Vernon Edward Osborne, and you'll straighten out this crazy business.

"There's a private entrance," Mrs. Evans said, weeping now. "It's not the way you came in. Please," she pleaded, "it's quicker that way, anyhow."

TREASURES

Eddy's hands just hung at the ends of his too-stiff arms. There was no place to put them. Walking around like that, you looked ridiculous. Mrs. Evans leapt for the Burberry raincoat that was always kept in the closet and draped it over his awkward hands. She reached up and kissed him, her wet nose brushing his jaw.

"God bless you, Mr. Osborne. He's a good man," she warned the intruders. "Be gentle with him," she said fiercely.

"Don't worry, lady."

So Eddy departed from the offices of Osborne and Company with one man ahead of him and one behind him. A plain black sedan was parked below, and no one in the hurrying crowd on the sidewalk saw the three men get into the backseat and drive away.

When they had traveled a few blocks, Eddy brought himself to ask where they were going.

"The United States Courthouse at Foley Square."

It was not a jail, anyway. Or did they have a jail there? He knew nothing of the law. How should I know? he asked himself. I was never in trouble, I hardly ever got a traffic ticket. This is rotten. Rotten. A man like me in handcuffs. Me.

Helpless because of his bound hands, he had to be assisted from the car. Mechanically, he moved through the broad halls past many doors; he had impressions such as one receives when in a moving car, a speeding blur of people clustered in corridors, waiting for something, of poor-seeming people, of brisk people with important briefcases, of body smells, odors of rain-wet woolen, stale cigarette smoke, of washing powder where someone was mopping the floor, and finally, of police in a room with green-white lights that glared over scuff marks on the walls and over brown scuffed furniture.

When they removed the handcuffs, he rubbed his wrists, not to ease pain, for there had been none, but rather to remove the feel of contact with something filthy. They held his splayed fingers firmly onto an inked pad; they stood him with a placard bearing a number on his chest and took his picture as if he were a rapist or a mugger, as if he had abused little boys or murdered his wife. As if he were not Vernon Edward Osborne. And through it all he did not speak a word, but promptly did what he was told to do while his heart's hammering did not abate, and he thought that perhaps it might stop or rupture something in his chest, and then all this would be over. When he had to urinate, somebody went with him to the men's room. For a moment in there he was sure he was going to vomit, but, mercifully, the sensation passed. They led him at last to a room where there was a telephone so that he could call Rathbone. Rathbone was already on the way. Somebody asked him whether he wanted to make any more calls, and with the asking, which to his inexperience seemed to be an unexpected kindness, he went all soft, fearful that tears might gather in his eyes. And he declined. Besides, he was not ready yet to talk to Pam; he needed time to figure out how he was going to say that the thing he had feared, while denying his fear, had happened.

In this room where people were coming in and out, he could see into more rooms and out into the bustling halls. What a place of misery and contention was here! Why would anybody ever want to be a judge or a lawyer or to perform any labor in such a place of misery? But when Henry Rathbone came in, Eddy put on the face that the world knew best, and was jocular Eddy Osborne again, whom nothing fazed.

"Well, Henry, here I am. What happens next, the guillotine?"

"No, no, Eddy. Don't worry, we'll have you out on bail in no time. You'll go home and sleep in your own bed tonight. Come with me."

"Where to?"

"We have to appear before a United States magistrate. He sets the bail. The U.S. prosecutor will be there too."

Rathbone was short, not much higher than Eddy's shoulder, and yet he felt like a child beside him. For Rathbone had authority in this place, and his walk showed it. That's the way I used to walk through the bullpen at Osborne and Company, Eddy said to himself, and then realized that he had already said "used to."

The magistrate sat high in a small courtroom, wearing his black robes. Even in that dingy, unimpressive room he looked— well, magisterial. He was supposed to, wasn't he? Perhaps it was the robe that did it. The United States attorney was a handsome man whose face would have been striking on a coin. It was a vote-getting face, perfect on television. And Eddy stood waiting and watching while the three men talked. It had begun to rain harder; a downpour sluiced long runnels on the dirty window. In spite of its fluorescent bulbs the room darkened, and to Eddy the effect of darkness was ominous. On the other hand, cheerful sunlight would have mocked him.

"The charges," said the handsome prosecutor, "warrant high bail, Your Honor. This man is charged on five separate counts involving, so far, more than three hundred million dollars. So far."

"Your Honor," responded Rathbone, "my client is not a hardened criminal. This is a first offense. If it is an offense at all, which I certainly do not concede."

"Your Honor," said the prosecutor, "I would like to ask that bail be set at five million dollars."

The magistrate's eyebrows went up, black eyebrows in a ruddy forehead. He looks as if he likes his Scotch, thought Eddy. On the other hand, it may just be high blood pressure. His mind wandered again. Now the rain was smearing patterns in the grime, circles and curlicues.

"That is most excessive, Your Honor," Rathbone was arguing. "Mr. Osborne has a home and a wife. He has relatives. His sister is married to one of the most prominent men in the city. He has roots. He's not going to run away."

"That can't be guaranteed, Your Honor," protested the United States attorney.

"It can, Your Honor. I would ask that reasonable bail be set. One hundred thousand dollars would be reasonable."

"Your Honor, in the light of the charges, that makes no sense. It is out of proportion, entirely out of proportion."

Rathbone persisted. "He is not going to flee, Your Honor. Can we not compromise?"

"Your Honor, we are poles apart."

"Well," said the magistrate, "we can't be here all day over this."

The man looked tired. Again, Eddy thought, I wouldn't take a job like this one no matter what it paid, and come to think of it, it doesn't pay much. And there was a long silence while the magistrate pondered.

At last he made his decision. "Bail will be two million dollars."

"May I consult with my client for a moment?" asked Rathbone. They went to the back of the room. "Have you got it? Can you get it?" he whispered.

"God no, you know I'm strapped. All the accounts were in Pam's name." Thank God he had been smart enough to do that.

"Your relatives? Berg? We could try a bail bondsman, but it would take time. Red tape and time."

Eddy thought. He hated to ask Martin. Forever after he would be miserable in Martin's presence, he would shrink. It was a bad thing to be beholden to a relative, even to one whom he liked well enough.

"The money would mean very little to your brother-in-law."

Eddy was silent.

"You know it would," Rathbone repeated softly.

Eddy looked off into the thick, smoky air beyond the window, and then back at Rathbone. "I dread asking," he said, and heard, despising it, the tone of appeal in his voice.

"I understand. Would it be easier if I were to ask instead?"

"It would help," Eddy replied with some relief. Then a thought struck him. "What if he isn't in?"

"Don't worry. I'll track him down. Berg knows me. At least, we've met more than once."

"Thank you, Henry. Thank you very much." And then a second thought struck dread, and he had to ask, "Do you suppose you could try to find my wife too? She's at her mother's in the country. Wait. Here's the number. Do you think you could sort of gently, sort of gradually, break the news to her? I never told her. I should have. She could have prepared herself, the way you prepare for a death when someone's been sick for a long time. This is like someone's dying of a heart attack with no warning. But I never wanted her to lose faith in me. Who knew it would come to this? Oh, this is the worst. It's killing me to think of Pam getting this news."

Rathbone nodded sympathetically. "I'll take care of it. And you take it easy, Eddy."

When Rathbone left, Eddy remained where he was, gazing out of the window at nothing, yet too much aware of the two men in the front of the room, the magistrate still on the bench, and aware, too, of another man near the door, some sort of guard, he supposed, to make sure that Eddy didn't try to escape.

It seemed interminable hours, but actually it was only a little more than twenty minutes before Rathbone returned and at once addressed the court. Bail had been arranged and would be delivered within the hour.

Then he walked back to Eddy. "Berg couldn't have been more helpful," he reported. "I only had to ask him once."

"I suppose he was pretty shocked. Stunned."

"I guess so, but he didn't show it. He seemed only concerned. Compassionate. And I tried to reach your wife, but she had left. Her mother said she was going to make some stops on the way and probably wouldn't be home before dinnertime. That'll give you a chance to wash up and rest before she gets there." Rathbone added kindly, "Take a stiff drink, sit down, and talk together as calmly as you can and then have a good dinner."

293

"Are we going to lick this thing, Henry?" Eddy asked, very low. "Tell me the truth, please. I can handle it."

"Eddy . . . We're going to do the very best we can, that's the answer."

The Filipino couple were in the kitchen. Ramón, with an apron over his white coat, was polishing silver, and María Luz was stirring something at the stove.

"How would you two like to take the evening out?" Eddy proposed, showing his most cheerful manner. "Mrs. Osborne and I have just been invited somewhere, so you might as well go."

"But the dinner . . ." María Luz was both doubtful and hopeful.

"Save the dinner for tomorrow." He gave them a jovial wave as he left the kitchen. "Go on. Enjoy yourselves."

The last thing he could tolerate right now was a ritual dinner, the elegance of which he ordinarily appreciated. But tonight there might be tears and recriminations. Who knew what tonight would bring?

In the library he sat in a vague sort of daze until he heard them going out at the back door. Then, as if obeying some peremptory command, he sprang up. In a pantry closet he found some cardboard cartons and pulled them into the library. He telephoned to the building superintendent and asked for more cartons, the largest he had and as many as he had.

"As many? We have a couple of dozen, Mr. Osborne, waiting for the trash pickup."

"Bring them all," said Eddy.

Back in the cleaning closets he found rolls of tissue paper, of brown wrapping paper, and balls of heavy twine. The house was well stocked with such practical items, for Pam was a good housekeeper, an efficient keeper of the house, the home that was now being destroyed. For no matter what Rathbone said—what had he said? Something like *I'll do my best*?—Eddy felt disaster in his bones. At the same time he could also remember moments when, even today, he had been certain that things would all turn out well in the end. But now, now at this moment, he felt only disaster.

When the superintendent had covered half the library's floor with cartons, Eddy saw the questions on his tongue. But they remained unasked; no doubt something in Eddy's face had deterred the man. As soon as he was gone, Eddy set to work, taking pictures down from the walls. There went the Sargent lady in her velvet dress; Winslow Homer's palm trees bending in a southern wind; the Pissarro's crowded, rainy street in Paris. These were his treasures and he was ripping them off his walls. There was even one that had not yet been hung, a nineteenth-century portrait of a horse that he had ordered from London for Pam.

For three hours he worked, going from room to room. He was frantic. Panic rose in him, and panic was cold; it ran up and down his arms and raised the hair on the back of his neck. Lifting, padding, cutting his fingers on twine, he sweated. He wrapped small objects, porcelains and ivories, emptying the twin lacquered cabinets in the drawing room; he began to take down his first editions, the leather-bound Dickens, the Walt Whitman, the—

"What in heaven's name are you doing?" Pam screamed. "Have you gone crazy? Crazy?"

He pulled himself erect and, ankle deep in paper, regarded his wife, his cherished wife, in her camel-hair coat and her alligator boots. And for the moment he was dumbstruck.

Stupidly, he said, "We're moving to Kentucky, you remember. So I thought, I had some time, I came home early. I thought I'd get a few things ready."

She grabbed his shirtfront. "Eddy, listen to me. I've known you were hiding something but I gave up asking you what. Do you think I'm an idiot? I've been so afraid. . . . Sit down here and tell me what's wrong. I want to know. Now! Now!"

His Adam's apple seemed to swell until it hurt. Nevertheless he had to begin. "I'm in trouble with the government, Pam. Some tax trouble. God, I hoped it would turn out all right! I wanted to spare you, but I can't anymore. I was arrested this morning."

"Arrested?"

"Yes. It was—well, it was quite an experience." And he managed a weak, shamefaced smile. "Fingerprints and all."

"But what have you done?" she cried.

"A few foolish things, I have to admit. But nothing criminal. I haven't hurt anybody. It's a tax mess, that's all, too complicated to explain. I'd need to show you reams of papers. My lawyer says we'll work it out."

"But if you were arrested, you must be out on bail."

"Yes. Martin put it up."

She was standing above him. And he looked up at her calm forehead under the velvet headband. Most women, hearing this piece of news, would be losing control.

"Why don't you get angry at me?" he asked. "I would feel better if you did. I deserve it. Don't be afraid of losing your temper. Yell at me."

"What's the point? What would it accomplish?" she responded wearily. Quality, he thought as always. Breeding. It shows.

In the street below, a fire engine passed with a long, terrifying wail, receded, and left a bleak aftermath of stillness. Pam was waiting.

"I got in too deep," he said. "I don't know how it happened. I thought I had a magic touch. I always did have. I knew my way around the market." He put his head in his hands. "Maybe I lost my touch. Things started to drain away. It was like a hemorrhage." And he made a little sound almost like a sob.

She stroked his hair. "Don't, Eddy. Aren't you the one who

296

always says anything can be worked out if you keep your wits about you?"

He raised his head. "Pam, I think it's possible that I might go to prison."

"Who's your lawyer? What does he say?"

"Henry Rathbone. One of the best in the city. He says it'll be okay." Had he actually said that? He had only promised to do his best.

"Did he tell you to pack up these things, to move?"

"He doesn't know I'm doing this. It's my idea to get things out of here in case anyone wants to come snooping after the paintings and antiques. The stuff's all yours, anyway."

"Louis XVI doesn't fit on a horse farm."

"Sell anything you don't want and take the cash. Oh, I'm glad I was smart enough to put this apartment in your name too. It's got to be worth four or five million by now."

The doorbell rang, making Eddy start. "Don't open it!"

"It has to be somebody they recognize downstairs, or no one would have let them come up," said Pam.

He supposed, after the morning's experience, that he would never again feel secure about who might be on the other side of a door. And then, when he heard the voices of Martin and Connie, he had the same feeling that had overcome him in the presence of Rathbone, that he was a child waiting to be scolded.

Connie stared about her. "My God, look at this ruin! Whatever possessed you, Eddy? Whatever?"

Martin waved her to silence. "How're you doing, Eddy? It's been a hell of a day for you."

"I want to thank you, Martin. If I can thank you, that is. But how can I ever for what you did?"

"Just see how you can work your way out of your troubles. That'll be thanks enough. Your sisters are beside themselves with worry. Lara phoned just now. She wanted to take the next flight."

"No, no," Eddy objected. Lara wouldn't say a word of condemnation, yet he felt he couldn't face her with this failure, not Lara, who had encouraged him from his days in junior high school up to now. "No, don't let Lara come," he repeated.

"We told her not to. With two children and the office work . . ." Martin shoved aside a pile of tissue paper and sat down on the sofa. "I only spoke ten minutes with Rathbone, so tell me, how deep in the hole are you?"

"I don't know exactly. A lot. I'd have to figure. It's complicated. I can't do bookkeeping in my head."

Martin frowned slightly. "But you must have some idea. Rathbone says one of the counts against you is that you played the stock market with your clients' funds. Haven't you any conception of your personal stock holdings?"

"I don't know. Maybe thirteen million. It varies, fluctuates. The market's been down the last couple of months. You know that."

"I know that," Martin said somewhat dryly. He nodded toward a Cézanne that was propped against a chair. "How much did that cost?"

Eddy followed Martin's glance toward the luminous blue-green Provençal hills. "About six million," he murmured, and wiped his forehead. "God Almighty," he blurted then, "I saved fortunes for my clients all the same! Everybody rushed to me. Didn't they love my four-to-one tax shelters? And now these same people will remember only my mistakes and won't give me the time to correct them. All I need is some time! God Almighty, I haven't committed murder, have I?" he demanded of the three who faced him.

"Well, if you've ruined people, that's almost the same thing, isn't it?" Connie said, sounding bitter. "Some of my good friends that I sent to you too."

Again Martin stopped her. "There's no point in that sort of talk," he admonished.

TREASURES

Pam sat rigidly, looking toward the window where lights twinkled across the street. Holding tears back, she blinked, and Eddy knew that the truth had finally just reached her.

"I don't understand," he said, "what started this government crackdown in the first place. What happened all of a sudden?"

"Somebody wrote an anonymous letter," Martin replied. "It was mailed from Vancouver to the SEC. Somebody who'd apparently lost money because of insider trading. I heard it from a man who has a brother with the SEC. Oh, it wasn't about you at all. But it started the ball rolling."

"Do you think I really have cause to be terribly worried?" Eddy asked.

Martin stood up. "I think I'm glad you have a top-notch attorney. Meanwhile, watch your health and use your head. Head over heart, you know."

Eddy nodded ruefully. "My mother used to say that, but she never did it."

"Well, you do it. Take a stiff Scotch and go to sleep." When Martin gave Eddy his hand, the grip was comforting. "Call me if you need me. Come on, Connie."

When they had left, Pam let a few tears fall, whispering into Eddy's shoulder, "Life was a ball, wasn't it? Such fun, being young and healthy and with no worries, just two hours ago. And now I feel a hundred years old."

"Remember what Martin just said, head over heart?"

"I know." Pam wiped her eyes. "I will. I just had to get it out of my system."

"Of course you do." And he understood that there must be within her, even as within himself, a turmoil of struggling contradictions, pity, fear, and anger. Of course.

"Life will be a ball again," he said.

"What happens next? To you, I mean."

"A trial. In about three months, Rathbone estimates."

"And he really thinks you'll win?"

"Lawyers have to think so, don't they?"

Smile, Peg always told her children. Smile even when you don't want to and it'll actually make you feel like smiling.

"Life isn't over," he said again. "Hey, I'm only thirty-four years old, and there's a long way to go. Let's see that photo of the Kentucky place. It's there on the desk. Looks like *Gone with the Wind,* doesn't it? Columns and all. And that copper beech on the lawn must be a hundred fifty years old." He hugged Pam closely. "Listen. I'm going to work out of this. And if I don't right away, if—if anything happens, why, you just go down there and live in the sun and wait till I get there too."

"He swindled people, didn't he? Tell the truth," Connie said on the way home. "I'm furious! How could he have been so stupid?"

"One word," Martin said. "Greed. It came too easily when he started, and he got too greedy."

"How will it end?"

Martin shrugged. "I'm not a lawyer, but my guess is that it'll end badly. From what I can see, he's committed four or five felonies."

"I'm angry at him, but I'm heartbroken too. Poor Eddy! He's got to be terrified. And I'm awfully sorry for Pam. Whatever will she do?"

"He told me once that everything belongs to her. Six of those paintings alone will give her at least twenty million. So I wouldn't worry."

"All the same, I'm sorry for her. They'll be ruined socially. Utterly ruined."

The federal district court was a far more imposing chamber than the one in which Eddy's first scene had been enacted. Everything seemed larger, the ceiling higher, the windows wider, the flag more prominent, and the bench more elevated. The

300

judge had the stern expression of the cancer surgeon who is about to operate. The jury's twelve chairs looked solemn in their rows, even when they were vacant. This was the place where severe punishments were meted out. Eddy's facetious remark about the guillotine did not seem absurd here. He wondered whether his heart, which had ceased to hammer—after all, how could it have kept hammering for the last three months?—and had merely subsided now into an irregular beat, would ever beat normally again.

All the chairs behind him, in row after row, were filled. He wondered why, and who the strangers might be who filled them. Directly in back of him in the second row sat his wife and his sisters; Lara, during the whole five weeks that his trial lasted, kept going back and forth from Ohio, although, knowing what effort it must take, he wished she wouldn't. Connie came in a sable coat, at least fifty thousand dollars' worth of coat, he knew, and hoped the judge and jury would not think this expensive lady was his wife. Pam, most sensibly, had worn her camel hair coat. She had remembered, too, that he had once said he felt uncomfortable when strangers sat directly behind him, where they could stare at the back of his neck, and so she took care to sit behind him herself. Pam was a princess, no doubt of it, in her dignity and reassuring calm. Pam was royalty.

Sometimes there appeared a few other familiar faces, friends and clients who had once been friends and were now enemies. Once he saw the puzzled, mournful face of Mrs. Evans, who probably was not sure now what she should think of the man she had served and protected from every small annoyance. In a brief passage of words during the court's recess, he gathered from her that Osborne and Company had been taken over by the government's examiners, who occupied almost every desk. And he hoped, although he did not say so, that no one would put his feet on his private desk, which was a treasure brought from an ancient house in Yorkshire. At the same time he knew perfectly well that the thought was foolish.

Nevertheless, his mind wandered foolishly again, veering between the closest, most tense observance of events and a dreamy escape into the changing sky, that was sometimes gray with a threat of rain and sometimes a cloudless, vibrant blue. In such moments, although he was seated beside Rathbone and his young associates with their boxes of sober documents on the table, he was entirely removed from them, not even there in the room at all. Then suddenly a word or an altered nuance of voice would jar him back into the time and place. He would let his eyes rove across the jury box, over the twelve who had been in turn challenged, faced rejection, and finally chosen with so much care. He wondered what it had been about each that had caused either Rathbone or the prosecutor to want him. He himself couldn't tell much of anything from their faces, although he tried to imagine what each might be apt to think about him. There was a very plain woman who could well be a social worker; there was a girlish-looking woman in her sixties who was probably rich; there was a black man in a suit that had come either from Brooks Brothers or J. Press; there was a seedy man with thin gray hair who reminded Eddy of his father. He had a flower in the buttonhole of his cheap suit. Pop had liked to wear one, too, goodness only knew why. Probably he had wanted to look carefree or jaunty, but he had only looked pathetic instead. That man would either understand Eddy or he would despise him. And Eddy had to look away. . . .

The hours dragged and the voices droned. The judge made a lengthy explanation to the jury about the securities business, giving them almost an elementary course in finance. They will never understand, Eddy thought. The only things that will stand out in their collective memory are the most simple terms: false information, altered dates, tax evasion. *If you decide that this is true. If you decide that this is not true, then you will not find him guilty.* Tax evasion is what would stick in their minds, the dollars deducted from their little paychecks. This would strike home.

The prosecutor struck home in his own way. ". . . the lifestyle, ladies and gentlemen, made possible by these defalcations is something one reads about, and, as ordinary working citizens, can only wonder at. This man maintains throughout the year, merely for occasional use by himself or his friends—palatial suites in the finest hotels to which he can go at a moment's notice and as the spirit moves him, in Florida, and in Arizona, in Cannes—that's a beach resort on the French Riviera—and in Gstaad—that's in Switzerland, a ski resort—and, oh, yes, I almost forgot, in Morocco too! Although what one does in Morocco, I certainly wouldn't know. Perhaps one goes there just for a change of atmosphere when one is bored." There were smiles from the jury at that.

"This man"—now he points at Eddy so that all twelve faces in the jury box turn their blank eyes toward him—"this man owns one of the finest art collections in this city, possibly in the entire United States. Just one of his automobiles, just one, mind you, cost over one hundred thousand dollars. You could probably fit all twelve of your homes and mine, too, into his East Side apartment and have room left over. And whose money bought all these marvels? I'll tell you: Not his! No, it was for the most part the money he received from investors who trusted him, whom he strung along, using fake account statements, so faked and fraudulent that his own accountants refused to serve him any longer. And I'll tell you who else's money." Here, the long finger swiveled back toward the jurors themselves. "Your money! You, the taxpayers of this country, whose taxes are paid out faithfully every fifteenth day of April. Oh, we're all too familiar with that date! But what did he do on that date? Well, I'll tell you. He did some fancywork, some juggling, deducting phony losses so that it turned out he didn't owe anything to Uncle Sam at all this year. It was put off till next year. Always next year. Only, next year never came! Do you see? Year after year, no taxes, or very, very little, a joke when you consider what his profits were. Yes, you can well sigh, for you were cheated. I was. We all were."

In back of Eddy a chair creaked, and there was a faint restless movement from his wife or from one of his sisters. And wondering what they were really thinking, he knew that because of their love for him, he would never be told what they were really thinking.

It was then Rathbone's turn. "I am going to rely on your common sense," he told the jury respectfully and persuasively. "These financial transactions are very complicated, but you are all intelligent people, and you will not be misled by name calling. The practice of deferring taxes is quite legal. It is standard, normal practice where losses have been incurred; neither my client nor his firm are the only ones who do this. It is by no means an evasion of taxes." He directed one of his young men to hold up a large chart, boldly printed on cardboard. "Let me show you. It will be quite clear. . . ."

But it will not be quite clear, Eddy thought, feeling his frail hopes ebb. Or rather, it will be clear in the wrong way. Rathbone is fighting a losing battle. Even if he is right about the tax shelters, what about all the other counts? No, it's no use. The girlish, sixtyish lady in the jury box was having a struggle to keep awake. The black man in the Brooks Brothers suit had a sardonic expression; he understands all too well, Eddy thought. Rathbone will get nowhere with him.

And so it went on and on, day after day. Eddy, well primed and well rehearsed, went on the stand and was carefully led by Rathbone. He performed well. On cross-examination he kept his calm demeanor, but he knew that he was floundering, and he was forced to answer some questions that condemned him.

"And did you on this date remove two hundred and sixty thousand dollars from the account of Mr. Marple and place it in your own?"

"Yes, but I replaced it a week later."

"I asked whether you removed it. Answer yes or no."

"Yes."

Why is all this taking so long? Get it over with! Eddy thought. These interminable hours were a torture, facing those twelve pairs of eyes and sometimes even meeting a passing glance from the judge, the sphinx in the black robes. And every day when it was over came the worst of all when, as he descended the courthouse steps, the reporters waited, and the photographers leapt to follow him, prancing like wild children playing horse, sticking the ugly snouts of their cameras into his face, so that if he had dared, he would have smashed their cameras and them too.

"Why don't you get an honest job?" he wanted to shout. "Vultures! Buzzards! Circling the ground where the animal lies dying. You can't wait to tear him apart, can you?"

When the end came in the fifth week, the verdict was guilty. Eddy, standing erect, did not look at the foreman who delivered the verdict, but met instead the bleary, weary eyes of the little man who reminded him of his father, and was sure he saw pity there; this was a man who knew what it was to be humbled and humiliated, who knew what it was to lose. And he slumped down, shaken, and reached up to grasp Pam's hand that rested on his shoulder.

Rathbone had approached the bench to speak. "I would like to ask, Your Honor, that in sentencing you consider that my client has been an exemplary citizen. He is known for his many philanthropies. If Your Honor please, I would like to say that it would serve no purpose for him to be imprisoned. A substantial amount of time to whatever worthy cause might best profit by his intelligence and energy, such as a drug rehabilitation program or service in a city hospital, would be far more meaningful in every way. I hope very earnestly that Your Honor will consider such an alternative."

The austere face revealed nothing. "I hear you, Mr. Rathbone.

Bail will be continued and sentencing will be"—here the pages of a calendar were turned—"in six weeks. You will be notified."

The same courtroom, even in the absence of the jury, looked as formidable as it had six weeks earlier. Eddy rose when instructed to and stood with Rathbone beside him to hear the sentence.

The words were meted out with no inflection and no emotion. "I suppose he can't let it show, but surely he must feel something," Eddy thought as the words fell into a thick silence.

"You have been found guilty on eight separate counts of conspiracy to defraud the Internal Revenue Service . . . your greed has been inordinate and without conscience . . . however, I do take into some account the number of letters I have received from character witnesses who testify to your charitable acts . . . there have been letters from simple citizens describing your personal generosity."

The janitor, Eddy remembered. He'd paid his wife's hospital bill. And Arthur Pyle. He'd saved his house from foreclosure.

". . . I take note of your counsel's request that you be permitted to render community service in lieu of imprisonment. But there has to be some deterrence of crimes like yours, which are occurring far too frequently in the investment community. Therefore, I sentence you to four years' imprisonment on each of the eight charges, the sentences to run concurrently. At the expiration of your sentence you will perform twelve hours of community service every week for one year, terms to be arranged. You will then have five years of probation. Furthermore, you will pay a fine of one million dollars in addition to back taxes. And you are forbidden ever to engage in the securities business as long as you live. Have you anything you wish to say, Mr. Osborne?"

"Nothing, Your Honor." What was there to say?

"Court is dismissed," said His Honor.

There was a scrape and shuffle of chairs and feet. Pam kissed him. Lara and Connie were stricken, as if they were seeing a bloody accident on a highway.

Rathbone asked softly, "Are you okay?"

Eddy nodded. "Okay."

"We'll appeal, of course."

"And if we lose?"

"I don't believe in thinking in those terms, you know that."

"But if we do," persisted Eddy.

"You'll be out in two years. You know, you could have gotten a lot worse."

"You're saying I got off easy?"

Rathbone shrugged.

"I didn't say that, Eddy. I only meant that it could be worse."

The two men, followed by the three women, moved downstairs and out onto the sidewalk.

"If I do get sent up," Eddy questioned in a low voice, "where will I go?"

"Minimum security. I'll ask for Allenwood—it's in Pennsylvania—and I'll probably get it. It's the least harsh. Not harsh at all," Rathbone added quickly.

"How long before the appeal will be heard?"

"It's hard to say, but maybe a year."

And Eddy blurted, "What the hell will I do with myself for a year, not knowing what comes next?"

Rathbone's reply was rueful. "There'll be no lack of activity: the government's suit for back taxes and penalties; suits by individuals to recover their losses; your own bankruptcy. The court will appoint a receiver for your assets, and I've already promised that you won't remove any of your possessions from the apartment. Is that understood?"

"Understood."

"Good." Rathbone gave him a slap on the back. "You'll get through this thing, Eddy. You're a good man, and you can't keep a good man down."

Platitudes, Eddy thought, and thanked him nevertheless.

They rode uptown in Connie's limousine. Eddy brought up the question that was in all their minds.

"Where shall we hang our hats for the year? I'm wondering."

"Kentucky?" Pam spoke tentatively. "There's nothing much more to be done in the house. It's quite livable."

"No." Eddy was decisive. "I don't want to go there, to the community where we'll be making our home, until all this is behind us. Maybe it's foolish of me, but I'd rather not. I want to start fresh."

"You can always stay with us," Connie said. "In the city or the country, or wherever you want."

"Thanks, Connie. I'd like to visit for short stays, but to be frank, your house is always full, and I don't particularly care to run into Wall Street types right now."

"There'll be no parties, no guests at all, whenever you are there," she assured him.

"My mother's?" Pam proposed. "Goodness knows there's enough room for us in that old barn of a house."

"No. Your mother's embarrassed by this mess. She's too much of a lady to say so, but she is, and I won't do that to her."

"Well, you've always got us in Ohio," said Lara, "if you can stand a noisy household."

"What I'd really like is to get far away. I wish we could go to Europe."

"Why can't you?" asked Lara.

"I'm out on bail. I can't leave the country."

"Oh," said Lara, flushing, "I didn't think."

No one spoke for a moment, and then Eddy said quietly, "I guess we'll just move where the spirit sends us."

Like a fugitive, he thought. Moving around.

So the months passed. Eddy and Pam spent a few weeks at the Bergs' Palm Beach house when no one else was there, and a few weeks out of season at a half-deserted inn on Nantucket. They flew back and forth to Lara's and found themselves most comfortable there in the easy atmosphere of the cheerful family. As much as possible they avoided New York; on its streets, in its theaters and restaurants, they were sure to meet people whom Eddy did not want to meet. Whenever, at Rathbone's summons, they had to be in the city, they stayed at the Hotel Pierre, for the apartment had been emptied out and its contents trundled away to Kentucky in two enormous vans.

Rathbone telephoned in shock one day. "Eddy! What the hell have you done? You know you weren't to remove any of your possessions! The receivers came in and found everything gone—"

"I wasn't supposed to remove *my* possessions, and I didn't. All of the stuff there was Pam's. It never did belong to me. I can show you the documents, legal documents. Incidentally, she has a buyer for the apartment too." Eddy chuckled. "I'd like to have seen that receiver's face when the super opened the door, and they walked through twelve empty rooms."

This was the one bright note in a long, dim year.

Vernon Edward Osborne, having lost his case on appeal, was given three days to report to Allenwood Federal Penitentiary.

Rathbone, at the sentence, asked permission to take his client there himself. "For," as he had explained to Eddy, who had protested that he didn't want to be a bother to Rathbone, "the alternative is to go to the U.S. marshal, be put in handcuffs, and maybe spend a couple of days first at the Metropolitan Correctional Center before they take you to Allenwood in chains. Not a pleasant prospect." Eddy closed his eyes as if he were seeing himself in chains. "We'll leave at the crack of dawn to get there early. That way you'll have a chance at the better jobs and room assignments."

"Jobs?" Eddy had not thought of jobs.

"All kinds. Kitchen work, cutting grass, office work, or the library. Anything and everything."

Eddy turned to Pam. "I don't want you to come along."

"Not me?" she cried.

"No. I don't want you to see me in that place."

"Families do visit," Rathbone said gently.

"No. I forbid it, Pam. I don't want you to remember me all our lives like that. I don't want that picture in your mind. I'm going to tell my sisters too. Just write to me. And Henry says you can phone. But don't come, any of you."

"Eddy, I don't care what you say, I'm going to visit you."

They spent the last night in a suite at the Hotel Pierre. Pam ordered flowers as if this were a bridal night, and a feast of a dinner with champagne in the suite. Afterward they sat together in front of the television set, watching a comedian who wasn't funny. Eddy lay with his head on her lap while she stroked his hair.

After a while she asked him softly, "Tell me, did you really do anything so very terrible?"

"Hell, no. . . . I mean . . . I suppose . . . Well, I didn't kill anybody," he said, as he had already said a few dozen times before.

"It's going to be terrible without you."

"The time will pass." He wanted to comfort her and himself too. "It will go by faster than we think, and we'll have the rest of our lives after that."

"We'll miss this." She put his hand on her breast.

Her breasts were warm, full, and firm under the lace negligee. He felt her body move beneath him, coaxing him to move, too, either to turn over on the sofa or else to get up and go with her to the bed. He wanted what she was waiting for; he always did want it; but the prospect of the long time, two years at the least —if he was lucky—was so daunting, unthinkable, and so chilling that he felt incapable of response.

TREASURES

"We need something to remember," she murmured in his ear. "Something to last us."

"Darling, I don't think I—"

"Yes, yes. You will. Don't you know I know how?"

So he followed her to the bed, lay down, and waited.

"No hurry. Just relax. We have all night." Her hands, soft and burning, moved upon him. "And if you fall asleep, that'll be all right too."

But he did not fall asleep. Slowly, slowly . . . Just let everything go. That's it. All the fantasies. The seduction, the lure. Was there ever a woman like this one? She was insatiable. There was no end. Her voice. Her words. And a tremendous power leapt within him at last; it surged, was satisfied, and surged again. He had no idea how long they were there together.

There was a Latin saying about man's sadness afterward. Always he had wondered about that, having never experienced such sadness. But tonight was different, he thought, when, after Pam had fallen asleep, he had gotten up and gone into the other room. The circumstances were rather special tonight, after all.

It was not yet midnight, and the city lay sparkling, wide awake below and beyond the window. Limousines were moving down Fifth Avenue, transporting people to late, gala functions. On Madison they would be going northward instead, transporting other people uptown to their silken homes. Eddy stood there staring at the cars, at the park, and at planes that crossed the night sky, bringing yet more people to this fabulous capital of the world. And he thought about the day when he had been a newcomer here himself, a nobody with almost nothing in his pockets. In the morning he would be leaving it with nothing at all in his pockets, unless one counted what he had given away to Pam.

Suddenly the city with all its glamor seemed to him like a place he had never known and would never know again. He

311

shook himself. The feeling was too strange, too eerie, for this night. "I'm giving myself the creeps," he said aloud. And then, "Hey, Eddy Osborne, get hold of yourself! You're down, but you're not out yet."

CHAPTER
FIFTEEN

❧

On a dark day in Thanksgiving week an early snow lay glistening on the lawns of Cresthill. It was Connie who had placed the bronze sculptures and the eighteenth-century folly at the foot of the parterre. It was she who had begun a neighborly tradition of inviting as many as could come for lunch on the Sunday after the holiday. There was something picturesque, she thought, something charming, in the sight of families arriving with their children, the little girls and the very tiniest boys wearing lace-collared velvet and looking like a chic advertisement in *Country Life* or *Vogue*. Last year Thérèse had worn ruby velvet with matching shoestring bows in her dark hair.

On this particular Sunday there was another kind of gathering in the house. Shortly after lunch the men had started to arrive, and so far Connie had counted fifteen of them around the conference table in the red leather library. Obviously, some tremendous deal must be approaching its climactic hour to have brought all these bankers, lawyers, accountants, and principals together. From past experiences she knew that they might well be here all day, which would mean dinner, and then possibly late into the night, too, which would mean pizzas. These country meetings were always held at Martin's house, although the De-Witt house was only half an hour's drive away. Very likely, Caroline didn't want the cigar smoke in her house, Connie thought with some amusement.

Cigar smoke was seeping out of the library now, past closed doors and into the adjoining sitting room where Connie had been asked to man the one telephone line out of the five in the house that had been left open. She had been provided with a short list of acceptable callers and was to summon Martin only if one of them was on the line. Yes, this deal had to be something extraordinary, she reflected, for Martin had been unusually tense during the last few weeks; his left eyelid had kept twitching.

Restless now, she got up and went to the window. Far down the slope a bright orange spot slid across the snow where Nanny was pulling Thérèse on her sled. And Connie had a curious recollection of being pushed down a little hill in a cardboard carton; it might have been Lara who had pushed her or, perhaps, her mother. How Peg would marvel today at the grandchild to whom all this splendor belonged, these wide, quiet fields and this great house! As always, Connie felt a wave of confused emotions: tenderness and fierce protectiveness, disappointment because Lara's child was beautiful and Thérèse was not, shame at having so mean a thought, and pride because Thérèse was so advanced for her age and had such an appealing personality. She might look like her half sister, but she would never be woebegone like Melissa.

Fresh snow began to sift through the sky in dry, slow flakes, whitening the parked cars. More cars were arriving. Here came Preston's old station wagon with a dented fender. You'd think it would bother him to ride around in a car like that. But he himself was immaculate, his thick hair ruffling in the wind as he strode across the drive, his lean face reddened by the cold. He would be perfect in an advertisement for country tweeds. Why, Connie thought, do I always imagine how people would look in photographs? No matter. Preston belonged indefinably to the

American aristocracy. Like Eddy's wife, Pam. You had to be born to it.

Poor Eddy, in that awful place. She had gone once with Lara to see him, and their presence had upset him terribly; it had crushed his pride. But over the telephone he still talked with his old bravado, as if he really hadn't done anything much, as if everyone were making too big a fuss about it, anyway. Two years ago he had been here with them, happy and boisterous, loaded as usual with gifts. Just there near the front door he had parked and called the butler to help him carry Thérèse's dollhouse. Poor Eddy. And she remembered him presenting her with the Mercedes on the day of her wedding, bidding for a Matisse at a spectacular auction, answering respectful questions at a fashionable dinner party.

What had it all meant in the end? A strange, sick feeling of loss swept through her, as if there were no purpose in anything. And Connie shook herself as if to rid herself of a dismal foreboding.

Now came a white Rolls-Royce. When the chauffeur opened the door, she saw white leather upholstery, at which she frowned. Flamboyant. No taste. This had to be Franklin Bennett, the famous Franklin Bennett. Martin's description fitted the broad, bulky man in the ankle-length mink coat who emerged from the car. Dreadful. And she frowned again.

The day dragged. She returned to the sofa and the Sunday newspaper. Delphine whimpered, wanting to be on the sofa with Connie, and she picked her up, thinking again what a picture that would make, the chintz sofa, the red poodle, and herself in her sea-green knitted suit. You often saw photos of women with their dogs in their drawing rooms or libraries. Her mind went suddenly to the day they had bought Delphine. "Why, I can almost fit her into my pocket!" Richard had exclaimed. She could hear the exact tones of his voice this very minute, although ten years had gone by. And she wondered what might be happening in his life now. It was strange to think how once his life had been joined to her own. *The shy young man, holding the tennis racket, said, Are you Miss Osborne?* And now here she sat in Martin's house with Richard's dog on her lap.

I dozed, she thought, when she was jarred awake. The low rumble of male voices that had been barely audible from the other side of the heavy doors was erupting into angry argument, now plainly heard.

"God damn it! Are you saying we're crooks? Is that what you're saying?" Unmistakably, that was Martin.

The answering voice, a youthful one, was just as loud, but even and controlled. "I did not say that, sir. I did not."

"You used the word *fake*, and I didn't like it. God damn, I didn't like it."

"I said, if you remember, that this money is fake stuff. These bonds are promises based on other promises that people may not be able to keep. So it's not real money. It's worth about as much, in my opinion, as Monopoly money."

"Oh," said Martin, icy cold now, "it's Monopoly money that we've been paying you, is it?"

"No, sir, I've been properly paid, and I know that. All I'm saying is, a lot of people in this country are going to end up not being paid at all."

Other voices entered into the commotion. To Connie's alarmed ears it sounded as if one man, the one with the youthful voice, was in opposition to all the others. She had never imagined that these eminent men would create such a tumult.

"This mountain of debt will someday crush the whole country—"

"Shit! Why don't you cut out the shit!"

"You're still wet behind the ears—"

". . . millions now, but there'll be a day of reckoning!"

". . . this firm was founded by my forebears when your grandfather was in his crib." That was Preston's voice.

". . . fucking bastards, throwing obstacles in the way of every fresh idea—"

Connie was thinking, "Even when Pop was drunk, he didn't talk like that."

". . . greed, brutal greed, is all—"

There was a crash, as of a fist hitting a tabletop. "Why the hell don't you shut up?"

"Calm down, will you? Go home—"

"That's the best idea yet." This was Martin again, calmer now. "We're getting nowhere like this."

And Preston said, "Go home, McClintock. Think things over, and we'll talk tomorrow at the office."

Piqued by curiosity, Connie went to the window again, to see a young man with coppery hair go running down the steps into a car and, with a crunch and spurt of gravel, speed away. She had always had excellent recall of people, and was sure she had seen him before.

Quiet resumed, and after another hour or so the meeting broke up, and Martin, with Preston, brought the man in the mink coat to Connie. Martin made the introductions.

"Pleased to meet you," said Franklin Bennett. His eyes touched her from head to foot. "Well, Berg, you sure know how to pick them. Nothing like a young woman to make you feel like a rooster again. How old are you, Connie?"

Appalled, she answered, "Thirty-four."

"My wife—my new wife's—younger. Twenty-seven. You remind me of her a little. Say, Berg, you've got a beautiful spread here. How many acres?"

"Forty-three."

"Oh, boy—worth a bundle, this close to New York."

"Well, it's home," Martin said modestly. "We like it."

"Why the hell wouldn't you? So, I'll be going." Bennett turned to Connie. "You must have heard that racket. Young son of a bitch lost his marbles."

317

"I regret," Preston said, "that the disturbance came from someone in our firm."

Martin added, "He's an interesting type, McClintock, and unpredictable, apparently. He started out as a poverty worker, then switched completely and has put some brilliant deals together. Looked like a rising star." Puzzled, he scratched his head. "I really can't imagine what happened to him today."

Bennett was magnanimous. "Well, it's not your fault. I've had to fire plenty of rising stars in my time, you can bet. The main thing is, we're getting somewhere." He reached for the door. "Got to be going. Can't keep the young missus waiting too long."

When the door had closed behind Bennett, Preston sighed in disgust. "What a horror that man is!"

Martin remarked that his biography would be fascinating, to which Preston answered that it would be if anyone dared to write the truth.

"He was reared by his grandfather on a Kansas farm after his parents died," Preston explained to Connie. "But he had no intention of staying there. His first job was at a cereal factory in the shipping office, but he didn't stay there long either. It only took him eleven years to become the company president. He's climbed, he's clawed, and he's got eyes in the back of his head. Incidentally, Martin, I hope you're going to fire McClintock tomorrow. That was inexcusable."

"I know," Martin said. "It'll be a nasty job, all the same." And he explained to Connie, "McClintock lost his wife in that bus accident upstate last summer."

"But he's outlived his usefulness," Preston said.

"I know," Martin said again.

"Son of a bitch!" he exclaimed as soon as Preston was out of the door.

"Who? Not Preston?"

"Yes, yes. Oh, I don't really mean it, but damn, he always expects me to do the dirty work. I'm the one who had to fire three hundred brokers after Black Monday, while he acted the gentleman."

Fire. They always knew when Pop had been fired, by the drag of his steps coming slowly and heavily up the stairs. Then he'd stand in the doorway, looking around from one to the other, and he'd cough before he got the words out. A shiver of pity ran through Connie.

"Why do you do it, then?" she asked. "You're as much a partner as he is."

"I'll tell you. Because I can do it more kindly than he can. I'll take McClintock out to lunch and break it nicely to him. Not that he deserves kindness, the damn fool. He could have lost the deal for us and sent six million in fees down the drain. You know what, Connie? A guy like that reminds me of my brother Ben, only McClintock seems to have just suddenly gone haywire, while Ben has always had his head in the clouds." Martin wiped his forehead. "I'm worn out. I need a cup of coffee."

When Connie brought the coffee into the library and set it on the table, which was still littered with papers, Martin said, "By the way, I haven't mentioned to you that Bennett wants to include your brother-in-law's plant in the deal."

"What? Davey's place? Why ever would he?"

"It seems that they've some patents that fit into Bennett's medical supply division. He wants them badly. He's already sent a man out to talk to Davey."

She thought for a moment and replied, "It's funny that you've never told me about it before."

"Why? I never bring business home."

"But this concerns Davey and Lara."

"All the more reason for you not to be mixed up in it."

"Davey will hate it if anyone tries to interfere with his plant.

319

It's like another child to him, you know that." And she said thoughtfully, "I wonder why Lara never mentioned it either."

"I guess she thought there was no reason for her to do so because they had turned Bennett's man down."

"Well, good. I should think they would. Bennett is abominable. I'd like to see him not get his way for a change."

Martin laughed. "That's irrelevant. He intends to make them a fantastic offer."

"Davey'll turn it down again."

"He'll change his mind when it's properly explained. Bennett said he may even fly out there himself to see the plant, and that's a highly unusual thing for the big boss to be doing."

"He must want it awfully badly, then. Funny. A little place like that."

"Not funny. It's the way conglomerates are assembled."

Connie shook her head. "Davey won't do it. Or Lara either. My sister's stubborn."

"It must run in the family." Martin laughed again. "I notice you didn't give up until you got your way and made me buy the London house." He bent down and kissed her. "Darn! It's only five o'clock. If I weren't afraid the baby might come looking for us, I'd take you up to bed right now."

"We'll go to bed early, darling." She had to pretend to share his impatience. But her mind was still elsewhere. "What would a deal like that mean for Davey and Lara?" she asked.

"A nice, big, tidy piece of change. That's what it'll mean."

CHAPTER
SIXTEEN

❦

I n Allenwood, Pennsylvania, the autumn weather had turned
suddenly warm, and families in their sweaters were picnick-
ing on a little stretch of brown lawn. Pam had brought a
basket with fastidious appointments and Eddy's choice of food,
French cheese, cold chicken, salad, red wine, and strawberry
tarts.

Regarding him anxiously, she asked him whether there was
anything special he would like her to send him.

"A couple of books. The library here isn't the best."

A husband and wife with two small boys were shaking out
their blanket and cleaning up the remains of lunch. Mother and
the children come to visit Daddy in jail, Eddy thought bitterly.
He could not comprehend how anyone could let his young children see him like this. It was bad enough to have a wife go home
with this picture of him in her head.

True, the place was not what he had imagined it would be. In
spite of Rathbone's description of "minimum security," many
things had surprised him here. The good food that they were
allowed to prepare for themselves. The freedom to use the telephone; why, a lot of the men here were actually carrying on
business by telephone. Working in the library was pleasant
enough, too, as was working in the yard on a summer day. He

had even learned to cook and clean up the kitchen afterward. The thought caused him to smile at this incongruous image of himself.

"What's so funny?" Pam asked.

"I was thinking how surprised you'd be to see me making dinner and cleaning the pots afterward."

She smiled, too, saying, "You won't have to when you're home again. I've found the most marvelous couple, even better than María and Ramón."

"All that seems like a century ago."

"I know." She put her hand on his arm. "Eddy, this will pass. You've been so brave."

He looked down at her hand with its short nails, so practical and yet so pretty, like little pearly shells. The diamond wedding band that they had bought in Paris on the Place Vendôme another century ago gleamed on her finger. It at least was the same, giving some measure of assurance that she really still belonged to him. And picking up her hand, he kissed each finger, one by one.

"You look so beautiful," he said. "You remembered to wear gray. I'll bet you thought I wouldn't notice."

"No, I knew you would."

Gray, a certain silvery gray, had purity. It was the color of rain, which he loved; it was crystal; it was the ocean at night; it was in some lights the color of Pam's eyes.

"It's terrible to be sitting here with you," he said, "and only touch your fingers."

"I know," she whispered.

"Sometimes at night I go almost crazy. I wish the work were harder so I'd be too exhausted to feel anything. One day I hauled stones in the garden; I wanted to knock myself out. That was the only night I didn't think of you."

"I don't know what to say."

"Is it the same for you too?"

"Eddy . . . you know me, so you have to know it is."

322

"I wish all these damn people would evaporate. I wish there was a hill or some woods where we could go right this minute."

"Please. You're tormenting yourself and me. Let's think of something else."

"You're right. I'm sorry. Then tell me things. Anything. Tell me what you did yesterday."

"Much the same as every day. The place takes a lot of attention. The stables are filling up. I'm breeding good stock. Last week I bought a lovely mare. The owner's moving to the city and wanted a good home for her. She's named Lassie."

"What color?"

"She looks like a caramel with white feet."

"When it's seven o'clock in the morning, I'm going to think: Pam's on Lassie now, taking the trail past the orchard and into the woods. Am I right?"

"Just about seven, unless I oversleep. I don't always fall asleep till very late. The house is so lonely. It's awfully big to be in by yourself. I don't even hear the help moving around, they're so far away."

No matter what subject they embarked on, it always seemed to lead back to the fact of their separation. And Pam, evidently aware of that, too, swiftly changed the direction of their thoughts again.

"People are surprised that I'm doing so well without raising hunters or racers. A horse is a companion for riding, I say, not to have its poor heart worn out at a racetrack. That's exploitation, that's cruelty. And as for hunting some miserable, terrified little fox—well, you know what I think of that." Pam's face grew stern.

"I love you when you go off on one of your crusades, although I suppose the hunters and the racetrack crowd must think you're some kind of nut."

"That doesn't bother me. Besides, I've got plenty of company to agree with me. I've made some nice friends, Eddy. You'll see."

The minutes were ticking away. Eddy pulled his sleeve over his wristwatch so he wouldn't have to see how late it was growing. And they sat on, talking volubly, wasting not even a minute in silence.

"The kitchen turned out perfectly. And the cabinets in your little office are perfect too. The man knows his business. Lara and Davey brought the girls. It's really just a hop over the river for them, about a four-hour drive. Peggy's darling, and Sue's amazing. I think she's going to be a scholar, she's that smart. Connie sent an enormous, extravagant silver epergne for our dining table."

"Whatever for?"

"House gift, darling. And it was really sweet of her. It must have cost a fortune, but you know your sister. She can't resist beautiful things. Like you with this picnic basket. Silver fittings!"

"Well, it's come in handy today," he said.

His remark was lame. Silver fittings for a visit to a jail!

They were the last people on the lawn, so it was almost time for her to leave, and he rushed to speak.

"I haven't asked you the only question that's at all important. How are *you*? Has all this changed you in any way, the you that I know? The truth, Pam."

Before replying, she paused. And then, slowly and seriously, explained. "In the beginning when you came here, reality hit me for the first time. It felt like running at full force into a stone wall. I saw stars. My head throbbed with the pain of it. And then I got angry—you will understand, Eddy?" When he nodded, she continued, "I was—well, I had a feeling of outrage that I'd been cheated. That it wasn't fair to have been given such a happy life only to have it snatched back in such a—a stupid way. Are you sure you understand, Eddy?"

"Yes. Yes, of course. It was natural."

Pam took both of his hands in hers. "Look at me. Look into my eyes. You asked me, so I told you. But I want you to know that's over. It only lasted for a couple of days, and I'm back where I was. And I love you, Eddy Osborne, and we're going to have a wonderful long life together again and—and I love you, love you—And now I have to go."

Before they parted, she said, "I'll be back the first of the month."

"It's too much for you, too long a trip."

"Let me be the judge of that. You can't keep me away."

He stood still looking after her. He had not said what he really felt! It's too much for me, seeing you so briefly, and having to let you go again. And it's not just myself that I'm thinking about, either, he thought. Why should a girl like Pam have to suffer because of my mistakes, mistakes that I regret, that I apologize for? I'm glad she's in Kentucky, at least. All the fine friends we had . . . they act as though we'd caught some foul, contagious disease. Oh, a few wrote nice letters to the court, that's true, but still the humiliation is hell. And I can't help her.

A couple of men had stayed outside to have a catch after the visitors left. He recognized little Bosch, who slept in the next bed. Bosch was in for a year and a half. In charge of office-supply purchases for the bank where he worked, he had set up a dummy corporation and pocketed half a million dollars before they caught him. Outright thievery, that was. And you'd never think it to look at him. He looked like a schoolteacher. Eddy supposed it would do him good to join them for some exercise. His flesh was willing to go, but his spirit was not.

He was in prison. All the guards might be dressed in navy jackets and gray flannel trousers, but they were guards all the same, regardless of their agreeable disguise. And they hated you, too, hated you because someday you were going to get out and return, very likely, to a comfortable life, while they would stay here. When they insulted you with their sarcasms, you had to take it and like it because if you answered back, they would put it on your record and that would affect your parole.

Yes, minimum security or not, this was a prison, and he was

immured. There were just so many steps permitted to the boundary. Beyond, just a little way, lay the Susquehanna River; it flowed all the way to Chesapeake Bay, where one of Eddy's clients had a fine colonial estate and used to invite him in duck-hunting season. Northwest a little way, near Bald Eagle Mountain, was Williamsport, where, flying to meet another client, he had been fogged in one afternoon and had to circle for an hour. He remembered being scared and vowing never to fly in a two-seater again. Well, "never" was a long time; he'd be glad enough to do it now. Two-seater or hot air balloon, anything to get out of here.

Immured.

Chapter
Seventeen

❧

"Now, who can that be?" Lara wondered, looking up from her desk, at which she was going over the Davis Company's monthly bank statement. It was not often that a stretch limousine drew up to the factory door—only when some important customer drove in from the airport.

A bulky man wearing, of all things, a long mink coat, got out and came picking his way up the walk through puddled, melted snow. A minute or two later she was summoned to Davey's office across the hall.

"Franklin Bennett," said the newcomer, "but call me Frank. I'm informal." He sat down, stretching his legs. "I never thought I'd find myself in the wilds of Ohio. I haven't been in a small burg like this since I grew up in one. The weather's nice today at least."

Neither Davey nor Lara had any comments to make to that.

Bennett lit a cigar and offered one to Davey.

"Thanks. I don't smoke."

"I don't usually visit every small operation," Bennett began, leaning back so far that the chair creaked. "But I hear you gave my man a hard time."

"I wouldn't say that," said Davey, very calmly. "I've never been known to give people a hard time."

"Well, you turned him down flat, didn't you?"

"That's my privilege."

"You could have listened to him, couldn't you?"

"I heard all I needed to hear, Mr. Bennett. This is our place, and we want to keep it that way."

Now Bennett switched to a smile. It doesn't look natural on his face, Lara thought.

"Well, I guess I can try to understand that. Your brother-in-law Martin," he said, indicating Lara, "has told me how you people worked to get this operation under way."

Martin! On the instant Lara's eyes met Davey's. So Eddy's gossipy, foolish-sounding rumor had been more than a rumor. After all these many months, during which Martin had made no mention of anything: Martin, the benefactor, the rock of strength! She felt as if she had been struck in the chest or pierced with something sharp and cold.

"You've done a nice job too. Very nice. But you don't want to stop here, do you? You want to grow, don't you?"

"Not particularly," Davey said. "We fit the town, we're part of it, the right size for it. We've got a nursery school on the grounds for the employees' kids, there's the Davis Ballpark—"

Bennett was impatient. "I know all that. Martin gave me the picture. But if you're so social minded, you ought to be thinking of all the good you could do by expanding."

It was Davey's turn to interrupt. "It wouldn't be expanding. It would be breaking up, and I don't want to do that, Mr. Bennett."

"Martin told me you were stubborn."

"Did he?"

"Oh, don't get me wrong! He didn't mean anything by it. He thinks the world of you both. He also thinks you'd be fools to turn down what we're offering."

Davey shrugged. "Then we'll be fools."

"You could find yourself worth millions in a couple of years."

"Mr. Bennett, you probably won't understand this, and it

seems that my brother-in-law doesn't, either, but neither my wife nor I have the least desire to be worth millions."

"My God!" Bennett said. He leaned forward so that cigar smoke rose into Lara's face. "You may not care about money, but your stockholders will care, and you can bet on that. All I need is to present my offer at a stockholders' meeting, and they'll vote to sell out."

"I guarantee that they won't. I know them, and you don't."

"I know human nature," Bennett replied.

Davey was silent. And Bennett resumed, "But I'll wait awhile. I'm not usually a patient man, though. I didn't get where I am by being patient."

"I can see that," Davey said.

Again his eyes met Lara's, speaking to her. Don't be afraid, they said, I've met bullies before.

"I'll give you a reasonable time to think it over, Davis. I'd like to avoid a fight on account of Berg. He's financed some sweet deals for me, and I appreciate that. And you'll find I know how to express my appreciation when people cooperate." Again a smile flashed across the florid face. "Well, I've got my plane waiting. Be seeing you," he said as he rose to go.

"Not if I can help it," Davey declared as the door closed. He stood still a moment as if to collect himself. "It's a raid, that's what it is, Lara."

"And Martin's part of it! I'm numb. Can you believe this? It's like suddenly finding out that your own father was a Russian spy. Oh, I don't know what I'm saying," she cried tearfully.

"Calm down. We have to think now. We have to take our time and think."

"But I'm just awfully, awfully scared. That man Bennett—he's brutal, Davey."

It was as if some wild, threatening vagabond had appeared at the front door of one's house and then, departing quietly enough, had left behind him the assurance that he would be back. After that, one would live with the doors locked and the shades down.

"What are we going to do?" she asked.

"Right now? Go home and eat."

Dropping the subject, she made the dinner hour as normal as ever. At the table Sue, now in eighth grade, posed a problem in math over which Davey and she had ten minutes' worth of discussion. Sue was at the head of her class and knew already that she wanted to be a scientist. Lara watched her with her eyes screwed up and her tongue in her cheek, drawing a diagram on a paper napkin. Such a serious girl she was, her childhood already almost left behind. And yet she had a delightful giggle too.

We've been so lucky with her, Lara thought. It's true, I have to admit, that we've put a whole lot of loving effort into her, but still the good material had to be there in the first place.

Sue was cutting Peggy's chicken. The care she took of Peggy was beautiful to see. Peggy was a toy for her, a pretty, movable toy. Sue sometimes has more patience with her temper tantrums than I have, reflected Lara.

After dinner Sue and Peggy went next door to the Burkes' and the parents took their coffee to the den. Lara looked around the comfortable room. Home. The curtains, warm, rose-flowered linen, were drawn against the evening; the sleeping sheepdog yelped once in his dreams; the children's photographs were ranked on the bookshelves. Home. They'd planned it so well, making it so snug and orderly a place. And now total strangers had come, daring to invade, to disturb, this chosen life. Total strangers! The outrage! Could such things be allowed?

The telephone rang and Davey picked it up.

"Hello, Martin. Yes, he was here this afternoon. What?" He nodded to Lara. "Take the phone in the kitchen. Martin wants you to listen."

Martin's voice, with its strong New York accent, had a powerful ring. "So, what happened? What did you think?"

"The first thought that came to me, Martin, was amazement that you're a part of this. You never told us."

Davey's voice trembled, but so faintly that only Lara would be aware of it. Only she could know the sense of outrage that he was suppressing.

"It's a very recent involvement, that's why. We weren't in it at the start. Bennett switched from some other people and then came to us to do a leveraged buyout."

"Well, either way," Davey said, still quietly, "it's come as a great shock to us."

"I'm sorry to hear that. It's a coincidence, that's all. And yet, not such a strange one. We are, after all, well-known investment bankers, and P.T.C. Longwood is naturally looking for the best help it can get." Martin spoke lightly, easily.

If only, Lara was thinking, we could speak our minds. But there are all the ties, the ramifications, the favors we accepted. And Connie. How to endure another breach with Connie?

"So tell me, what did you think?"

"I thought he was an awful man."

Martin laughed. "I can't disagree with that. But if you had to love everyone you met in the business world, you'd do mighty little business."

"True. Only, I don't want to do business of this kind with anyone."

"If you don't like the deal, I can get him to sweeten it, you know that. Leave it to me. What part of it didn't you like?"

"We didn't get to any of the parts. I didn't want to hear them. I'm not interested."

There was a pause until Martin said, sounding incredulous, "That's impossible."

"It's true, Martin."

"Listen, Davey. I realize that he must have turned you off. Nobody likes the man, but everyone admits he's a phenomenon.

331

In the entire corporate world there's nobody who can even come close to what Bennett's accomplished so fast."

"I believe you, but we want to keep what we have, just the way it is."

There was another long pause, and then Martin said, "Listen, I'm going to fly out on Saturday and see you at your house. We're family, and we don't talk formally in offices. Can you pick me up at the airport? I'll phone you when I get in."

"Martin, we—" began Davey, but Martin had already hung up.

Lara came in from the kitchen. "He's so determined! I don't want him here on Saturday."

"I wish he weren't your sister's husband. I wish he hadn't been so good to us. Then I could tell him to go to hell."

The car had scarcely stopped in the driveway before Lara was at the front door, watching the two men come up the walk and scanning Davey's face, for a hint of his mood. But on both faces there were only smiles of greeting, especially as Peggy appeared beside her at the door, shrieking.

"Uncle Martin! What have you got for me?"

For Martin had two white glossy boxes in either hand. During her stay with the Bergs, Peggy had quickly learned the ways of their household. She knew that whenever Martin came into a room where the children were, it was with some sort of gift, if only a few pieces of chocolate.

"Peggy!" Lara gave the obligatory reproof. "That's not nice!"

Martin laughed, stooped down, and kissed the child. "For you, for all of you. I brought a box of candy, not to be opened until after lunch. And these," he said to Lara as he put the boxes down on the floor, "are some things Connie bought in Paris for you, Peggy, and Sue. She flew over to the openings with Bitsy Maxwell for a couple of days last week."

Lara said the expected "Oh, she shouldn't have!"

TREASURES

Bless Connie as always! The sumptuous clothes would be nothing that anybody would wear in an average American town, but the thought and the love were there.

Lunch was a cooperative effort. Sue had set the table very nicely with the best new china and helped Lara with the salad and the lemon custard. After a week of heavy rain the sun had come out. And from the dining room's bow window one saw a spread of bright grass. The mild light dappled the pretty table.

"Well, this is nice," Martin said when they sat down.

It is nice, Lara thought, and a pity in such a setting to be as frustrated and resentful as she was.

"I can read," Peggy announced, apropos of nothing at all. "Uncle Martin, did you know I can read?"

"No," said Martin in great surprise. "Well, that's wonderful."

"I'll show you," Peggy said, starting to climb down from the chair.

"No, no," Lara ordered. "After lunch you may show how you can read, but don't bother people now."

The child, surprised at the unusual reprimand, sat down. Martin promised to hear Peggy read later, and then, diplomat that he was, asked Sue how she liked school.

"It's pretty good. I like science and math the best."

"Sue keeps her grades up," Davey said. "We never have to remind her to do her homework."

Martin nodded sensible approval. "It's great that girls are going in for the sciences. There never was any reason why they shouldn't."

And so the conversation went, a civilized, amiable family conversation, while all three adults pretended that there was no tension among them.

When lunch was finished, the three went to the living room. Lara set a coffee service on the table before the sofa, and Martin settled back with a cigar.

"Yes, yes, you've got a nice place," he repeated. "Homelike. A lot more so than an apartment on Fifth Avenue."

Lara was inwardly amused. As if Martin would trade the Fifth Avenue apartment for this!

"We like it," Davy said. "But then, we've always lived here."

"It's a good place to bring up kids," Martin observed. "And you've got a beautiful family, with Peggy back to normal, thank God. Sue's an especially appealing girl too."

"Yes, we've been lucky," Davey acknowledged.

There was a pause. Now that these amenities were accomplished, Lara was just wondering how long it would take to get to the point of the visit, when the point was abruptly reached.

"Well, let's begin. You know why I'm here," Martin said.

The two looked up from their coffee cups without responding. Martin cleared his throat, blew his nose, and replaced his handkerchief. It occurred to Lara that she had never before seen the man ill at ease about anything. Then to her surprise he addressed her individually.

"I've never said this to you, Lara. I know Davey has a clear picture of the Longwood proposal in his mind. We had a good talk in the car. But I wondered whether you really have one. And since I know he won't do anything without your approval, I've concluded that maybe you're the reason he can't quite make up his mind. And that's why I'm here, to go over the whole thing in detail and specifically with you."

"But we have both made up our minds," Lara said. "I thought you knew that."

Martin turned to Davey, who still said nothing, but stirred his coffee and looked thoughtful. What was the matter with him? Why did he not speak up?

Martin began again. "Davey, I understand very well how you built this business and what it must mean to you—"

Now Davey interrupted. "The idea for the business was actually Lara's. I'm just an inventor. And then it was Eddy who developed it, who showed us how to run it."

"Oh, Eddy," Martin said with a slight shrug.

The shrug, however unintentioned, irked Lara, bringing her at once to the defensive. "Yes, Eddy. He never had anything but giving in his heart."

Martin nodded. "True. But then came greed, and it ruined him. Very sad."

"That's why we mustn't let greed ruin us," Lara said gently enough.

"We are digressing." Martin laid the cigar in an ashtray and shoved the coffee cup aside. "Let us get back to my subject. I have to tell you, I won't be able to stave this matter off. Franklin Bennett is not the easiest man in the world to deal with. Nor are all the bankers, or the lawyers. A project like this involves more people than you perhaps imagine."

Lara, trying to meet Davey's eyes, had no success. He was deliberately avoiding her. It was infuriating to see him so impassive, offering no responses, no opinions; quiet man that he was, man of a few words, he could nevertheless express himself very firmly indeed, whenever he wanted to.

Martin was waiting for someone to answer him. So she said, "Martin, I hate being negative. After all you've done for us! You must think I'm ungrateful, as if I'm not even decent enough to give thought to what you've proposed. But I have thought. We both have. Believe me when I say we've thought very, very deeply."

"You made a clear statement a moment ago, about not letting greed ruin you. You can't have given the proposition much thought, Lara, if you can say a thing like that."

Still quietly, Lara persisted. "But greed is what I see in these takeovers. Wouldn't it be greedy to sell out, to close down a plant that has brought so many jobs to this town and done so much for the town, greedy to sell out, to grab our money and run? What about Bennett himself or the money shufflers on Wall Street? Not greedy?"

At that Davey spoke anxiously. "Lara, not everyone is—you don't mean—she doesn't mean," he said to Martin, as if, Lara thought, he were apologizing for me, as if I were not responsible for my own words.

She was not to be hushed. "I was not being personal, Martin. I was only telling you what I see is happening in this country. We don't want to be part of it. That's all I meant."

Martin flushed, and she realized that he had indeed considered himself insulted. Nevertheless, she continued.

"Maybe you don't understand a town like this one. People here resent it when they read about others taking golden parachutes and then abandoning everything. People giving themselves millions while their companies are drained away."

"Envy," said Martin. "Envy pure and simple. It's exaggerated and ridiculous."

Lara shook her head. "No, Martin, not envy. Oh, maybe some of it is, I suppose. But I'm talking about a friend from my school days whose husband works at our plant. If we close up and he loses this job, they'll lose their house. That's what's happened to her sister's family in New Jersey, and she's terrified. If our plant closes, we'll mangle this town, Martin. We're the largest factory in it. So many people have come to depend on it."

"They can be relocated," Martin argued. "P.T.C. Longwood has plants in Michigan and Tennessee—"

"But they don't want to be relocated." She could hear the pleading in her voice. "And you know they wouldn't relocate all of them, anyhow. You know that, and I know it. I've read enough about it."

Martin sighed and appealed to Davey. "What's the sense of going down fighting? You can't win, Davey. Take my word for it. You'll be best off if you accept the buyout. Take the money, and a damn big hunk it is. Think with your wallet. Your wallet is your friend in need, and never forget it."

"We're joint owners," Davey said, indicating Lara. "We'd have to agree on anything we do."

"Well, you'd better come to a quick agreement. That's all I can say." Martin looked at his watch and stood up. "I've got to fly back. DeWitt, my partner, lost his wife, and the funeral's tomorrow." They went to the door. "If you're the one who's holding this up, Lara, you're making a big mistake. Go along with Bennett, and Davey can have a big job with the company. Make an enemy of him, and you'll regret it. Because I warn you, although I've told you before, when this offer is formally tended to the stockholders, they are going to vote against you." He made a thumbs-down gesture. "I've got to hurry. Will you take me back to the airport, Davey?"

And Martin left, left in cold anger, Lara knew, scarcely shaking her hand.

Within her also, while she waited for Davey's return, anger mounted. By the time he came home, it was ready to erupt.

"What do you mean," she demanded as he came into the kitchen where she was furiously polishing silver that needed no polishing, "by letting me take the brunt of all that? You hardly opened your mouth. You acted as if you agreed with him, for God's sake!"

"Maybe I felt discouraged, Lara. Maybe it's occurred to me that it's smart to know when you're beaten."

She stared at him. "I don't believe you! Beaten!"

"You know the prayer, 'Lord, give me the courage to accept the things I cannot change'?"

"I'm not ready to accept this. We can change it. We can."

"You heard what Martin said. You heard what Eddy said when this business was first proposed. The stockholders will vote to accept Bennett's money. You know the shares can triple in value overnight, don't you?"

"You can win them over if you try! You've always said they're your friends."

At this Davey held up a weary arm. "Stop. They *were* my friends."

For a moment she was stunned. "Oh, you're such a defeatist!" she cried then. "Do you actually *want* to give up? You sound as if you already have given up, as if you're just resigned to walking away from the Davis Company. Yes, go hand everything over to that creep Bennett. I'll tell you something, Davey Davis: If those people win I won't take a penny of their goddamned money. I won't."

"Maybe it's you who want to walk away. Walk away from this house and we'll all go live in a tent, I suppose."

"Of course I don't want to."

"Then stop talking like a child."

"It's not talking like a child to say that I won't live here with a small fortune in my pocket while the people I grew up with have lost their livelihood through our fault. I'll fight first."

"Oh, fight! Big talk!" Davey glared at her. "When you've got a few million dollars so you can outbid Longwood's offer and buy all the stock yourself, then come to me with your big talk about fighting. But since you haven't got the millions, we'll do a hell of a lot better to let them take the place and get paid so you and your kids won't starve even if I should die tomorrow."

"I'd never starve. I can work."

"Tough talk, Lara. I didn't know you could be so tough."

She was not quite sure whether this was sarcasm, but she answered nevertheless, "Well, now you're finding out."

"Yes, and Martin's finding out too."

"Don't think I enjoy being at odds with my sister's husband. It's pretty awful."

This time the sarcasm was unmistakable. "Especially since he's done a few small favors for us."

"One thing has nothing to do with the other."

"It has plenty to do with it. Think about it. If Peggy were—"

"Now stop right there, and listen to me. A while ago when we thought she was doomed, I understand how you could say you didn't care what happened to the plant. I didn't agree even then, but I understood. Now that she's well, though, you've no excuse for talking like that—unless somebody's brainwashed you or something. Yes, Martin's brainwashed you, I see that."

Davey turned on his heel. "Enough. I'm going inside to lie down. Keep the kids out of the den. My head's splitting." At the door he paused. "This has got to be decided one way or the other, Lara."

"You're right. But we're deadlocked. We're fifty-fifty. Deadlocked."

"One of us has got to give way."

"It won't be me, Davey. I won't sign anything. And it's not only because of my social conscience. Oh, no! It's you too—your product, your brains. *I* won't give them up even if you're willing to."

Davey slammed the door.

Lara put the silver away and went outside into the waning afternoon. A chipmunk, surprised no doubt by the unexpected warmth when spring was still far off, emerged from his home in the stone wall; only his striped head with its bright black eyes was visible. Unmoving, the woman and the tiny creature observed each other. He, she thought, is probably thinking of going back for more of the birdseed that drops from the feeder, while I —what am I thinking? That I could possibly be wrong and Davey right?

Through a gap in the hedge she could glimpse Peggy and her friend playing in the friend's yard. The yellow jacket darted, the treble voice was lifted now in laughter. Had it ever seemed, during those dark months, that she would be running and screaming like this? Davey had lost hope, Lara thought. To tell the truth, I did, too, almost; and yet there was always something else inside me that said, Wait! It's not over till it's over.

A little ruefully, she had to smile. Maybe I get that from Peg, who never stopped believing that Pop would learn to stay sober, or even—who knows—from Pop, who never stopped believing that prosperity was just around the corner.

Presently she got up and went back indoors. Davey was still lying on the sofa, but hearing footsteps in the room, he opened his eyes.

"Angry?" she asked.

"Oh, I suppose not." He never could be angry too long. "Just terribly worried."

"I know. I am too. It seems that the minute you get over one awful thing, another comes along." She sat down on the sofa and smoothed his forehead. "Don't wrinkle it like that."

"Can't help it. I'm thinking. Is it possible that I'm giving in too easily?"

"Funny, I had just been thinking for a moment that maybe you could be right."

"Only for a moment?"

"Yes. And then I thought, No, it's not over till it's over."

They were both silent. Then Lara asked, "Shall we wait and see? Do nothing as long as we can?"

"I'm willing. To tell you the truth, I don't seem to have enough energy for much else."

News spread through the town. Someone from P.T.C. Longwood had planted an item in the local paper, attracting startled attention. The item, during the months that followed, was repeated and expanded. Davey was interviewed and coped with the rumors by affirming some, denying others, and carefully avoiding any definite conclusions. Stockholders and employees wrote letters to the editor. Nine out of ten, indignant, righteous, reasonable, or pathetic were against any change in the Davis

Company. An editorial deploring the talk of a leveraged buyout gave unsavory details about Bennett, Bennett's life-style, his salary, and the "disgraceful" perquisites that such a man enjoyed at the public's expense.

Rumors were picked up by the statewide press in a series of articles about the takeover mania. From these it was deduced that the Davis Company's plant was to be shut down and five hundred people put out of work. The news, spreading over one weekend, resulted in a great protest rally, led by schoolchildren carrying banners in the high school stadium, and attracted a crowd as large as the one that had assembled there for the Thanksgiving Day football game.

Lara worried. "Three women stopped me on the street this morning. The latest talk is that the Japanese are going to buy the place and move it to North Carolina. Millie Corning was practically hysterical, telling me how her sister's husband lost his job through a restructuring deal and then started to drink and hit the kids and how her sister attempted suicide. 'Why doesn't Davey tell us if something really is going on?' she kept saying. It was awful."

"Well, what answer did you give her?"

"I said of course you'd tell them if there was anything to tell, but that you had no intention of selling. People should know that by now."

At an emotional meeting of his employees and their families, Davey spoke. With hands clenched and tears in his voice, he promised to fight Bennett and whip him. But driving home together afterward, he said to Lara, "We can't win. I've canvassed, and I've had friends canvassing the stockholders for me. The stock's already risen on rumors alone. So what do you think will happen when the offer's on the table in black and white? They'll take the lollipop instead of the good bread, and I'm certain of it. The damage has been done; they don't trust me."

"Davey, I don't believe it for one minute. The business with

341

Eddy is past and over. Everybody understands what really happened. People don't hold anger forever." She waited for comment, but since none came, she asked thoughtfully, "Don't you think it's mighty strange that we've heard nothing from Martin since he was here?"

"Not at all. Undoubtedly he expected to hear from us. Undoubtedly he's angry. So they're going full-steam ahead, and he doesn't want to go through any more emotional useless meetings with us." Davey put a hand on hers. "Everything all right between Connie and you? You haven't said, and I've been afraid to ask."

"We spoke three times last week, but not about this. You and I agreed not to talk about it, didn't we? But anyway I have the definite impression that she has no idea what's going on."

"He probably wants it that way. It's got to be a subject he'd like to avoid with her. Anyone would if he could."

"They're going to the London house for a few weeks over Christmas." Lara hesitated. "Do you think we'll know anything by then?"

"I imagine so. I imagine we'll receive the final offer at the stockholders' meeting next week."

It will be a strange Christmas at the plant if we lose, Lara was thinking as they drove into the garage, a red-and-gold bonanza for a few and a bleak, gray loss for the rest.

The principals sent their representatives to the meeting. A fleet of rented cars came from the airport and disgorged a dozen or more prosperous young men with bulging burnished leather briefcases. These were the lawyers, bankers, accountants, and corporate executives of the upper-middle echelon. No Bennett, no Berg, or others from the pinnacles appeared. These did their work well, however; although their documents were loaded with statistics and complexities, their oral presentations were lucid and easy to understand, presenting in essence one simple fact:

Do you want to take your golden dollars now, this minute, or are you satisfied with modest gains and future hopes?

In vain did Davey, when his turn came, point out that the golden dollars and the whole edifice of P.T.C. Longwood were founded on a gigantic pyramid of debt.

"Pull out one stone from the base, and the whole thing will tumble," he warned. "One stone after the other will fall, all the way back to the banks who lent the money for the tenth-rate bonds that are financing P.T.C. Longwood. Whereas here"—and he gestured about him to the length and breadth of the room— "you have four tangible, debt-free walls where people work and make things that you can see and touch with your hands. No concealment here, no flim-flam—"

He was interrupted by a brief titter, suppressed but unmistakably mocking, nevertheless. Lara could have strangled them all, the cold, confident young men from the city, along with the gullible locals who were listening to them.

"You've been earning good interest on your money. We're growing, providing products for which there is real need. And there are more plans on the drawing board, you all know that. Why else do you think this monstrous megacorporation is so eager to engulf us?"

But the audience, Lara saw, was unmoved, even though Davey was speaking more eloquently than he had ever spoken before. She was stricken. These were the people who had been so eager to buy stock, so confident of his talent. Such intelligent people, too, or so one would think, a banker's widow, a school superintendent, a doctor, an architect—

"Have you lost all confidence in me?" Davey pleaded. "It surely looks that way. Yet you have no reason to. We're prospering, aren't we, under my direction?"

And he looked from face to face as if to ask one of the ten to reply, but the faces were either blank or turned away. They were impatient. The evening was late; they were in a hurry to vote for their quick money and go home.

So, close to midnight, the vote was called. They hardly needed to take the trouble to count it, for the result had been predictable from the moment they sat down.

In the corridor afterward Ben Levy and Doc Donnelly were the only ones who even looked in Davey's direction.

"Davey, I feel your pain," Ben said. "I want you to know I'm sorry I had to do what I did."

"It's not that we in any way doubt your *honesty*," the doctor explained. "I know I personally feel some guilt about deserting the ship, but frankly, the way most of us see it is that if you could be taken in by that Osborne fellow, why then—it's a question of judgment, you see. So we want out, we'll feel safer, and this is a perfect opportunity."

Ben added, "You know we all lost a big bundle on account of him and this is a chance to recoup in a big, big way. It's not a question of *blame*, Davey, but—"

"Osborne left a bad taste in my mouth," Dr. Donnelly said, more sharply. "In all our mouths."

Davey's face, Lara saw, was stone-white. And she, too, spoke sharply to the men. "Enough's been said, hasn't it? Good night. Come into the office, Davey."

Alone there with him, she asked, "What happens now?"

"Berg and his people will meet in New York with Bennett and his people to finalize it. It shouldn't take more than a month, if that. And then they'll send me a check for our share of the stock. And then I guess I'll start hunting for a job somewhere."

Yes, she thought bitterly, it's my family that's done this to him. He's only sparing my feelings, because surely he must be having the same thoughts. Eddy and Martin, but Eddy first, have brought him down.

She could not look at him. Later, when they were at home together, she would put her arms around him, but not here while the enemy was still under this roof in the process of making its noisy, triumphant departure.

"Wait here till they're all gone. I don't want to look any one of them in the face," Davey said.

With their coats on they stood behind the office door until the last chair had scraped back, the last voice sounded, and the thrum of the last motor died away.

Theirs was the only car in the parking lot when finally they came out. The night was very cold, very still, and bright with stars. Light shone on the white building, the thriving, wintry trees, and the holly hedge, now thick with red berries, that Lara herself had planted when they had bought this derelict old warehouse.

When they reached the outer gate and were passing slowly through it, as if of one mind they both turned back for a look at the entrance. There, above the imposing double doors with their double Christmas wreaths the light fell clearly upon the carved inscription: THE DAVIS COMPANY.

"Dead in the water," Davey said, and Lara had such a lump of tears in her throat that she could not answer. Anyway, there was nothing to say.

Then he gunned the engine and turned the car toward home.

CHAPTER
EIGHTEEN

❧

E ddy lay on the bed alone in the room, skipping dinner. He had worked all afternoon in the kitchen and had no appetite for food; it seemed as if the smell of Patsy's garlic sauce was still on his clothes. He had no taste, either, right now, for the nightly conversation about deals in the making, opportunities pending, opportunities lost, lawyers and their fees, pleas and appeals, the whole gamut of life in minimum security, a gamut that always seemed to end with family tales.

Family was the most miserable subject of all. It seemed that whenever he heard from his own people, they had painful things to tell. It was like seeing a house on fire across the street while you were tied to a tree and couldn't even get to a telephone to warn or rescue the sleeping people inside. No, that was not fair! The fact was that neither Pam nor his sisters ever wanted to talk to him about troubles; it was he himself who insisted on knowing everything, by telling them that keeping things secret was a greater torment to him, and forced him to guess worse things. So it was that he now could have a graphic picture in his mind of Davey's worried face bending over columns of figures and pages of complex legalese, none of which he was able to understand. He felt for Davey. To lose the business that was one's brainchild! Even though the circumstances were so entirely different, the

346

loss of Osborne and Company brought its own anguish; the visual impression of nail holes where the fine brass nameplates had been removed from the door was a sharp one, hurting as sharp things hurt when they pierce the skin.

The difference was, though, that he, Eddy Osborne, had no one to blame but himself for his debacle, whereas Davey had— face it, Davey had Eddy Osborne to blame.

I caused him to be vulnerable. With those lousy tax shelters that I made him sponsor, I lined up a phalanx of enemies for him. How could they trust him to head a company after that? Lara had been so sure it had all been forgotten. But Lara doesn't know the world. I knew they wouldn't forget. And a brother-in-law in prison makes a bad connection, anyway. Fair or not, disgrace rubs off on the rest of the family.

It was Pam alone who had the power during these hard months to cheer him. That was as it should be; if a man's wife couldn't sustain him, who should? She phoned, she wrote about the house and the horses, about new friends and the life they would have together. It was her letters especially that warmed him; her voice was gone the instant he left the telephone and walked away, but her letters endured and were reread uncountable times. There were more than a hundred of them by now, and when he read them over, it was almost like being in bed with her. He smoothed the pages on which her hands had rested, and held the paper to his nose as if he could recapture the delicate fragrance of her body.

The magic wasn't working tonight, though. He didn't know why, and perhaps it was absurd, but he'd had, the last few times she'd come to visit, a queer sense that there was something different about her. She'd seemed nervous, he thought. Or would "preoccupied" be more descriptive? And he tried to remember the nuances that had left him with that restless feeling. She had been as affectionate as always to the extent that one could be under the eyes of the damned guards. She wasn't ill, she looked the same, but—what?

Oh, probably nothing. Maybe it was the weather that depressed him. It had rained in sheets for the past three days, and he was feeling a sense of permanent incarceration, as if he were in some gulag and would be here for the rest of his life. Nonsense, of course, but nevertheless, it was the way he felt.

It was so unlike him, so much against his principles to give way like this! Abruptly he sat up and reached for the newspaper that lay at the foot of the bed.

It was all the same stuff; couldn't they ever find anything new to write about? Wrangling over the budget; drug wars in Brooklyn; a kid shot while he was playing in the hallway; more investigations on Wall Street; the same stuff—but wait! Wait! What—

"Man hurls himself from eighteenth floor. . . . Sometime between midnight and five o'clock when his body was discovered, Richard Tory jumped from his apartment onto the empty, silent street. . . . Police found a suicide note in the apartment. . . . Formerly in the advertising business, he had lately been unemployed. . . . Neighbors said he had suffered financial reverses."

Eddy's heart pounded, and he dropped the paper. Good God! Was this his doing, his, Eddy Osborne's? ". . . had suffered financial reverses," it said. Yes, yes Richard had. He had lost—how many thousands, hundreds of thousands? And gotten back what? Ten cents on the dollar. Perhaps not even that. It was all a blur in Eddy's red-hot brain. Then he went cold, and trembled.

It occurred to him that Connie might not know. It seemed to him that she ought to be told. And he went to the telephone.

"I hoped you wouldn't see it in the paper," Connie said.

For some reason this offended him. "Don't baby me!" he almost shouted at her. "Tell me what you know."

"There's nothing—" she began.

"The fellow he lived with, he'd know. What did it mean that he was unemployed? It doesn't make sense. He had a great job."

"Eddy, you're all upset, and you don't need anything to upset you more. I hoped you wouldn't see it," she repeated.

Then he repeated, louder this time, "I said, don't baby me, Connie."

He heard her considered pause. Then she said, "All right. I called his friend, and he told me the story. I don't suppose you ever knew, because I never said much about Richard's family, but—well, they didn't know about his being homosexual, and they're the sort of people—at least his father is—who would be horrified and unforgiving. It's a long story. Anyway, what happened was that Richard had taken all his big inheritance from his grandmother and invested it, and—"

"Invested it with me."

"Well. Yes." There was another pause. "So when it was—lost —his father found out. I don't know how, probably from the bank he had taken it out of. Yes, that was it, and he came up to New York in a fury and found that Richard was living with his friend. Found out about him, you see. He thought Richard had been living with a girl. But it was really the loss of the money that was the worst humiliation. All hell broke loose. Richard went into a severe depression. He felt worthless. And he quit his job. He went to pieces." Another pause. "It just shook me. I couldn't stop crying. But that's all I know."

"It's enough," Eddy said.

"Eddy?"

"Yes?"

"It wasn't your fault."

"No?"

"His father was brutal."

"Yes."

"Families are supposed to stand together, to forgive."

"Yes."

"I know I shouldn't have told you. Now I've made you miserable."

"Yes, you should have told me. I'm all right. Just—it's so sad. So goddamn awfully sad." For a moment Eddy pulled himself together. "I'm all right, Connie. Really. It's chow time. I have to go."

When he replaced the receiver, he went back and lay facedown upon the bed.

How was it possible to look down from that height and find the courage to jump? It made you sick to your stomach even to think of it. How many seconds till you struck, and were you terrified, did you scream in horror, did you want to change your mind at that last instant when it was too late? Good God! Not wanting to live! Even on his worst day, standing there in court while the judge castigated him before strangers and all those hostile reporters, even on the day Rathbone had brought him to this place and the gates had closed behind him, even then he had wanted to live.

"I killed him," he said aloud. "Poor, trusting innocent, I killed him."

He was still lying there when he heard men coming into the room.

"Hey, Eddy, are you sick?"

"I'm all right," he replied into the pillow.

"The sauce was great. You want a dish of pasta in here?"

That was Louie, Big Louie, the labor leader, in for extortion. Funny how a guy like that liked to mother people.

Now he tried to roll Eddy over, and in trying, caught the tears on Eddy's cheek.

"Hey! Something happen?"

"Louie, for God's sake, leave me alone a minute, will you?"

"He's got the chills. Look at him shake." That was Bosch's nasal voice.

"Cover him. Leave him alone."

TREASURES

Somebody dropped a blanket over Eddy's back. Then he heard them leave the room and shut the door. Tough guys. Mothers.

They like me, he thought. People always do—or did. That's why they trusted me. Nice guys like Richard trusted me. And I killed him. I always say, why am I here? I never raped anybody or broke into a house or mugged anybody, did I? But still, I killed Richard as surely as if I had mugged him on a rainy night outside of his front door. Richard, and how many others? How many? Well, I guess I know how many funds I dipped into. I've had enough time here to tally them up. I killed something in every one of them, even if their names didn't get into the newspapers, even if they're not exactly dead. Still, something must have died inside them. Trust. Richard gave into my hands everything he had in the world, almost. Yes, I would have paid them all back, I always say that, too, don't I? I mean every word of it, and I would have done it, only there wasn't time. Still, that's like saying, after you've run somebody over with your car, I really meant to stop. . . .

God, if I had it all to do over again! If I could get out and do something, not just lie here and think and think and be sorry, while life races on outside.

And he saw Richard Tory plainly as if he had been standing here in this godforsaken room, saw the golden, athletic look of him, the dapper clothes, the open, naive, friendly face. That poor soul, looking down on the empty street in the middle of the night in the dark. Looking down. Letting go.

For a long time Eddy lay there. After a while he got up, made himself ready for the night, and then lay down again, praying now that sleep might come without dreams, to relieve him, if only until morning, of the pain.

CHAPTER NINETEEN

❦

"**W**hy don't we change the subject?" Ben suggested.

The two brothers had been having a wild argument all through dinner. It had been Martin's idea to invite Ben to the house in Belgravia. Connie had objected, certainly not to being in the company of her brother-in-law, who had just arrived for a semester of study at the London School of Economics, but to dining here at this house, in this lofty hall with the stiff new butler in attendance.

"He'll be far more comfortable at a restaurant," she had proposed.

Nevertheless, Ben was here, as earnest as ever, and perhaps a little ill at ease with the complicated array of silverware in front of him.

"Brokerage fell way off on Wall Street after the crash," Martin said. "Investors were scared. The only business that's really holding up is the leveraged buyout."

Ben's eyebrows rose. "A poor excuse, especially from a man who already has more than enough of the world's goods."

Martin gave a short laugh. "What's 'enough'? Does anyone ever have it, even in academia?"

"Yes," Ben said, repeating then, "Why don't we change the subject?"

TREASURES

Martin never wanted to change a subject once he'd gotten his teeth into it. Like a bulldog, he hangs on to the end, to the final word, Connie thought. Bored, she took another spoonful of raspberry sorbet, sliding the satisfying sweetness over her tongue, and concentrated on her surroundings, which were also satisfying.

The entire house had been restored to its early-nineteenth-century splendor. From the Palladian windows to the classical moldings and the crystal drops that festooned the chandeliers like flounces on a ballgown, all was perfection. Beyond the dining-room doors she could see into the hall, where statues stood in marble niches and the floor was laid with enormous squares of marble, cream and beige. Everywhere in the house there was more marble, which Connie loved, on tabletops, and on bathroom walls. Between one drawing room and another, interior columns copied the temples of ancient Greece. Nowhere but in Britain would one find a house like this one. There was surely nothing like it in the States, she declared silently. Whenever she was abroad, she liked to refer to her country as Europeans did: the States.

"We get rid of dead wood. We tighten production when we buy out," Martin was saying.

"That's why we're doing so well in world markets," Ben countered sarcastically. "Why, damn it, our whole manufacturing capacity is oozing away across the Pacific!" And making a sweep of his arm in the direction of that ocean, he upset a water goblet. His embarrassed gaze fled toward Connie.

"Oh, heck, sorry! Clumsy. Sorry."

The butler hastened to mop up with a napkin.

"It's nothing. Don't think about it," Connie said. Oddly enough, given their cool nonrelationship to one another, she pitied the man's embarrassment. Besides, it was only water, and thank goodness, not red wine.

"Coffee in the little rose room," she directed then.

In the rose room, so named because of the carpet and the

seventeenth-century still life over the mantel, a genial fire snapped behind the screen, accentuating by its heat and brilliance one's awareness that outside these walls a dingy, wet fog was creeping, chilling the streets.

Martin shivered and held his hands toward the flame. "I wish to hell I didn't have to go flying back home," he grumbled.

"I wish you didn't either. Why must you?" asked Connie. "Of all times to go flying off, with Melissa coming from Paris to be with you, and the reception at Lady Bartly's that you know I've been dying to go to."

"I told you, I've got a deal on. What else? It's finally gotten all its pieces together after a year and a half, and the principals want to close it fast before Christmas. I'm not taking chances with any more delays or slipups. Anyway, I'll be back in a couple of days."

Connie became suddenly alert. "You're not talking about that man Bennett's deal, are you?"

Martin nodded.

"Are Davey and Lara still one of the pieces? Are they?"

"They are, and struggling to the very end."

"I thought the deal was dead."

"What made you think that?"

"You never talked about it."

"Do I usually discuss my deals with you?"

"Do you usually make deals that involve my sister?"

Martin lit a cigar. He took a few puffs on it, removed it, examined the soggy tip, replaced it in his mouth, and talked around it.

"Connie, I kept you out of it on purpose. I foresaw the possibility of trouble, although I hoped there wouldn't be any. The one thing I wanted to avoid was a family squabble. That's all we needed on top of everything else."

"So you thought sneaking was the better way."

"That's a damn nasty word, *sneaking*!"

"All right. Disguising, then," she said sharply.

A picture seemed to rise out of the fire and hover there before her eyes: Bennett in the mink coat; all the clever men in their dark suits sitting around the table in the Westchester house; superimposed somehow upon these were Lara and Davey standing over Peggy's bed.

"How can you do this?" she cried. "Forcing people . . . You might as well hold a gun to their heads." And she heard Lara's voice pleading, almost, "Don't let this come between us, Connie." This, then, was why Lara hadn't told her anything either.

"Gun, gun, bullshit. Know what you're talking about before you say things like that, Connie. You make a fool of yourself otherwise. Davey's stockholders voted in our favor, and that's that. It's not my fault if he can't see reason."

"Whether it's reasonable or not isn't the point. Davey's worked for years to build that business, and you're taking it away from him."

"Don't be an idiot. He's been offered more than he could earn if he worked in that place for the next fifty years."

"He doesn't *care*, Martin! Why can't you get that through your head? Davey and Lara are different from you and me. They don't want the money."

"The more fools they." Martin turned to his brother, who had withdrawn into the copy of *Country Life* that lay on the table next to his chair. "This is quite apropos of what we were saying at dinner. You should approve of Connie's brother-in-law, Ben. He's got this dinky little business that he hates to let go of even though it's to his best advantage."

Ben laid the magazine down. "An inventor of surgical instruments?"

"Yes. How did you know?"

"I met them at your wedding. We spoke a few words together."

"They're the salt of the earth," Connie cried. "Both of them."

"Connie," Martin said impatiently, "I never said they weren't."

"Then why don't you leave them alone?"

Sighing, Martin made a gesture of resignation. "She doesn't understand business," he told Ben.

"Business or businessmen?" replied Ben. "There's a difference."

"So? What are you driving at now?"

"I may be a professor of economics, but I still can't understand why businessmen want to wreck American business. To say nothing of the human factor, the cruelty."

Connie broke in. "Then you're on their side? Lara's and Davey's?"

"I would have to be," Ben said quietly, "thinking the way I do."

No one was speaking when the butler brought in the coffee service and set the silver tray between the twin sofas at the fireplace. An odd melancholy settled in the room.

When the man had left them, Connie answered Ben, "You're surprised. You never thought I could be on the same side as you." And she saw that he was too startled, perhaps too embarrassed, to find the quick reply. "Come," she said, "be honest. You haven't liked me much. I don't mind if you say so."

He found words. "It's possible that I didn't know you."

"I don't say that I'm always on your side. Probably I am only because this is very personal. After all, it concerns my sister. And I want to see justice done."

"Well, Martin, what about that?" asked Ben.

"Connie is dramatizing. We are not in never-never land. This is a practical world, and the man's been outvoted, that's all there is to it."

Bitterness was a taste in Connie's mouth. "You don't care. You take away the thing he built, and you break his heart. And you don't care."

Martin tossed the cigar into an ashtray. "If you want to know what I think, I think you're all crazy. Making much ado about nothing."

Ben got up and stood with hands in pockets like a child about to recite in class; he had, too, a child's clear, open gaze, belying the beard and the creased forehead. He began to recite.

" 'And they shall build houses, and inhabit them;

And they shall plant vineyards, and eat the fruit of them.

They shall not build, and another inhabit;

They shall not plant, and another eat.'

"Do you remember, Martin? Friday nights and Papa reading in the front room after the Sabbath dinner?"

"Please," Martin said wearily. "Please. Spare me."

"Isaiah. He was our father's favorite prophet, Connie. Papa must have known the book by heart. Well, a good half of it, anyway."

"And you must know the other half," Martin said. "Lord, how can two brothers be so unlike?"

Ben began to walk toward the door. Martin grabbed his arm.

"Oh, for God's sake, Ben, where are you going? Do we have to let this get personal?"

"No, no. I've got early classes tomorrow, that's all. But this is between you and Connie, anyway. Thanks, Connie, for the good dinner. Thank you both."

When they had seen Ben to the door, they went upstairs.

"Speaking of 'holier than thou,' " Martin remarked.

"I didn't think he was. As a matter of fact, I liked him tonight. I never thought I would, especially."

"Because he agreed with you. Why else?" Irritably, Martin began to undress, talking as if to himself, pacing from closet to bathroom and back again. "I wonder how early the airline offices are open. And how the hell am I going to get a seat? There must be a couple of thousand students going home for Christmas. I wish I had our plane here. Just my luck the damn thing has to be in for overhauling. Just when I need it."

"Where's the company plane?"

"Preston has it in Vail. He'll be flying back for the closing tomorrow."

"Don't you think we need a new one for ourselves, Martin? We have to get to Mykonos for the Byrds' house party next month and if ours isn't ready by then, it'll be awkward because I've offered Bitsy Maxwell's whole group, and the hairdresser, and—"

"All right, all right! I'll order a plane, for God's sake. I'll charter one." Martin stopped in front of the dressing-table mirror, before which Connie was sitting removing her makeup. "Look at me. I look like hell."

Two deep lines had carved themselves into his cheeks, lines that she had really not been aware of until this minute, in the glare of the makeup light.

"Well, don't I look like hell?" he demanded.

"You look tired, that's all."

"This business is wearing me down. I'm getting to be an old man before my time."

"Well, I always tell you not to work so hard, but you won't listen."

"Get off that subject, will you? I have to work. You spend so much that no matter what I earn, it's never too much. Huh! Barely enough, I should say. Ten million it cost me to do up the Fifth Avenue apartment, and now there's this place. There's never any end to it. I've never worked so hard in my life as I do now. You're the last one to talk to me about working so hard."

She sprang up from the bench. Astounded and hurt by what she took to be an implication, she screamed at him. For the first time in their life together, she was really furious.

"Just because your first wife was a dowdy, dreary mess who

didn't spend, a joy killer who doesn't even know how to bring up a daughter—"

"Leave her out of it!"

"Well, that's what you meant, isn't it?"

"Nah, I don't know what I meant. Yes, I do know. This whole damned evening was a bomb. Ben, with his holy conscience making me feel like a—like a thief or something. And you—you fall right in with him. I never would have believed it."

"I didn't 'fall right in with him.' But I have a right to agree with anybody I want when I choose. And he made a point. That business about one person planting and another one eating. He was right."

"Oh, back to Lara and Davey again, of course. Lara and Davey, all evening. Maybe that's the reason I feel so wrung out."

"I doubt it."

"Well, I don't. I'm tired of being nagged about them."

"I never nag, and you know it. I'm too smart to nag," she said coldly.

"Well, good. I'm glad to hear it. And now I'm tired. I want some sleep."

In the morning there would be no time to talk. Then he would be gone, and the next day in New York, the deal would be closed. In Ohio, Lara would be waiting with Davey for the telephone to ring with the news. Probably, they would be waiting at home in the little den; Peg's photograph was on the table near the telephone. There would be snow on the ground outside, and a white glare coming through the window.

"Martin, Martin, listen to me. I don't want to fight with you. But listen. It's only a piddling little company. There's no reason why that man Bennett has to grab it, with all he's worth."

"It's not so piddling. I've told you ten times that it fits into the whole combine; he wants it, and I'm not going to upset a multimillion-dollar deal and look like an ass besides, just because that stubborn, stupid fool happens to be my brother-in-law."

"He is stubborn, I agree, and so is Lara. And personally, in their position, I might go along with the offer and be glad about it. But that isn't the point." She felt herself floundering. Surely he must understand what she meant! And she pleaded. "You said yourself that Bennett's a horror. Preston said so too."

"One doesn't have admire everybody with whom one does business."

A sense of futility overcame Connie then, as Martin, with his back turned, went searching through his tie rack. And she cried out, "I'm not going to let you hurt them, Martin! I'm not! How can you be so hard!"

He whirled upon her. "I? Hard? You can say that after all I've done for them, for the child?"

"Yes, it was wonderful, but that has nothing to do with this."

"You're right, it hasn't. This is a question of money and nothing else."

She stared at him. This man, who almost never turned down an appeal, and the daily mail was flooded with them. . . .

"Money," she said. "I remember what you said about poor Eddy, how greed undid him. And now what are you doing?"

"You're comparing me with Eddy? After he swindled people? Filed false returns? God damn you, Connie, this I never could have expected to hear!"

"I didn't accuse you of anything like that, did I? But if you make people wretched, if you destroy them in their hearts, I don't see that it matters much whether what you did is legal or not."

Her words had enraged him. She hadn't meant them to, had meant rather to touch him, but the effort had misfired and failed.

"You and your hard-luck family! Your brother and your sister . . . nothing but trouble."

"That's not true. And at least we care about one another. We talk to each other, not like you and your brother Ben—"

"Now leave me alone. I've heard enough," Martin said. "I need some rest. I'm sleeping across the hall."

The door closed sharply behind him.

She wanted, she needed, to fling herself onto the bed and cry out her frustration. And for a moment she stood undecided. But then she would look frightful in the morning, with her eyelids puffed red above dark rings. Frightful. And she had promised to take Thérèse to see Santa Claus; after that there was a luncheon at the Savoy with some delightful English ladies whom she had just met. No, no, Connie. Cream your face as you always do. Drink some hot milk, climb into bed, and swallow the tears. Be sensible.

The plane roared up out of Heathrow and climbed northward toward Scotland and the Atlantic. Martin had been lucky to get the last seat in economy class. The Concorde had been filled, as apparently was every seat in every class on every westbound plane, and he had spent hours waiting for this lucky cancellation.

It had been years, he could truly not remember how long it had been, since he had ridden in tourist class. He was terribly tired. He had scarcely slept all night in that strange bed, he was that upset about having argued with Connie, and he was tense, too, about the closing. Indeed, when it was all over, when the final signatures had been affixed, there would be triumph and exhilaration, but there was always so much to be gotten through until that moment, so much wrangling over last-minute demands and bothersome minutiae, so many withdrawals into corridors and men's rooms for whispered conferences among lawyers and accountants, an army of them on either side. He had been through it all so often.

He laid his head back, but he was too cramped to fall asleep, and anyway, his mind was too perturbed. So he ordered a drink to soothe himself, but was still miserable.

He hadn't said good-bye to Connie that morning. She had

been asleep when he had gone into their room to get his clothes. Then he had just had time before running to the airline office to see Thérèse; he'd kissed her on the run and gotten a spot of grape jam on his tie where she'd grabbed it, wanting him to stay. He felt bad about having left them both like that. And, too, he'd said some nasty things to Connie last night, to his good-natured, good-hearted Connie. Well, she had said some pretty nasty things too. Still, they hadn't been as nasty as what he'd said, about her spending so much, for instance. God, Connie could spend whatever she wanted as far as he was concerned! When you loved a woman, you wanted to give her things, didn't you? Anyway, admit it, he liked to spend as much as she liked to. They were both caught up in spending. "Expenses rise to meet income." He'd always said that, and it was the truth.

As to her family, the fact was that he admired their warmth; to their credit they stood fast to each other in a tough, chilly world. But to hear Connie you'd think he had attacked them! It had been queer to see her in agreement with Ben, or Ben in agreement with her.

And it's funny, too, about Ben, he thought. He can be so hard sometimes, so sure he's right, and yet he can also be so soft, quoting Papa, remembering the words exactly. He can remember a hundred things that I've forgotten or buried someplace, being too busy to keep them in my head: what we ate on those Friday nights when Papa read to us; all those fine singing words, mostly about charity and loving-kindness. Well, nobody can possibly say that Martin Berg doesn't give! But it's not just the giving, Ben always says, it's the accumulation, the first taking that enables the giving. And if the accumulation is all wrong—

Abruptly, Martin became aware that his nervous fingers were drumming on the armrest. He removed his hand and held it on his lap.

It's a game with you, Ben says. It's a war. You're tensed up all the time, waiting to go to war.

TREASURES

And then something made Martin remember that fellow Mc-Clintock. Something? Why, those had been McClintock's words, almost exactly. *You guys are playing a game with money, a war game, and most of the money isn't even yours.* And Martin wondered what had become of the man after they kicked him out. Just about a year ago, it was. *This kind of high, wide, and handsome financing can't hold up, and when the day of reckoning comes* —He had taken a chance with that kind of talk, McClintock had, and Martin had been as furious as everybody else in the room. Maybe he'd been even more furious because common sense told him—and if you read the signs throughout the country, you had to see—that McClintock was right. One knew it, and one didn't want to know it.

Maybe that's what had been bothering him lately, nagging like an ulcer, not so much in the stomach—although here too—as in the head, if that were possible. Just one more big deal, real fireworks, and then quit. Quit in the fullness of power. Celebrity status. I bet half the people on this plane right now would recognize my name if it were called out, he thought.

Now, above the general babble and noise, he caught a snatch of conversation between two grown boys across the aisle.

"My dad hasn't lost his job after all. So that was great news."

"I'll bet."

"I can't wait to get home."

That last time in Ohio, Davey had been more worried about his men losing their jobs than about almost anything else. The original innocent, that was Davey. The innocents of the world. "Nice guys finish last." What if that kid's father—and out of the corner of his left eye Martin could see the kid's nice, eager face and his cheap imitation leather windbreaker—what if that kid's father had lost his job? When you thought about it like that, really looked at a flesh-and-blood person, not a statistic, it did something to you.

How could he have forgotten? He, a child of the tenements

363

. . . How could he? Why, it was easy, because he had wanted to, that's all. Hadn't things always been like this, as far back as the Roman Empire or farther?

A vague sadness, an unfamiliar pity, filled Martin's chest. He could not even try to analyze it. Fragments of thought, like dispersing cloud shreds, floated through his head. Thérèse, his little darling. And his Melissa, his heart. The son who hated him because of the divorce. Connie, his joyous Connie. He wished he could turn the plane around, go back to London, and tell her how much he loved her.

"Even with," he'd say, "even with that troublesome family of yours." But he'd laugh when he said it.

He had been so angry at Lara, really disgusted, baffled by her stubborn resistance. And yet—he had to admit it—a part of him had been filled with admiration all the time. One had to admire the human being who went down fighting because he believed he was right.

It was funny to think of little Lara Davis, a small-town woman who'd never gone any farther from home than New York, defying the firm of Fraser, DeWitt, Berg. Or, more than that, defying the great Franklin Bennett and his multibillions. Amazing, when you considered the contrasts.

God, what a loathsome thing was Bennett! He was probably flying back from Acapulco right now, licking his chops over the deal, while ordering his cohorts to wait on him. Cohorts like Martin Berg who'd gladly wait on him provided that the fee was big enough. Well, that, too, had probably been no different back under the Roman Empire.

Wouldn't it be something, though, to turn on him one day and out of a bright, clear sky, tell him to go to hell? Think of those astonished, popping eyes, the jowls gone slack in disbelief, the spluttering fat lips!

And think of being able to say to Connie, "You know what? You're right. I'm not going to destroy Davey's work or quench his dreams. I'm not. For what? For Bennett and his kind? No, or for Fraser, DeWitt, Berg either."

Now Martin let his imagination go free. Suppose he were to walk into that meeting tomorrow and announce that after much thought, he had concluded that he couldn't approve this buyout? They wouldn't believe him! And he could see them all sitting around the table with their faces turned to him, staring, thinking that they couldn't have heard aright, so that he would have to repeat his words. Preston would be speechless. At first they would all think he must be having some sort of nervous breakdown, and then when they finally understood that he was perfectly sane, they would be wild with fury. There would be a battle such as the venerable firm of Fraser, DeWitt, Berg had never seen before. They would search their minds for motives, they would suspect him of some kind of double-cross. They would drive themselves crazy trying to figure him out.

It would be a new kind of battle, one that he might even, in a way, enjoy. He would be fighting this time not for profits, but for people. For Peggy, who had returned to life. And in a curious way, for his own Thérèse; he hoped she would grow into the kind of person who would understand. It would not occur to them that a man could simply and suddenly undergo a sea change.

So, here at last he stood with his decision. And an inward chuckle began to bubble to his throat, where a few moments before a lump of sadness had lain. He knew exactly what he was going to do the moment he landed.

"I'll phone Connie first," he said to himself. "Then I'll call Davey and tell him I'm going to buy his firm out from under the syndicate and give it to him. 'Pay me back whenever you can. I don't care when,' I'll say. Imagine his face, and Ben's and Connie's when—"

Pan American flight 103 went down over Scotland in clear weather at three minutes after seven o'clock in the evening.

CHAPTER
TWENTY

I n those terrible minutes during which one airplane blew
apart in the sky, another one headed toward a smooth landing at the airport outside Louisville, Kentucky.

Anyone who had not seen Eddy Osborne for the past few years
would have noticed at once as he emerged from this plane that
he had altered. His features, obviously, could not have changed,
and his vivid eyes were as striking as ever. His hair, too, was still
as thick and fair. But there was something remarkably different
about his expression, a reserve, a quietness, that one had never
associated with Eddy in the past. His posture and his gait were
different too; the jaunty step, the almost rollicking sailor's
bounce, was no more. He walked through the airport toward the
car-rental counter with the deliberate, measured manner of a
thoughtful man.

There was no one to meet him. Having been discharged from
the prison a few days earlier than he had expected, he had
thought he would surprise his wife, perhaps ring the bell and
have her find him at the door, or perhaps be sitting there when
she came home.

Under a wide, light sky the mild winter day was utterly beautiful. He thought as he drove that any day, under any kind of open
sky, would be beautiful from now on if only because he would be

free to come and go in it. No one could possibly feel the full meaning of those words *free to come and go* who had not once been unfree.

Now, that's a cliché sure enough, he reflected, laughing as he did so. It had been said a million times before, yet it was nonetheless true for all that, as every cliché was true. And filled with thankfulness he laughed aloud again, clapping himself exuberantly on the knee.

He began to whistle, and stopped. He switched on the radio and turned it right off. It was better to hear the wind rush through the open windows, for he had quite forgotten the sound it made, almost like singing, one long, soft note, sustained. The air was clear and sweet. Having passed from the suburbs and into open country, he became deliciously aware of space, just space. The only confining walls were the rail fences that divided the fields from one another. Among the fields stood clusters and groves of trees, and in the sheltering shade of each of these stood a house, white clapboard or dark red brick, fine houses in a rich countryside. His own home was white; he remembered that they had discussed what color to paint the shutters and wondered now what Pam had finally done about them. His heart began to beat faster at the thought of home and Pam.

By the time he reached the stone pillars and the long graveled drive that led up to his house, his heart was drumming so that he imagined he could hear it. A sudden fear struck him, that he would show tears and seem foolish. He parked the car and looked up at brilliant green shutters. On the second floor on the far side was the room where he would sleep tonight. He blinked and steadied himself. And another fear almost overwhelmed him, that perhaps he was dreaming all this, that he wasn't really here but was still in Allenwood. Then he counted the five steps up to the front door. He walked up and seized the brass knocker; it was a lion's head, and warm in the sun.

"Oh, my God," said Pam when she opened the door.

He stood for a moment, awkward at the sight of her. There flashed before his eyes an impression of long hair lying on her shoulders, of a white shirt and white riding breeches; these flashed, then his eyes filled and he took her in his arms.

"Oh, you shocked me," she murmured against his cheek. "I didn't expect you until next week. I've been counting the days."

"Rathbone asked the judge to let me go before Christmas, and since I've been a good boy," he said, mocking himself, "he let me go."

Kissing, they trembled against each other. "Oh, Eddy. I'm glad," she said. "I'm glad."

They held each other apart, examining each other.

"You haven't changed," he told her. "What about me? Have I?"

"I can't tell yet. Come, sit down. Are you hungry? Thirsty? Let me get you something."

"No, I had stuff on the plane."

He leaned back against the pillows in the corner of the sofa. All of a sudden there was nothing to say, or rather, there was so much to say, covering two years of their separated lives, that the task was daunting. And he remembered how many hundreds of times he had imagined his homecoming, bounding into the house, seizing and carrying her off to bed, there to quench a bursting, unbearable desire. And now that the moment had come, he wanted only to sit here and look at her.

"You do look different," she said. "I didn't notice it so much when you were—up there."

"A lot happens in two years."

She said softly, "I know."

"How different am I, do you think? I haven't gained or lost any weight."

She scrutinized him. "It's something, I can't say exactly what. But there's a change. . . . Tell me, was it awful? I never wanted to ask you. But now that it's over—"

"Not the way they treated me. You saw. It was more what goes on inside one's head that's—that's—"

He stopped, and she, seeing his struggle, said quickly, "It's past. Let's not talk about it. Not ever, unless you want to. For now it's best to look forward."

She gave him the encouraging smile that one gives to an invalid or to a troubled child, and he saw how hard this hour was, not only for himself, but for her.

"I'm required to do a year of community service, you remember? So I thought maybe I might work in a hospital here as an orderly or something, according to what they need. I should think that would be acceptable service. But I haven't been told yet."

She took his hand and held it between both of hers.

"Whatever you do, darling, whatever, things are going to come right from now on."

He gave her a smile, a small wan upturning of closed lips.

"You guarantee it?"

"Absolutely! You and I are going to have fun again. We are, Eddy! Oh, I've been so sorry about it all, so sad for you . . . but it's going to be good again. I know. I promise."

Her eyes were anxious; she was appealing to him. And understanding that, he assumed a brighter air.

"I believe you. Now tell me things. Anything. Tell me about the horses."

"Oh, we have some beauties in the stalls! Yesterday we had two foals born, both treasures. And I've finally found a perfect man for the stables after having three absolute disasters in a row, one too lazy to get up in the morning, one more often drunk than sober . . ."

He was only half listening. The exuberance that he had felt while driving had suddenly flattened, as bubbles flatten when the bottle is opened. He tried to analyze his feelings. Was there a trace of some vague fear inside him?

Looking around the room, over her head into the wide hall and beyond it, he saw that the dining room table was set with flowers and candelabra. At this distance it was not possible to see how many places were set, but it was obvious that guests were expected.

Pam, following his glance, explained, "I asked a few people to dinner tonight for a pre-Christmas party, people I've been owing. I thought I'd get it over with before you came home. I didn't think you'd want to have guests right away."

"No, I wouldn't."

"So I'll just run to the phone and cancel. I'll be right back and when I come, I'll bring a tray of goodies for you. Even though you say you're not hungry, I don't believe it. You can't have had a decent meal since—"

"Since I went to prison, you mean. It's all right to say it, Pam."

"We are going to forget it, Eddy Osborne." She kissed him. "Now, stay there and rest. I won't be long."

When she had gone, he closed his eyes again. The room was scented with the pine branches, garlanded for Christmas, that hung from the mantel. There was, besides, a whiff of Shalimar on the shoulder of his jacket. At Christmas he had always put a bottle of it in the toe of her stocking. He could see her now, could see them both, sitting on the floor scattering ribbons and tissue paper as they opened each other's gifts. They hadn't had a care. Would it really ever be that way again?

At that he became angry at himself. Life wasn't over, for heaven's sake! Pam was right in urging him to look only forward. He had never in his life been moody, and he wasn't going to succumb to moods now. And he forced himself to stand up and feel energetic, to be glad, glad, as he had been on the drive from the airport.

He began to look around the room again. It was odd how changed an object became when it was transplanted. He had to look twice to recognize some things. For that matter, the house itself was strange to him. He had been in it so briefly, after all, and then it had been in disarray with painters and plumbers coming and going. He walked out into the hall, which was airy, light, and long enough for a man to take a good run in. The staircase curved up to a landing where stood a tall clock from his collection. The Waterford chandelier that had once hung in Pam's sitting room now descended from a thick silk rope two stories long.

Then he crossed into the dining room, where poinsettias were heaped in Connie's great epergne at the center of the table. He counted the place settings. There were twelve. He noted that the Royal Crown Derby service plates, which had always been kept for special occasions, were laid out, as was the heavyweight vermeil flatware. The furniture was eighteenth-century English, and he wondered what had happened to the marble-topped French pieces they had used in New York. If she had sold them, they must have brought over half a million dollars, he reflected. But she had not sold his favorite paintings. His Berthe Morisot hung over the fireplace, and the two Mary Cassatts had been placed between the triple windows.

As he went on through the rooms, it pleased him to see how she had kept his favorite possessions and that they were safe here, protected like children in this solid house.

From the pantry her voice carried as she telephoned her guests. Surely it was good, he thought, for her to have had some pleasures while he was away. On a table in the library a magazine lay open to a double page of photographs. There was the fine, symmetrical facade of this house, with Pam in riding clothes standing on the front steps. There was Pam at the stables under a clock and a gilded weather-vane. And Pam again, taking the jumps at a horse show. Finally, Pam in evening dress, the Grecian, columnar sort of dress that she always wore, standing in a group at—Eddy bent to read the caption—"the benefit for the

371

hospital, the high point of the social season." He was reading further when she came in.

"I'm sorry it's taking so long to go through the list, but anyway, the coffee's on in the meantime—oh, you're looking at that silly article." And she said, apologizing, "It must seem to you that all I did was enjoy myself, while you had nothing."

"There was no reason why you shouldn't enjoy yourself. You couldn't have helped me by locking your door and pulling the blinds down."

And yet it came to him suddenly that his entry into this life that she had established here might not be easy for her. Nor easy for him either.

"Why don't you sit down and read the paper while I finish my calls."

"Maybe I will."

However, he was too restless to sit, and laying the paper aside, he went upstairs to explore. It pleased him again to see things like his Rowlandson prints in the hall and his pink jade Chinese horse on Pam's chest of drawers. By the braided trim on all the curtains he recognized the hand of their New York decorator, who had been persuaded—for a handsome fee, no doubt of that —to come to Kentucky. His was, however, the hand of a master, and that pleased Eddy too.

Then something caught his attention, a pipe lying in an ashtray on a small lamp table in the bedroom at the end of the hall. It might have been his eyes that found it first, or it might have been his nose, scenting the pungent tobacco. For a moment he stood blankly seeing the thing, not comprehending it. Then, despising the immediate, crowding thought, the unworthy, stupid, cheap suspicion, he turned away. But it happened also that the closet door which faced him was ajar, and the unworthy, cheap suspicion drove him to reach out to the knob. Then he withdrew his hand. Then he seized the knob.

In a tidy row hung a man's riding clothes, half a dozen suits, a raincoat, an overcoat, tweed jackets, and a silk bathrobe, an entire wardrobe. Pajamas hung on a hook. For some crazy reason, Eddy was afterward to remember, he did not want, in that first instant, to believe what he saw. A cousin, perhaps, some relative who had come to live with her? But she had no relatives. . . . And then he became frantic; he ran to the chest and opened drawers. There were underclothes, there were socks, sweaters, and shirts with London labels. In the adjoining bathroom there hung a terry cloth robe. On a shelf were shaving things, a brush and a comb.

He understood. For the first time in his life he thought he would go mad. He understood, too, that it was in every man at some time or other, to kill. These were not stale words; it was perfectly possible to kill. If the owner of these pajamas were within reach, he would do it. He knew he would. Afterward he was to consider the fact that it was the man, and not Pam, whom he would have attacked. Was it because he knew her, while the other was an unknown? A statistic?

He ripped the pajamas off the hook. They were expensive silk pajamas that very likely the man had not even worn, for Pam slept naked. . . . Her nightgowns were only for show, for five minutes' worth of wearing. Eddy's rage shook him. His hands became so strong that he tore the trousers from waist to ankle with one stroke. Then he tore the top, leaving a heap on the floor in the center of the room. After that he sank down on the chair and covered his face with his hands.

His thoughts were fragmented: Connie, coming home and finding Richard. It was a queer enough possible parallel to this. . . .

And he remembered the men at the tennis courts and the riding school, long ago. Who knew the truth about them?

He was still sitting there when he heard Pam calling from the downstairs hall.

"Where are you? I've got soup and a smoked salmon sandwich."

Smoked salmon. A delicacy intended for the evening's party, which his arrival had spoiled. No doubt the owner of the pajamas would have been at the party. Perhaps the party had even been planned for him.

"Eddy? Where are you?"

He did not answer. Then he heard her come up the stairs in search of him. And still he did not move. What would he say to her? What would she say to him? Would she lie? Of course she would, as anybody would.

Her glance from shocked, wide-open eyes took in the closet, the bureau drawers, and the rags on the floor. Then it came to rest on Eddy, who looked back in silence.

So lovely, she was! So fastidious in white with those long legs and the long hair and that pure, patrician face. His patrician lady, now no longer altogether his. The diamond wedding band glittered on her finger; he saw an instant picture of her hand, wearing his ring, doing intimate unmentionable things upon that other man's body. And a surge of nausea made him tremble.

"Oh," she said very softly. "Oh. But you've misunderstood! Sometimes I have a guest who stays overnight, that's all! He likes to ride on these trails. We have some marvelous trails. I'll show you. . . . He lives in town, so he leaves his riding clothes here."

"And his suits and his underwear and a stack of shirts? Enough for a year's use?"

She said nothing.

"I see that at least you have enough decency to blush."

She began to cry. "You don't believe me. I know how this might look to someone who didn't know me—"

"But that's just it, Pam. I do know you."

"Whatever can you mean by that?"

Thick, shining tears slid down her cheeks unheeded and fell on her clothes.

"Ah, Pam, Pam, be truthful with me now! At least you can do that much for me." And he tried to meet her eyes, but she turned away to stare down at her fingernails.

Presently, in a harsh whisper, she spoke. "He's nobody. I mean *nobody* to me. He's nothing. He was nice to me when I came here, not knowing a soul. It was so lonely. You can't imagine how it was. It's one thing for a bright young couple to arrive together in a new place and start fresh. But for a woman to come alone without a husband—"

"Or a husband in jail."

She did not answer.

"Tell me, Pam, is he good in bed? How does he compare with me?"

She had been standing, and now she flung herself on the bed, flung herself so hard that the bedframe creaked, and then lay there with her face hidden in the bolster.

He walked to the window. The grass on this winter afternoon was still bright, but he was only half seeing it, was only barely conscious of this pastoral sweetness. His thoughts were the old ones, old thoughts of early days, riding on the beach, dancing among Pam's golden, lucky crowd and going home to make love at dawn. Highs, tremendous highs . . .

Then he whirled around. "He lived here with you, didn't he?"

"He comes and stays a few days at a time. He never *lived* here."

"What's the difference?"

"There was never any commitment. This is your house. He always knew you were coming back."

Numb now, Eddy turned back to stare at the grass, where a flock of strutting crows searched for seeds. After a while the bed creaked again as Pam turned. Lying on her side with her cheek resting on her arms, she began to address the wall.

"I didn't plan for it. It just happened. And not as often as it may seem either. I was always sorry every time. But I told you—I was so alone. And he was kind to me."

"Yes. I imagine he would be."

"I don't love him, Eddy. I never did, not for one minute. It wasn't love."

"If you did, there would be more of an excuse. This way it's worse."

"Why worse? Can't you see that this was only—"

He heard himself sneer. "Only what? Fun?"

"Well, yes. You could say that. Yes, fun. Sex. Eddy . . . two years are a long time."

"I'm rather aware of that."

"Oh, I'm sorry. Sorry! It was stupid of me, cruel of me! Please, Eddy, I wasn't thinking when I said it. And I'm so ashamed. Ashamed of it all." Now with piteous eyes she looked fully at him. "It's so rotten. It's unspeakable. I've been thinking for weeks, for months, and you must have, too, how the minute you got here, we would just lock the door and— Now, now it's all spoiled. Oh, my God, it's all spoiled!"

Our twisted lives. How is it possible for everything to go wrong? he asked himself. Everything.

Pam sat up and held out her arms to him. "But I won't let it be spoiled! I won't let it, Eddy! Come. Come here. Please. Will you? Can you? Please."

He felt himself flinch. "I can't," he said very low. It was an effort to speak; even his voice was exhausted. "I'm only thinking that if I hadn't found this out, you'd have let me live the rest of my life here not knowing that another man had been with you in this house. A man whom in my ignorance I would undoubtedly meet and sit with at somebody's table, with everybody knowing except me. That's what you would have done to me, isn't it?"

She flung herself back into the pillows, facedown. "Why must you do this, Eddy? I can't bear it. I can't. You hate me! I see it in your eyes."

He shook his head. "No. A minute ago, I did. But that's gone." So quickly had the rage, the outrage, drained away. "I'm only so damn sorry for us both, that's all. Do you remember when we were in the kitchen at your mother's house and I asked you about other men and you said—"

"You're not really going to rake that up, are you?"

"You said something about how long and lonesome the week was when I stayed in the city and we didn't see each other. You missed being 'admired,' I think you said. You didn't mean admiration, though. You meant sex."

And now it was Pam in whom rage fired. She sprang up and stood before him shaking with it, her fists clenched, her eyes furious.

"Who are you to rummage around with your ancient suspicions? Is your past so lily-white? Is it? There's enough I could say, God knows!"

For a minute or two he stood and looked at her trembling shoulders. He could think of no answer. There was none. So, carefully, he closed the door behind him and went downstairs. He had no idea where he was going.

A servant was clearing the table in the dining room. The woman looked up and he nodded but passed her. There was no need to get acquainted. And he walked on. The house was very large with many rooms and long passageways. Wall after wall displayed his treasured paintings, and precious sculpture stood in lighted niches. Beautiful, they were, each one a marvel; none had lost the power with which it had first moved his heart. And yet he wondered however he could have cared that much to possess them. He stood there, staring about him, feeling empty. The zest of ownership had gone. It would be enough to see these things in a museum.

After a while he went out onto the veranda. The sun had moved far to the west, leaving a last spot of light and warmth where a group of chairs stood at the end. He sat down. His spirit was numbed and dulled. All through this momentous day, he reflected, his moods had been veering, as if he were on a sailboat tacking in an erratic wind, answerable only to the wind. And he sat still, waiting for what, he did not know.

Presently, after an hour or more had passed, he heard the door open. Pam came out and sat down. Her eyes were swollen and her voice was thick.

"What now, Eddy?" she asked quietly.

With equal quietness he answered, "I guess you'll want a divorce."

"Why? Do you really think that's what *I* want?"

"I don't know. I know I can't stay here, so I suppose you will want one."

"You do hate me, Eddy, don't you? The truth."

There was such a heaviness in his chest that he could hardly breathe.

"No," he said. "No. I don't hate anyone. I told you."

She was in a rocking chair, and now, perhaps unconsciously, she began to rock. Back and forth the chair went, rumbling over the wooden floor.

"Oh!" she cried. "Who could have thought it would end like this? It was such fun in the beginning. Didn't we have a lot of fun together?"

"Yes. Yes, we did."

Faster and faster, the rockers went. Eddy put his hand on the arm of the chair to stop it.

"You'll rock yourself off the edge of the porch," he said gently.

"What will you do, since you said you can't stay here?"

"I guess I'll go back to Ohio. There was a fellow in—in that place whose brother-in-law has a large firm of accountants in Columbus. They offered me a job. I turned it down, but now I'll take it. I'll take them up on the offer."

"You'd like that?"

He shrugged. "I always loved numbers. I've been pretty good at numbers, all considered." And he managed a wry smile.

She wiped her eyes with the back of her hand as a child might do. The gesture was curiously touching.

"I'd have a steady salary," he said, thinking aloud. "I'll get an apartment, have a budget, and live within the salary. No worries. It'll feel good."

A silence, sorrowful and heavy, fell between them. After a while Pam broke it softly.

"You'll be needing things for the apartment."

"Not many."

"There's plenty of stuff here. The attic's full. Even though I sold five million dollars' worth, there's enough left for another big sale."

"Sell it, then. Get the cash."

"I'm hardly in need of cash, am I?"

"Hardly."

And now an idea struck Eddy, an illumination, as if a light that had been flickering uncertainly had flared into a brilliance. "I was thinking, with all that money tied up and doing nothing, if it were sold, then some of the people I took from could be paid back."

"You don't have to do that. You've been discharged in bankruptcy. You're cleared."

"I know that, but I don't feel cleared."

"I don't see why not."

He saw, but there was no need to tell her what he saw, or how Richard and some special others haunted him yet. So he said simply that he had had much time to think and that it was the right thing to do.

"Perhaps so, for a saint or an angel. How many people do you know who'd do it?"

"Not many, it's true. But still, I thought you might agree. You were never attached to things as I was."

"That's true, too, but I'm attached enough not to give them away."

He was too tired to argue further. Anyway, he had no power over her possessions.

"That doesn't apply to you, though. I want you to look through everything and take whatever you like, Eddy." There was a glisten of tears in her eyes, and he had to look away again.

"I can tell you right now. I'd like my desk. The little one that stood in my den. And that's all."

"All? That's ridiculous," she said, very gently.

"No, it's all I want," he insisted, thinking. "I need to be free and clean. I need to divest myself of all the reminders."

"What about paintings? You could take some to sell, and then *you* sock away the cash."

"I'll have no use or space for treasures in the kind of little place I'll have, and I don't want the cash."

"You can find room for some good pictures. Take them!" She was almost pleading. He understood how sorry she was for him, for everything. "They're yours. You bought them. Remember?" And she gave again that small, sad smile. "You're the one who earned them."

"Let's say, rather, that I acquired them. That's more accurate," he said bitterly, wanting to hurt himself, wanting to reach the last threshold of pain.

"All the same, I insist. Select some art. You loved it so much."

If anyone could know how he had loved it, Pam could. She knew everything about him. . . . And he thought for a moment. "All right. I will take one. The small Renoir with the woman who looks like my mother."

Peg, who always saw the bright side. What would she have to say about all this?

"I don't understand why you're refusing to take more."

"I don't know that I can explain it, Pam, so you'll have to believe my word. Please."

"Isn't there anything I can give you? Anything at all that I can do?" she asked in a rising, wavering little voice.

He thought again, considering the weight of what he was about to suggest.

"Yes. Yes, there is something. I was thinking about Davey and Lara. You've kept in touch, so you know as well I do what's going on. Would you be willing to lend them enough to buy back all the stock? Or you could buy it yourself and then release it to him, so he can beat those people who want to take him over? I don't know exactly how much is needed. It's a big sum, but not more than you can afford, I'm sure. And you know Davey. He'll pay you back ahead of time. Do you think you can do it?"

"I'll think about it. I've always loved Lara. You know that."

"It would mean so much. They've struggled so and gotten so far. I'd hate to see them lose out."

"I think Martin Berg's too rotten for words."

"I don't know. I don't judge anybody anymore." Eddy could hear the rueful sound of his own voice. "I only know how easy it is to get caught up in the rat race. 'Business is business,' after all."

"Lara held out to the end. Didn't I always say she's the tough one? You wouldn't think it to look at her. But I told you so long ago."

"Davey had to take the pressure from the stockholders, don't forget. And then there was all the trouble with Peggy. Too much pressure."

"Lara had it too. I wish," Pam said wistfully, "I wish I had her guts. Just plain guts. But I don't know. . . . This trouble of yours was just too much for me, Eddy. It's humiliating to have to admit it. But maybe I was just meant to be good for you in good times."

"Maybe so." And he thought, If the truth had to come out, it's better for it to have come out now instead of when we're sixty.

The short afternoon was coming to a close. Rusty clouds

edged with silver fled toward the horizon, and a damp wind rose. Pam stood up.

"It's getting cold. Come in and get ready for supper."

"I'm still not hungry, and I have to see about getting back."

"You have to eat, Eddy."

"Okay. I'll just take a little walk around first. It's a long time since I've done much walking."

And he thought, as he started off over the lawn, I suppose this is what is called a civilized parting. Well, if it was, he wondered how anyone ever bore the pains of a savage one. Then, in a return of his old practical tendency toward letting reason prevail over emotion, he reminded himself that Pam, at least, would survive very well. She was healthy, young, and rich. Yes, she would certainly survive, he thought, half in despair and half in gratitude. God, all he had ever wanted was for her to be safe! As for himself, he would manage. Somehow . . .

It felt good to walk, stretching his legs in long strides, feeling that he could keep on walking, if he chose, to the end of the earth and meet no barrier, no wall, no locked gate. No one was watching him. His feet crunched on gravel, then trod on grass, and, following a track, he seemed to recall that it led to a pond. At the edge of the pond all was still; even the wind had died there. Then something splashed, a frog or a fish, and the stillness surged back. He stood there, hearing the stillness.

"I loved her so," he said aloud. And he remembered how it was said that after an amputation, the lost limb still ached.

After a while, as thick dusk fell, he walked back toward the barns and the house. A single horse was still out in the stable-yard, drooping its head over the rail fence. He could barely discern the gleam of its dark, tranquil eyes. The horse whinnied softly, and Eddy went up to lay his hand on the warm head. On some impulse, then, he put his own head against the animal's long cheek, and rested there. He had a sense of kinship, of perfect trust. It was as if the animal could feel the man's trust, for it did not move or pull away. The innocence, Eddy thought, the innocence.

"What are you doing here?" Pam said. "I thought I heard steps on the gravel."

He started. "Nothing much. Just talking to the horse."

"His name is Baron. I'm boarding him temporarily. He's won three blue ribbons, and he's worth a fortune."

"I wonder whether he would be happier if he knew."

Pam gave him a queer look. "I've come to tell you something. I will pay. Not just Davey and Lara, but the people who lost through you. Just let me know whom you owe, and I will pay."

He was too astonished to speak.

"But of course it will mean selling this huge place."

"You're really willing to do all that, Pam?"

"Yes, if you're willing to try to forgive what I've done, and begin again with me. No, Eddy, hear me out," she said, as he started to reply. "I've been thinking about us. I've been sitting upstairs thinking, maybe the way you'd think if you'd been in a terrible car smash-up and by some miracle found yourself still alive. We were never very grown up, were we? Not even grown up enough to start a family, to be responsible for kids. At least, I wasn't. I married you because you were handsome, and we had great sex. I never really thought about *you*, about what drove *you*. If I had, maybe I could have helped you. I wouldn't have let you make a mess of things."

He was infinitely moved. "Don't say that. I've no one to blame but myself for what I did."

And I, he thought, I married you because you were beautiful and you had a family tree that I didn't have and that I envied. Crazy, wasn't it?

"I have no one to blame but myself," he repeated.

"We had fun, didn't we?" Her voice trembled. "And fun is fine, but that's about all we did do with our lives."

He could have wept. Instead he swallowed hard.

"Eddy? Do you think we can ever be what we were?"

"I don't know. There's so much I don't know anymore."

"I'm willing to try if you are."

To be what they were? To go upstairs now and take her in his arms? A shudder went through him. No, not possible.

"If you would just stay here. Just for a while. We'll be selling this place and there'll be the moving, and—"

"You'll need help, I know."

She did not answer. She's giving up all this because I asked her to, he was thinking. And it seemed to him that he owed her something in return. Why not stay, then, if that's what she wanted, or needed? We're being civilized, aren't we? I can live amicably in my own room at the end of the hall; I can get a job here as well as anywhere, and go away again when she's settled and I'm ready.

"I'll stay awhile," he said. "Just fix a room for me."

"I understand."

"And, Pam—no anger. No recriminations. I can't speak for you, but I'm too tired for any more anger. I don't want to feel anything. I don't want to feel."

"I understand that too."

A gust of wind came suddenly out of the north, shaking the trees, and Eddy shivered.

"As long as I'm to stay, I'll take the hot drink you offered me before," he said courteously.

"Of course," she answered with equal courtesy. "We'll go right in."

CHAPTER
TWENTY-ONE

∽⟨⟩∾

T he first person whom she saw among the little crowd that awaited her plane's arrival at Kennedy was Preston, whose silver-white head loomed above all other heads and shoulders. He stepped back to let Melissa, who had just flown in from Paris, reach her first.

"Oh, Connie! Oh, Daddy!" Melissa said as they embraced.

The girl's homely face was swollen with weeping. It flashed across Connie's mind that here was the one person who had really deeply adored Martin. And this thought, this genuine pity, added to her own shock and grief, brought tears to Connie also, so that the photographers, coming forward at just that moment, were able to catch for tomorrow's newspapers an appealing picture of the sorrowing young widow holding the hand of her seven-year-old daughter.

Preston, grasping the other hand, kissed her cheek. "You must be exhausted. I've made special arrangements to get you through customs first."

"How thoughtful you are. . . . There's no luggage except our little carry-ons."

When one had so many houses and did so much traveling between them, it was only sensible to maintain a complete wardrobe in each.

"I thought you'd like to keep together in one car, so I've got a stretch limo waiting. Seats for six." Preston counted: Connie and the two girls, Nanny, Connie's secretary, and himself. "Yes, just right. Come. We'll be out of here in no time."

"So good of you," she murmured, following him.

"We're all just devastated, Connie. There are no words for it."

In the car on the way from the airport the only desultory conversation was held by Thérèse and Nanny. When Preston, sitting across from Connie, met her glance, he turned considerately away. The bleak December day rolled past: joggers along the waterfront, choppy olive-green bay-waters, high-rise apartments, rows of uniform houses with plastic snowmen in their front yards and windblown tinsel decorations.

"My brother's coming for the memorial service next week, but I wanted to come now," Melissa said in a near whisper.

Connie nodded. She was thinking, when someone dies suddenly, people absurdly say, "Why, I was only talking to him on the phone yesterday," or, "We were supposed to go to lunch next Tuesday," as if the banality of these connections could make the sudden death more shocking. Yet, for the last four or five days, she had been doing the same thing herself: "I was reading to Thérèse at the very instant the plane went hurtling in pieces through the sky, and I was thinking how many hours it would take before I could phone him in New York and say how sorry I was that we had fought before he left."

Oh, God! How sorry! Gulping, she closed her eyes. That awful fight! And then the horror. The horror. No one would ever know what those people had felt, whether they had lived for minutes as they fell five miles to earth or they had only one unspeakable instant before they died, or—

"Daddy promised me a boy doll to be brother to my Annie." Thérèse's voice chirped now in the silence. "He told me. Did you know?"

"Yes, yes. We'll talk about that later," Nanny said quickly.

"Why don't you take a little nap? Here. Put your head on my shoulder."

She would have to ask a child psychiatrist what Thérèse should be told and how to tell it. Oh, the horror. The horror.

Such a good man, a kind man! No woman could have wanted a more devoted husband. The terribly sad thing was that she had not been anything more than fond of him, had never returned his love, not in her heart, although, thank goodness, he could have had no way of knowing that. If she had loved him fiercely, desperately, with the kind of love one read about, she would have been wanting now to die. And she was filled with guilt because she did not now want to die. . . . If only they had not parted in anger! If he hadn't left in such a hurry, she would have made things up the next morning.

But she had tried to be a good wife, that much at least was undeniable. Impulsively, she reached forward for the limp hand that lay on Melissa's lap and squeezed it, vowing, I will take care of Martin's daughter, for she needs me; that much I can do for his memory.

In the apartment's foyer the servants were lined up, making a phalanx of black wool, black silk, white aprons, and respectful mournful faces. Behind them the rooms all appeared to have been banked with flowers. They're like diplomats at a dignitary's funeral, Connie thought.

The butler took a step forward. "Madam, on behalf of us all, I want to say that our hearts ache for you. Mr. Berg was—we shall miss him."

"Thank you, Marston."

"Will you have tea, Madam? Is there anything we may do?"

"Tea please, Marston. In the red library. You'll stay awhile, Preston?"

"Of course. Unless you want to rest."

"No, no, stay."

Felice, Connie's personal maid, took off the sable coat and Preston went with Connie into the library.

"I look a wreck," she said, passing the Venetian mirror.

"Nothing could make you look a wreck, my dear."

On a table next to the sofa stood Martin's familiar cigar humidor, burled walnut with a monogrammed gold plaque on the lid. Preston followed her glance.

"You need have no worries about his affairs," he said gently. "He left everything in perfect order. But you must know that."

The humidor had to be taken away. Perhaps Melissa might want it. The thing, the very scent of it, made too many pictures: Martin in the hospital when Thérèse was born, Martin in the courtroom when Eddy was convicted, Martin clasping the new sapphires around her neck, Martin talking to the doctor when they flew Lara's poor baby east, Martin . . . She put her face into her hands.

"Shall I leave you?" asked Preston after a while.

She raised her head. "No. I'm sorry. Please talk to me."

He seemed to reflect. Then, "It's curious," he said, "a terrible irony that he had to die while rushing back to consummate a deal that was to fizzle anyway."

"What? The P.T.C. Longwood buyout?"

Preston folded his long hands together over his crossed knees. "Ah, yes, and after two years' work. Naturally, as soon as we heard the awful news, we arranged to postpone the closing for a week, but then, two days ago, we learned that your brother-in-law had bought back all the stock for just a trifle over what we were prepared to pay. If we had known, we'd have upped our offer."

"That's incredible," murmured Connie. "How could he have managed to do it?"

"I'm sure I don't know, but he did, and Bennett was furious. He refused to go ahead without the inclusion of the Davis Company's patents. So the whole thing went up in smoke. And we've lost, I haven't calculated yet how much in legal and accountants' fees. Up in smoke."

Connie restrained a smile. How on earth could Davey have come through with all that money? But she said at once, "Yes. It must be terribly disappointing for you."

"To say the least." Preston sighed. "Well, you can't win them all, I guess." There was a poignant silence. "One thing, though," he said, just as Marston appeared with the tea tray, "I want you to know you're not alone, Connie. I'm here to help you in every way I can. Remember that."

Connie Berg made a stunning widow, slender in black with a single strand of eleven-millimeter pearls around her throat under the sweep of her pale hair. Mourning clothes were old-fashioned, yet for just that reason they had a kind of elegance reminiscent of Jacqueline Kennedy's widowhood. When the weather turned warm in the second half of the year, she changed to cream color, heavy linen or thin silk. People turned to look after her when, on Nanny's day out, she walked on Fifth Avenue with Thérèse and the three small poodles.

By the beginning of spring her telephone began to bring discreet invitations for quiet evenings. "Just a few friends at dinner, that's all, since you are still in mourning." From such quiet evenings came other invitations, most of which she turned down, from unattached men, some of them too young, some too old, and some just simply fortune hunters. Connie knew about fortune hunters.

Anyway, she was not interested. Still numbed by the unpredictability of death, by the daily immanence of it, which she had quite forgotten since the long-ago death of her mother, she was now feeling a need only for the protective comfort of the familiar. Lara and Eddy had of course come at once to New York and thrown their arms around her. It was then that she learned how Pam, through Eddy, had rescued the Davis Company. Her feelings on learning of it were mingled of tenderness toward her brother—how changed he was, still steadily optimistic, but with all the cocksure, boastful swagger gone!—and a confused sense of shame that it had been Martin who would have driven Davey to the wall.

"What bothers me," said Lara, "is my memory of Martin's last visit to our house. It didn't end with the most friendly feelings, and I'm sorry."

There was no way for Connie to answer that, since her own last memory of Martin was what it was. And for a while the three were silent in the red library, where a newly enlarged portrait of Martin in a baroque silver frame gazed out at them.

What a year it had been for the three, each in his own way! A year of trials and tests. It seemed to Connie now that they were merely pausing, resting as the world rests when a terrible winter seems to have passed, but there is still no certainty that another storm might not be on the way.

Drawn by this need for the familiar, she made a few impulsive trips in Martin's plane to Ohio and Kentucky.

Davey's plant was going full blast, but Lara worried nevertheless.

"The debt load is horrendous, Connie. To think that Davey had to borrow such a sum to save his own place! We're making just about enough to meet the payments he promised Pam. And after that, we barely squeeze by. It doesn't seem to make any sense."

"I can't believe Pam would press him, though. Not with all she owns."

Lara shook her head. "No, no. But I don't understand it! Ninety percent of their splendor's gone. It's very queer. Wait till you go there, and you'll know what I mean. It's almost as if she'd stripped herself when she made the loan to us."

"That's too saintly to be real. Nobody does that. And surely not for a brother- or sister-in-law."

"Well, wait till you see," repeated Lara.

What Connie saw that first time was a neat white house of moderate size with no grand driveway, columns, wings, or terraces, surrounded by ten level acres of grazing grounds, stables, and riding rings. By the side of the country road above the mailbox a sign read: OSBORNE HORSE FARM, RIDING, BOARDING, SCHOOLING. Pam, familiar in boots and breeches, came out and led her around, explaining the new order of things.

"We don't raise racers, only a few horses for show. Eddy's turned against racing, and I see his point, because it's just gambling, really, and cruel to the horses besides. Riding for its own sake is the true sport."

Connie, feeling dainty and citified, hurried to keep up with Pam's long stride. "How's Eddy getting on in the new job?" she inquired.

"Very well. It's only a three-member firm of accountants, no problem for him."

Pam's tone was flat. Connie thought she sensed a reluctance to touch on Eddy's work. But that was probably understandable. Osborne and Company, the computers, the consoles, fax machines, row on row of young men, avid, nervous, and concentrated, bent above them, these were what Pam must be remembering.

"Quite a change," she said sympathetically.

"Yes. Come see the house. You'll find that quite a change too."

Here indeed was no southern mansion, merely the usual basic rooms, along with an office decorated by framed photographs of horses. Connie recognized most of the furniture, although some pieces were too simple ever to have been in the New York home; they must have been bought to replace the gilt and marble. However, it was all very tasteful, and Connie was gratified to recognize familiar things, too, some of the finds that Eddy had discovered at auction, a few pieces of the silver that he cherished, and some paintings.

"Oh, the Winslow Homer!" she cried on entering the living room. "I always loved that so."

"Yes," Pam said rather shortly. "Would you like the whole tour? Upstairs?"

"Of course. You know how I love to see houses."

On the second floor a narrow hall ran across the back of the house. From it there opened a sunny master room at the end, three more bedrooms, and a small office.

"Eddy's office," Pam said. "Eddy's bedroom next to it."

The women's eyes met. Connie turned hers away. Was there something Pam wanted her to know? If so, why not tell her outright?

But no more was said. They went downstairs, had tea with small talk, and waited for Eddy to come home to dinner.

After dinner, when Pam had to talk to a customer in the stables, the brother and sister were for a while alone. And presently, after many circumlocutions, Connie came to her point.

"This retrenchment—I don't mean that you aren't living very nicely, but the change is dramatic, isn't it? What's the reason? Why?"

Eddy's faint, short-lipped smile was wry. "Reason? Have you any idea what it cost Pam to outbid P.T.C. Longwood for Davey's company?" Then as Connie's flush rose to her face, he said quickly, "It's a painful subject, I know, but you mustn't let it pain. It's past and done with. Business is business. It always was. I blame no one, least of all Martin. Who would I be to cast the blame, anyway?" he finished.

"But I don't understand," said Connie in a low, hurt voice, "why she made such a sacrifice. It's staggering. I can perhaps understand why you would, although even that would be astounding, but why she would hand over almost everything . . . Was it simply because you asked her to?"

"Because I asked her to." Eddy's mouth closed in a hard, stern line.

"Extraordinary." She looked around the room as if a real explanation might be hidden somewhere behind the curtains. "And you are back where you started. Living on what you earn from day to day, I mean."

"As most people do. Although for us it's not quite like that. We have Davey's payments. He began making them from the start, every month."

"It's terribly hard for them, I think."

"Pam doesn't press them. It's they who insist."

"They would, of course."

At that moment Pam came back, and the subject was changed.

"You'll stay a few days, I hope, Connie?" she asked.

"I'd like to, but I have things to do at home. I try to spend every minute I can with Thérèse, so that she won't miss her father too much. And then I have to look into colleges for Melissa because she wants to come back and make her home here with me. She says she feels happier here."

All the way home Connie was bothered by what she had seen and heard. It seemed to her that in some way she had inherited a responsibility for making good the damage that Martin's firm had done. And she said as much the next time she saw Preston, who had taken her to dinner a few times at the Carlyle Hotel, not far from her apartment. Carefully and courteously he listened, as was his way, considering his reply before he gave it.

"Frankly, I can't see why you or anyone should feel responsible. Your brother-in-law chose to take the hard way. He could have given in and walked off with a small fortune, plus a salary with P.T.C. Longwood, if he wanted. To be rich is no bad thing, and to my mind he was foolish."

"That's what Martin said."

"And Martin was right. So now he's struggling."

Connie interrupted. "I hate to see him struggling."

"What are you thinking? That you should buy up the loan yourself?"

She regarded Preston's quizzical, amused expression. There wouldn't be much one could hide from such a man. "You're a mind reader, Preston. Yes, I have been thinking that. After all, I'm Lara's sister. Pam's only a sister-in-law."

"A remarkable thing for a sister-in-law to have done, especially since you tell me it meant such a sacrifice."

"Evidently Eddy wanted her to do it." Yet they're sleeping separately, she thought. And the atmosphere in that house had been in some way formal, in some way not quite right. . . .

"People don't impoverish themselves, relatively speaking, simply because a husband or wife asks them to. Judging by what I've seen of human nature, there'd have to be a quid pro quo," Preston said.

"Meaning?"

"That she owes him something. You look puzzled."

"Well, I am. Anyway, I really want to buy the loan from Pam. I really do."

"Go ahead, you can certainly afford to. Especially if you plan to sell all that property. Do you?"

"Yes, what do I want with a huge house in London? It's just a responsibility. And an Arab has offered me an enormous profit."

"Take it. The real estate market is about to drop, all over the world. What about Palm Beach, and the ski house?"

"I'm selling them. It's so much easier to take a suite in a hotel when you want to go somewhere. All I want to keep are the apartment and Cresthill."

"You've done well for yourself in this world, Connie."

"I guess I have."

"You guess! You know you have. But you deserve it. Beauty deserves its rewards."

"Thank you."

"And you've got a lot more than beauty. You make people feel happy when they're with you. You've got heart."

"Heart? Funny, that's a thing I really think I haven't got enough of."

"What? Why, Berg was mad about you. He talked about you constantly."

She thought, you're missing the point. For all the man's shrewdness he had failed to see that she had not loved "Berg."

"And look at the good heart you have for your sister, now."

"That's different. That's a blood tie, like Thérèse."

"It must have been a touchy business for Martin, having to deal with his wife's family. We all appreciated that in the firm."

"I'm sure it was. . . . I was thinking, Preston. I could take Davey's repayments, after I've assumed the loan, and put part away for Lara's children. It would have to be secret because he and Lara would never accept it otherwise. Can that be done?"

"Easily. We'll set up a trust. Just tell me when."

She smiled at Preston. "It's good having you as a friend. I hate dealing with lawyers. They always come in batches of three or four, and they're so pompous, taking ten words to answer when two would do."

She meant what she said. It had become easy to talk to Preston. Even as recently as a few months ago he had still been the slightly forbidding patrician gentleman, a little too distant, too chilly, for a woman who was accustomed to the ebullience of Martin. Something had changed him.

"Then let's be friends. I'd like that very much, Connie. I was rather waiting for you to emerge a bit from your first mourning."

They were a distinguished couple. In restaurant and theater lobbies, wherever there were mirrors, Connie glimpsed them in passing, he with the elegant white head and aquiline young face above her head. Women stared at him. Women had never stared at Martin. Once when she heard a woman whisper, "Look at that stunning couple, the woman in white," a shiver of excitement ran down her back. Power. Preston was power, and unlike some who had it, he looked the part.

One evening in late May, when it was still light after dinner, he said abruptly, "How about driving to my place in the country for a nightcap? It's only about an hour and a half away."

"I'd love it. I was never there," she remarked.

"Well, you know—how shall I put it? My wife had her ways."

Preston's Buick sedan was not new. An old blanket had been tossed on the backseat. "For the collie," he explained. "I took her to the vet yesterday. She sheds like the dickens."

It was a soft night. Preston put on a tape; the music was as soft as the air; the car whirred softly northward. Neither spoke until they came to a familiar intersection and went past it, when he said, "The road to your place."

"I know. I'll be there for the summer as soon as Thérèse's school is out."

"We're only twenty minutes apart."

"That's all?"

Invisible from the road, Stonycroft lay behind a massive border of wild growth that, to Connie's eyes, appeared unkempt.

"Observe the hedgerow," Preston said. "It's not like the ones you see in France or England—they've taken centuries to grow— but I think this is pretty good for only seventy-five years' growth. My grandfather began it."

It seemed odd that such a tight-woven tangle should be preferable to a landscape architect's pattern of rare shrubbery, but Connie made no comment. Nor did she remark upon the sheep who were cropping the grass right up to the stone balustrade that encircled the house, nor upon the flagstone entrance hall with its boot racks, dog beds, and foul-weather gear hung on clothes trees.

In the long drawing room two great Newfoundlands and a shaggy collie sprang up from the sofas and came forward to greet them. The chintzes were faded, and next to a wing chair an Oriental rug showed a large hole. Connie, quite taken aback, followed Preston through halls hung with portraits, past a two-storied library darkly paneled, through a vast dining room lined with cabinets in which massive silver gleamed, and finally into an enormous kitchen that had not been altered since the 1920s.

Preston fixed drinks, carried them back to the main room, and shoved a dog off a sofa to make room for Connie and himself. From somewhere again, music played, very low.

"Cozy, isn't it?" he inquired.

"Very." She raised her eyes to a portrait opposite; two women, one gray haired with a sweet face, the other barely out of her teens, sat on a rustic garden bench in the shade of a stone house wall. "That's very lovely. Eighteenth century, isn't it? By anybody I ought to know?"

"No, some itinerant painter did it in Yorkshire one day just before the younger woman married and emigrated to America."

"Oh, you actually know the provenance? How exciting!"

"I ought to. They're my great-grandmothers, five and six times removed."

Connie felt a flush of embarrassment. "And all those others on the walls? The man over the fireplace?"

"He's only my grandfather. Yes, all the others. The DeWitt side were Huguenots; we don't have every one of them because some were too poor to have their portraits done. I don't like putting up phony ancestors," Preston added.

"Do you mind if I look some more?"

"Go ahead."

On each painting a small brass plaque gave names and dates: Amelia Ann Cornwallis, 1767; James Todd Cornwallis, 1880; Marie Laure DeWitt, 1814. These were the real thing, a jumble of the family's generations. No doubt the furniture was too. No decorator would have juxtaposed this Elizabethan chest with those Victorian Gothic chairs, that was sure. And yet, beside the "cozy" feeling that Preston had pointed out, the whole possessed a certain elegance. Strange. And those huge dogs with their dirty paws on the furniture! Martin would have had a fit, Connie thought, and so would she.

"It's a lovely house," she told Preston. "It looks—well, *real*. I can't think of a better word."

"It's lived in, anyway. And meant to be lived in, not to impress people with."

Had that been, possibly, an oblique rebuke? She looked up quickly, to find that there was nothing in his expression that could indicate anything but an honest statement.

"I wonder," he said suddenly, "whether you will do a favor for me?"

"Why, you know I will. What is it?"

"A little great-niece of mine is being presented in Charleston at the St. Cecilia Ball, and I'd like to send an appropriate gift. Will you do the shopping? I thought perhaps a strand of pearls, suitable for a girl of eighteen, would be the best unless you have another suggestion."

"Pearls are always good. And if she should already have some or should receive some, they can be worn wound together. You'll need to tell me how much to spend, though. Whether you want a diamond clasp and—"

"No, Arabella's too young for diamonds. Her parents wouldn't like that. They're very quiet, conservative people. My niece married into one of the oldest South Carolina families."

"Oh," said Connie, who had just bought pearls with a huge diamond clasp for Melissa's birthday. "I suppose the St. Cecilia Ball is a formal charity affair?"

"Formal, and by invitation only. It's a local tradition. One can't buy tickets for it. It's not a New York charity bash."

Connie was feeling that she had walked into yet another world. Worlds beyond worlds, barely and only touching here and there when necessary, as Martin's had touched Preston's. She had not even been aware that there were people who thought a diamond clasp wasn't proper.

Back home that night she kept thinking about those people who could live secure in their shabby grandeur and drive an old Buick, while their millions piled up in the bank. "Curiouser and curiouser." So said Alice in Thérèse's favorite story, as she explored the rabbit hole.

One stage followed another. Full summer came, Connie moved to Cresthill, Preston stayed full-time at Stonycroft, and the cars traveled back and forth between the two houses. Both had pools and tennis courts. Both had chairs and tables at which, after strenuous sport, a hot afternoon could be whiled away in the shade. They talked. Connie spoke freely about herself and her background. It pleased her that Preston DeWitt would find her so interesting, pleased her to be turned, in his eyes, into someone charmingly unfamiliar and exotic. On her part his casual mention of places to which she could never have gone with Martin, to which even first-generation corporate executives like Bitsy Maxwell's family had no access, was tantalizing. Mount Desert was where one summered, not Southampton; Hobe Sound was where one wintered, not Palm Beach.

"Of course," he said, laughing a little at himself, "it all began in America with the Gilded Age after the Civil War. The unspeakable vulgarity of Newport's so-called cottages! It takes two or three generations to learn how not to show off."

Damn decorators, Connie was thinking. Telling me that the best houses had to be French! And she wondered what Preston really thought of Cresthill.

One evening in late July he gave a dinner at Stonycroft. Having been at one of his dinners before, she knew this time what to expect: tall men in perfect dinner jackets and tall women in plain, expensive dresses three or four years old. Here were seen no fads like Lacroix's pouf skirts. So she dressed accordingly in the kind of white silk that Pam had always worn, with a pair of barrettes in her hair, and was rewarded by Preston's praise.

"Very becoming. Very well chosen. You've matured, Connie."

She understood that he meant, and was too clever to tell her outright, that she was learning to look as if she had been born in a house like his.

After the dinner, when the other guests had gone, he asked her to remain.

"Sit there a minute. I'll be right back."

In a curious way, while wondering just what the request portended, she felt that it portended some sort of important change. A few minutes later he returned with a leather box in hand, apologizing for the delay.

"I had to take down a picture to get at the wall safe. Anyway, here it is."

And on the coffee table he displayed a ruby necklace, an elaborate arabesque of splendid stones set in platinum and diamonds; long pendant earrings matched.

"Caroline's parure," he explained. "But it came from my grandmother."

Nothing in Connie's possession, no matter how costly, could equal this. These were museum pieces. Royalty could wear them; royalty had perhaps done so. She could only gasp.

"I'd like you to have it, Connie."

She looked at him, disbelieving. "I don't understand. It makes no sense."

"Yes, it does. I have no daughters and no granddaughters. I don't need money, so I'm not going to sell it. It lies in a dark vault. Why shouldn't such jewels see the light of day? Or I should say 'night,' shouldn't I? But don't wear them in the country, you do know that, don't you? They belong in a parterre box at the opera on opening night."

She was bewildered. "Preston, I can't. I shouldn't. It isn't right."

"At least let me see how you look in them. Try them on."

Before the mirror she watched him clasp the necklace, his handsome face concentrated. Then she put on the earrings and turned to him, saying in a kind of self-conscious, awkward tension the first thing that came into her mind.

"This dress is too high necked. You can see it's wrong."

"Pull it down so the jewels rest on your skin."

When she did so, he smiled. "That's better. Actually, do you know how it should be worn? Wasn't it under one of the Louis in France that women exposed their breasts? I don't remember. Anyway, that would be sensational."

Connie laughed. "It's against the law."

He laughed too. "Not here and now in this room."

And saying so, putting both hands on her shoulders, he stretched the white silk down past her breasts, exposed the lace brassiere, and unfastened it. Now at the cleavage lay the largest of the rubies, blood-red, rose-red, hot and glittering. For a moment she stared at it, then slowly turned her eyes toward Preston, who was examining her with questioning curiosity. She had long ago perfected a quiet, steady gaze into which a man might read whatever degree of meaning he wished.

"We'll go upstairs," he said.

She followed. It was as if she were watching another woman mount the great curving flight of steps beside him, as if she were clinically analyzing that woman's emotions, her triumph at having conquered so desirable a man—and at the same time her total absence of desire. To tell the truth, it had been a long evening, and that woman really would have preferred sleep to what was coming. But she also knew what was expected of her and was prepared to perform well.

The room into which he led her contained a high old bed with carved mahogany hung in dark green damask. Sir Walter Raleigh might have bedded Queen Elizabeth in it. Or had he ever slept with Elizabeth? No, not Raleigh. Essex.

401

From far away then, she seemed to hear Preston's voice ringing with delight. "This is the number-one guest room for VIPs."

She heard the slither of silk as the coverlet was removed; from the open window felt the rush of cool air on her skin as he removed the rest of her clothes and carried her, naked except for the rubies, onto the bed.

"On second thought, I seem to remember it was in Napoleon's time that women bared their breasts," Preston said as they rested together.

"I don't remember."

"Well, no matter. But if it was Josephine I'm thinking of, I can tell you Napoleon would never have gotten rid of her if she'd known some of your tricks."

Twinkling—Preston DeWitt actually twinkling!—he regarded Connie. A sudden vision of him in bed with his late wife Caroline, that *prune*, brought a tremble of a smile to Connie.

"What are you smiling at?"

"I'm remembering something. The very first time I met you, before I married Martin, I thought you were the handsomest man I had ever seen."

"I remember. You wore a beige suit, and your eyes sparkled. I've wanted to do this for a long time, Connie."

"Why didn't you?"

"Good Lord, I wouldn't poach on my partner's territory!"

Playing the coquette, she said, "I wouldn't have let you."

"Don't you think I know that? But it's different now, isn't it?"

"Yes. Different now."

In the morning, for some absurd reason against which, because it seemed so childish, she fought and lost, she felt a need to speak to Lara.

What she said was, "Lara, don't be shocked, but I do believe Preston DeWitt will ask me to marry him. I had to tell you."

There was no answer.

"Lara? Are you there?"

"I'm here."

"You're shocked. I know you are."

"I don't know what to say. It just seems—it's not nearly a year yet."

"I know. I didn't say I would actually do it now. I meant that I see it coming, that's all I meant."

"That's better." There was a long pause. Then Lara said, "I barely remember him. Is he white haired and quite tall?"

"Yes. Distinguished. And very sweet. You'll like him, Lara. Really."

"Never mind me. It's you who matter. You can't really be in love again so soon, can you?"

"Well, as you say, it's so soon. But one can tell. . . . You know how it is."

"Maybe I don't know."

This conversation had not been entirely satisfactory, Connie thought when she hung up the telephone. It was rash to have spoken out now, after all. She couldn't be sure of what was in Preston's mind, could she? Yet after last night, could she not?

And she allowed a little drama to unroll. When the year was well past, perhaps next spring, there could be a very small private ceremony at Cresthill, after which the place would be sold, for he certainly wouldn't sell Stonycroft with all his grandfather's trees. It was actually his great-grandfather who had bought it. Thank goodness he was a widower; there'd be no exasperating divorce to delay things as there had been with Martin. . . . So Connie reflected.

Her prediction was fulfilled. About a month after the night of the rubies, Preston outlined a plan exactly like the one Connie had imagined.

"Of course, we have to wait until next spring," he said, complaining, "but it's damned hard. Can't sleep together at my place except on maids' nights out, and can't ever sleep at yours on account of the child. However, it will pass. Patience, patience. Damn," he said again, "I may have to go abroad for a month. We're expanding our facility in Tokyo. In fact, it's not 'may have to,' it's 'must.' Since we lost Berg, there's been nobody to take his place. I'd love it if you'd come along."

"I can't leave Thérèse, Preston. She's starting school again at the end of the month, and I need to be here."

He nodded. "I understand, of course. But I'll miss you."

"I'll miss you too."

Yet, when he vanished through the departure gate at Japan Airlines, she turned away with no feeling at all, except perhaps the pleasant anticipation of a quiet evening at home with the telephone shut off, a long bath, a book, and bed. For some reason she had been feeling depressed during the last week or two. I'm getting tired, she thought suddenly, of simulating emotion; it takes all one's energy to be passionate and vivacious when one isn't feeling either way. For now that Preston was 'caught,' and was an accomplished fact in her life, the first miraculous excitement had just seemed to drain away. Where could it have gone? Perhaps she was simply getting older. . . .

Then she thought: No. I'm only thirty-five. This has got to be a delayed reaction from last December's shock. That's all it can be.

One day Connie happened to drive past the hospital where Peggy had been cared for. Quite naturally, then, that whole experience raced like a motion picture through her memory: the arriving airplane, the unconscious child on the stretcher, the room on the second floor, Lara's shrunken face, the day of the miracle when the child's eyes opened, and in the corridor the nurses' and the doctors' running steps.

He was a nice man, that Jonathan Bayer. I remember thinking, she said to herself, that I'd like to know him. I can't say why exactly, but he just seemed interesting. At our picnic that Fourth of July I had the feeling that he liked me.

And driving on with the top down and a fresh breeze blowing, she felt a sudden heat rise to her cheeks. Absurd, Connie. Where do you think you are? In junior high school?

There was a choice of three routes from Cresthill to the village, the most circuitous of which was the road that passed the hospital. Nevertheless, driving one day with Thérèse in the car, she took that route again.

"Look, Mommy. That's where Peggy was when she was sick."

"Yes, I remember."

"We used to bring toys and cookies."

"You're right, we did."

"We used to bring things for lots of other children, Mommy. You said they didn't have enough toys."

"You're right, we did. Would you like to buy some toys and bring them there again?"

"Yes, let's."

Whatever the motive, whether the child really had generous feelings or simply liked the fun of visiting a toy store, the project was a good one, and ought to be carried out. Besides . . .

But how foolish! He probably wasn't even there anymore. And if he was—so what?"

"We'll go tomorrow," Connie said.

They had half a dozen cartons filled with dolls, toy cars, simple puzzles, and other toys suited to recuperating children, when they returned the next day. It took several trips from the parking lot to carry all of these indoors. On the last one Connie, dropping a carton, was rescued as Jonathan Bayer came hurrying through the lot.

"What's going on? It's not Christmas yet," he said.

Connie explained. "We have a special feeling for this place, because of Peggy. My sister's child, if you remember."

"Remember? Of course I do!" He looked surprised.

What a stupid remark! Naturally he remembered. And annoyed with herself for being so awkward, she made amends.

"When she came, she might as well have been dead, and when she left, she was whole again. It was a miracle."

"Yes, miracles do happen, but not often." They set the bundles down in the front hall and stood there for a moment. There was an odd sense of uncertainty about what to do next.

"Shall I have these distributed, or do you want—?" began the doctor, when Connie interrupted hastily, "No, no, I don't want to. That's too much like Lady Bountiful. Oh, no."

He laughed. "Good for you. I'll see to it, then. We're always in need of toys, and we surely thank you. Especially you, Thérèse."

He went down the hall fast, almost running, as Connie remembered he had used to do.

Outside on the lawn patients, singly and in groups, with nurses or relatives, sat in wheelchairs or made arduous efforts to walk. A little boy about Thérèse's age was sitting on the grass with a woman, fumbling over a puzzle.

Thérèse stopped. "I have that game," she told him, and uninvited, sat down beside him. "I'll show you how to do it."

Connie said quickly, "No, no, don't bother the little boy."

The other woman looked up, smiling. "She just wants to be friendly. We don't mind, if you don't."

So the two mothers sat watching while Thérèse, with astounding patience, demonstrated to the disabled boy how to tilt the box so that the little silver ball would run through the maze into the hole. And Connie, listening to the other woman's tale of disaster in an automobile and long, discouraging recuperation, was struck by wave after wave of gratitude for, and fierce protectiveness of, her own feisty little girl.

Presently, Dr. Bayer came down the walk and stopped to watch the children. When at last the silver ball fell into the hole, the boy laughed, and Thérèse clapped and stood up.

"Time to go now," said Connie.

Dr. Bayer, also going in the direction of the parking lot, remarked as Thérèse ran ahead, "You have an unusual child."

"Yes. She's always been quick and bright."

"Like you."

"Thank you. But she's like her father."

"I see the kindness too."

"I'm lucky to have her, I know." And she added, "We live alone now, the two of us. Her father was on Flight 103 that went down over Scotland last winter."

"Oh!" he cried. "Your husband—that vital man!"

There was such genuine pain in his single "Oh!" that she turned to look at him. What she saw was an expression of extraordinary gentleness.

They reached Connie's car. When he had seen them into it, Dr. Bayer stood at the window. She had not yet started the motor. And again there was that sense of uncertainty, as if neither quite knew how to end the brief encounter.

She said, "The things you do here . . . When I remember my little niece, I feel so grateful. I wish I could do something to show it. Better than bringing a few toys, I mean."

"You could volunteer," he told her.

"Why? What could I do?"

"You could do pretty much what Thérèse did just now. The nurses don't have enough time for all that should be done, especially on weekends."

"Really? I think I'd like to do that."

"Well, if you're interested, come see me about it. They've made me medical director since you were here. I'm on the ground floor."

"Congratulations!"

"Thank you."

"Let's go, Mommy!" Thérèse cried impatiently.

"All right, we're going."

For once, Connie was glad of the child's impatience.

407

*   *   *

She asked to be with children, so on the following Saturday she was given a ten-year-old girl in charge who needed someone to walk with her around the grounds. This was such simple work that it was hardly work at all, and yet one knew how valuable it was. It might, in another sense, be thought rather odd for Connie to be spending the afternoon with a strange child while her own child was being cared for by a nanny. And she knew, of course, that the only reason she was not at home with Thérèse was Jonathan Bayer.

He came upon her just after she had brought her charge back to her room.

"Where's Miss Thérèse?" he asked.

"Oh, playing with friends."

"Well, how do you like this work?"

"It's hardly work, but I do feel I've done something worthwhile."

"You have." He looked at her quizzically. "I'm off for the rest of the day. Would you like to have a drink with me?"

"That would be nice."

"There's a place down the road. We can sit out under an umbrella, if you'd like."

"That would be nice."

Where was her vaunted "personality"? She was as tongue-tied as a girl on a first date. They got into his car, drove, and found themselves at an umbrella table on a gilded September afternoon with nothing but silence swelling between them to fill the afternoon.

"Why do you keep looking at your feet?" he asked abruptly.

She hadn't been aware of doing so, but she found an answer. "I thought I saw a hole in my stocking."

He laughed. "And if there were? What then?"

"Nothing, I guess."

"The trouble is, we don't know what to say to each other."

Her heart pounded. "There's nothing wrong with being quiet."

"No, you're right." And he looked away across the little lawn, bisected by a gravel path on which a couple of pigeons were foraging for crumbs.

Her mind, as she observed him, spun through time, through all she had known of life. He had none of Preston's Roman-coin symmetry, none of Martin's vigorous enthusiasm, and surely none of Richard's—poor Richard!—sunny, boyish charm. What then? She could not say, did not understand, knew only that something powerful had taken hold of her, that she felt eased while she was drawn to him, and yet that she feared this thing, so fearfully unfamiliar.

"Do you still live in the same house?" he asked abruptly.

"Yes, in the summer."

"It's very beautiful. Very grand."

"Yes."

Again the silence fell. There had been something in the way he said "grand" that disturbed her. Suddenly she saw her palace through his eyes, as his eyes would have seen it. And it seemed to her that she knew, without having been told anything about him, how his eyes would see the world.

They finished their drinks and drove back to where Connie's car was parked at the hospital. He took her hand on parting.

"This was only our first time," he said. "We'll do better the next time."

There were three more times, a tea, a lunch, and a dinner. And the talk began to flow more easily between them, talk about movies, politics, about books and places Connie had never seen, such as the inside of a hospital for Cambodian refugees in Thailand. She learned that he had always wanted to be a doctor from the time he'd been nine years old. She learned that he had never been married; for some reason that pleased her. But then she had to give him in turn the bare facts of her own life, about her family and her marriages.

She said nothing about Preston DeWitt, who would be home in a week.

After the dinner date, in the dark of the hospital parking lot where she had kept her car, he kissed her. It was a light brush on the lips, the obligatory kiss, and that is all it was. He couldn't know it, but if he had asked her to, if there had been a private place for them to go, she would have lain down there on the grass with him, would have cried out the marvel that it had taken all these years for her to feel, really to *feel*, at last. . . . She scarcely recognized herself. . . . And driving home alone through the quiet night, she wept.

Although he was tired after the flight from Tokyo, Preston came straight from the airport to Connie's apartment. In the familiar red library they talked.

"I really missed having Berg along, I'll tell you. He knew how to get things done, he was a brain. Oh, a mite too aggressive for my taste, to be honest about it, but let me tell you, what he did for our firm was stupendous. We're richer by a couple of billion dollars because of him, and that's not all bad."

"It's not necessarily all good, either, is it?" When he looked at her with astonishment, she added, "When you see what's happening to the country, all the bankruptcies and the unemployment, you have to wonder about a lot of things."

Preston shrugged. "Cycles. Everything goes in cycles. If you're smart, you prepare for the downturns. And we're prepared. We'll be as busy as we ever were in the eighties, only we'll be on the other side. We'll be deleveraging. Doing financial rescues. So I'm not worried, not a bit."

When I was in India, said Jonathan, I saw such things, such criminal neglect, that I felt an anger I had never known I was capable of feeling.

410

TREASURES

Preston swirled the brandy in the snifter, contemplating the sunny liquid. "Yes," he reflected, "the eighties are almost over, but greed isn't and never will be, so one might as well survive by taking advantage of it."

"Isn't that rather cynical?" she asked quietly.

"Not at all. It's true."

"Not of everyone. Not of Davey and Lara, for example."

"You still talking about them? Babes in the wood. Berg himself said so."

"Sometimes lately," she said slowly, "I have a feeling that at the very end, Martin would have taken Davey's side, that he wouldn't have pushed through with that deal."

"That's ridiculous, Connie."

"Maybe. But I do have the feeling, given the man Martin was."

Preston shook his head. "Never. Not with all that money at stake."

We are miles apart, she thought. He was turning and turning the snifter, warming it between his long hands. How could I ever have thought otherwise? It seems so clear now, the crazy extravagance of the Bitsy Maxwells, and yes—of Martin—and yes, of Eddy—and then the reverse snobbishness of Preston's friends in their old dresses. False, all false. All of it.

What has happened to me?

"How are the Davises doing, by the way?"

"They're struggling, paying me back on the first of every month. But they're very, very happy."

"How can they be so happy, when they're living with a load of debt on their hands?"

"Because they're together. Do you understand? Together in every way?"

I never married, said Jonathan. I always said I never would until I found the woman I couldn't live without.

411

"Something has changed you," Preston said. "You're dissatisfied."

She did not answer.

"Tell me."

She rose. "I have to give you something first."

From the wall safe in her dressing room she removed the box with Preston's rubies and returned. He was cold and would not be devastated by her rejection, yet he was a decent man, and she wanted to be gentle. She knelt on the ottoman at his chair.

"Please take these back. You were very generous, but I mustn't keep them."

He raised his eyebrows. "Why? Have you found someone else?"

Truthfully, wistfully, she replied, "I think I may have, although very likely nothing will come of it."

If it meant anything that Jonathan was her first thought in the morning and the last at night, if it meant anything that she felt panic at the idea that he might go away, if it meant anything that she would go with him gladly to Borneo without a penny, then indeed she had found someone.

"Rather a sudden development, I should say."

"Yes. Sudden."

Cold or not, this man was very proud, and no human being suffers a rejection gladly. His lips tightened, while his fingernails made small, clicking sounds as they tapped the arm of the chair.

"I'm truly sorry, Preston. I respect you and admire you, but— something happened, that's all. I can't help it. I'm truly sorry."

"Is it—may I ask—anyone I know?"

"I'm not sure." Jonathan at one of Preston's dinner parties!

"Have you known him long?"

"A couple of years. That is, I met him," she stumbled. "But I don't—didn't know him much until last month."

Preston frowned. "The whole thing sounds odd, to say the

least. Not," he said quickly, "that it's any business of mine, but do you expect to be married or just—"

"I'd like to get married," she said simply, "but I really don't know whether I will. Probably not."

A despondent, anticlimactic silence fell, during which Preston's nails kept clicking. After a while he stood up, ready to leave.

"You can understand that I'm fairly disappointed. I thought we had firm plans. But I suppose I must wish you good luck, anyway. I'm still fond of you, Connie, and I hope you're not doing anything foolish."

So that much was over, and not too painfully. But—oh, Connie, Consuelo, she asked herself, Peg's own late-blooming romantic daughter, are you indeed a fool?

After two weeks there was no word from Jonathan Bayer. She was sure she had given him her New York address, and in any case, he could easily have found it if he had wanted to.

I don't understand it, she thought over and over during the quiet hours. She had many quiet hours in the days that followed the parting from Preston, all desire for activity having left her. So, walking in the park with Thérèse or sitting with a half-read book on her lap, she pondered. He had called her "gentle" and "comical" and "kind." "When we get to know each other better," he had said.

She felt a cold sense of loss. The man had reached her as no man ever had, yet that was not to say that she had reached *him* in the same way, was it?

One night, not sleeping well, she got up and walked through the apartment, turning lights on and off as, on thick, muffling rugs, she went from room to room. The place was lonely. For so many months it had been deserted, its long rooms filled with plump, padded, and now vacant chairs. She heard again the air resounding with imperious chatter, the boasts of those who had "made it," hoped to make more, and were there to let the world know how importantly they existed. The place was a museum, too, its walls and corners, its cabinets and niches, crammed with brilliant objects, collected in superfluity that all might see how well their owner had "made it."

The place was useless. It was dead. Like the pyramids, it was dead.

How strange it was that, living here, she had never before felt its deadness!

"I will telephone him in the morning," she said aloud into the midnight silence. "Pride or not, what more have I got to lose?"

If he should agree, they would have dinner together at Cresthill tomorrow.

It was still light enough when Jonathan arrived to see the gold leaves tremble slowly onto the leaf-speckled grass. From the window nook in the library where Connie had arranged that they would dine simply at a small round table, he gazed out at a vast view of lawns emblazoned with ornamental trees, with gazebos, ponds, and statuary. During the last few minutes, after an animated start, he had become quiet.

She had told herself that she would be very open; for the first time in her life she would bring no wiles, no calculations to bear upon a man. And so she asked bluntly, "What are you thinking? What are you seeing out there?"

He turned to her with equal honesty. "Do you really want to know?"

"Yes."

"I am thinking that this place reminds me of Versailles."

"And you don't like it."

"Versailles was fine for Louis XIV in his time. No, I take that back. It wasn't fine, even then."

"I want to sell it," she said abruptly.

"I thought you loved it."

"I did once." She hesitated. "It was a binge. An addiction, like drugs."

He listened while she let her thoughts speak, thoughts that not long ago she would have said she could never have. All that money, flowing in and spilling over . . .

"In the end," she said softly, "it has no meaning. The treasures, the rich prizes, have no meaning."

Without answering he kept his gaze on the window and the scene beyond, where it was rapidly growing dark. With every one of her senses she was aware of him, aware of the black, curving eyelashes, of the cleft chin that gave a sweetness to the powerful face, of the long hand that rested on the table, the white cuffs, the—

He stood up suddenly. The coffee had grown cold in the cups. "May we sit elsewhere? I need to talk to you."

Fifty people could sit comfortably in the library. At one end a fire had been lit against the early autumn chill, and there she led him to sit.

"Connie," he began, "I know you wondered why I didn't call you. You knew, we both knew, that something was happening to us."

"Then it was cruel of you," she cried. "I waited—"

"Forgive me," he said, vaguely pleading, "but I was so afraid."

"Afraid of what?"

He waved his hand toward the enormous room. "Of this. I don't belong here. It seemed incongruous to think of myself with a woman who did. I knew who Martin Berg was—a decent man, I'm sure, but worlds apart from me, and I thought that a woman who had coveted all this couldn't possibly be happy with my ways." He stopped.

Connie's heart was hammering. "Go on," she said, not taking her eyes away from him.

"You don't know how I fought with myself. I remember think-

415

ing how warm you are, with all your vital joy. And still I asked myself whether I really knew you."

"And do you think you do now?"

"Much better. Oh, much better. What you said just then about the treasures, 'the rich prizes' I think you said, that seemed to open the way for me to see you clearly."

She got up and stood before him, trembling. "What do you see? Tell me what you see."

"I see a woman. A real one. Oh," he said, "I know I wouldn't have held out. I kept thinking, I mustn't lose you. Then I thought, but what if we start out together and then I lose you? How much worse that would be!"

"You won't lose me, Jonathan."

"Oh," he cried, and rose to meet her.

For minutes then they stood together, clasped while he kissed her eyes, her cheeks, and her mouth, his hands moving gently on her body, and neither of them able to stop or to let go. So this had been here in the world all the time, and she had never known it!

When at last he loosened his arms, she was thinking, I shall have so much to make up for, and the thought made her laugh, a little tender laugh mingled with a few bright tears.

"Shall we? Shall we now, darling?" asked Jonathan.

"Yes. I've left Thérèse in the city, so there's no one here." No wiles, she thought again. There'd be nothing but bold honesty this time. And she said, "You see, I wanted it to turn out like this. I wanted it so. With all my heart."

Thanksgiving, one year later.

With huge pleasure Lara looked down the long table. At the far end sat Davey; ranked on either side were Eddy and Pam, Connie and Thérèse and Jonathan, then Melissa Berg and her own two children. In the center was a splendid mound of chrysanthemums, baby pumpkins, and dried Indian corn.

416

TREASURES

"I always wanted a really big tableful, really big," she said, "and this year I have it."

"Next year, if you invite us," Eddy said, looking significantly at Pam's visible, enormous pregnancy, "it will be even fuller."

"No, you'll come to our house," Pam said. "We must start a tradition of taking turns."

A sliver of pie remained on the plate in front of Lara. "Does anyone want the last piece?" she asked. "If not, I guess we can all get up and stretch."

At the living room window Connie stood looking out at the yard, where the pin oaks' leaves, turned to brown, would hang on all winter through the snow, to be shed contrariwise only in the spring. At the far end of the property stood Davey's new workroom, much like the shabby original in size and shape, but painted white with green window boxes that Lara would plant with geraniums again. Connie smiled to herself.

"He gets his best ideas when he can work at home in a quiet place," Lara said, coming up beside her. "The plant's too busy."

Davey overheard. "Thank God, it's busy. I hired ten new men last week. Have you heard about P.T.C. Longwood, Connie?"

"No, I don't hear about those things anymore."

"Well, it was in the papers. Bennett's selling to the Japanese."

"A few more billions for his coffers," said Connie, scoffing.

"Connie, you've become an idealist," Lara observed tranquilly.

"Well, I have. It's disgusting when people are addicted to piling up millions that they can't possibly use."

"It's an easy addiction to get," Eddy said, "and hard to break."

"None of us is exactly impoverished." That was Davey.

"We've finally sold Cresthill," Connie announced abruptly. "And the apartment too. We're going to close the deal on our new house this week."

It pleased her that they all wanted to know what the new one was like.

Jonathan replied with a smile. "It's a beautiful colonial near

417

the hospital and Thérèse's new school, a little larger than I wanted and a little smaller than Connie wanted, so we compromised, since each of us paid for our half of it."

"There's just enough room to hold you all, including Melissa when she's home from college, and then even a nursery for Pam's baby," Connie assured them. "Are you positive you haven't got twins in there, darling?"

"I'd be delighted if she had," said Eddy, taking his wife's hand.

"What a wonderful day it's been," sighed Lara, with that same lovely, tranquil look on her face.

"I've been thinking of Peg," Connie murmured. "If she knows that we're here together like this, she's very, very happy."

And Eddy added typically, "Yes, we haven't done too badly. We've had our ups and our downs, and nobody's won a Nobel prize, either, but we haven't done too badly."

Connie caught her husband's eye. So you like us? went her silent question.

Yes. And you, you I love, came his silent answer.

The moment caught Connie's heart. She must remember it exactly, its familiar faces, its well-known voices, and even the way the late sun fell, to touch with its blessed light these whom she held most dear, all these, her living treasures.

Treasures

Plain, Belva